MAPPING THE END OF EMPIRE

Mapping the End of Empire

AMERICAN AND BRITISH STRATEGIC VISIONS
IN THE POSTWAR WORLD

Aiyaz Husain

Harvard University Press

Cambridge, Massachusetts
London, England
2014

Copyright © 2014 by the President and Fellows of Harvard College
All rights reserved
Printed in the United States of America

Library of Congress Cataloging-in-Publication Data

Husain, Aiyaz, 1977–
  Mapping the end of empire : American and British strategic visions in the postwar world / Aiyaz Husain.
     pages cm
  Includes bibliographical references and index.
  ISBN 978-0-674-72888-2 (alk.paper)
 1. Decolonization—Middle East. 2. Decolonization—South Asia. 3. Geographical perception—Middle East. 4. Geographical perception—South Asia. 5. Palestine—History—1917–1948. 6. Jammu and Kashmir (India)—History—20th century. 7. Great Britain—Foreign relations—1945–1964. 8. United States—Foreign relations—1945–1953. I. Title.
  DS63.18.H86 2014
  956.04—dc23   2013037069

For my parents

Contents

    Introduction 1
1. All of Palestine 23
2. Remapping Zion 52
3. The Contested Valley 78
4. Keystone of the Strategic Arch 105
5. Imperial Residues 129
6. Two Visions of the Postwar World 161
7. Maps, Ideas, and Geopolitics 187
8. Joining the Community of Nations 218
9. From Imagined to Real Borders 242

    Conclusion 262

    Abbreviations 277
    Notes 279
    Archives Consulted 349
    Acknowledgments 353
    Index 357

MAPPING THE END OF EMPIRE

Introduction

The close of the Second World War marked a triumph of the victorious Allied powers in a global contest against the forces of fascism. But victory presented immediate challenges: effective postwar cooperation to prevent the recurrence of a total war with its massive human costs, and assorted political, economic, and territorial questions prompted by the end of hostilities. In a series of wartime conferences, the United States, Great Britain, and the Soviet Union had discussed the need for international cooperation to address postwar concerns. Those discussions led in 1945 to the creation of the United Nations Organization, which the Allies hoped would cement world peace after the second global conflict within half a century.

But the challenges of postwar diplomacy extended beyond just questions of interstate war and peace. The dispositions of vast European colonial possessions throughout the Middle East, Asia, and Africa remained indeterminate, despite growing calls for self-determination from active independence movements pitted against colonial governments exhausted by the trials of war. Moreover not all Allied great powers were equal at war's end. The most basic feature of the new international balance of power was the glaring disparity between the economic and military might of the United States and that of its European allies Britain, France, and the Netherlands. While the Netherlands and France lay physically devastated by occupation, bombardment, and Allied liberation, the economic costs of the war accumulated in monumental sterling balances that threatened to crush the British Empire under their weight.

An immediate consequence of this state of affairs was the impending withdrawal of those European powers from territories they controlled in the Middle East and Asia. But how would those power transfers occur, and what state or interstate authorities would manage them? While these questions remained unanswered, the basic outlines of one of the impending global shifts were clear. If the *Pax Britannica* was giving way to the American Century, the geopolitical evidence of that change was now clearer than ever.

The British Empire was firmly in retreat, overburdened by the monetary cost of imperial defense, which had contributed to a foreign debt burden that soared to some three billion pounds—over a third of Britain's gross domestic product. Britain was vacating its strategic presence in Egypt, the cornerstone of its Middle East policy, leaving the Labour government with vexing quandaries about suitable locations that could sustain a residual force. At stake was nothing less than Britain's access to the region's vast oil reserves and the security of the Suez Canal Zone and the eastward sea route to India. Palestine, Cyprus, Cyrenaica, Iraq, and Transjordan were all possible candidates to offset the impact of the loss of Egypt and direct British control of the Canal Zone. And as the loss of India loomed ever larger in the minds of British strategists in the postwar years leading up to 1947, the Middle East seemed an obvious strategic foothold from which to secure the growing British interest in Africa—and thus as a justification for the maintenance of ever costlier fragments of empire. But whatever alternatives remained for preserving influence in the Middle East, the finality of the British Empire's looming withdrawal from Egypt was clear. Decades of British rule there, the keystone of the crown's presence in the Arab world at the intersection of three continents, and a prerequisite for control of the Sudan would be at an end after the removal of British forces to the Suez Canal area. The costs of holding India were also mounting to unsustainable levels, while Indian nationalism surged after the wholesale defeat of the Axis powers and the successful defense of the subcontinent, toward which Indian troops had contributed significantly.[1]

Against this backdrop of Britain's hasty retreat from the Middle East and Asia unfolded the counternarrative of America's expansion to fill distant, residual spaces vacated throughout the postwar world by defeated Axis enemies and imploded empires. American power reached its apogee after the Second World War, as the United States contemplated a new role in a changed international landscape. It was American credit that would finance the Marshall Plan and American military manpower and materiel that would shoulder the postwar reconstruction of Germany and Japan. After the United States secured petroleum supplies through concessions on the Arabian Peninsula negotiated by President Franklin Roosevelt with King Ibn Saud, the synergy of Middle Eastern oil and American industrial output began to power global economic recovery and rehabilitate war-torn Europe and Asia. Marshall Plan aid soon flooded across the Atlantic to help resurrect European allies, while billions of dollars of additional U.S. assistance flowed to China, India, Japan, South Korea, Indonesia, the Philippines, and Pakistan.[2]

The displacement of British influence in the world by expanding American economic and military influence thus was somewhat inevitable, as the United States sought to secure key strategic points and access to the raw materials of the third world that the Truman administration considered essential in case of a future global conflict. Moreover fears of a growing confrontation with the Soviet Union as the early cold war began to divide East and West soon supplied a powerful new rationale for an expanded U.S. global posture: the need to safeguard the free world from communist influence and subversion, especially after the promulgation of the Truman Doctrine and the American assumption from Britain of the responsibility for economic and military assistance to reinforce ailing democratic governments in Greece and Turkey. But as this book argues, the disparity in their material power aside, both Atlantic powers—one falling, one rising—also adhered to distinct geographical conceptions of their security needs in the new international order, conceptions that helped shape their respective postwar foreign policies.[3]

Great Britain's sense of its own interests in the world had been curtailed by war's end but remained decidedly colonial. The new British role in the postwar world was predicated on realism and oriented around shielding a contracting empire's territorial integrity and remaining possessions. Saddled by outsized defense costs while the domestic economy slumped, Britain sensed that its shrinking imperial reach was inevitable. And with that sense of a newly circumscribed international position came a revised geographic conception of Britain's postwar interests: more limited, more practical, and more concerned with only the most vital interests. Crown rule was crumbling in the empire's outposts in the Near and Far East, from Palestine to India, leaving strategists scrambling for alternative military basing postures and redefinitions of British security requirements.

Meanwhile America's ascent to a new era of global influence prompted, in turn, the reinterpretation of *its* core postwar objectives. Those interests would be defined in terms of an expanded view of America's international role, one commensurate with new economic and military interests in corners of the world suddenly vacated by retreating empires, demobilizing allies, and defeated adversaries. With a worldview more ambiguous and ill-defined than the reconfigured British one, officials in the Roosevelt and Truman administrations began to shape the global foreign policy that would come to be framed by the strategic thought of a young Sovietologist, George Kennan. Its basic precept, the "containment" of communism, would guide American foreign policy for the remainder of the century.

Importantly these parallel and divergent geographical conceptions of international interests and security emerged from both official policy deliberations as well as popular conceptions of geography at the time. Both embedded themselves down to deep operational levels in the respective foreign policy establishments in London and Washington as sets of ideas about geographical interests that guided foreign policy.

Colored maps of the British Empire around the Second World War revealed the extent to which a binary worldview of the bounds of the empire, on the one hand (usually colored red in official maps), and the world beyond, on the other (often colored beige), penetrated British thinking about overseas territories. Moreover the continual linkage of British interests in the Middle East and South Asia by British government and military officials revealed assumptions that underpinned a view of key parts of the empire as an almost geographically contiguous political unit rather than sprawling territories linked only by trade routes and military lines of communication. Thus the end of the war prompted suggestions of consolidated diplomatic arrangements to secure strategic areas in which British military presences could no longer act as the cohesive force ensuring stability and the defense of imperial interests.[4] And the conceptual linkage of foreign policy priorities across myriad colonies, possessions, and other non-British territories increasingly appeared in British diplomatic correspondence. In the minds of some British strategists, it was widely accepted that "Turkey and Greece, Palestine and Egypt, Iran and Arabian oil, are all really wrapped up in the same package." It was a trend in British policy toward what that this book calls a new *regionalism* that both pared down the key geographical nodes that anchored British defense planning and drew spatial linkages between them.[5]

Conversely U.S. officials revealed the mental maps and frameworks that underpinned their own worldviews in framing postwar foreign policy problems. The contours of the Roosevelt administration's earliest plans for postwar international organization did not delineate a segmented world of geographically dispersed regional alliances. It was rather a vision of a global peace overseen by the world's most powerful states, "Four Policemen," in Roosevelt's formulation, patterned after the Concert of Powers that presided over Europe after 1815 but whose extrapolated responsibilities now spanned the entirety of the globe.[6] Here was a conception of American interests that entered the popular imagination through millions of wartime maps published by *National Geographic* and that reflected the basing needs of the "air age" dawning on U.S. civil and military aviation alike. Its essential blueprint also materialized as the iconic azimuthal equidistant projection map on the flag of the United Nations, a body whose structure emerged in part from the designs of the Council on Foreign Relations' Advisory Committee for Postwar Foreign Policy, whose work products would later be folded directly into the State Department's postwar planning efforts in the prelude to the San Francisco Conference of 1945. Throughout the process the global scope of postwar American interests became increasingly clear, guided by the thinking of officials like the influential geographer of the United States, Isaiah Bowman, who the anthropologist and geographer Neil Smith argues "moved more and more away from seeing a U.S. global future in terms of territorial blocs and regional trading spheres and toward a global vision."[7]

Thus a receding British Empire gave way to a new U.S. role in the world guided by what Smith, Stephen Ambrose, and other historians termed a new *globalism*, one that echoed the manifest destiny of nineteenth-century frontier expansion and suggested aspirations toward a worldwide Monroe Doctrine for a new era of American primacy. While American globalism would be limited by the onset of the cold war and Soviet competition for allies and influence that penetrated the third world by the mid-1950s, the global outlook of the U.S. foreign policy establishment had been fundamentally shaped by war's end and was reflected in the early postwar national security state. The geographic assumptions in this globalism came to shape postwar American grand strategy. As James Lay, the executive secretary of the National Security Council wrote in 1952 in the pages of *World Affairs*, the administration had realized early on that "policies developed for the security of the United States have far-reaching impact throughout the world. Likewise, events throughout the world affect our national security. Policies, therefore, can no longer be decided solely within geographical limitations."[8]

These American and British geographic definitions of security interests were fundamentally distinct. It was thus no surprise that they collided haphazardly at the Dumbarton Oaks and San Francisco conferences, which finalized the blueprints for the United Nations Organization. In deliberations on myriad aspects of that new institution's design, from voting and membership to provisions for the administration of former colonial territories, British and American officials clashed over the ideal structures and procedures for the UN machinery that would address fundamental outstanding postwar questions.

The United States sought a system of international trusteeship geared toward helping liberated and former colonial territories achieve independence and opening up the postwar world for the spread of American trading interests and overseas influence. British diplomats worked instead to insulate colonial territory from the intrusions of the UN system and to avoid overt references to rights to independence for imperial possessions. Those differences were understandable given the primacy of the competing geographic worldviews shaping the aspirations of both powers. The United States saw in the United Nations (and institutions like its Trusteeship Council) a world body that would strip the colonial powers of dependencies, open new markets to American products and industrial output, and oversee an international peace safeguarded by a balance of power largely allied with America and the Western democracies. As the historian William Roger Louis put it, "The ideology of trusteeship was easily forged into a weapon of American defence."[9] Britain meanwhile considered the new organization a tool with which to manage the decolonization process and unburden itself of responsibility for territories in key areas like the Suez Canal Zone in a manner agreeable to British interests but that would still not force the official British hand. For Foreign and Colonial Office officials in London, UN mechanisms for managing dependent territories and peoples offered hope that Britain might preserve a measure of influence over former colonies and protectorates as League of Nations mandates expired and they edged toward independence.

These divergent American and British geographic worldviews impinged heavily on postcolonial questions such as the futures of Palestine and Kashmir, affecting Anglo-American discussions on both issues just as ideological differences about colonial rule and self-determination did. As their underlying logics gained wide acceptance, globalism and regionalism came to mirror concomitant trends in strategy grounded in specific assumptions about geography—assumptions that determined which territories and human populations clustered together in the minds of British and American officials entrusted with the solution of key postcolonial problems, and how they did so. They also profoundly affected the French and Dutch empires in the Levant and the East Indies, respectively. Both found themselves sandwiched between Britain's receding worldwide presence and a symmetrical American expansion pushing openly to dislodge their authority.

This work of international history explores how British and American perceptions of the greater Middle East and South Asia shaped Anglo-American strategy in Palestine and Kashmir and helped drive out the remnants of French and Dutch colonial rule elsewhere. While the prejudices, biases, and experiences of specific diplomats and military officers likely shaped their mental maps of specific world regions, broader sets of assumptions shaped the globalism and regionalism through which larger groups of officials in Washington and London viewed the postwar world. Evidence of these assumptions in official and public records alike reveals the lasting importance of such conceptions of geography for policymakers, administrators, and thinkers on both sides of the Atlantic as the final acts of the decolonization of the British Empire began to unfold in the Middle East and South Asia. It alludes to the diverse origins from which such perceptions and their underlying assumptions formed: the geographic terminology conceived by diplomats and policymakers; the military necessities forcing the hands of generals; and the imaginations of academic geographers, geopolitical theorists, and public intellectuals. This book also reveals the lasting institutional legacies of mental maps as *ideas* that, while partly shaped by the realities of material power, also hardened into actual bureaucratic structures and policies. It shows how ideas about geography came to shape national foreign policy agendas like U.S. plans for global refugee resettlement after the Second World War; how they drove organizational changes like the creation of the British Middle East Office in Cairo; and how they congealed into international bodies like the UN Security Council and its associated rules of procedure.

Two of the most important implications of the argument concern the impact of perceptions of geography and their value for comparative historical analysis. First, the findings of this book suggest that the diverging

American and British geographic conceptions of the postwar world deeply impacted Anglo-American policies during decolonization. The trends toward globalism and regionalism were rooted in specific worldviews that surrounded the thoughts and actions of midlevel and senior policymakers alike. As such this book argues that assumptions about geography came to form key underpinnings of the geographical "official minds" driving American and British postwar foreign policy and the strategic thought behind it. Importantly it also argues that individual mental maps (as opposed to collective worldviews shared by foreign policy establishments) drove the thinking of anticolonial nationalists like David Ben-Gurion and Muhammad Ali Jinnah—as representations of ideal end-states guiding the trajectories of the nationalist movements that they led. Second, this book suggests that perceptions of geography can serve as useful metrics for sizing the overseas footprints of great powers like the United States and Great Britain. Such metrics help define politico-military "overstretch" concretely in terms of key bases, air and sea lines of communication, and other geographic realities in tangible ways that could prove relevant for gauging the proper U.S. overseas footprint in the world today and framing it in historical context.

Both these implications suggest that collective perceptions of geography can provide a powerful comparative framework for the study of national foreign policies during complex processes like decolonization, a framework that goes beyond more simplistic explanations of such phenomena that highlight single factors like domestic opposition to empire, international norms, or the strength of individual nationalist movements. A brief discussion of each of the cases of decolonization examined in this book helps illustrate the degrees to which American and British mental maps of the colonial world impinged on Anglo-American policies at the time.

PALESTINE

The voluminous literature on the British withdrawal from Palestine almost defies comprehension.[10] British Foreign Office officials principally saw Palestine as a possible strategic outpost in the wake of a withdrawal from Egypt, a foothold for the defense of India, and strategic depth for guarding British interests in Africa. Historians like Louis have even characterized Ernest Bevin's foreign policy in the Middle East as tantamount to a search for replacements for the vacated British foothold in the Suez. But in the course of that search, the Foreign and Colonial Offices, which shared responsibility for the administration of Palestine, and most of all the Chiefs of Staff, recognized the key constraint that any political solution for Palestine had to be sufficiently amenable to its Arab populations lest it provoke a revolt throughout the Levant and wider Middle East, and perhaps even among the Muslims of India. The ramifications of such a revolt were obvious in the augmented policing needs for Palestine and the problems it would pose for the maintenance of British relationships with newly independent states in which no direct imperial or mandatory administration would exist to protect British interests, only client states. As Herbert Samuel, former high commissioner in Palestine, put it in 1948, "On the relinquishment of direct British and French administration of the Middle East, country by country, Great Britain has patiently built up a whole block of Arab states within her sphere of influence."[11] Should a Muslim revolt consume the heartlands of Islam, Britain would have only its relationships with those states to contain and subdue it.

The perception of interdependencies linking the states of the Arab and Muslim world naturally led the Foreign and Colonial Offices to develop a holistic view of the crescent of Muslim populations stretching eastward from the Levant through Iraq and the Arabian Peninsula into Iran and southward into the Indian subcontinent. As Bevin himself put it, the Middle East extended all the way to Pakistan. This regional conception of British interests within a single territorial swath of predominantly Arab, Persian, Pashtun, and Punjabi Muslim populations was perhaps an unsurprising product of a British official mind seeking to manage a retreat from key strategic points that dotted Southwest Asia and the Persian Gulf. But it diverged sharply from the way American counterparts across the Atlantic perceived the Middle East.[12]

Like the historiography of British policy at the end of the mandate, a huge body of scholarship has explored the complex story of U.S. involvement in the Arab-Israeli conflict leading up to the Truman administration's recognition of Israel in May 1948.[13] The United States, in contrast to Britain, viewed affairs in Palestine in the context of the wider world situation. Washington's vital interests in the Middle East centered around the extraction of Middle Eastern oil to fuel global economic recovery, the defense of the region's energy reserves in case of another global war, and the preservation of access to sea lines of communication and their corresponding defense from the encroachments of the Soviet Union. The State Department's Policy Planning Staff cautioned that U.S. efforts to assist in the enforcement of a partition of Palestine might lead to the loss of U.S. basing rights and financial concessions in the strategically critical region, endangering the Marshall Plan, given its heavy dependence on Middle Eastern oil supplies to Europe. Regional stability was the critical requirement for continuity in the preservation of those rights. During the war the U.S. Joint Chiefs of Staff (JCS) had warned of the dangers of the rapid dissolution of European colonial authority in the region in terms of the instabilities that could arise, weakening the very powers whose help the United States would depend on not only to ensure access to the region's petroleum but also to balance Soviet power.[14]

As early as June 1946 the JCS had notified Truman of what they perceived to be the dangers of a U.S. commitment to employ military force to carry out certain recommendations of the joint Anglo-American Committee of Inquiry on Palestine. JCS fears of instability aside, the United States might well have been committed to the departure of colonial authority from regions like the Middle East. But too hasty a departure of existing British and French forces in the region could trigger a security vacuum counterproductive to broader American interests, the military warned.[15]

The Joint Chiefs' concerns with the wider geopolitical implications of any Palestine settlement echoed a separate linkage in the minds of State Department policymakers and especially White House officials between the situation in Palestine and liberated Europe. The nexus between these concerns led Truman administration officials to urge their British counterparts to submit first to increased quotas for Jewish immigration and ultimately, at the behest of Truman and his closest advisors, to the partition of Palestine in the service of the creation of a Jewish state in 1948. For some U.S. officials, the resettlement of Jewish refugees from occupied Europe in postwar Palestine was one natural solution among myriad others that would have to be hashed out to accommodate the necessary territorial adjustments, population transfers, and economic infusions in the service of peace. Moreover any delay in considering the implications in Palestine would only aggravate the situation. As Secretary of State James Byrnes told Ernest Bevin in October 1945, "This Government fears that any inquiry directed to an examination of conditions not only in Palestine, but other countries outside of Europe would result in delaying the alleviation of a situation which requires prompt remedial action."[16] Truman expressed his sentiments directly to Prime Minister Clement Attlee after stunning his British counterpart in his Yom Kippur statement of October 1946 reiterating the call for an additional 100,000 Jewish refugees be admitted to Palestine.[17]

While much has been made of the sensitivity of the Truman administration to the Jewish vote in the United States in the upcoming November 1948 presidential election, the geographical connection the administration drew between the flood of European Jews out of occupied and newly liberated territory and their potential resettlement in Palestine has been examined less closely. That strategic link in the minds of administration officials reveals a more integrated conception of postwar problems whose solutions would have to be implemented across continents—from population transfers in Western Europe to the Balkans, the Far East, and the Pacific. When superimposed onto the map of the Middle East, this outlook produced a quasi-Braudelian view of the Mediterranean region but also a distinctly American image of a region central to U.S. global interests in terms of its ample supply of energy reserves and arable land to accommodate refugees fleeing war-ravaged Europe. It was an image that contrasted sharply with British cartographies of the region that partitioned Europe from the Eastern Mediterranean and bounded the Levant and all that lay east of it into a self-contained sphere of influence extending from the Bosporus to the Indus—a closed system of sorts in which strategic basing needs and constraints were linked and where dissent and unrest had to be regulated at a delicate equilibrium in the face of dwindling economic and military resources.

KASHMIR

The Indo-Pakistani conflict over Kashmir likewise revealed the contrasting worldviews dividing the American and British official minds, despite a closer convergence of Anglo-American policy on the issue at the United Nations than was the case with Palestine. Again the view from London was very much of a dispute whose repercussions were considerable for the Arab Muslim world, in which Britain remained heavily engaged and on which it was dependent for military basing and trade connections in the wake of Egyptian independence. These primary considerations prompted many British officials to initially favor a settlement that would not sow discord among Pakistani Muslims, discord that they realized could quickly spread throughout the Arab world. By 1948 the Foreign Office feared that a settlement involving a Pakistani retreat from Kashmir, especially given the recent United Nations decision to partition Palestine, could deal yet another blow to British influence in the Islamic world as a whole.[18]

But Arab Muslim identification with the plight of their Kashmiri coreligionists was only one side of the coin. The strategic and territorial implications of close ties with Pakistan was the other. The Anglo-Pakistani relationship would prove a key consideration inside the crucible in London, where Labour was forging its imperial defense strategy. As Olaf Caroe, governor of the Northwest Frontier Province, recalled in his memoirs, the region from Turkey to Pakistan constituted "the Northern tier" of British defenses against Russian, Iranian, and Afghan influence threatening to penetrate the continent and displace authorities friendly to British interests. The role that the subcontinent's mountainous upper reaches played as a defensive bulwark protecting the Northern Tier ascribed additional importance to the resolution of the Kashmir dispute. The observations of officials like Caroe are insightful in revealing a British mind-set concerned with the Arab-Muslim "arc of crisis" stretching eastward and southward from the Levant down to its eastern end point in the mountainous northern edge of the subcontinent, a theme repeated by other British officials in references linking the issues of Kashmir with those of Palestine and other Muslim Arab lands.[19] From this frame of reference, the Kashmir settlement was one whose geographical and religious repercussions had to be contained lest they spread to adjoining regions of strategic importance for Britain and its relations with the wider Commonwealth.

Scholars of U.S. policy in South Asia have argued that the relative insignificance of the Indian subcontinent as a theater of the global cold war accounts for the apathy on the part of the United States to apply more forceful diplomatic pressure for a full settlement in the resolution of the Kashmir conflict. American interests saw the subcontinent as a secondary strategic asset in the cold war whose value lay principally in its raw materials and manpower. The conflict in Kashmir was distant from vital U.S. postwar interests in Europe and the Middle East, so much so that U.S. policy at the United Nations in the settlement of the question fell in line closely behind British policy. But U.S. government sources reveal that, to the extent that Washington took an interest in Kashmir, it was shaped by the need to prevent the Indo-Pakistani dispute over that territory from opening the Indian subcontinent to Soviet penetration. In assessing the source of South Asia's importance for the United States, American analysts highlighted four principal elements: the region's proximity to the Middle East, its large pool of manual labor, its mineral resources, and its potential as a market for stimulating the economic recovery of Europe and Great Britain.[20]

For these reasons, U.S. strategic calculations in the Kashmir conflict led Washington to remain mindful of the importance of Pakistan in its diplomatic efforts. U.S. intelligence officials had concluded that Pakistan possessed significance as an area that could benefit "U.S. offensive capabilities in the early phase of hostilities" in a potential world war.[21] But State Department officials conceived of Kashmir as only one of a number of issues that the partition of the Indian subcontinent had precipitated and that had to be dealt with as part of a broader settlement of postcolonial concerns in the wake of the British departure. Framing the problem as such, the Department bound the resolution of the Kashmir dispute to deliberations over "meeting a possible Soviet attack upon the Indian sub-continent through the strategic northwest frontier region."[22]

Thus while the State Department expressed some concerns similar to those of the Foreign Office about the nature of the tribal regions to the north and west of the North Indian plateau that shielded the subcontinent from invasion, U.S. concerns were founded less on regional stability requirements and the volatility of Muslim sentiments than on the security of raw materials and manpower resources of value in another potential world war. And whatever that potential value amounted to, from the perspective of Washington, the subcontinent was only one corner of the periphery of the developing worldwide struggle against international communism and its allies. Washington's interests were diffused over much larger territories than just the subcontinent, where quiescence was a necessary but insufficient precondition for the Kantian peace that America hoped to oversee.

THE LEVANT AND THE EAST INDIES

British and American views of the Palestine and Kashmir conflicts were thus shaped by two very different worldviews, affixed to regionalism and globalism's distinct geographical lenses of analysis. But the contracting British Empire, with its more restrictive geopolitical ambitions, and the new America bestriding the global stage to secure strategic access points and open new markets were not the only powers on the international scene; their interactions in the colonial world were affected by a class of "middle" powers. Wedged between British retreat and American expansion stood France and the Netherlands—obdurate empires both oblivious to overstretch in the Levant and East Indies, respectively, and unwilling to recalibrate their imperial footprints to fit a changed world.

One of the forces impinging on French wartime control over Syria and Lebanon was the introduction of British military presences into both mandated territories, which had both declared their independence in 1941. While the Free French Forces under Charles de Gaulle hoped that Allied cooperation would lead Britain to facilitate the reestablishment of French administration in the Levant, such anomalous amity could hardly take root against the grain of the long and acrimonious history of Anglo-French imperial competition dating back to nineteenth-century friction. The prospect of expelling France from the Eastern Mediterranean, where it could challenge British influence in Iraq and Palestine, was just too tempting for Whitehall to resist.

In May 1945 demonstrations in Damascus and Aleppo against the French-backed Troupes Speciales du Levant forced the British government to decide whether and how to respond to the crisis. Instead of pursuing a course of support for French authorities or even one of benevolent noninterference, Britain chose to dislodge the French foothold in the region by leveraging the utility of its wartime occupation dating back to the Allied landing four years earlier. When Syrian nationalist sentiments finally boiled over at the close of the war, Britain seized the opportunity to intervene militarily to restore order, threatening to occupy Damascus. The ensuing campaign ended in a cease-fire order from General de Gaulle and the eventual withdrawal of both French and British forces by the end of 1946, ending French colonial mastery over the newly independent states.[23]

If the intervention by a calculating British military in full-fledged postimperial retreat helped *pull* the French out of the Levant, the active encouragement of Syrian and Lebanese nationalism by the United States worked simultaneously to *push* them out. The Roosevelt administration's recognition of Syrian and Lebanese independence in 1944 showed that Washington would not pay lip service to French colonial rule over those states as it did to other French possessions. As a result Syrian and Lebanese nationalists found in Great Britain and the United States two allies to help them realize their aspirations to independence. One was an imperial power willingly curtailing its ambitions in the region that sought to drag the influence of its colonial competitors out with it. The other was a declaredly anticolonial power eager to promote the ideals of the Atlantic Charter throughout the postwar world.[24]

A similar fate would befall the beleaguered Dutch administrators in the East Indies, where the withdrawing British Empire again hastened the reluctant retreat of overstretched colonial rule. Unlike in the Levant, the East Indies were subjected to two foreign occupations: first by Japanese forces, under which a nascent Indonesian state bureaucracy came to function with surprising effectiveness, and then by liberating British troops, when jurisdiction for the archipelago fell to the Southeast Asia Command (SEAC). Another difference was the complex set of considerations weighing on the Foreign Office's East Indies policy. Here the situation was not simply one of supporting a nationalist struggle at the expense of a rival European imperial power but a delicate balancing act between the maintenance of law and order, respect for Dutch colonial authority, and circumspect non-involvement in the simmering Indonesian nationalist movement. A particular concern for British policy in the East Indies was the precedent it might set in an increasingly restive India, whose troops, if forced to pacify ethnic Indonesians on behalf of the Dutch imperialists, could sow massive unrest throughout the subcontinent and incite a rebellion against British rule. Eventually a measured British policy driven by regional considerations shaped largely by the situation in India spurred the Dutch government to engage nationalist leaders in a dialogue on the devolution of power and the future of Dutch rule in 1946.[25]

In a sense America had expressed its tacit lack of interest in the Indonesian archipelago by transferring responsibility for it to British command. For the overarching American goal in the Pacific theater was the maintenance of stability, while focusing on the critical postwar questions in Europe. But unfortunately for Dutch colonial authority, stability for Washington did not mean a simple reliance on America's wartime ally and Marshall Plan aid recipient to do as it saw fit to pacify the islands. Early U.S. policy did rely on British and Dutch efforts to fashion a reasonable settlement, but over time the Truman administration came to condemn the excesses of Dutch policy and promote an international settlement of the Indonesian question that led eventually to independence and a defeat for Dutch colonial rule. America's very reliance on two European allies to handle the vexing postcolonial problem of the East Indies revealed a willingness to lean on a decentralized system for the management of global security responsibilities in far-flung corners of the postwar world. But the anticolonial objectives in the eventual U.S. push for Indonesian independence were unquestionable.

In the Levant and the East Indies, therefore, the French and Dutch found themselves facing similar quandaries. Unwilling to withdraw hastily and cut short their wartime losses through geopolitical contractions, both governments came to recognize the need to downsize their imperial presence only when confronted with geopolitical pressures. One source of this pressure was the transitional effect of temporary British military occupations in the closing years of the war, occupations that limited the reach of imperial power and provided glimpses of postcolonial futures to nationalists eager to confront imperial overlordship in the era of the Atlantic Charter and its ideals. Another was the reach of American power—both hard and soft—coupled with the historic anti-imperial ideology that had characterized American foreign policy from George Washington to FDR.

THE UN ORDER AND POSTCOLONIAL STATEHOOD

The geographically distinct American and British conceptions of postwar security that produced varying degrees of Anglo-American conflict and cooperation in the cases of Palestine and Kashmir and helped dislodge France and the Netherlands from other parts of the colonial world had to be reconciled at the wartime conferences that created the United Nations. After all, the great powers also had to agree at the decisive moment of 1945 on the new institution's internal geographical organization. The Security Council, with its five permanent members, would preside over questions of international peace and security; that much had been determined by the time of the Dumbarton Oaks Conference of 1944. The UN machinery for managing the decolonization process, meanwhile, consisted of a Trusteeship Council and "regional arrangements" to handle issues local to regions of the world that did not need to be brought before the Security Council. All of these structures reflected to varying extents a tension between American globalism in pursuit of a central postwar organization that could manage international peace and the distinct, territorially limited aims of its counterpart trend toward regionalism driving British strategy.[26]

After American and British geographic conceptions of the postwar order were reconciled in the UN Security and Trusteeship Councils at San Francisco in the summer of 1945, the United Nations Organization and its subsidiary bodies provided an institutional forum for multilateral cooperation on postcolonial questions. But the differences dividing the two allies as to where their postwar interests lay outlived the creation of the United Nations. In walking a fine line when it came to sovereign statehood for former colonial dependencies and mandated territories, the United States had formulated a careful policy balanced precariously between the precepts of realism and idealism.

But Great Britain too had to tread carefully, between the Arab and émigré Jewish claims to self-determination in postwar Palestine, and rival Indian and Pakistani claims to sovereignty over Kashmir, where the future disposition of the territory of Jammu and Kashmir remained unclear. Intriguingly an analysis of the ways the British and American official minds subscribed to varying geographic perceptions of the postwar world goes a considerable length toward explaining the policies that Great Britain and the United States pursued on postcolonial matters, including at the United Nations. At one level, an America eager to adopt a global national security policy now faced a Great Britain judiciously tending to its newly circumscribed territorial needs. When the time came to decide the inherently politicized questions of the fates of redistributed postcolonial territories and the redrawing of colonial-era maps to accommodate newly independent nations from the Middle East to South and Southeast Asia, this book argues, it was primarily from these distinct ways of seeing the spatial distribution of political interests that the rationales and policy divides separating American and British plans emerged.

In exploring these strategic worldviews and integrating them into the stories of the anticolonial protagonists themselves, the arguments in this book span three broad themes. The first centers on the role of geography in international politics and the rise of geopolitics as an academic field around the Second World War, especially in the United States. The second concerns ideas about postcolonial nationalism in the third world that came to shape struggles like the Zionist movement and the call for Pakistan. The third revolves around the craft of international history and the interconnectedness of the histories of decolonization, the early cold war, and the creation of the United Nations.

GEOGRAPHY AND INTERNATIONAL POLITICS

Scholars have long recognized the centrality of geography as a driver of international politics. Some of the foundational works of geopolitics that influenced postwar U.S. foreign policy appeared between the late nineteenth and mid-twentieth century. Alfred Thayer Mahan, Halford Mackinder, and Nicholas Spykman all acknowledged the importance of geography in shaping historical processes, though they disagreed on the relative importance of sea and land power and held differing conceptions of the earth's principal land masses and peripheral coastal regions. Contemporary observers have increasingly focused on the importance of geographical factors in shaping international relations.[27]

Despite the postwar decline of geography as a scholarly discipline in the United States in parallel with the rise of region- and language-specific area studies, historians have recently emphasized anew the centrality of territorial sources of power and the spatial dimensions of international relations. Such lines of inquiry have highlighted geographical factors shaping both the broadest patterns of world history as well as the course of the West's rise to preeminence in the modern world over the past five centuries.[28] Neil Smith's *American Empire* applied the lens of geographical analysis specifically to the first half of the twentieth century and America's rise to "globalism." Other scholars have built on the work of geopolitical theorists to consider how representations of geography in maps and in the minds of policymakers have impinged on the policies that they have pursued, especially in the age of civil and military aviation and increasing global interconnectedness after the Second World War, as well as how historical factors have shaped the development of cartography and pictorial representations of territory. This work has emphasized the importance of the rise of the academic field of geopolitics in the United States during the early 1940s, after the publication of Spykman's *America's Strategy in World Politics*. It has also explored how maps on the pages of magazines like *National Geographic* and Roosevelt's wartime call on every American to buy a map and follow the war effort helped flesh out everyday Americans' geographical knowledge of the wider world. This body of work provides a firm foundation with which to examine the strategies and policies conjured by official minds, codified into bureaucratic processes, and bound by organizational jurisdictions.[29]

THE RISE OF POSTCOLONIAL NATIONALISM

Globalism and regionalism entailed assumptions about real geography—geography that not only existed at the spatial, territorial level but also connoted meaning in terms of human geography, demographics, and individual identities. Colonial subjects and free citizens alike populated the far reaches of the British Empire and the new markets for American goods in its postcolonial successor states. The postcolonial sources of identity considered in this book (Muslim, Jewish, Arab, Israeli, Indian, Pakistani, etc.) underwent fundamental transformations in the immediate postwar years once relieved of the pressure of British colonial overlordship from above and buffeted by American anticolonial rhetoric from afar.

Historians and theorists alike have offered insights into the origins of anticolonial nationalism in the twentieth century and the movements with intellectual roots stretching back to the nineteenth century that undermined colonial authority before, during, and after the Second World War. Partha Chatterjee and his fellow proponents of subaltern studies opened an early debate on the complex process by which anticolonial struggle in India appropriated the "derivative discourse" of the nation-state as idealized by Enlightenment rationalism, with attendant conceptions of values like liberty and ideas like philosophies of history. But as the international histories of movements like Wilsonianism have shown, the national liberation struggles that sprung up in each postcolonial territory evolved along unique narrative trajectories with distinct histories. Indeed nationalisms came in many flavors, as the colonial powers soon came to realize in the years after 1945. And the ideological bases for nationhood in the new international order were manifold and distinct. Thus national histories exploring each movement in depth have unearthed fine-grained details about their intellectual and social foundations.[30]

Scholars of Zionism have traced the complex evolutionary path of that movement, from Theodor Herzl's original appeal for a secular, neutral, egalitarian Jewish state as a sanctuary to afford Jews protection from anti-Semitic persecution to the more exclusivist vision of David Ben-Gurion and his contemporaries, who accommodated orthodox religious parties in postmandatory Palestine and supported the expulsion of Palestinian Arabs in the course of his state-building enterprise. Critically the twentieth-century Zionist movement soon split between those for whom settlement was the key to the destiny of the Jewish people and those for whom the attainment of sovereignty became the paramount concern. In contrast, other thinkers, such as the Jewish philosopher Hannah Arendt, supported the idea of Palestine as a Jewish homeland, but a *binational* one that accommodated Arabs and was stripped of any unitary Jewish sovereignty, the conferral of which she believed would transform European Jewry from oppressed into oppressor.[31]

Muslim nationalism was the driving force behind the Muslim League's goal of a state of Pakistan. But exactly *what* the idea of Pakistan—as framed by Muhammad Ali Jinnah, the nation's founder—connoted is a historical problem that scholars have long debated. Indeed British India Office officials openly speculated that a degree of ambiguity helped Jinnah rally Muslims against their political opponents in the Congress Party and British colonial authorities without having to specify what exactly his demands were. Muslim identity posed no more acute a problem anywhere in British India than in the princely state of Jammu and Kashmir, whose accession to India through the signature of its ruling maharaja triggered a postcolonial war between newly created India and Pakistan. Like Zionism, Muslim nationalism reaffirmed the importance of identity beyond territoriality as a potential basis for nationhood caught up in the swirl of shifting postwar power balances and the Hegelian clash of competing ideologies in former colonial territories.[32]

Similarly, though their exploration in depth exceeds the scope of this book, other (perhaps more contestable) bases of national identity drove revolts in both the Arab Levant and the East Indies, where French and Dutch colonial power lost control of prewar possessions suddenly in the turmoil of rapidly demobilizing British military occupation and succumbed to the influence of expansive American military basing, air transport, and commercial presences radiating outward into former colonial spheres of influence. The search for Indonesian nationalism and its origins is perhaps the most complex in this regard, amounting to a grassroots movement uniting a rich milieu of ethnicities and languages strewn across the archipelago that reached a critical mass during Japanese occupation and subsequent liberation. In this regard the extraordinary coherence of the nationalist movement under Sukarno and Mohammed Hatta, and the degree to which it gave rise to functioning local government by the time of British reoccupation under the SEAC, is perhaps a testament to the complementary role that identity played to that of territory in shaping the Indonesian anticolonialism that displaced the Dutch empire-in-denial that had clung to the East Indies.[33]

Works on the independence of Syria and Lebanon have documented the parallel experiences of both those former colonies in the Levant while the Indonesians waged their own independence struggle. While Albert Hourani and other scholars have cited the strong impact of Arab nationalism in driving the Syrian and Lebanese bids for independence, especially given its roots in the nineteenth-century notion of *asabiyya* (community) as it developed among Christian middle classes in the tea houses of Damascus and Beirut, other scholars have attributed less consequence to Arab identity as a nation and more importance instead to the heavy-handedness of French colonial policy.[34]

DECOLONIZATION, THE COLD WAR, AND THE UNITED NATIONS

The historiographies of decolonization, the early cold war, and the birth of the United Nations have largely evolved as separate subfields, yet their synthesis is central for international histories that account for the interplay of these broad currents. The connections between them reveal how postcolonial nation-building intersected with the nascent cold war superpower rivalry played out in a new multilateral order supposedly predicated on formal cooperation. The works of William Roger Louis, John Darwin, Robert F. Holland, and others have helped explain the geographical contraction of Britain's foreign policy under Attlee and Bevin, which led primarily to a policy of nonintervention in transfers of power in the Middle East, including in Palestine. Despite championing that nonintervention, Bevin, in particular, was sensitive to the logic of the cold war and the specter of Anglo-Soviet competition in the Middle East in the wake of a British retreat from the region. Into its vacated spaces rushed America's policy of "containment" of Soviet power and the attendant global geography of competition that underpinned it.[35] Without an explicit focus on the colonial powers and their possessions, cold war historians John Lewis Gaddis, Bruce Kuniholm, and others have shown how Soviet policy—especially in the Middle East—shaped U.S. national security policy toward former colonial territories and newly independent states in the lead-up to and after the promulgation of the Truman Doctrine in 1947.[36] And scholarship on the history of the United Nations has shed important light on the aims of the U.S. State Department for the new international organization and how the United States perceived its role in the management of international security, including postwar territorial questions. Robert Sherwood's Pulitzer Prize–winning *Roosevelt and Hopkins* remains the standard treatment of FDR's dispute with Winston Churchill over the meaning of self-determination as referenced by the Atlantic Charter.[37] Institutional histories of the creation of the United Nations are likewise useful in explaining how intragovernmental American and British policy disputes were resolved neatly into predictable positions, such as the American insistence on trusteeships dependent on international supervision and monitoring and British support for national trusteeship schemes that would not impinge on colonial jurisdictions. The work of historians like Robert Hilderbrand, Christopher O'Sullivan, and Townsend Hoopes and Douglas Brinkley clarify U.S. intentions for the colonial world as formulated by Cordell Hull, Sumner Welles, Leo Pasvolsky, and Isaiah Bowman at the State Department and Churchill's and Bevin's determination to thwart them.[38]

Seams between these works have occluded integrative international histories of the postwar period that show how great power competition and a new multilateral order shaped early anticolonial struggles. At a minimum, any holistic account of Anglo-American efforts to redraw borders in the postwar world must meld insights from across all three of these subfields. But a complete history of Anglo-American policy toward the colonial world during this period must advance even beyond such a synthesis. It must also take account of the fundamental impact of perceptions of geography on both American and British strategies toward colonial territories throughout the world as well as the goals of individual protagonists engaged in independence struggles in order to explain how the visions of great powers and anticolonial nationalists clashed in the course of their collective efforts to map the end of empire.

ONE

All of Palestine

The first Arab-Israeli War was the climax of a decades-long struggle between Arabs and Jews in Palestine. For Britain, the war was a catastrophe. Arab unrest fueled by continued Jewish immigration into Palestine, accelerated by both Nazi persecution and Soviet pogroms, coupled with the postwar costs of overseas military deployments and manpower shortages throughout the British Empire, had pushed to the limit British forces in the mandated territory and in the region as a whole. Meanwhile U.S. support for the continued immigration of Jewish settlers into Palestine and the eventual recognition of the state of Israel in 1948 raised the temperature and demographic pressure in Palestine to new highs. The combustible situation meant that it was only a matter of time before the pragmatic Labour government in London seeking to implement Foreign Minister Ernest Bevin's policy of nonintervention and economic development in the Middle East would beat a hasty retreat from Palestine.[1]

THE BALFOUR DECLARATION AND
MANDATORY PALESTINE

The modern roots of the Arab-Israeli conflict date back to the aftermath of the First World War and the resulting peace settlement that accorded the British Empire rights to League of Nations mandates to Iraq and Palestine.[2] Great Britain had long coveted the Eastern Mediterranean for its intrinsic strategic value, given its proximity to the Suez Canal and the

Levant's principal trade routes. As early as 1917 British officials, including Prime Minister David Lloyd George, an ardent Zionist, and his advisors, had subscribed to the notion that a partnership between Great Britain and Jewish émigrés seeking a national homeland in Palestine could help fashion a peace after the war consonant with British interests in the Near East, as Britain began to feel the pinch of creeping imperial costs and to countenance new strategic risks imposed by the burden of imperial administration. By the end of the war a number of these officials—including assistant secretaries of the War Cabinet like Mark Sykes and Leo Amery and an influential member of Parliament, William Ormsby-Gore—came to the conclusion that the coexistence of an Arab Palestine and a national homeland for Zionist Jews within the same borders was both desirable for Great Britain and a feasible diplomatic objective.[3]

As is now well known, that objective proved infamously difficult to reconcile with wartime promises to the leaders of Arab tribes to which the Foreign Office had assented for the sole purpose of inducing a revolt that might decisively turn the tide against Britain's enemies, the Ottoman Empire and the Central Powers. During the years 1915–1916 the British high commissioner in Egypt, Sir Henry McMahon, conveyed to Sharif Hussein of Mecca (the leader of the Arab Hashemite clan) Britain's intent to support Arab independence throughout the Levant in exchange for leading a revolt against Ottoman forces. Specifically McMahon delineated territories promised to Britain's Arab allies in a document known as the Damascus Protocol, which assured the Arab leader of "the recognition by Great Britain of the independence of the Arab countries lying within the following frontiers: North: The Line Mersin-Adana to parallel 37N. and thence along the line Birejek-Urga-Mardin-Kidiat-Jazirat (Ibn 'Unear)-Amadia to the Persian frontier; East: The Persian frontier down to the Persian Gulf; South: The Indian Ocean (with the exclusion of Aden, whose status was to be maintained). West: The Red Sea and the Mediterranean Sea back to Mersin."[4] As mountains of historical research have argued, McMahon's vague message seemed to directly contradict parallel assurances that London would soon thereafter provide to Zionist leaders eager to settle in Palestine. Perhaps motivated by the hope that Russian Jews would reinforce Tsar Nicholas II's support for the war effort and that American Zionists would persuade President Woodrow Wilson to enter the war in support of the Entente powers, the British government issued the Balfour Declaration on 2 November 1917 in the aftermath of an energetic campaign of lobbying by international Zionist groups, the start of a global advocacy effort that would continue throughout the first half of the century and culminate in the creation of the state of Israel. The Declaration all but committed the British government to the establishment of a national Jewish homeland in Palestine, paving the way for the emigration of Jews there at an increasing rate over the next two decades. In issuing the Declaration the Foreign Office probably also considered its effect on President Wilson, who, it surmised, might have been subjected to pressure from American Zionists to enter the war on the side of the Entente powers. Whatever its motivations, the Declaration encouraged a wave of emigration to Palestine over subsequent decades. It was largely the population shifts and displacements spurred by this emigration en masse that sowed the seeds of the Arab-Israeli War of 1948 and the modern Israeli-Palestinian conflict.[5]

After the First World War the great powers, convened at the San Remo Conference of 1920, agreed that Britain would be responsible for postwar administration of the territory of Palestine.[6] But just what constituted "Palestine" first had to be defined before the mandated territory could be topologically demarcated—which raised the corresponding issue of the precise obligations connoted by the Balfour Declaration. In a May 1922 conversation with the Colonial Office, the first high commissioner of Palestine, Herbert Samuel, pleaded with British officials to assuage Arab concerns by outlining three conditions. First, Samuel proposed limiting the Jewish national home to areas west of the Jordan River; second, he suggested abandonment of the principle of a state with a Jewish majority; third, he suggested that future Jewish immigration under the mandate be limited to "the economic capacity of the country." When His Majesty's government published Samuel's draft document on 1 July 1922, the resulting Churchill-Samuel White Paper came to represent the official British definition of the extent of mandatory Palestine. That week the House of Commons accepted the mandate, paving the way for its approval by the League of Nations on 29 September.[7] A year later the League of Nations approved Britain's rights to a formal League "mandate" for the territory of Palestine. While the settlement did not grant the Zionist movement a free and independent Palestine to settle at will, the League Council echoed the Balfour Declaration and acknowledged "the historical connection of the Jewish people with Palestine." It also made reference to the legitimacy of the Zionist movement in "reconstituting their National Home in that country." Moreover the British would "use their best endeavors to facilitate" continuing Jewish immigration and settlement. Notably, though, the mandatory language refrained from any direct mention of the Arabs in Palestine, describing the territory's other inhabitants only as "non-Jews."[8] The language was significant in its omission of a reference to the Muslim Arabs inhabiting Palestine, who constituted a sizable majority.

In a sense the omission of an overt reference to the Palestinian Arabs cast further immigration into Palestine in the rhetoric of frontier settlement, as opposed to the narrative of neocolonial usurpation and territorial appropriation, to which the Arabs of Palestine subscribed. These opposed narratives with disparate geographical implications—one of overseas settlement of fertile soils, the other of illegitimate invasion—would soon collide in violent confrontation leading to open war.

Over the subsequent decade a cascade of violence over continuing Jewish immigration began to threaten the tenability of Britain's presence in Palestine. Throughout the 1920s and early 1930s Arab-Jewish clashes such as during the May Day riots of 1921, the Wailing Wall incident in 1929, and other encounters led officials in London to rethink their policy vis-à-vis the Palestine mandate.[9] The continued immigration of Jewish settlers into Palestine had worsened drastically the security situation in Palestine, a series of British government White Papers concluded. But the leaders of the Zionist movement maintained that the notion of Palestine's "absorptive capacity," as a static limit, was an illusory one. "How are we to interpret the principle of absorptive capacity?" David Ben-Gurion wrote in 1933. "In the eleven years since the [1922 Churchill-Samuel] White Paper appeared, the rate of admission has fluctuated considerably—in some years, over 10,000 Jews arrived, in others, only a few thousands; one year more than 30,000 immigrants; another year more emigrants than immigrants."[10] The notion of absorptive capacity was ambiguous, Ben-Gurion and his Zionists maintained, and a construct of the British "Official Mind" to stem further Jewish immigration.

The British government's response to the deterioration of the situation in Palestine entailed convening a series of commissions of inquiry, elaborate undertakings by appointed senior officials that produced massive periodic reports on the situation and laid out recommendations for resolving Palestine's ultimate status. But the spiral of events in Palestine and beyond began to sweep away any hope of Arab accommodation of incremental Jewish settlement. After the National Socialist Party's accession to power in Germany triggered additional waves of emigrating European Jews, Arab opposition to the Jewish influx hardened reflexively, further defining itself in the process. Led by the ardent Nazi sympathizer and grand mufti of Jerusalem, Hajj Amin al-Husseini, Arabs turned en masse against the perpetuation of British rule. Organizing under the banner of the new Istiqlal Party, Palestinian Arabs now demanded institutions that would secure what they perceived as their increasingly embattled majority in mandatory Palestine. By the mid-1930s what was brewing among Arabs was a more virulent, reactive, anti-Zionist nationalism that now, like many of the Zionists it targeted, lay claim to *all* of Palestine in the name of Arabs.[11]

These sentiments boiled over into violent riots in 1936 in which the Arabs in Palestine revolted against British rule in a conflict that would last for three years, sparking a guerrilla war between Palestinian Arabs and Jewish settlers. The event was significant not only for its scale but also for the Arabs' appropriation of the rhetoric of political independence as a specific demand.[12] The following year the influential 1937 Palestine Royal Commission (the "Peel Commission") issued a report based on an inquiry it conducted recommending the partition of Palestine into Arab and Jewish areas to allow the internecine conflict to subside before it reached the level of a full-blown civil war. The report concluded, "While neither race can justly rule all Palestine, we see no reason why, if it were practicable, each race should not rule part of it."[13] But the idea of partitioning off elongated slivers of Palestine failed to fully satisfy either Arab or Zionist demands and left unaddressed the issue of the demographic pressures elevated by the continued immigration of European Jews there.

Some British officials believed at the outset that Palestine could not be partitioned, leading the Foreign Office to retreat from the Peel Commission's findings almost upon their release. At the outbreak of the Second World War in 1939, Great Britain issued another White Paper on Palestine, a document that would profoundly affect the fate of displaced European Jews in the war and arouse the most vitriolic Zionist opposition Whitehall had yet faced. Its recommendations were threefold. First, it called for the creation of an independent state in Palestine after a transitory ten-year period; second, it tightly circumscribed the continued purchase of land throughout Palestine by Jews seeking to settle there; third, it called for the restriction of Jewish immigration into Palestine subject to Arab acquiescence within five years, over the course of which no more than 75,000 Jews were to be admitted.[14]

In stipulating that "political and psychological factors must be taken into consideration" in determining future immigration quotas, Zionists lashed out that the 1939 White Paper represented a complete British capitulation to Arab demands. The prominent Zionist and British chemist Chaim Weizmann, leader of the World Zionist Organization, had first glimpsed some of the provisions of the eventual White Paper at the 1938 Tripartite Conference convening British, Arab, and Jewish delegations to discuss immigration. There an invitation to a lunch hosted by the British government intended only for the Arab delegations was inadvertently sent to the Jewish participants. After reading the letter, Weizmann's reaction characterized that of many Zionists: that "Arab terrorism had won its first major victory."[15]

But was agreement on an acceptable rate of immigration to accommodate the outflow of Jews from Europe the principal objective of the Zionist movement? Or were its goals more fundamentally irredentist in nature, in terms of the reclamation of an ancestral homeland? It so happened that the 1930s saw the transformation of not only the Arab political consciousness in Palestine but also that of Palestinian Jewry. The continuing (and accelerating) Jewish immigration into Palestine and the punitive British policies hastily fashioned to limit it had unearthed and sharpened new political aims of the fluid, international Zionist movement.[16]

ZIONISM AND ITS POLITICAL AIMS

The idea of a collective return to Zion reentered public discourse among Jewish intellectuals as early as the late nineteenth century. Critically it had a defined territorial component.[17] The modern Zionist movement, founded by the Hungarian journalist Theodor Herzl, undertook to establish a national homeland for Jews in Palestine in the wake of upsurges of anti-Semitism in Europe as manifest in the form of mass rallies in Paris following the Dreyfus Affair. In 1896 Herzl published *Der Judenstaat* (The Jewish State), laying out his vision. The following year the first World Zionist Congress convened in Basel, Switzerland. As early as that first gathering, it became clear that two distinct mind-sets separated the international Zionist movement. While both saw the settlement of a territory where Jews would become a national majority as their ultimate objective, one group focused squarely on the acquisition of international legal sovereignty as its principal goal—even before the achievement of a demographic majority. The other focused on the *act of settlement* as the primary task at hand. The Basel Program adopted at the Congress sought to reconcile these views by framing the Zionist mission as "the establishment of a home (Heimstaette) for the Jewish people secured under public law in Palestine."[18]

When the 1903 Kishinev pogrom against Jews in Bessarabia stirred Russian anti-Semitism and open acts of violence, some 40,000 Jews answered Herzl's calls and migrated to Palestine. So began the modern Zionist settler movement, which continued through the interwar period until it vexed and inextricably bound American and British policymakers within a half century. As settlers purchased land from Arab landholders, the influx of Jews into Palestine began to disrupt the livelihoods of Arab tenant farmers, who in some instances were forced to abandon the land they tilled and accept compensation for the tracts they inhabited when landlords sold off their holdings. By the end of the First World War the fledgling Jewish settler population in Palestine, "the Yishuv," numbered about 55,000. But from 1919 onward the Third Aliyah (or "homecoming") immediately began to populate the Jewish community at an increasing rate. A thousand new Jewish settlers fleeing persecution and other forms of civil unrest in European homelands flooded into Palestine each month by 1920, and a total of some 37,000 arrived between the years 1919 and 1923.[19]

A critical mass of the Zionist movement had envisioned a future state in Palestine for themselves and for Jewish refugees from Europe. During the negotiation of the Balfour Declaration with the British, Weizmann had played a delicate balancing act. Though he denied that the Zionists sought to create a Jewish state in Palestine as an immediate objective, he persuaded his fellow Zionists that the Declaration was not the final achievement of the Zionist project, but merely one step in a longer process.[20] That did not stop other Zionist groups like the Jewish Revisionist Party in Palestine, founded in 1925 by Vladimir Jabotinsky, from focusing almost exclusively on the establishment of a Jewish state as its goal. Did the Revisionists' statist agenda explicitly espouse what was only implied in the wider Zionist movement, or did it embody a widely shared, core commitment to a Jewish state at the heart of the Zionist project? The historical trajectory of Zionism dating back to Herzl's own writings seem to suggest that the goal of an independent Jewish state lay at the core of Zionist ideology.[21] But irrespective of the movement's original intellectual underpinnings or direction, many mainstream Zionists clearly shared Jabotinsky's vision, and the Nazi persecution of Jews in occupied Europe only hastened their existential drive to realize it. The year of the great Arab revolt, Ben-Gurion, chairman of the Jewish Agency and de facto leader of the Yishuv, told the

Zionist Executive Council that it needed to continue working with British mandatory authorities, acknowledging that, despite their faults, the British had done much for their cause.[22] But by the issue of the 1939 White Paper, a fissure between those who pursued continued immigration and settlement as their core objective, and others now squarely focused on the maximalist vision of a Jewish state in all of Palestine, opened and began to widen.

That fissure was conspicuously evident at the Twenty-first Zionist Congress in August 1939. Ben-Gurion and his hitherto moderate Labor wing of the movement now vociferously asserted Jewish national identity in Palestine in conjunction with the Revisionists through open calls for a state. "The White Paper has created a vacuum which must be filled by the Jews themselves," Ben-Gurion thundered in his typically impassioned style. "The Jews should act as though they were the State in Palestine, and should so continue to act until there will be a Jewish State there."[23] He later reflected that it was in these years between the White Paper and Palestine's abandonment at the United Nations that he and Weizmann parted ways ideologically. "It is my belief that from the beginning of what we can call the White Paper epoch—spring of 1939—up to the United Nations Partition Resolution of November 1947, Weizmann was beset by a gnawing inner confusion and stress, and he failed to find his way," Ben-Gurion later reflected.[24]

Herzl himself had alluded to the difficulty of maintaining a distinction between the goal of a national homeland and the separate political objective of establishing a sovereign state. Jewish settlement of Palestine in the late 1930s was scattered. The extent of Jewish landholdings as of 1937 was captured visually for the massive 1945–1946 *Survey of Palestine* conducted for the Anglo-American Committee of Inquiry (figure 1). But it was unclear whether it was geographically delimited in scope. With regard to the potential limits on the term *Jewish National Homeland*, Herzl felt that there was "no need to worry. . . . The people will read it as 'Jewish State' anyhow."[25] This shift was significant in that it recast Jewish identity in the symbolic and concrete trappings of a state; territorial borders, national institutions, and a proprietary language were acquiring a new importance in what was a modern redefinition of Judaism.[26] The vision rapidly acquired momentum, associating the power of a specific territorial space steeped in religious historical significance with the existence of the Jewish people.[27] During the Second World War Zionist activists led by Ben-Gurion sought "to have the Zionist leadership in Palestine, namely himself, direct the movement toward statehood," as one historian put it.[28] And while official Zionist documents often assiduously avoided references to Jewish statehood, Ben-Gurion's own writings echoed that focus on a state as the movement's ultimate end: "I don't regard a state in part of Palestine as the final aim of Zionism, but as a means toward that aim."[29] He also later confided to his wife that even if a Jewish state was not established throughout all of Palestine at first, "the rest will come in the course of time. It must come."[30] Ben-Gurion's view gradually displaced those held by his more moderate contemporaries, such as Weizmann, who had hitherto espoused slower, steadier gains on the road to Zionist statehood.[31] In a sense Weizmann represented a more advanced stage of Zionist thought than Herzl, having tied Herzl's abstract vision of a homeland specifically to the land of Palestine, which in Weizmann's mind was "the only land in which Jewish sovereignty could and must be revived." Weizmann's parting of ways with Ben-Gurion had occurred over the former's concerns with the difficulties that would beset the Jewish people in their efforts to fulfill the Zionist dream.[32] But by 1942 even Weizmann seemed to be coming around to the idea of statehood. In January of that year he published an article in *Foreign Affairs* that demanded a "Jewish Commonwealth" throughout the whole of Western Palestine.[33]

Paralleling this radical shift in the movement was a surge in activity by Zionist extremist groups like the LEHI (Fighters for the Freedom of Israel) and the Irgun, who launched violent attacks against British police and other official targets. In the United States Weizmann's associates organized a vastly successful 1942 conference in New York's Biltmore Hotel, where they called for entrusting control over immigration into Palestine to the Jewish Agency. Public American sympathies for the Zionist cause crested to new highs, especially after news of the Holocaust and atrocities committed against Jews in occupied Europe began to spread throughout the world. By early 1943, though the movement's center of mass had now coalesced behind Ben-Gurion and the activist wing of the movement, Weizmann joined his colleagues in calling on Britain to rescind the White Paper. Rumors of British collusion with the Arabs to establish a pan-Arab federation of sorts prompted him to write to Churchill to appeal for a reversal of British policy. Indeed Anglo-Arab postwar plans to partition the Levant loomed large as one of the Zionist movement's greatest fears.[34]

In the prelude to the 1944 presidential election in the United States, both the Democratic and Republican parties' platforms swiftly subsumed the Biltmore Conference's call for the establishment of a Jewish homeland in Palestine.[35] Interestingly the State Department also took note of the opinions of many American adherents of Zionism who were nonetheless opposed to the creation of a new Jewish state in lieu of continued resettlement in the existing territory of mandatory Palestine.[36] But the allure and historical resonance of the call to statehood proved irresistible, drowning such sentiments under waves of international support for the Biltmore Program. By the end of the war the Zionist project to construct a Jewish state in Palestine had thus not only congealed around a concrete ideology; it had also mobilized internationally in the service of realizing its aspirations to sovereign statehood. And the center of mass within that movement was accelerating toward a violent, revolutionary activism. The U.S. Office of Strategic Services concluded that Zionist militancy was "in the ascendant."[37] In May 1945 Weizmann again appealed to Churchill, beseeching him to open the floodgates of immigration into Palestine at last and anoint all of it as the Jewish homeland that the Balfour Declaration had promised: "Every passing week, every reply in Parliament which treats the White Paper as law, increases the prescriptive interest of our opponents in that fatal document. This is the hour to eliminate the White Paper, to open the doors of Palestine and to proclaim the Jewish State."[38] As a matter of fact, Weizmann maintained, demographic reality presented its own self-fulfilling rationale for seeking a state in all of Palestine: the population pressure generated by the presence of the Jews who had reached Palestine by war's end, barely tolerable during the war, now meant "confinement to a territorial ghetto consisting of five percent of the area of Western Palestine."[39]

That confinement in an increasingly tight area became a rationale for outward territorial expansion and a sort of frontier settlement. It was in this context of increasingly ambitious postwar Zionist designs that Anglo-American policies clashed over the future of Palestine.[40]

ANGLO-AMERICAN POLICY IN POSTWAR PALESTINE

In the minds of American and British policymakers alike, no postcolonial question likely loomed larger as the war drew to a close than that of Palestine. But extraordinary constraints curtailed their freedom of action over the fate of the narrow sliver of land on the Mediterranean littoral. Instead, as the former mandate-era high commissioner Herbert Samuel put it, Palestine's future would hinge "largely on the relative strength of the pro-Zionist and anti-Zionist forces throughout the world as a whole. Little is to be gained at this stage by traversing once more the sterile plains of promises, rights and desiderata," Samuel thought, adding that "no new approach to the Palestine problem is possible today." Still, the stalemate precipitated by the clash of forces in support of Arabs and Jews need not worry British officials, he maintained. For irrespective of whether a change in the status of the mandate was effected, Britain would continue to maintain preponderant influence "on both sides of the Red Sea route to India."[41] Moreover the disorder in Palestine could even benefit British interests: "Without imputing any [M]achiavellian desire to foment disorder or to divide and rule, the mere existence of perennial trouble in Palestine, while it may require the employment of several divisions of troops from time to time to restore the peace, does simultaneously strengthen British control of a very desirable base for the protection of British sea and air communication with India and the Far East."[42]

Samuel's pessimism, despite his grim contentment with the potential strategic side benefits of the status quo, probably echoed across the rank and file of the Colonial and Foreign Offices and perhaps the Near Eastern Affairs Division of the U.S. State Department. But it was also drowned out by the clamor of voices demanding that Palestine's status be actively addressed. As the war drew to a close, Zionists had begun to push for more active British involvement in the resolution of the Palestine problem, and Weizmann actively lobbied the Eastern Department of the Foreign Office for a separate meeting on Palestine akin to the Simla Conference on Anglo-Indian discussions.[43] British officials in the region likewise recognized the need to formulate a Palestine policy with dispatch. As the minister resident in the Middle East, Sir Edward Grigg, pointed out, the failure to swiftly take a position on the mandated territory threatened to squander gains that the war effort, and not least the imperial contribution to it, had achieved at such incredibly high cost.[44] But another reason was the continued Jewish agitation about increasing immigration to Palestine. Irrespective of which position His Majesty's government took, a delay in the consideration of the question alone might trigger destabilizing waves of new émigrés. Grigg noted that the ramifications of potential British military involvement to suppress such a conflict were considerable given the limitations on power projection imposed not only by the lingering British military presence in Syria but also by the continuation of the war with Japan.[45]

The broad outlines of the possible courses of action that Britain could pursue in Palestine crystallized into the 11 June "Memo on Palestine Policy" by the Foreign Office. In considering a range of five possible courses of action, the memo represented the state of British thinking on Palestine at the conclusion of the war. In his own comments on the memo, Grigg noted the importance of maintaining Arab goodwill toward Britain.[46]

Another consideration was the fact that the United Nations Conference had yet to produce consensus procedures for the administration of international trusteeships—which could imperil one of the principal policy options (among other schemes, such as sole British trusteeship, international controls on immigration, and partition). This would mean that new terms would have to be drafted and the nature of the trust agreements might have to change if Britain chose to enact preliminary provisions before the UN machinery was finalized. More important, other powers could cite those new multilateral mechanisms later to challenge British policies that predated them.[47]

Some in the Foreign Office believed that UN involvement could actually legitimize policy on Palestine and address immediate concerns, such as the plight of Jews seeking to emigrate there. For Gladwyn Jebb, private secretary to the permanent undersecretary, five-power deliberations limited to the immediate question of whether emigration should continue, even before Palestine's final future status as a trusteeship or otherwise was fully considered, could be utilized to strengthen international political support for dealing with "other troubles that might arise." The bottom line for Jebb was that by relying on the United Nations, "we might be able to invest ourselves with the whole authority of the world organisation, and if we were able to accomplish this the danger of disturbances or civil war in Palestine would be very greatly diminished, if not eliminated altogether."[48] Thus, ultimate arrangements for Palestine's final status aside, the glass was also half full: perhaps limited UN involvement could solve basic, near-term problems.

Such were the domestic and international political factors complicating British strategy on Palestine in the middle of 1945. They were byproducts of the reality that the Palestine question had come to a head at a moment of fundamental change in the international system. Britain's accelerating retreat would reach full speed in the next two years, and the parallel emergence of the United Nations, which now was literally holding up British decision making (until the San Francisco Conference issued its proceedings), made clear that new international provisions would fundamentally shape the decolonization process. But for the Foreign Office, perhaps the greatest of these complicating factors was the position that the United States would take on Jewish emigration and the future of the mandate— and the extent to which that position helped resolve or exacerbate the British policy conundrum.

Pressure had begun to mount from European Zionists seeking to abolish the terms of the 1939 White Paper and secure the right to emigrate to Palestine. A June 1945 appeal from the chairman of the Assembly of the Romanian Section of the Jewish World Congress to the British Mission in Romania was emblematic of the mood among European Jews at the time. Moreover the international breadth of the Zionist organizations that mounted this pressure was not limited to Europe but stretched as far as Greece, Argentina, and beyond, revealing the global scope of the Zionist endeavor. Yet that lateral reach notwithstanding, the Zionist Association in Egypt had also already begun to organize in the region by early 1945, seeking to teach Hebrew, encourage emigration to Palestine, and organize informal get-togethers. Pressure from the large American Jewish population could be critical if Zionist ambitions were to be contained in Palestine. But the activities of Zionists in America so alarmed the Foreign Office that they even prompted a proposal to monitor and publish texts of broadcasts by the Haganah's Voice of Israel in the United States. And the Foreign Office realized that organized Zionist elements in America, far from exerting a moderate influence in urban centers like Cairo, could pose the greatest threat to a tenable Palestine strategy.[49]

For Churchill and Foreign Secretary Anthony Eden, the way to mitigate the possibility of American adventurism in pursuing a policy too sympathetic to Jewish aims in Palestine was to involve the United States as a stakeholder in Palestine's future more directly than mere membership on a future body overseeing a trusteeship. As it stood, the United States possessed a great deal of leverage over events in Palestine. Half of international Jewry lived in the United States, and included among its august ranks were prominent intellectuals, statesmen, and titans of finance. Unsurprisingly most international funds that flowed to Palestine came from the United States. Yet despite that leverage, to British observers, their American counterparts were curiously absolved of having to bear more responsibility for events in Palestine. As Lord Halifax put it from his perch at the British Embassy in Washington, "For the Americans to be able thus to criticise and influence without responsibility is the most favourable and agreeable situation for them, and, I must suppose, the exact converse for us."[50]

Especially in the event that Palestine's future was to be determined by some international trusteeship body or other multilateral mechanism, Eden believed that the United States should assume "some form of responsibility more direct than the mere possibility of United States representation on the International body, or than indefinite responsibilities for maintaining the peace through the World Organisation."[51] Churchill agreed that it would serve British interests to involve America more directly in the resolution of the Palestine problem. Great Britain should not continue to handle the difficult situation in Palestine "while the Americans sit back and criticize." Moreover the British strategic position in the region vis-à-vis the United States would grow stronger "the more they are drawn into the Mediterranean."[52]

In response to Churchill's request, the Chiefs of Staff examined the question of American assumption of responsibility for the Palestine mandate. Their analysis assumed United Nations knowledge of the transfer as well as the willing American obligation of the responsibility. In assessing the strategic importance of Palestine, the resultant document cited the centrality of Palestine's geographic importance for the linkage of the United Kingdom with the empire in the east and its co-location with one of the Eastern Mediterranean's oil terminals. But unlike the independent states of the region with which the United Kingdom enjoyed sovereign treaty relationships, the loss of Britain's predominant position in Palestine could likely not be recouped easily through a future treaty. "Such an abrogation of our predominant position would be looked upon by the world, and especially by India and other eastern countries, as an indication that we were no longer either prepared or able to accept our responsibilities. The psychological effects of this are incalculable." They thus determined that "in considering this problem, therefore, we must recognise that the abandonment in favour of the Americans of our present position in Palestine will adversely affect our position, not in that country only, but throughout the Moslem world." Britain's strategic needs in Palestine in the event of a transfer of responsibility to the United States were five-fold: control of the eastern exit of the Mediterranean; security of oil sources and supply lines; airfields and other air facilities supporting routes to India, the Far East, and Southern Africa; control of sea lines of communication; and a base for stationing a strategic reserve in the region. On the one hand, backing up the security of the region with the credibility of American involvement would bolster British security, the Chiefs concluded. However, "we could not guarantee that the policy which the Americans would pursue would be such that our interests were preserved."[53] The question remained: Would American involvement really be to Britain's benefit? And how balanced or subservient to Zionist interests would America's Palestine policy really be?[54]

The Roosevelt administration had decided to postpone dealing with the Palestine situation until after the war. But the expiration of the immigration clauses of the 1939 White Paper five years after its issue meant that dealing with the issue of continued immigration was coming to a head. British and American representatives accordingly met in April 1944 in London to discuss a wide range of outstanding questions pertaining to Middle Eastern affairs, the most prominent of which was the future of Palestine. Representing the State Department were the director of the Office of Near Eastern Affairs, Wallace Murray; the influential geographer of the United States, Isaiah Bowman; Murray's deputy, Foy Kohler; and Robert Coe from the American Embassy. The delegation met with Undersecretary of State for Foreign Affairs Sir Maurice Peterson; Murray's British counterpart, C. W. Baxter; and Baxter's subordinate, the astute R. M. A. Hankey.

The discussions considered the first-order questions confronting Palestine. Peterson opened the meeting by explaining that he did not yet deem the situation in Palestine "urgent," because some 27,000 immigration certificates had yet to be issued, but he went on to insist that a permanent solution had to be crafted at the war's end. Discussions soon turned to the shape of a prospective plan. Peterson envisioned a binational state in which the Jewish population would be limited to minority status, with local Jewish and Arab communal governments under a mandatory power or similar arrangement entrusted to a single power, such as Great Britain. Bowman suggested the idea of an international trusteeship, in which the Foreign Office expressed a measure of interest, despite not being able to speak for British parliamentarians. While the meetings featured some discussion of a draft joint statement on the future of Palestine, Peterson explained that the issuance of such a statement at that time might "irritate rather than calm the Zionists" in the United States. Murray agreed, and the matter was left for later consideration.[55]

But waiting to exhaust the White Paper quotas did not mean an indefinite delay, and even the United States was beginning to feel the consequences of the rising tensions. In the winter of 1944 swelling bipartisan U.S. support for the Zionist movement had inflamed Arab sentiments throughout the region. Demonstrations in Syria were accompanied by the boycott of a visiting economic mission, and press campaigns took to the airwaves condemning American trade and policies. "If this trend should continue," Secretary of State Hull wrote to Roosevelt, "it would seriously prejudice our ability to afford protection to American interests, economic and commercial, cultural and philanthropic, throughout the area. It, of course, would have a very definite bearing upon the future of the immensely valuable American oil concession in Saudi Arabia, where the King's opposition to Zionism is well known."[56]

Nevertheless, in the State Department's view, at least four factors still warranted the continued postponement of a decision on the course of Palestine policy. First, the continuation of the war effort was paramount, and this meant the avoidance of "any action which would be likely to create a situation in the Near East" that might endanger it. Second, the president had assured King Ibn Saud and other Arab leaders that they would be consulted before any change in the "basic situation in Palestine." Third, the British government's official policy was to consult with both concerned Arabs and Jews before entering into any commitments about Palestine. Fourth, it was the State Department's understanding (however inaccurate this later proved, given revelations about Stalin's intentions) that Soviet officials remained opposed to the creation of a Jewish state in Palestine. The Department accordingly recommended that Roosevelt take a noncommittal line with Churchill in any discussions on Palestine that might arise at the Potsdam Conference of August 1945.[57]

Meanwhile Zionist leaders continued to beseech the State Department to endorse expanded Jewish immigration into Palestine, given that the situation was now becoming "unbearable," while dubiously attempting to assure Henderson and his staff that subsequent immigration would not unleash a cascade of violence "if the Arabs were given to understand that Great Britain and the United States had taken a firm stand and would not be swayed by force or threats of force."[58] Tensions in the region remained elevated in the summer of 1945 as both Jewish and Arab groups remained armed and ready to take violent action pending a British decision on immigration in the wake of the White Paper.[59]

At the close of the war, when the victorious powers convened the San Francisco Conference from April to June 1945, many Arab states naturally wanted to see the great powers speedily address Palestine's fate. As a product of the decolonization of British dominions throughout the world, the question of Palestine, in the minds of American policymakers, was certainly ripe for resolution and germane for consideration under UN auspices.[60] U.S. strategists recognized the importance of Palestine, situated as that territory was near the known oil reserves of the Middle East in northern Iraq, Iran, and the Persian Gulf. But in helping shape a durable political settlement, State Department officials urged the Truman administration to take into account the interests of both Palestinian Arabs and Jews. They likewise underscored the need for a U.S. policy mindful of and consonant with British expectations to the extent possible, akin to how Washington followed London's lead in South Asia and other former British dominions.[61] As the San Francisco Conference got under way, Secretary of State Edward Stettinius alerted the newly inaugurated U.S. president Harry Truman to the prospect of calls from Zionist leaders for unlimited immigration into Palestine. But he warned the president, "The question of Palestine is, however, a highly complex one and involves questions which go far beyond the plight of the Jews of Europe." Stettinius accordingly counseled Truman to seek fuller information on the issue before issuing any such call. He also pointed out that the San Francisco Conference deliberations on the new system of trusteeship could be relevant for the formulation of Palestine policy, given that Palestine might be among the territories whose future status the United Nations had agreed to consider at a later date.[62]

Stettinius's cautionary note alluded to the severe tensions that would strain the State Department's relationship with the White House over the issue of the future state of Israel. Cognizant of the problematic implications of British promises to Arab leaders like Sharif Hussein of Mecca, and increasingly worried by the violence in Palestine, especially after the 1936–1939 revolt, Stettinius and his advisors had continually provided Arab governments with reassurances that their concerns would be taken into account before major U.S. policy decisions affecting the future of Palestine. The concerns in the Arab world were acute and widespread that U.S. politicians were succumbing to Zionist influence and that American policy might drift away from the promises of the Roosevelt administration and the principles embodied in the Atlantic Charter.[63]

To a considerable extent, those concerns were well founded. As the White House increasingly came to be influenced by electoral considerations, as Eden had feared, Truman's sensitivity to his American Zionist constituents was heightened. In response, American Jewish groups capitalized on the opportunity, utilizing the support of Eliahu Elath (Epstein) at the Zionist Organization's Washington office, who came to regularly brief Truman's influential special counsel Clark Clifford and presidential advisor David Niles. Niles maintained such regular contact with the Jewish groups that he came to be known as the Truman administration's "portable wailing wall."[64] The pressures from the legislative branch had been clear from the previous administration, in which the agitations of Representative Sol Bloom and other members of Congress produced widespread congressional resolutions supporting Jewish immigration into Palestine and the creation of a Jewish commonwealth there. Moreover, the influence of American Zionists aside, the difficulties of reconciling American and British policies on Palestine were clear right from the early stages of the Truman administration. The limits on Jewish immigration agreed to in the 1939 White Paper were now close to exhaustion, and the new president's briefing paper on Palestine for the Potsdam Conference noted that British policies that inflamed Arab sentiments were often attributed to American pressure. Accordingly the State Department suggested that the United States might press Churchill on clarifying that any British proposals on future immigration were attributable to the British government alone.[65]

As the summer of 1945 wore on after the elections in Britain, Truman and newly elected British Labour Party prime minister Clement Atlee both felt increasing pressure to deal with the worsening situation in Palestine. Zionist officials, having heard that Roosevelt had indicated to Rabbi Stephen Wise during their last meeting in March 1945 that the Palestine question might be settled in San Francisco, were keen to apply pressure on the Truman administration to address the issue before the representatives gathered at the world body's first congress. The onus of securing a permanent home for the displaced Jews of Europe after the Nazi occupation had become the overriding consideration for the international Zionist movement, which in turn applied increasing pressure in London and Washington to decide swiftly on the future of Palestine and accommodate their demands. The United States had named representatives from both the American Jewish Conference and the (non-Zionist) American Jewish Committee as consultants to the American delegation to the San Francisco

Conference. They demanded that one million Jews be admitted to Palestine as quickly as possible. The State Department estimated that the number that would be seeking emigration would likely not exceed half that figure, since the Soviet Union was unlikely to permit emigration of Soviet Jews and many of those fleeing Europe sought to relocate to the United States instead. Meanwhile the housing situation in Palestine had deteriorated to the point where, even without additional immigration, accommodations would have to be arranged for some 200,000 persons in the immediate future.[66]

Unfortunately for the Zionists, despite the dire state of affairs, the Palestine issue was not addressed by the United Nations. Nor did Britain possess the means to provide redress. Over the summer the British Chiefs of Staff weighed in on how developments in Palestine could get out of control, especially if unrest in the Francophone Levant escalated to the level of attacks against British forces. "The forces at present located in the Middle East would be insufficient to meet this emergency even if the development of Arab Nationalist sentiment did not preclude the use of Indian troops to deal with Arab/Jew conflicts," they concluded.[67] One of the most dangerous courses of action, the Chiefs of Staff predicted, was the implementation of the partition of Palestine, as then favored by the Colonial Office. Importantly the Chiefs of Staff reminded the Colonial Office, "there would also be very grave reactions in India."[68] Reports from British diplomats in the region confirmed the Chiefs' assessment. According to diplomatic channels, the Egyptian reaction would be "very violent." Iraqi Arabs would meet the policy with "immediate and united opposition, resulting in "consequent disturbance which could only be suppressed by force." And King Ibn Saud "would regard the scheme with complete hostility."[69]

The situation of potential Jewish-Arab violence in Palestine, compounded by the French presence in the Levant, of which the Foreign Office was deeply mistrustful, left the Foreign Office grasping for answers in the face of the San Francisco Conference's silence on the Palestine issue. In a sense the refusal of the convened United Nations to address colonial questions was a blessing of sorts for the Foreign Office. At the time, the Chiefs of Staff were preoccupied with Britain's withdrawal from Egypt and the attendant implications of the proposed UN Security Council's substitution for the defunct Council of the League of Nations as the arbitrator of an Anglo-Egyptian dispute over control of the Suez Canal Zone. While the Chiefs of Staff were fairly confident that the existing alignment of great powers would likely not take a position in the new Security Council at odds with British interests in the Canal Zone, concerns about foreign involvement should the issue be deemed a "threat to the peace" permeated British calculations.[70]

Such a precedent could of course pose significant consequences for the resolution of the Palestine issue. As the Chiefs of Staff noted, a UN security scheme for the defense of the Middle East in which the new provisions for trusteeship were adopted could be advantageous to Britain, "provided that France and Russia were excluded." But on the other hand, as the Foreign Office would realize in the course of the subsequent year and a half, the United Nations also served as an institutional forum in which Britain could absolve itself of intractable postcolonial problems. And U.S. membership in an international body entrusted with the oversight of a trust territory in Palestine might both introduce a voice that the Arabs looked upon favorably in the discussion and "silence that uninformed criticism which might at any time impair Anglo-American relations" by imposing a cost on U.S. support for an irresponsible policy of continued immigration into a territory for which the United States was now held accountable.[71]

THE ANGLO-AMERICAN COMMITTEE OF INQUIRY

United Nations involvement in the Palestine problem would not be obviated, merely postponed. By October an initial response to the pressing need to resolve the issue of Jewish immigration came from London in the form of a British proposal to establish a joint Anglo-American Committee of Inquiry to examine the situation in Palestine.

Twelve committee members—six each from the United States and Great Britain—would study the question of Palestine's future, including the issue of Jewish immigration, and publicly present their findings. Among them were American academic Frank Aydelotte, director of the Institute for Advanced Study at Princeton University; James McDonald, who would later become America's first ambassador to Israel; and Judge Joseph Hutcheson, who chaired the group. The British chair was Sir John Singleton, also a court justice; members included Sir Frederick Leggett of the International Labour Office and a Bevin confidante, and Richard Crossman, coeditor of the *New Statesman* and a socialist Labour MP who converted to the Zionist cause in the course of the proceedings, and whose accounts of the Committee's work have become standard treatments.[72] The Committee's specific objectives were to assess the plight of European Jews, estimate the number of them that would have to be resettled outside their countries of origin, explore the possibility of resettling them outside the European continent, and look for other means of "meeting the needs of the immediate situation."[73]

As the Committee commenced its hearings, the population of European Jews displaced by war now totaled some 100,000. Refugee interviews indicated that an overwhelming majority of those consulted sought resettlement in Palestine. A Foreign Office memorandum presented to the Committee laid out a balanced view of the Zionist rationale for the establishment of a Jewish commonwealth in Palestine and the abolition of limits on settlement there.[74] The Committee's American and British representatives, who spanned a wide range of views on the Palestine issue, visited Palestine and researched the situation over the coming months. In his address to the Committee, Ben-Gurion rooted the case for a Jewish state deep in the annals of Jewish history: "Sir, our case seems to us simple and compelling. It rests on two elementary principles. One is that we Jews are just like other human beings, entitled to just the same rights; that the Jewish people is entitled to the same equality of treatment as any free and independent people in the world. The second is that this is and will remain our country. We are here as of right. We are not here on the strength of the Balfour Declaration or of the Palestine Mandate. We were here long, long before."[75]

In a September 1945 meeting with Weizmann, U.S. Secretary of State James F. Byrnes had offered the vague promise of U.S. assistance to deal with the plight of 100,000 immigration certificates that were deemed necessary to deal with the overflow of European Jews in excess of those permitted to emigrate under the terms of the 1939 White Paper. The issue, because of the Democratic Party's large Jewish constituency, was one of paramount domestic political concern for the Truman administration. As Byrnes phrased it, while "he had no right to speak on behalf of Mr. Truman, he could tell [Weizmann] that their people would help."[76] Understanding that the United States viewed the plight of European Jewry displaced by the war and the Holocaust as linked with the future of Palestine, Weizmann lodged a hopeful appeal with Byrnes after their meeting, beseeching the Americans to assist with the immigration of more than just the 100,000 additional settlers under consideration. He told Byrnes the following week that their "immediate anxiety is to see the White Paper regime abrogated: that would mean the repeal of the Land Regulations of 1940 which constitute a discrimination against Jews and forbid us to acquire land in by far the greater part of the country. With regard to immigration, we would like to see the doors of Palestine open for all Jews desperately in need of a home."[77] Soon thereafter Weizmann appealed to the Jews in Palestine to show patience and perseverance despite the incremental progress in establishing a Jewish state. He called on them to reject violence as a tactic and to "continue our struggle by persuasion, negotiation and constructive effort till our position as a free nation in its own country has been firmly established—till the Jewish State has become a reality."[78]

By the fall of 1945 the differences in Anglo-American policy that Weizmann had perceived led to candid discussions between Washington and London over how to address the issue of continued Jewish immigration into Palestine. When the new Labour government took office, Attlee and Foreign Minister Bevin promptly adopted a liberal policy of nonintervention in the Middle East, predicated on the economic development of the region and diplomatic amity. Bevin believed that British policy in the region had hitherto "rested on too narrow a footing, mainly on the personality of kings, princes or pashas." He envisioned for the future a new liberal British policy in the Middle East predicated on more equitable diplomatic relationships, cooperation, and British support for the extraction of the region's human and material resources for its own betterment. His tentative ideas included the possibility of a joint Anglo-Egyptian defense force, grant assistance to the Sudan, and the convocation of periodic meetings in Cairo of Middle East experts with counterparts from as far afield as the United States and even India.[79]

Bevin's sweeping, regional approach sought to holistically consider the interconnected policy challenges that impinged on British policy, within a clearly articulated set of principles, without treating problems in piecemeal fashion. The Cabinet's Palestine Committee shared his vision and the extent to which the new Labour policy relied increasingly on Arab complicity with the extension of British power and the preservation of its interests, flatly acknowledging, with regard to the future of Palestine, "The attitude of the Arab States to any decision which may be reached is a matter of the first importance."[80]

British power in the world was now constrained in new and painful ways, and Labour's policy for the Middle East recognized its limits. But during a fall 1945 trip to the United States, Bevin also picked up on the seething Anglo-American tensions over the fate of Palestine, arguing to Lord Halifax at the British Embassy in Washington that Truman was playing politics on Jewish emigration to Israel.[81] Fundamentally, continued Jewish immigration into Palestine was not conducive to British regional interests as reconfigured under Labour. A few weeks earlier Attlee had let Truman know as much in no uncertain terms. And the new prime minister reminded the president of Roosevelt's promise to consult with Arab leaders before embarking on a course toward any future settlement for Palestine. In his letter Attlee raised concerns about the potential spillover effects should the Palestine conflict spread to the region as a whole.[82] Even the Colonial Office was mindful of the dangers of a rapid policy swing that could turn friendly Arab governments in the region against Britain, endangering the entire Labour policy of nonintervention and the cultivation of informal relationships to protect imperial interests whose positions were growing more precarious.[83]

The rationale behind the British appeals did not completely fail to resonate within the U.S. administration, nor even with Truman himself. At times, despite the advice of advisors Niles, Clifford, and White House Counsel Samuel Rosenman, Truman seemed flabbergasted by the extent of Jewish demands. In an extraordinary note to Senator Joseph Ball of Minnesota that Truman requested be filed but not sent, he remarked, "I told the Jews that if they were willing to furnish me with five hundred thousand men to carry on a war with the Arabs, we could do what they are suggesting in the Resolution—otherwise we will have to negotiate awhile."[84]

While the Committee was meeting, and even before it had weighed in on the issuance of 100,000 additional immigration certificates for would-be emigrants, American Zionists held firm on their demands, stipulating in the press that immigration quotas were no substitute for what by then had become their common goal of a state. Dr. Abba Hillel Silver, president of the Zionist Organization of America, declared, "It should be clearly understood by everyone, and more especially by members of the Anglo-American Commission of Inquiry now meeting in Washington, that the rescue of a certain number of refugees alone, however vital and urgent, is not Zionism nor is it the Balfour Declaration nor the Palestine Mandate."[85] But there was a growing disparity between the inflamed public rhetoric of Zionists like Rabbi Silver and rank-and-file Zionists, and the sober, calculating realizations of Zionist leaders. As the British first secretary in Washington observed, an increasingly widespread belief in the lack of a national homeland as "the fundamental cause of the Jewish tragedy" was taking hold. Its attendant implications were impractical: they entailed the creation, by force if necessary, of a Jewish state partitioned out of Palestine that would be difficult to defend and would be incapable of meeting the requirements for Commonwealth membership (and indeed would go against "the ethos of British political evolution"). Yet this belief on the part of the general public now seemed to contrast with a growing realism on the part of Zionist leaders that compromise was necessary for a historic breakthrough. As Nahum Goldmann, the Jewish Agency's representative in Washington, told a Zionist gathering in London, "I do not say that we will get 100 per cent of what we want. We will have to make a reasonable compromise."[86] After the tortuous deliberations during and after the war, it seemed that at least some Zionists were ready to pull back from the demand for "all of Palestine."

In proposing such a compromise, the recommendations finally issued by the Anglo-American Committee of Inquiry sought to respond to mounting international pressure to accommodate additional displaced European Jews *in Palestine* despite growing Arab discontent there. To relieve the pressure to resettle the huge numbers of displaced former residents of occupied Europe, the Committee of Inquiry subsequently called for the issue of 100,000 corresponding certificates of immigration to Jewish refugees.[87] The Committee either underestimated the impact of the influx of these refugees or envisioned some idealized, future Palestinian state inhabited by both Arabs and European Jewish émigrés in balanced proportions. But its decision flew in the face of the intensifying unrest and the outbursts of ethnic violence in such events as the May Day Riots of 1921, the Buraq uprising of 1929, and the 1936 revolt, which still burned in living memory.

It hardly came as a surprise that the Committee recommendations profoundly perturbed the U.S. military leadership, who were especially preoccupied with the attendant commitments that the plan to admit 100,000 additional Jewish settlers could entail for America's armed forces, entangling them in the Palestinian quagmire even as the British were desperately seeking to extricate themselves from it. In a memorandum to the State-War-Navy Coordinating Committee, the Joint Chiefs of Staff warily counseled the Truman administration of the dangers of introducing American troops into the volatile state of affairs in Palestine, explicitly urging "that no U.S. armed forces be involved in carrying out the Committee's recommendations" and "that in implementing the report, the guiding principle be that no action should be taken which will cause repercussions in Palestine which are beyond the capabilities of British troops to control."[88] Interestingly, even before addressing the dangers of increased Soviet leverage in the Middle East as a result of a military deployment to Palestine, the Joint Chiefs lodged a separate concern: the potential backlash that could result from the redeployment of U.S. military forces in the Middle East. The JCS analysis stemmed from two basic assumptions: one was the general lack of confidence in the British military's ability to maintain control of the situation as security broke down in response to further Jewish immigration; another was the corollary expectation of major repercussions resulting from American participation in any international military forces introduced to help stabilize the situation. With regard to the latter, the JCS hoped to warn the administration of potential Arab (and even wider Muslim world) reactions against the United States triggered by the reappearance of American troops. The collective sentiments of U.S. military planners were clear: the British were unable to control the situation in Palestine, and the United States should not attempt to succeed them as occupying powers in the postwar period.[89]

The memorandum is revelatory of U.S. strategic considerations aside from those associated with the developing cold war with the Soviet Union and American policymakers' concerns about Soviet penetration of the region. For it seems that the danger of a confrontation with Moscow in the region aside, a separate concern tempering the inclination of the U.S. military to deploy armed forces in Palestine was the possibility of a hostile reaction against an American troop presence in the Middle East after the tumult of the Second World War. This reticence signaled discomfort on the part of U.S. military leaders to take either side in what was a postcolonial struggle between rival claimants to the territory of Palestine. Moreover it rationalized a "do no harm" policy that assumed levels of security that could be guaranteed with only the British military presence in Palestine, without additional reinforcement. Such an argument from the Joint Chiefs of Staff suggests that they favored, as in the case of regions like postcolonial South Asia, a U.S. policy that deferred to British interests in their former colonial possessions.

But the course of that British policy itself was unclear. The Foreign Office firmly opposed any incitement of a Palestinian Arab backlash. In keeping with his strategy of a sea of friendly successor states spanning the

Middle East, Bevin had divorced the plight of European Jewry from the future of Palestine. Concerned primarily with the defense of the empire and Commonwealth, from the foreign secretary's standpoint the disruptions induced by a large influx of Jewish emigrants from Europe would precipitate needless upheaval and local strife with which Britain could not contend. But the Colonial Office, under Colonial Secretary Arthur Creech Jones, was responsible for the supervision of the mandate within Palestine and still subscribed to as "pro-Zionist" a view as existed within the British government, believing that partition was the optimal solution for Palestine. This line of thinking held that moderate Zionist aims could be accommodated if the creation of Jewish and Arab states was swift and decisive, thereby preempting the outbreak of a civil war. But even Creech Jones stopped short of sympathy for the maximalist Zionist dream of converting Palestine into a Jewish state outright and favored partition only as the most practical of a set of unfavorable policy options.[90] The Chiefs of Staff sided largely with Foreign Office views under the Labour government, conjecturing that the British army presence in Palestine on which requisite security conditions for partition would have to depend was becoming increasingly untenable. Thus a single British strategy for Palestine had yet to emerge, although the course of events from the fall of 1944 to the spring of 1947 would force the government to fall in line behind Attlee's mental maps and Bevin's master plan.[91]

But others too were contemplating fateful policy shifts. The White Paper limits on immigration and the general worsening of the plight of Jews in Palestine had spurred the Irgun, which had hitherto focused its attacks on Palestinian Arabs, to now target British authorities in Palestine. On 6 November 1944 an underground Zionist terror group, the Stern Gang, had taken the dramatic step of assassinating British Colonial Secretary Lord Moyne. June 1946 saw the terrorist organization kidnap five British officers in Tel Aviv. The incident occurred one month before the infamous bombing of the King David Hotel in Jerusalem, which housed the British government offices—another attack attributed to the Irgun. British military personnel had become fair game for militant Zionists within two years of the war's end. These attacks were not just a manifestation of the maximalist struggle for immediate statehood that the rhetoric of Ben-Gurion and Weizmann had adopted in the years after 1939 and anointed with their blessing in the Biltmore Program. Churchill began to consider the fuller implications of the new Zionist militancy and whether his long-standing support for the cause of a Jewish state in Palestine was still tenable. Like Churchill, many American Zionists who had long supported the cause were deeply disturbed by Palestine's descent into Zionist terrorism in the wake of November 1944. A number of them, including Treasury Secretary Henry Morgenthau, Supreme Court Justice Felix Frankfurter, *Washington Post* editor Eugene Meyer, financier Bernard Baruch, and attorney Benjamin Cohen, were horrified by the use of more extreme militant Zionist tactics, such as violence against civilians.[92]

As the new high commissioner in Jerusalem Sir Alan Cunningham observed barely a week into his assignment in Palestine, the situation had worsened dramatically. Moreover "in regard to the Jews local Jewish leaders are intransigent and intractable and both they and press are carrying on an intensive propaganda campaign vilifying as barbaric the use of force by the Mandatory while directly or indirectly praising and encouraging resort to violence by the Jews themselves." Still, Cunningham kept true to the trajectory of British mandatory policy in retaining a focus on a settlement that did not inflame Arab sentiments: "To attempt to solve the Palestine problem, and to bring to that country large numbers of Jews, without the consent of the Arabs, will result in increasing racial bitterness and hatred. If there are to be peace and good will prevailing in the Middle East, the problem of Palestine must be solved by consent and not by force."[93]

Given both the doubts that circulated even within the British government over whether to maintain a military presence in Palestine and the escalating costs of that occupation (which amounted to some 40 million pounds per annum) piled atop the security threats, His Majesty's government was running out of ideas for sustainable solutions. Unfortunately the Anglo-American Committee of Inquiry also failed to supply one, recommending the immediate immigration of 100,000 Nazi victims into Palestine and the conversion of Palestine into a United Nations Trusteeship territory in which Arabs would be elevated to economic and cultural parity with Jews, with neither side dominating the other. The implications of these findings were clear to the British government, especially the Chiefs of Staff: such a policy would destroy Arab faith in British goodwill; that trust deficit, in turn, would jeopardize critical defense requirements in the region, such as the preservation of communications and access to oil supplies in the wake of the withdrawal from Egypt. Neither did the continued stationing of a British military presence to enforce the settlement seem realistic. The estimated costs of maintaining the force levels in Palestine alone stood at 96 million pounds sterling, 38 million more than the price of maintaining all other forces in the region—which meant securing an American loan.[94]

Diplomatic reporting from the region validated the British military assessment of the likely regional reaction. His Majesty's minister in Jeddah characterized the report as "disastrous," noting that, tragically, it failed to appease either side. The State Department supplied Truman with similar accounts of the uproar over the report's alleged "repudiation of Arab rights," as reported in Cairo, and the organization of a general strike in Baghdad.[95]

When the Committee formally recommended the admission of 100,000 additional Jews to Palestine, Truman hastily endorsed the plan on 30 April without weighing in on the report's other recommendations regarding the establishment of a binational state. His selective concurrence enraged the Foreign Office. But the Truman administration, acting on the guidance of close White House advisors Clifford and Niles, grasped at the elements of the recommendations that appealed to it most clearly and directly, refusing to weigh in at all on the provincial autonomy scheme.[96] Attlee was furious over Truman's failure to consult directly with the British government before issuing the statement. In his meeting with Secretary of State Byrnes, Bevin told his counterpart that the Committee's recommendation to distribute 100,000 additional immigration certificates would lead to security concerns that Britain could not manage alone. In the view of British military strategists, the new influx would require the reinforcement of the British army presence by two infantry divisions and an armored brigade—even beyond the equivalent of two and a half divisions Britain had in Palestine—units that His Majesty's government was not in a position to procure. Bevin's message was clear: if Washington was adamant about endorsing the Committee's immigration recommendations, it would have to help deal with managing the security consequences of the changed demographics, as Churchill had suggested it should. Moreover that involvement should take the form of both financial and military assistance.[97]

British Cabinet discussions revolved around how to handle the issue of Palestine in the wake of the report's publication. Bevin firmly maintained that a referral to the UN Security Council would be tantamount to "a confession of failure" that "would have unfortunate effects on other aspects of [British] foreign policy." Yet an interminable delay in referring the problem could open the door to others bringing the issue before the Council, involve the Soviet Union, and precipitate other unwanted action. Cabinet members generally agreed that continued Anglo-American policy coordination on Palestine had to follow as the next logical step. But certain ministers advocated for informing the Security Council that the Palestine issue would be brought before it if Anglo-American efforts failed to achieve a settlement. Thus the Foreign Office would mount one last bid to achieve consensus with Washington before directly putting final proposals to the parties to the dispute.[98]

By the end of the war America had thus maintained a guarded distance from the Palestine issue despite Churchill's appeals to involve the United States as a bigger stakeholder. As the new U.S. ambassador in London, Averell Harriman, put it to Secretary of State Byrnes before the dispatch of envoy Henry Grady to London for joint talks on the Anglo-American Committee of Inquiry's findings, "Any military discussions between the British and U.S. on the specific subject of Palestine are most undesirable at this time."[99] Grady later recalled that the American delegation interpreted the Committee's provincial autonomy plan as an interim step toward the final partition of Palestine into Arab and Jewish states, an assumption that the British officials receiving the Grady mission did not share. But he conveyed to Byrnes that the provincial autonomy scheme was still the only one proposed that could ensure that the 100,000 additional Jews would be able to emigrate to Palestine, the issue under study by the Committee that preoccupied the White House the most.[100]

Whatever its flaws, the scheme endorsing provincial autonomy as an interim solution crafted by Grady and Herbert Morrison, chairman of the British Cabinet's Palestine Committee, represented the last chance for a negotiated Anglo-American settlement. This final prospective compromise would be laid at the feet of the Arab Higher Committee and the Jewish Agency. If it failed, Britain and the United States had little recourse but to refer the matter to the United Nations.[101]

TWO

Remapping Zion

By the summer of 1946, British and American officials alike found themselves running out of ideas for a lasting solution to the problem of Palestine. As the cold war took hold and Soviet military presences encroached from Eastern Europe and Central Asia, the stakes for securing the energy-rich Middle East rose ever higher. Pressure mounted at the Foreign Office and the State Department to generate constructive ideas that could break the deadlock. But the course of Anglo-American diplomacy to resolve the Arab-Israeli dispute that began with the 1946–1947 London Conference and ended with the creation of the State of Israel in 1948 proved just how differently those two organizations conceived of the territory of Palestine and its immediate regional context.

THE LONDON CONFERENCE

At the behest of the Foreign Office, Jewish and Arab representatives converged on London in September 1946 and met periodically until the pivotal month of February 1947 to discuss the Anglo-American Committee of Inquiry recommendations.[1] The Jewish delegation had refused to participate unless the establishment of a Jewish state could be agreed as a basic prerequisite to the meeting, opting instead to conduct separate, concurrent discussions with the British government. The conference was a moment for British reappraisal. The Chiefs of Staff maintained their consistent line in steadfast denial of the prospects of any partition. But Sir Alan

Cunningham, the high commissioner in Palestine, wondered whether some form of partition might not be the only way out of the cul de sac into which British policy had stumbled.[2]

Truman compounded Britain's dilemma by reiterating his 30 April statement of support for the admission of an additional 100,000 Jews to Palestine in an October speech delivered just before Yom Kippur, so that the contents of the speech would be addressed in sermons throughout synagogues across America. Arabists at the State Department had warned Truman of the inherent dangers of such a statement—or any in favor of the imminent partition of Palestine. Despite the efforts of Zionists like Rabbi Stephen Wise to lobby Truman vigorously for such a statement, Byrnes, Harriman, and others in the Department counseled strongly against any such utterances that "yield to the pressure of highly organized Zionist groups."[3] But the White House went ahead with the statement nonetheless, and again the announcement blindsided the British government. Truman expressed his remorse directly to Attlee: "My feeling was that the announcement of the adjournment until December 16 of the discussions with the Arabs had brought such depression to the Jewish displaced persons in Europe and to millions of American citizens concerned with the fate of these unfortunate people that I could not even for a single day postpone making clear the continued interest of this Government in their welfare."[4]

The sessions, in which British intercessors relayed proposals back and forth between the two sides, were unproductive to say the least. Before any coordinated policy could be agreed, representatives of the Colonial and Foreign Offices and the Jewish Agency for Palestine met in the closing informal sessions of the London Conference, hoping to bridge the gap between an acceptable British solution and a satisfactory settlement for the Zionist Executive. The fiery January 1947 meetings between the delegation of Jewish Agency representatives and British government representatives held at the Colonial Office represented a last chance for a negotiated solution to the Palestine problem. But a common British front had still not been forged, and, not unlike the policy discord across the Atlantic, a divergence of views on Palestine extended to the highest echelons of power in London. In the broadest sense Attlee and the Labour government had adopted a firm stand to extricate Britain from its entanglements in the Levant. But Bevin, torn between pragmatism and a new hard-headed cold war realism that tapped his populist inclinations, warned the prime minister against beating too hasty a retreat. "What you propose is a reversal of the whole policy I have been pursuing in the Middle East, with the assent of the Cabinet, since the Government took office," he told Attlee. Instead what was necessary was strategic patience.[5]

Interagency discord also pervaded the bureaucracy below the cabinet level. The Colonial Office remained dug in on its opposition to a provincial autonomy scheme into the new year, while the Chiefs of Staff now hedged their assessment of regional defense needs on the assumption that the crown would retain basing rights through treaty arrangements with successor Arab and Jewish states should Palestine be partitioned. British strategy in the Middle East hinged on two key needs: a defensive bulwark safeguarding British possessions in Africa and a forward offensive presence. Egypt and Palestine remained "the two strategically important countries."[6] These requirements were central for postwar imperial defense planning and remained unchanged as the Palestine drama unfolded. Of course they severely limited British military resources after the ravages of global war and the heavy reliance on the Indian army for the defense of the empire. Attlee's growing concerns about overstretch in the region led him to mandate that the study of security needs in the region be located in the wider context of core British defense needs and the threats posed by long-range weapons to the British Isles. But short of "an unacceptable reduction in the forces required to ward off attacks on Britain from Western Europe," even the noninterventionist Labour government and its prime minister recognized the need to remain engaged in the Middle East to defend its bases and lines of communication.[7]

In their final report on Palestine before the London Conference talks concluded, the Chiefs of Staff noted that British strategic interests in the region would be "gravely prejudiced" if the military presence in Palestine had to vacate. But the proposal for a temporary trusteeship was dependent on the goodwill of the Arab people, and up to two full divisions would be necessary if Arabs and Jews entered into open war. The key requirement was holding Egypt, which was most critical for security in the region—and Egypt could be defended from the north only by holding Palestine.[8]

Moreover, as the Chiefs of Staff pointed out in their assessment of the provincial autonomy proposals, Arab opposition to any settlement would impede the movements of British forces throughout the region, a basic strategic requirement. In certain respects, from a military standpoint, provincial autonomy could be even more disastrous than partition with respect to alienating Arabs and exacerbating security concerns. It also became clear that the Jews of Palestine would not readily accede to a provincial autonomy scheme given the adherence of the majority of their leaders to the maximalist demand for a state of their own. Over the following week the Cabinet decided that the optimal course of action would be to encourage both parties to accept provincial autonomy only as an interim step with a view toward eventual independence for Palestine. In the meantime a British military presence would remain to ensure security and a smooth transition, supported by the international justification that it could assist with the preservation of regional stability if the new United Nations Organization needed it as part of any future defense scheme.[9]

The proposed way ahead seemed the only possible means to simultaneously preserve British strategic interests, mitigate the flagrant incitement of either side as the result of the perceived unjustness of a settlement, and preserve international legitimacy for British actions and a measure of flexibility for the future. Now the task at hand was to sell the scheme to the Jewish Agency and the Arab Higher Committee.

In his remarks to British government officials during the pivotal closing sessions of the London Conference, Ben-Gurion began by stating that the Jewish Agency's objectives in Palestine were the return of the Jewish people to their homeland, the rebuilding of Palestine to the maximum possible extent, and the attainment of national independence. His egalitarian view of this last requirement held that the world's Jews would never enjoy identical status with the citizens of the world until they were conferred citizenship in a state of their own. While 70 percent of Palestine's arable land remained uncultivated, he reminded his counterparts, 1.2 million Jews in Europe and Asia were suffering under conditions that were no longer tolerable. Colonial Secretary Arthur Creech Jones responded that he felt "the profoundest sympathy with a great deal of what Mr. Ben Gurion said," but that "practical difficulties" prevented the simple adoption of a "comprehensive policy" of the sort Ben-Gurion espoused. Creech Jones instead wondered about the viability of Bevin's last-ditch plan for a binational, unitary Palestine in which the Jews and Arabs lived together and cooperated, an abstract form of the idea discussed with American representatives in the preliminary talks before the London Conference. Ben-Gurion responded that Arab and Jewish social and economic cooperation was not only possible; indeed it already existed between the two peoples to some extent. But *political* cooperation was not likely, and the central question was one of continued Jewish immigration. Pressed by Bevin as to the rate at which he expected it to continue, Ben-Gurion maintained that it would depend on the natural growth of the Yishuv and the trajectory taken by its development. Continued immigration, if sanctioned by the United Nations, need not threaten Palestine's Arab neighbors, Ben-Gurion said, for a UN-sanctioned settlement would leave the Jewish state as secure as any other. While a Jewish state would not be able to join the Arab League, Ben-Gurion assured the British government that it would cooperate with the organization. Importantly, in delineating acceptable compromises short of statehood for the whole of Palestine, Moshe Shertok, head of the Jewish Agency's Political Department, assured his British hosts that sovereignty over the full territory of what did remain of the eventual Jewish state was the only compensation to which the Zionists could agree in return for the loss of truncated territory.[10]

Over the course of the meetings, the Jewish Agency representatives presented their arguments for why the Anglo-American Morrison-Grady scheme for a binational state could not be the basis for subsequent discussions, and both sides presented and debated their own maps for how Arabs and Jews could practically inhabit Palestine together. Ben-Gurion lodged complaints with the various schemes presented by the British representatives at the Conference as merely variants of the same unitary state idea. Despite Shertok's assurances, the maximalist aim of partition seemed to have firmly settled into Ben-Gurion's mind. He showed little inclination toward the "reasonable compromise" that Nahum Goldmann had told the British Federation of Zionists would be necessary in 1946. The state of displaced European Jewry and the escalating tensions in Palestine meant that the Zionists had reached a point of no return, and Ben-Gurion decided to press for partition with all the political capital the Zionist representatives held.

The critical element of his demands concerned their geographical scope. While the Jewish Agency supported the notion of a unitary state, Ben-Gurion said, it could not occupy one in which they were confined to one part of the territory. He likened what he saw as the absurdity of such a notion as akin to the prevention of Welsh settlement outside of Wales, or of Scotsmen outside of Scotland. Ben-Gurion then launched into a long history of the Zionist claim to *all of Palestine*, as he was wont to do, stemming from the Balfour Declaration, through the 1922 creation of Transjordan, to the withdrawn 1937 Peel Commission's partition proposal and the 1939 White Paper measures. Ultimately he did acknowledge that the Jews were willing to consider compromise solutions, but only those in which they would have complete control of immigration, could define the nebulous notion of "absorptive capacity" themselves, and be permitted to make treaties with other nations like any other sovereign power.[11]

By the end of the meetings the locus of the impasse was clear. An explosive 6 February exchange between Ben-Gurion and Bevin about Britain's responsibilities as the mandatory power resolved the size of the gap that both sides sought to bridge. According to the official notes of the meeting:

> MR BEVIN asked whether the Jews suggested that His Majesty's Government should create a Jewish state?
>
> MR BEN GURION replied that His Majesty's Government should carry out the Mandate. They were failing to do so. The White Paper policy whereby the Jews were condemned to remain a minority in the country, was still in force. The objects of the Jews were two-fold, to secure their future and to restore friendship between Jews and British. . . .
>
> MR BEVIN went on to say that there was nothing in the Mandate providing for the unlimited immigration of Jews into Palestine and thereby enabling them eventually to dominate the Arabs. His Majesty's Government had tried to reach an understanding between the two communities but they were still at loggerheads. The Jews had never submitted any scheme of partition to His Majesty's Government. The British people would never consent to the creation of a Jewish state in the whole of Palestine at the expense of the Arabs.[12]

The meeting on 6 February 1947 not only marked Bevin's last effort to draw the line with Ben-Gurion with regard to what the British government would accept in the way of a settlement that would partition Palestine and create a separate Jewish state; it also represented the achievement of the first consensus British government view on Palestine. For Arthur Creech Jones and the Colonial Office had given in at last, having acknowledged that it would be next to impossible to partition Palestine into "viable" Jewish and Arab states that would coexist peacefully given the demographic realities. After Arab and Zionist leaders formally rejected the "Bevin Plan" for a five-year UN trusteeship that would lead to an independent state, the defeated foreign minister issued a statement on 18 February that the London Conference had failed.[13]

Despite Bevin's hard-headed convictions that had enabled him to assert the Foreign Office's priorities over the relatively meek Creech Jones, the collapse of the London Conference dealt his and Labour's grand strategy in the Middle East a crushing blow. Britain had effectively quit Palestine, and the United Nations now remained the only possible recourse.[14]

By early 1947 even Creech Jones's staunch opposition to the idea of abandoning Palestine to the international organization had collapsed. Realizing Palestine's changing demographics meant that partition would no longer be viable; the colonial secretary had conceded the Foreign Office's position. Out of options, British policy had at last converged on one course of action. Still, the British Chiefs of Staff expressed skepticism about the prospect of seeking to preserve military rights to Palestine; where they deemed unlikely the emergence within five years of an independent state friendly to Britain and amenable to concluding a treaty with it.[15] Though powerless to shape the final settlement in the way it had hoped, the Labour government had turned to the international legitimacy and political support that the United Nations offered as a last resort to dispose of Palestine. But the strategic considerations that shaped British views of ideal outcomes remained: Palestine was a critical alternative to Egypt and the Suez for basing, access to oil, and the defense of imperial lines of communication and transit. Moreover any final settlement had to take into account the sentiments of the Muslim populations of the Arab Middle East and the Indian subcontinent. In the closing week of February 1947 Bevin announced that Britain would relegate the future of Palestine to the United Nations.[16] On that day he drew a parallel between the Jews and Arabs in Palestine and the Hindus and Muslims in India, pointing to the difficulty of reconciling a territorial settlement with the underlying demographics: "I cannot alter the balance of people in a State—that is impossible—any more than one can alter it between Nehru and Jinnah today in India," he lamented.[17]

UNSCOP, AMERICA, AND THE ROAD TO PARTITION

That fateful year of 1947 saw the establishment of the United Nations Special Committee on Palestine (UNSCOP), comprising representatives from eleven UN member states. Over the course of nine months, from February to November 1947, UNSCOP formulated its recommendations for the future of Palestine. Meanwhile British policy had crystallized over the spring and summer after the February Cabinet decision. Its fullest and most thoughtful explication appeared in an August memo entitled "Palestine: The Autumn Session of the General Assembly." In it the Foreign Office individually considered the basic options at hand. They were, in order of preference from the standpoint of British strategic needs as laid out by the Chiefs of Staff: British trusteeship for Palestine, the creation of a unitary independent state, partition of Palestine into separate Arab and Jewish states, and international trusteeship. Having gotten wind of UNSCOP's inclinations toward its final majority recommendation, the Foreign Office explained the difficulties of partition. One central problem consisted of the uncertainty associated with which and how many states in the General Assembly would support the proposal, and whether the required two-thirds of the body would indeed fall in line behind such a recommendation. If Britain supported partition and it failed to pass, it might incur the wrath of the Arab would. Alternatively, if the proposal passed *despite* British opposition, the outcome would harm Anglo-Zionist relations and British diplomacy toward the new Jewish state. In short, the preservation of British diplomatic relations with the possible successor states that emerged from the settlement—at the opposite, western endpoint of the arc of crisis from India's Muslim territories—was the principal consideration shaping Whitehall's policy toward partition. As such, "there would seem to be a strong case for abstention on this issue in all circumstances," the Foreign Office concluded.[18]

The thinking went that Britain would neither advocate vociferously for a position for which international support was unclear or had yet to amass, nor stand in the way of the Committee's recommendations in a way that would arouse a strong anti-British reaction from Arab or Jewish quarters. This was more or less the policy that the Foreign Office ultimately pursued, viewing the implications of the Arab-Jewish dispute through the lens of regionalism, which focused on the conflict's proximal effects on a contiguous territorial area stretching to South Asia and on the Muslims within it. This most basic of imperial concerns was one that Attlee had warned Truman about two years earlier, telling his American counterpart, "I know you realise that as things are the responsibility of preserving order with all the consequences involved rests entirely on this country. . . . In addition to this problem we are engaged upon another related one and that is India. The fact that there are ninety million Moslems, who are easily inflamed, in that country compels us to consider the problem from this aspect also."[19]

Across the Atlantic, Washington's views on Palestine had parted ways with Britain for good. The inherent political and diplomatic difficulties of solving the Palestine problem aside, a deep domestic dispute also divided American policy on the issue. Bureaucratic discord penetrated to the deepest levels of the decision-making structures of U.S. foreign policy, beginning with the American delegation to the United Nations itself. Ambassador Warren Austin's deputy on the Security Council, John Ross, was one of the greatest skeptics of UN efficacy in producing a viable Palestine settlement, irrespective of the body's lack of international military forces to enforce a decision. As Ross put it to his superior, "With regard to other international political problems, e.g., Palestine, Kashmir, Indonesia, Greece, Korea, these are on the whole all being dealt with reasonable effectiveness by the United Nations, and I do not think it likely that we could deal with these questions with any greater effectiveness if we had the [UN Charter] Article 43 forces."[20]

Interagency positions on Palestine also diverged outside of Foggy Bottom. Like the Foreign Office, the State Department and the Joint Chiefs of Staff remained wary of the pitfalls of any decision that might inflame Arab sentiments in the region. American support for such a plan, these policymaking circles held, could endanger a wide range of U.S. interests in the region—from military basing rights to the security of American citizens overseas, to the continuing presence of U.S.-sponsored institutions in the Arab world that represented conduits for the exercise of what today would be termed "soft power." Locating Palestine in a global context, the Joint Chiefs went so far as to warn that advocacy for a partition plan might even endanger the Marshall Plan itself, given the dependence of the European Recovery Program on Middle East petroleum exports to power Europe's reconstruction and economic growth.[21] In stark contrast, the Truman White House strongly supported the creation of a Jewish state in Palestine, partly at the behest of presidential advisors like David Niles, who was actively involved in the Zionist movement in the United States, and of course Clark Clifford. Endorsement of partition was essential for the continued support of American Jews for the Truman administration's reelection bid, and this domestic consideration became a principal rationale for the endorsement of the Zionist claim to statehood. The appearance of the Palestine question before the United Nations in late 1947 thus set the stage for an epic bureaucratic struggle that would radically alter the trajectory of American policy in the Middle East and transform the region.

Over massive opposition from Near East Affairs director Loy Henderson, Secretary of Defense James V. Forrestal, and others, Truman directly instructed the U.S. delegation to the United Nations to support the UNSCOP majority report on 11 October. Pressure from Zionist groups in the United States probably weighed heavily on the decision. Truman recalled in his memoirs, "I do not think I ever had as much pressure and propaganda aimed at the White House as I had in this instance."[22] On 25 November the majority report passed the UN Ad Hoc Committee on Palestine (set up to deliberate on the report) by a vote of twenty-five to thirteen, with seventeen abstentions, failing to pass adoption by the General Assembly by a single vote. Four days later, after the Thanksgiving weekend had passed and a series of eleventh-hour diplomatic appeals by the United States to Greece, Liberia, the Philippines, and other countries that had abstained from the vote the first time around, the UN General Assembly voted on 29 November thirty-three to thirteen in favor of the Committee's majority plan to partition Palestine.[23]

The Committee's recommendation was perhaps the last straw for Britain's ordeal in Palestine. London had finally concluded that it could no longer resolve the Palestine question itself. Devastated by the war effort and exhausted by the postwar burdens of empire, Britain took the decision to abandon Palestine as an admission of the limits of its overseas power projection capabilities. The powder keg had been lit for the first Arab-Israeli War, sparks already having begun to fly. But Britain had already commenced its military withdrawal.

In the weeks before the General Assembly vote, while American Zionists lobbied member nations intensively, the Colonial Office had expressed concerns about the early termination of the mandatory regime, lest both Arabs and Jews contest British authority during that interval. Even if violence were to break out, the thinking went, at least it would not be directed against the vestiges of the British mandatory administration and its officials. What was absolutely essential for British interests was to prevent the entanglement of the residual British troop presence in the enforcement of the UN settlement—a concern that paralleled the U.S. Joint Chiefs' preoccupation with U.S. military entanglement in Palestine. Moreover, in accordance with the Ministry of Defense's concerns with the prospect of unrest in Egypt, Iraq, or Iran in the course of the British withdrawal, an additional brigade would be left in Egypt for the first half of 1948 as a precautionary measure to preclude a regionwide backlash against the UN vote.[24]

The concerns revealed a regional sense of the implications of escalating violence in Palestine that stemmed naturally from the geographical and strategic realities confronting the British Empire in the Middle East and that might have consumed the work of the British Middle East Office in Cairo, entrusted as it was with the consideration of regional questions (in lieu of the piecemeal treatment of individual bilateral policies). But the foresight and associated precautionary arrangements could hardly prevent the outbreak of chaos. While delaying the expiration of the mandate until the British withdrawal precluded a direct challenge to formal British jurisdiction, reserve British units were completely ill-equipped to preserve order in the wake of the UN vote.

Violence still engulfed Palestine over the subsequent months, in which clashes between Zionists and Palestinian Arabs gradually escalated. As Benny Morris put it, what unfolded was a civil war from November 1947 to May 1948, followed by a conventional regional war between Israel and the combined, but hardly uniform, support of the joint Arab armies. The situation on the ground flagrantly defied the international community's appeals for restraint. Raids by Arab irregular forces across the border into Palestinian territory commenced in January 1948, and the CIA assessed that some 8,000 Arab volunteers had entered Palestine. Within the first three months of the conflict, the war had claimed over 1,000 lives, mostly Arabs. The CIA considered a number of possible options for an international force to uphold the partition decision but rejected all of them, deeming them impractical.[25]

The equivocal nature of U.S. policy toward the dispute over Palestine was manifest from early 1948, well before the Israeli declaration of independence. At a press conference in January, Truman refused to elaborate on whether the United States would commit military forces to Palestine. While the president acknowledged that an international force might be dispatched in accordance with the course of action recommended by the United Nations, he refused to confirm whether he envisioned that such a force would materialize, or whether the United States would contribute militarily to such a hypothetical force.[26] Subsequent discussions by U.S. officials grappling with the issue confirmed the ambivalent attitude of the Truman administration vis-à-vis the formulation of foreign policy toward Palestine and the prospect of an Arab invasion. Some State Department officials seemed ready to admit that "armed interference in Palestine by the Arab States to prevent the implementation of the [UN General] Assembly's resolution would clearly be aggression contrary to the obligations of those states under the Charter. . . . The United States cannot avoid its responsibility as a permanent member of the Security Council to act within the limits of the Charter to prevent this type of aggression from outside Palestine."[27] In a sense U.S. officials thus admitted that if the letter of the law of the UN Charter was to be upheld, then the prohibition on the use of military force in Article 2(4) had to be enforced. And it was incumbent upon the United States as a signatory to the Charter and permanent member of the Security Council to act to prevent the combined Arab militaries from flouting the article's provisions. But the State Department's Office of United Nations Affairs espoused a somewhat cautious "wait and see" approach. It was the responsibility of the Security Council, these officials reasoned, to determine whether the violence in Palestine amounted to a threat to peace, a breach of peace, or an act of aggression. Accordingly such a determination by the Council should precede any action taken by the United Nations, and concomitantly the United States, to address the situation.[28]

Not surprisingly, calls for the boldest course of action came from the White House. Clifford appealed directly to Truman on 6 March, proposing that the president *himself* instruct the U.S. mission to the United Nations to seek a resolution in the Security Council, grounded in the actions of the Arab states. Clifford also suggested that Truman urge Great Britain to comply with the arms embargo on Palestine and advocate for the creation of an international volunteer force to restore the peace there.[29] Two days later Clifford presented Truman with a longer memorandum on the basic issues at stake in Palestine. Refuting the concerns of State and Defense Department officials opposed to partitioning Palestine, including Henderson and Forrestal, Clifford maintained that support for partition was consistent with the Balfour Declaration, preserved continuity with U.S. policies dating back to the Wilson administration, and constituted "the best hope for a permanent solution" and "the only course of action with respect to Palestine that will strengthen our position vis-a-vis Russia."[30]

George Kennan and his Policy Planning Staff viewed the prospect of a Security Council finding of aggression in Palestine to be fraught with peril. Three days after the memo discussing "armed interference in Palestine" by Arab military forces, Kennan warned against a willingness to find an act of aggression in the provision of arms and assistance to Palestinian guerrillas by the Arab states. He further reiterated the Staff's recommendations to steer clear of the deployment of international UN or member state armed forces for the purpose of enforcement action within Palestine.[31] Defense Department concerns about the repercussions of introducing U.S. troops into Palestine, which would ostensibly be part of any international force, also worried Truman. Whatever the U.S. position on an international force, one with an American contingent was largely out of the question for the administration, despite French and Soviet willingness to contribute to a force and of course the beleaguered receding British presence already in Palestine.[32]

Despite the internal U.S. government debate, when the Palestine issue arose before the Security Council in February 1948, American officials formally recognized the potential need for international armed forces to be deployed to quell the violence should the Council determine such an enforcement action was necessary. If so, the United States would, in theory, consider consulting other potential troop contributors in accordance with Article 106 of the Charter about joint action "for the purpose of maintaining international peace and security." The reason for such consultations was "the fact that armed forces have not as yet been made available to the Security Council under Article 43."[33] As late as the end of February, it seemed as though the Truman administration was ready to countenance the prospect of the dispatch of UN-sanctioned military forces to Palestine if need be. But was it in actuality willing to sanction such forces, even without U.S. troops?

The following day, in a statement to the Security Council, Ambassador Austin laid out the U.S. position on the scope of Security Council authority in taking action on the Palestine issue. For Austin, the critical point was that the Security Council had to act to preserve international peace and security, but not act as a surrogate authority for the enforcement of a partition plan.[34] The distinction the State Department sought to draw was between the global responsibility entrusted to the Security Council by the UN Charter and the altogether distinct issue of wrongfully invoking that authority to enforce what was merely a recommendation of the General Assembly. But the great irony in Austin's argument was evident, given the White House's simultaneous efforts through the likes of David Niles to prod Security Council members to adopt precisely the latter course and enforce the partition plan.

American concern with enforcing partition was of course bona fide, given the pressures to which the State Department felt America's Palestine policy was succumbing at the time, and the British experience with attempting to maintain order in Palestine that Washington had just witnessed as violence and chaos consumed the final months of the mandate. And though the Department felt that the deliberations on the Palestine issue at the Security Council linked U.S. involvement in the resolution of the dispute to the credibility of the new United Nations Organization, the prerogatives of American policy could not be circumscribed by a preoccupation with the prestige of the new international organization. "To the extent that we move in this direction," the Policy Planning Staff concluded in a report, "we will be operating directly counter to our major security interests in that area."[35] Moreover CIA analysis of the various contingencies at play in Palestine was pessimistic about the prospects of a forced settlement on Palestinian Arabs. "The Arabs can never be forced to acquiesce in a Western-sponsored movement which they believe is threatening the twentieth century renascence of their indigenous civilization," one of the Agency's reports had concluded in February.[36] These grounds for caution credibly justified any reluctance of U.S. officials to employ international armed forces to carry out the partition of Palestine in 1948. The ramifications of the potential finding of a breach of the peace and the attendant obligation to intervene would be severe enough; the last thing on the minds of State Department officials was intervention on behalf of the partition plan. Moreover, what if U.S. support for a proposed international force triggered international calls for an American military commitment, thereby implicating the credibility of the new international organization? A more practical consideration than the politics of the conflict in Palestine was the availability of adequate U.S. ground forces. Near the end of the Second World War the U.S. army, with 3.5 million troops in sixty-eight divisions, had demobilized to but 400,000 troops in less than a year. As U.S. planners feared the need to deploy troops to areas afflicted by postwar instability, such as Greece, which was besieged by communist insurgency, the Joint Chiefs estimated that between 80,000 and 160,000 troops would be required to enforce the UN partition plan. Given such needs assessments, the prospects for U.S. military involvement, and correspondingly, perhaps, those for a Security Council determination of a threat to or breach of the peace, became all the more unlikely.[37]

Interestingly, in contrast to its aversion to the introduction of international armed forces to enforce partition or address breaches of the peace, it seems that even some within the State Department were for a time willing to countenance the idea of at least the temporary deployment of an international force to ensure sufficient security for the transition to a trusteeship or "federal state" while Jewish emigration into Palestine continued in the early spring of 1948. As the Policy Planning Staff (which had conceived of the idea) framed it, "If necessary, this proposal should include provision for an international force to maintain internal order during a transitional period."[38] An April assessment by the JCS had even explored precisely the question of, inter alia, "what armed forces would be required to be supplied from outside of Palestine in order to maintain law and order under a temporary trusteeship."[39] It is interesting to speculate on the composition of the force proposed by Kennan's staff in this document. The Joint Chiefs suggested a force comprising two equal contingents of American and British units totaling 46,800 personnel each, which would amount to 90 percent of the force, along with 10,400 French troops to provide the remaining 10 percent "because France is one of the remaining members of the Allied and Associated Powers."[40] Austin's remarks at the United Nations had drawn a distinction between U.S. reluctance to commit troops to enforce the UNSCOP partition plan and the deployment of U.S. troops to provide security in Palestine under other circumstances, to which Truman remained coyly noncommittal. But the force envisioned by the Policy Planning Staff, albeit one marshaled to protect a unified Palestine transitioning to trusteeship or federal status (an idea with which the State Department was much more comfortable), was still not likely one in which U.S. forces would be a constituent element for the principal military and strategic necessities elaborated by the JCS. Still, the suggestion was a tantalizing allusion to the prospect of an international force, perhaps one acting under the auspices of the United Nations Security Council, to secure postmandatory Palestine if the partition scheme was ultimately abandoned by the international community. But for that to occur, the Council would first have to have acted in its quasi-judicial capacity to determine that the peace had been breached in the first place—before calling on member states to act to restore it—neither of which occurred. An examination of statements made and informal P-5 deliberations at the Council provides some clues as to why the turn of events at the Council never led to such a finding.[41]

The State Department, angered by Zionist interference with the UN vote and the dismal state of affairs, had in effect proposed a last-ditch effort to resolve the conflict: international or UN-administered trusteeship over Palestine until the formation of a permanent government.[42] But days later Truman issued a public statement on 25 March clarifying that "trusteeship is not proposed as a substitute for the partition plan but as an effort to fill the vacuum soon to be created by the termination of the mandate on May 15. The trusteeship does not prejudice the character of the final political settlement. It would establish the conditions of order which are essential to a peaceful solution." Truman also called for a cease-fire, as the fighting was escalating beyond control.[43] Given considerable ambiguity about the transience of the plan as an interim measure, the trusteeship idea seemed to some observers to contradict the U.S. commitment to partition, which Truman had reaffirmed to Weizmann in a private meeting the week before his public statement. As a result, in the confused days after the announcement of the trusteeship proposal, pro-Zionist elements lambasted Truman for betraying them, while a blindsided State Department came to grips with the new course the White House seemed to have charted.[44]

Trusteeship ultimately foundered on the inability of the UN to obtain a cease-fire ending the violence, despite the passage of a 17 April resolution establishing a Truce Commission consisting of U.S., French, and Belgian consular representatives.[45] During the last month and a half or so of hostilities before the outbreak of open war, the Haganah, the Jewish proto–defense ministry, launched a counteroffensive against Palestinian Arabs that culminated in its consolidation of control over the entire territory accorded to the Jewish state by the partition plan. This area included the regions of Tiberias, Nazareth, and Besian in the northeast of present-day Israel, a strip of the Mediterranean coast that comprised Haifa, Tulkarm, and Jaffa, and portions of Ramallah, Gaza, and Beersheba to the south. Upon the declaration of Israeli independence, Syrian, Iraqi, Transjordanian, and Egyptian military units crossed the borders of partitioned Palestine. But Arab involvement in the conflict was neither instantaneous nor driven by immediate consensus on the need to come to the aid of Palestine's Arab Muslims. Riven by divisions and conflicting loyalties, the Egyptian-led intervention in Palestine occurred only after a key decision in Cairo hinging on the scale of the escalating violence, the corresponding reactions in the Arab world, and the implications for Egypt's role as the leader and international political center of the Arab world. Violence in Palestine had grabbed headlines on the Arab street in the prelude to the Israeli declaration. And the now well-studied massacre at Dayr Yasin and the flight of Palestinian refugees spurred massive protests in the region, including a 100,000-strong gathering in Cairo.[46]

Mobilization stirred young Arab and Jewish men to arms in the service of the nascent war effort. Attacks and counterattacks perpetrated by both sides led the leaders of the Haganah to adopt a policy of "aggressive defense" that assumed a more assertive posture than its hitherto dispersed, withdrawn positions defending Jewish enclaves. In January 1948 a force of some 2,000 Arab Liberation Army irregulars had crossed the Syrian border to aid Palestinian forces. But the conflict had yet to be formally "internationalized" in the sense of large-scale Arab military involvement. Egyptian leaders proved initially hesitant to engage in the Israeli-Palestinian "civil war," owing to its stated claim, however incredible, of defense requirements mandating that Egyptian army forces remain positioned for potential use against the lingering British military presence in Egypt (whose departure from Egyptian soil and the repudiation of the 1936 Anglo-Egyptian agreement Cairo had long sought). Egypt also feared that its prospects for victory were slim in the face of the well-trained and well-equipped Israel Defense Forces. King Farouk eventually overruled his military advisors and Prime Minister Muhammad Fahmi an Nuqrashi Pasha and ordered the invasion. Nevertheless Arab military assistance would ultimately be for naught. After two short campaigns in May–June and July, punctuated by a UN-brokered truce, the nascent Israeli military forces had beaten back the Arab invaders and consolidated control over the West Bank, the northern end of the Gaza Strip, areas south and west of Jerusalem, and Acre to the north.[47]

THE LIMITS OF GLOBALISM

Did the actions on the ground in Israel and Palestine amount to a threat to the peace, a breach of the peace, or an act of aggression of the sort that would trigger the enforcement provisions in the UN Charter? The United States certainly deemed the actions of the Arab states to constitute at the very least a breach of the peace and tabled a draft Security Council resolution stipulating as much. The draft, however, was voted down by other members of the Council. The Council instead decided that the situation as of 15 July constituted a threat to the peace but did not assign responsibility in making that determination.[48]

In reality the legal questions at the heart of the war were staggeringly complex. First and foremost was the question of the international legal personality of both the Jewish Agency and the Arab Higher Committee as actors before the Council. Both parties had indeed been recognized by the League of Nations as representatives of their respective communities in Palestine. These communities, according to the Institute of International Law in 1931, were "subjects under international law."[49] But of course there existed no past practice establishing precedence for such bodies asserting their right to raise matters of peace and security before the Security Council.[50] A second consideration was the invocation of the principle of self-determination to claim sovereignty over the territory of Palestine. On this point interpretations among legal scholars diverge widely. The Jewish Agency's and the Arab Higher Committee's rights of self-determination necessarily proved mutually exclusive, grounded as they were in claims to the same physical territory. Scholars like John Quigley have maintained that the Palestinian Arabs' claims to the land of Palestine was historically based on occupation and dominion, grounds on which the Jewish Agency and Zionist settler claims were more weakly established. But others, like Michael Reisman, maintain that Arab self-determination rights could not be applied to areas in which the state of Israel already enjoyed sovereign authority, an infringement of Israel's rights that "would involve a comparable deprivation of the Israelis who themselves have their own historical trauma and have established a state for reasons which are well known."[51]

There was a third legal question: of the historically long-standing but newly codified right of self-defense in Article 51 of the UN Charter.[52] A fourth and final matter at issue was what actually constituted aggression. After the collective Arab invasion of Israel in May 1948, there was perhaps a case to be made for armed aggression perpetrated by both sides. Some analysts have deemed Israel the victim of Arab aggression in the spring of 1948, arguing that the Egyptian-led invasion and violation of Israeli sovereignty entitled Israel to invoke the doctrine of self-defense to repel its enemies. This rationale seemed to resonate within the Truman administration, including even at the U.S. State Department, where the "globalists" viewing the problem in a wider context than the Arabists in the Division of Near Eastern Affairs brought it to bear on deliberations about Palestine policy at the United Nations. Nevertheless the Arab states also ostensibly held claims to the right of collective self-defense, perceiving themselves as coming to the aid of their Palestinian Arab brethren at the latter's request.[53]

Ultimately the UN debates on the invasion focused less on the legality of the armed interventions by both sides and more on the practical considerations concerning the current and future status of Palestine. And in a sense, the United States and other permanent members of the Security Council arrived at their chosen courses seemingly oblivious to the apparent legitimacy of either side's claims in international law. But despite that aversion to debating interpretations of Charter law or acting in accordance with the merits of each side's case, the Council revealed its respect for the gravity of the problem of determining whether Palestinian self-determination rights trumped those of Israel in the most obvious way (or its claims to sovereign authority over Palestine, for that matter): by refusing to address that ultra-sensitive question at the Council table.[54] A brief synopsis of the debates reveals the salience of political-military and ideological considerations over precise legal distinctions, despite the consensus that quickly formed that events in Palestine clearly threatened international peace.

Beginning on 8 March the five permanent members of the Security Council commenced a series of consultations to coordinate their policy on the unfolding crisis in Palestine. Interestingly the convergence toward Great Power consensus proceeded fairly rapidly throughout the early rounds of talks. As early as the sixth meeting of the group, on 17 March, a number of the representatives present, including both Austin and his Soviet counterpart, Andrei Gromyko, arrived at the consensus view that the situation in Palestine constituted a threat to international peace that the Security Council needed to address. Gromyko seemed to share Austin's sense and went so far as to support American language that the Council should "take further action by all means available to it" to end the violence.[55] In contrast, the French ambassador to the United Nations, Alexandre Parodi, expressed his view that there was "a sort of threat to the peace" extant at the time. Tsiang Tingfu, China's representative at the discussions, stressed the need for the Council to provide a balanced assessment of the situation that did not ascribe blame solely to either side. The deliberations disclosed the extent to which the permanent members of the Council saw the situation in Palestine through the same lens of a rapidly escalating postcolonial conflict in which no one wanted to intervene decisively on either side, despite the strong cases to be made for international legal infractions incurred on the parts of some, if not all, of the belligerents. The meeting subsequently turned to the issue of measures to which the Security Council could resort, given a putative threat to the peace. Austin beseeched his counterparts to examine the full spectrum of actions the Council could seek under the scope of Chapter VII. After all, he observed, the five permanent members "would never be able to maintain a situation permanently by a ring of bayonets" in as hotly contested a dispute as the one engulfing Palestine.[56] In his statement to the Security Council two days later, Austin echoed that sense of flexibility, reminding members of the broad range of actions afforded them by the Charter. Austin, of course, had a motive for opening up the discourse to the consideration of intermediary options within the policy space between military enforcement action and apathetic inaction. The Department had armed him with the ill-fated trusteeship proposal prepared in February, which he now suggested that the United Nations adopt "without prejudice to the character of the eventual political settlement," in lieu of the continuation of the partition plan.[57]

As noted, neither the Arab Higher Committee nor the Jewish Agency consented to the trusteeship proposal. But if a basic consensus had emerged among the five permanent members that the situation in Palestine threatened international peace, as Austin's deliberations with his French, British, and Chinese counterparts suggested, why did the Council fail to invoke the more robust collective security provisions placed at its disposal by the Charter? The imposition of the UN-sponsored truce was within the scope of the Charter's provisions, but in a sense the Council had failed to meet as egregious a threat to the peace as could be conceivable, given both the Arab invasion as well as Haganah operations against Palestinian Arabs in territory slated for the Jewish state. One reason was the perceived or real lack of military forces available for this purpose—not only troops placed at the disposal of the Security Council under the nonexistent Article 43 agreements but even troops volunteered by member nations for the purpose of enforcing the Council's will. Considering the hypothetical case of an Arab invasion of Palestine, Austin remarked to Secretary of State George Marshall on 8 May 1948 that it was clear to British and Canadian colleagues that "there would probably be weak legal basis for sanctions against Arabs. In any event if by sanctions we meant force this [would be] impossible because [the] forces required would be very large and are not forthcoming."[58] But given the strains of postwar economic upheavals, including British and French indebtedness, coupled with the ordeal of raising new troops for foreign deployment in the midst of global demobilization, of course the provision of military forces under UN command was one obstacle to surmount. That practical consideration aside, it seems that other factors also dampened Council members' enthusiasm to introduce international military forces into the region to repulse invading Arab forces and temper the extent of Haganah reprisals.

In a personal appeal to Austin, UN Secretary General Trygve Lie explicitly reminded the American representative of the Council's obligations and its corollary responsibility for maintaining international peace. "A failure of the Security Council to act under these circumstances can only result in the most serious injury to the prestige of the United Nations and hope for its future effectiveness in keeping the peace elsewhere in the world," Lie contended.[59] By this time the Truman administration had at least contemplated the need for international armed forces to be deployed to Palestine—despite the concerns of the JCS and the raging internal debate over enforcement of partition as opposed to the deployment of an international force simply to restore the peace. Nevertheless Kennan again warned Secretary Marshall of the dangers of recent U.S. policies toward the Palestine issue—specifically those precipitated by the entanglement of the U.S. military in an effort to oppose Arab aggression in the region by virtue of American UN commitments.[60]

The United States and its fellow Security Council members thus found themselves carefully weighing the costs and benefits of inaction in the face of a multicountry invasion of Israel with the dangerous consequences of embroiling American military forces in an Arab-Israeli civil war in Israel and Palestine. In the end, for Washington the proposed solution was not a military response but a diplomatic overture. On 14 May, with U.S. support, the General Assembly voted for a United Nations commissioner for Palestine to exercise his good offices for the benefit of Palestine's population, the protection of its religious sites, to promote a settlement on Palestine's future, and to work with the new Truce Commission for Palestine established by the passage of General Assembly Resolution 186.[61]

Interestingly two days after the war broke out, the United States did introduce a draft resolution in the Council acknowledging that a "breach of the peace" had occurred, without apportioning blame to any of the parties involved in the hostilities. The resolution ordered "all Government and authorities to cease and desist from any hostile military action and to that end issue a cease-fire and stand-fast order to their military and paramilitary forces to become effective within thirty-six hours after the adoption of this resolution."[62] But it immediately became clear that the text failed to muster the sufficient votes to pass. And by this time Council members seemed to have adopted the attitude that the introduction of international armed forces was growing increasingly unlikely. Perhaps an international consensus was forming in accordance with the U.S. view, supported by the bleak JCS assessments of the prospects for enforcing a settlement.

Austin relayed to Marshall that the draft resolution as it stood would not garner more than three or four affirmative votes given that Council members knew of the U.S. reluctance to commit troops to enforce any such finding and to deploy military forces to restore peace.[63]

The Council had essentially called America's bluff in testing the credibility of the body's binding decisions. By the end of August, as sporadic violence continued, despite the fact that the war had largely ended for all intents and purposes, the State Department continued to support efforts to resolve the dispute led by Count Folke Bernadotte, who had been appointed to the post of mediator under the auspices of the General Assembly resolution. The Department thus essentially had acquiesced to the Joint Chiefs' warnings. America's commitment to the United Nations, validated by the ultimate test—its willingness to contribute to the military burden to enforce the new body's will—came down to a cost-benefit analysis that hinged on the virtues and pitfalls of deploying U.S. military forces to resolve a postcolonial dispute Department officials feared might pull them into a wider conflagration.

Manifold concerns weighed on the minds of U.S. policymakers considering the upshot of American military action in the Levant. The Joint Chiefs had laid out their fears of Soviet penetration of the Middle East on 19 August in a report, NSC 27, which maintained that "it would be incompatible with the security interests of the United States to have either United States or Soviet or Soviet satellite forces introduced into Palestine."[64] Critically it had also highlighted the global impact of a deployment to Palestine on U.S. military power projection. It was thus not only Great Britain that faced strains on military manpower and materiel. As Forrestal told the new U.S. National Security Council, "Participation in enforcement of peace in Palestine by United States armed forces, no matter of what strength, must be viewed as the quite probable genesis of a series of United States deployments to Palestine which might ultimately attain such proportions that our military responsibilities in other parts of the world, which are vital to United States security, could not be either promptly or effectively met."[65] However, Forrestal noted, despite the passage of the Security Council resolution of 15 July, the United States was not yet obligated to contribute military forces to Palestine because it had not yet agreed to the relevant troop contribution commitments.[66]

The State Department pointed out additional political considerations that likely factored into U.S. strategy—considerations that seem to have influenced the Policy Planning Staff: "Apart from the specific threats indicated above, United States security would be seriously prejudiced by large-scale fighting anywhere in the Middle East, but particularly in Palestine. Continued warfare between Jewish and Arab forces would undermine the gains which have been made in Greece, Turkey and Iran, might permanently alienate the Arab world from western influences, and might impose upon the United States a basic re-examination of its own world security position."[67]

The internal policy dispute in Washington revealed the variegated degree of influence that the new globalism in American strategy had across executive branch agencies. For the National Security Council and the advisors at the State Department concerned with UN and multilateral affairs, globalism—and the linkage of Palestine to the plight of European Jews—meant at least considering an international force presence in the Levant to enforce a UN partition plan. But others, like the Arabist camp in Foggy Bottom and the JCS, were concerned that the reintroduction of U.S. troops as part of such a force into the Middle East in the aftermath of the Second World War could cause considerable turbulence in the region and beyond, threatening U.S. interests throughout the Near East, tarnishing impressions of the United States throughout the Muslim world, and sowing the seeds of conflict that could destabilize the region. The optimal course of action, Department officials reckoned, was one that fell short of the use of armed force: the Security Council should instead make use of other measures from the full spectrum of action afforded it by Chapter VII of the UN Charter, such as the institution of economic sanctions or arms embargoes to quell the violence. While the Security Council did eventually find a threat to the peace in Israel in July 1948, the Haganah by then was well on its way to routing the combined Arab military forces that confronted it.

Given the immediacy of the presence of American troops in the Middle East in the closing stages of the Second World War, some "regionalists" among U.S. policymakers surmised that the reintroduction of such troops into the region might instigate a hostile response throughout the Arab world, and potentially beyond, in other Muslim countries. This line of reasoning seems to have profoundly influenced military officers advising the Truman administration's national security establishment in the years immediately following the war. Hence the remarks of Colonel A. J. McFarland about the potential instability that a renewed U.S. military presence in the region could precipitate.[68] Understandably postwar demobilization gave rise to strong disincentives against the redeployment of Western military forces in the former theaters of the global conflict—disincentives that directly discouraged states from upholding their military commitments to the Security Council. While these concerns did not shape overall postwar American foreign policy, which focused on building up NATO and funding the Marshall Plan, they did partially slow the outward expansion of American influence driven by globalism, proving weighty enough to blunt that expansion when it came to the most sensitive questions, such as whether to employ American military power to reshape the Middle East.

ANGLO-AMERICAN STRATEGIC DIFFERENCES

The analysis of Anglo-American policy in Palestine reveals that the distance separating London's take on Palestine from Washington's was considerable and was rooted in basic differences in strategic outlooks. Those differences were the internalized rationalizations of policymaking establishments that employed widely different mental maps of the Middle East based on different conceptions of security interests, power projection capabilities, and other material realities.

For most American officials, the significance of the Middle East was truly global. The critical importance of the region's petroleum reserves for the continuation of the European Recovery Program and the reconstruction of Western Europe and Japan, as well as for the general well-being of the industrialized economies, was a principal maxim of policy. Adequate supplies of petroleum were essential to offset looming shortages in the Western Hemisphere in the postwar years. Oil reserves were likewise critical prerequisites for U.S. war-planning assumptions.[69] As a result American oil companies maintained a vested interest in imports of petroleum from Arab countries, and the stakes were sufficiently high that the U.S. government would go as far as the subversion of domestic antitrust legislation to protect them. In addition, American military contingency plans for potential war with the Soviet Union called for the use of air bases in the Middle East, as well as Britain and Okinawa. Due to its proximity to Soviet oil refinery installations, American planners coveted the Suez area in Egypt. Believing Soviet radar capabilities in the region to be weak, Anglo-American war plans rested on access to the region as a staging area for launching strategic bombing runs by the U.S. Air Force.[70]

However, it is critical to understand that the global context of U.S. perceptions of the Middle East also led to other policy conclusions. While the requirements for cold war contingency planning and worldwide energy needs for European and Japanese reconstruction led the Joint Chiefs to conclude that the support of the Arab states was essential for any lasting settlement in Palestine, the Truman White House considered the Palestine question in the context of its own global strategy, albeit one that led it to favor continued Jewish immigration and eventually to recognize the independence of Israel. Globalism led officials at the White House and some even in the State Department to connect the plight of Jews fleeing Europe with the future of Palestine. In the minds of White House officials like Niles, Clifford, and even Truman himself, and the State Department's advisors on the United Nations, the European Jews were potential settlers who were geographically linked to the reconstitution of the Jewish national homeland in Palestine.

But as American interests expanded geographically in the aftermath of the war, so did Britain's correspondingly contract. In stark contrast to his observations in the summer of 1945, as war engulfed Palestine in the aftermath of the UN partition plan, Herbert Samuel now held that "there is thus little strategic advantage to Great Britain in holding the Middle East, except to protect the oil fields and to prevent a Russian advance into Africa."[71]

The shift he cited was perhaps not pervasive throughout the British government. Indeed the Chiefs of Staff continued to maintain that the Middle East possessed significance for Great Britain because of the strategic requirements of the defense of the empire. But the Labour years had overseen both a military and a psychological retreat from the region. British strategic thought now felt the pinch of the economic and military pressures squeezing the empire's ability to preserve its influence in the East. The consequences of this shift are visible in Whitehall's Palestine policy.

As the geographical scope of British interests was curtailed to fit this more modest "regionalist" vision, the sober realism of Labour's approach to the Middle East tightly delimited its policy objectives, including in Palestine. Thus the overriding concern for a settlement became the continued goodwill of the Arab states—goodwill that was necessary for both geopolitical advantage and to account for demographic realities. As the looming retreat from Egypt triggered a scramble for alternative basing presences, the prospect of negotiated basing arrangements became a key concern for policy in Palestine, which some in the military considered a suitable substitute for the Suez. And as imperial strategy was recalibrated to focus on maintaining the integrity of the land and sea routes to India, preserving calm across the predominantly Muslim populations "from the Bosporus to the Indus" became a paramount concern, preoccupying the Middle East Regional Office entrusted with considering the regional effects of flashpoints like Palestine across the states, territories, and peoples of a shrinking British sphere of interest.

THREE

The Contested Valley

One of geographer Ellsworth Huntington's first observations about Kashmir in his 1906 survey concerned the region's physical isolation and the attendant effects on the history of the Kashmiri people. "Kashmir presents one of the best opportunities for the study of the relation of man to his surroundings," he noted, "for from the earliest-known times the basin has been occupied by a single race. The people are Aryans allied to those of northern India in blood and language, but far less subject to outside influences because of the high mountain barrier, which has not only made invasion a rare occurrence but has restricted external trade and migration."[1] Huntington's prescient observation about the isolated region southwest of the towering Karakoram Range applied only to the central valley that constituted the core of the modern state of Jammu and Kashmir. But that state had expanded into a far more complex polity over the eventful century culminating in the trials of partition in 1947.[2]

The princely state of Jammu and Kashmir came into existence in the nineteenth century as a political unit under the rule of the upper-class Hindu Dogra dynasty of northern India. Partly the result of conquest, territorial consolidation, and territories relinquished by the Sikhs and the English East India Company, the state became an authoritarian fiefdom comprising myriad ethnicities and religious groups that echoed the cosmopolitan heydays of Mughal rule. Kashmir came under nominal British imperial administration in 1846 after the first Anglo-Sikh War, when the Battle of Sobraon saw the defeat of Sikh forces at the hands of the British military with the assistance of the nominally neutral Dogra ruler of Jammu,

Gulab Singh. The terms of the settlement in the 9 March Treaty of Lahore specified Sikh concessions to the East India Company that included the surrender of the Vale of Kashmir. In return for the Dogra ruler's assistance in the war, and lacking any interest in administering the territory directly itself, the Company subsequently consented to acknowledge Gulab Singh's "independent sovereignty" over Kashmir in the 1846 Treaty of Amritsar. Shortly after he successfully suppressed a rebellion with the help of Herbert Edwardes, assistant to the British resident in Lahore Sir Henry Lawrence, in the span of about two years Gulab Singh became the maharaja of the expanded princely state of Jammu and Kashmir.

After 1846 the consolidation of Dogra rule over Jammu and Kashmir conjoined a patchwork of ethnicities and religions that lacked other ties binding local identities, unlike in more homogeneous stretches of the empire, such as predominantly Sunni Muslim Bengal. Subsequent years after the Treaty of Amritsar would see even further expansion of Jammu and Kashmir, northward and eastward to encompass Gilgit, Hunza, Nagar, and other areas adjacent to Afghanistan and China. In addition to the Vale of Kashmir, the eventual state borders subsumed primarily ethnic Tibetan and Buddhist Ladakh; Shia-populated Gilgit Agency and Baltistan; and later the state of Poonch, along Kashmir's western border. Poonch, which the court of the Dogra ruler Ranjit Singh had awarded to Gulab Singh's brother, Dhyan Singh, merged with Jammu and Kashmir only in 1935 as the result of a lawsuit by the last maharaja of Kashmir, Hari Singh. This complex process produced the territorial state of Jammu and Kashmir that existed at the moment of the subcontinent's partition.[3]

The Dogras would rule Kashmir on behalf of the British Empire throughout the century between the Treaty of Amritsar and the cataclysm of partition in which Kashmir proved the most critical flashpoint. But the restiveness of Kashmiri Muslims against the heavy-handed rule of their Hindu overlords, who presided over an impoverished, largely uneducated Muslim peasantry, had worried British officials for decades. Their concerns intensified when the state's officials prevented Kashmiris from fleeing the drought and subsequent famine that gripped the Vale of Kashmir in 1877. Growing increasingly uneasy with the maharaja's callous and feckless administration, the British government recast the officer on special duty in Kashmir, who had hitherto represented British interests, as a full British resident akin to the one serving in Lahore. Despite stripping some of the powers of governance from the maharaja (which were later restored by Viceroy Lord Curzon in 1905), decades of the maharaja's oppressive rule had irreparably damaged relations between the Dogras and Jammu and Kashmir's predominantly Muslim population.[4] And growing Muslim discontent would begin to mount ever more daunting challenges to the Hindu state administration right up to the communal violence that gripped Jammu and Kashmir during partition.

One of the most charismatic agitators against the excesses of Dogra rule was the six-foot, four-inch Sheikh Muhammad Abdullah, a schoolteacher who had failed to find work as a government civil servant upon the completion of his degree. In the early 1930s Abdullah and his fellow Muslim activists grew increasingly vocal about the state's treatment of Muslims as second-class citizens, who remained largely illiterate, unorganized, and unable to engage in public discourse or ascend to the ranks of the military's officer corps. Their collective political consciousness awoke violently in the summer of 1931 at a riot by Kashmiri Muslims demanding they be allowed to present a list of grievances. The maharaja's guards responded by opening fire on the mob and killing twenty-one protestors.[5]

In the aftermath of the massacre, the maharaja consented to the formation of a commission to investigate the source of the uprising and propose reforms to accommodate the growing discontent. From November 1931 to April 1932 a commission, led by B. J. Glancy, then head of the government of India's Foreign and Political Department, investigated the causes of the 1931 riot. When the Glancy Commission findings emerged in the spring of 1932, they centered on the basic roots of Kashmiri grievances: the lack of rights to free speech and press, the state's administrative bureaucracy, the system of land tenure, the lack of education, and the taxation structure. Unfortunately the princely state did little to implement the Commission's recommended reforms, essentially preserving its authoritarian character.[6] But the report revealed that the state administration denied basic rights across various spheres of activity to all Kashmiris, irrespective of their communal or religious affiliations. Soon after the Commission released its report, in October 1932 Abdullah became a founding member of the All Jammu and Kashmir Muslim Conference, a political party that hoped to unite Kashmiris in their demands for freedom of the press and political assembly from the state's Hindu ruler and his British masters. Jailed in the decades before partition because of his outspoken platform against the maharaja, Abdullah in 1938 changed the name of the Muslim Conference to the National Conference to render it more representative of all Kashmiris. Pandit leaders like Prem Nath Bazaz and some Sikh leaders echoed the recast agenda of the National Conference reformists, which sought to de-emphasize the communal divisions among Kashmiris in their efforts to force the state to address common grievances. But the change incurred the resentment of conservative Muslim elements within the Conference, who grew increasingly distrustful of Abdullah's secular bent and split off to form their own faction, adopting the organization's original name. Abdullah's stock nonetheless continued to rise among educated Kashmiris, and he immediately impressed Indian Congress Party leader Jawaharlal Nehru in their first meeting the same year the National Conference came into existence. Responding to pressure from the Muslim (and also the National) Conference, the maharaja consented to a new Kashmiri constitution in 1939, which expanded the number of parliamentary seats to an amount that would theoretically enable Kashmiris to elect a majority. But the control of candidate nominations, limits on enfranchisement, and other measures ensured that the maharaja maintained his tight grip over electoral outcomes. The constitution thus proved a dead letter of sorts, despite the symbolic accommodation of rising pressure to reform dating back to the violence of a decade earlier.[7]

The pressures from below emanating from the Muslim Conference and National Conference, coupled with the refusal of the state authority to accommodate them, threatened to bring the temperature to a boil after the start of the Second World War. As Indian troops deployed to the eastern theaters to defend the British Empire, the maharaja announced that new Kashmiri elections would be postponed until after the conflict. But Abdullah refused to let that defiance of constitutional limits go unchallenged. When the Cabinet Mission arrived in India to discuss reforms in the government of India, Abdullah used the occasion to pronounce the invalidity of the 1846 transfer of the Vale of Kashmir from the British to Gulab Singh. The announcement led to Abdullah's arrest, along with two of his associates, and a trial that subsequently sentenced him to three years' imprisonment. But his declaration had sparked a "Quit Kashmir" movement that challenged the authority of Britain and the maharaja in a bid for independence by war's end. Abdullah's trial and politically motivated sentence catalyzed the movement, which gathered momentum throughout the last years of the Dogra dynasty. Indeed Nehru had attempted to visit Abdullah in custody in June 1946 but was denied entry into Jammu and Kashmir. After asking the viceroy to intercede with Maharaja Hari Singh, the Congress

Party leader was successful in his second attempt, in July, when he was finally able to attend a portion of Abdullah's trial and visit with the incarcerated leader.

Nehru had grown fond of Abdullah and admired the young activist's leadership abilities. Abdullah had risen to prominence among Kashmiris who identified politically with their respective confessional groups and ethnicities and imbued them with a wider collective identity. His appeals to extend the reach of the Muslim Conference by secularizing it, his calls for freedom of political expression and the development of a robust press that educated Kashmiris could leverage for civic awareness and action, and his passionate defense of citizens' rights mirrored the struggles that Nehru saw across India on the cusp of independence. But what remained to be seen was whether parties like the National Conference and the Congress Party could bridge the divides between religious identities, and the extent to which the appeals of Abdullah and Nehru would resonate vis-à-vis those issued by the likes of Muhammad Ali Jinnah.[8]

Those unresolved Hindu-Muslim tensions came to a head during Britain's postimperial moment in India. Kashmiri Muslims first revolted against the Hindu maharaja of the state of Jammu and Kashmir in spring 1947 in Poonch. The uprising grew in severity after the partition of India and Pakistan in August, when violence spread to India's Punjab region and Pakistan's Northwest Frontier Province (NWFP). Despite the signing of an agreement between the maharaja and the government of Pakistan establishing Pakistani oversight of telegraph lines, postage, and the provision of food to Jammu and Kashmir, attacks by neighboring Muslims on Kashmiri Sikhs and Hindus upset the precarious state of accord. In October Pashtun tribes launched an attack on the state of Jammu and Kashmir, and the maharaja appealed to the Indian government for assistance. On 26 October he signed an instrument of accession to India, which smoothed the way for India to supply military aid to Jammu and Kashmir and maintain the maharaja's political office. These hostilities marked the start of the conflict that would draw in the United Nations Security Council the following year.[9]

Lord Mountbatten had first recommended that a plebiscite for Kashmir be held under UN auspices on 1 November 1947, as a condition for Kashmir's accession to India. Pakistan's first leader, Muhammad Ali Jinnah, had complained that with an Indian military presence on the ground, Kashmiris would lack the courage to vote to join Pakistan. Despite his misgivings, Prime Minister Liaquat Ali Khan caved in to British proddings. Although Nehru had also opposed the idea of a plebiscite at first, by the end of the year he too eventually consented, along with the Indian Cabinet. But when the parties failed to agree on the terms on which it would be held, the deadlock froze in time the unanswered question of Kashmiri self-determination. That question, in turn, touched on a wider issue that the Kashmir crisis had brought to light in 1947: whether the unity of postindependence India would last or whether it would divide into what one member of the UN Commission for India and Pakistan described as "two ways of life, two concepts of political organization, two scales of values, two spiritual attitudes." One man had nurtured a closely guarded sense of what the latter of those two opposing visions of India's future might connote for the Muslims.[10]

JINNAH, "PAKISTAN," AND MUSLIM SELF-DETERMINATION

Muhammad Ali Jinnah was one of eight children born into a Karachi family whose lineage not only drew from Punjabi and Gujarati roots but also stretched westward into Iran, and reflected a mix of both Rajput and Shia Ismaili traditions. Schooled in Karachi, Jinnah moved to London at the age of seventeen, where he worked briefly for a trading firm in business with his father, before pursuing studies in law. Acquiring an interest in political affairs in London, he returned to India in 1896 to practice as the first Muslim barrister in Bombay. Jinnah proved eager to participate in nationalist politics upon his return and joined the Congress Party. He quickly became known for his inclusive platform within the party and as an "ambassador of Hindu-Muslim unity." After joining the All-India Muslim League in 1913, Jinnah helped broker the Lucknow Pact between the Congress Party and the League three years later and secure 30 percent representation for Muslim representatives in India's provincial governments. The Pact, in the wake of the British decision to reverse the partition of Bengal, represented a breakthrough in cooperation between the two parties, as well as a gesture of reconciliation between the radical and moderate wings of the Congress Party. Under its auspices Congress and the League vowed to renounce violence and agreed to work together to seek representative government and a list of specific proposed reforms from the colonial authorities while preserving harmony within India, including a separate electorate for

Muslims. But the early cooperation proved short-lived after the colonial government refused to adopt many of the Pact's recommended reforms in the Montagu-Chelmsford Report of 1918, thereby weakening Jinnah's credibility and marking the beginning of a decade-long decline in the Muslim League's political fortunes.[11]

The period after the First World War saw the League eclipsed by groups like the pan-Islamist Khilafat movement, dedicated to the restoration of the Ottoman caliphate as the sole seat of global Islam. To the Sunni Muslims of India, the future of the seat of the universal Islamic caliphate in Istanbul resonated powerfully with their own destiny, as if its permanence somehow ensured their own continuity as a people and as a religious minority. The converse of this idea of course implied that the caliphate's disappearance might somehow strand them in a state of historical displacement like many European Jews, bereft of hope and homeland. But the movement also reflected the growth of a new religious fervor in India that accompanied the ascendancy of Gandhi, who opted to join forces with the Khilafat Muslims in exchange for their espousal of his principle of nonviolence. In this changing milieu the Muslim League lost considerable support to the Congress Party, which emerged as the new mainstream secular party rallying Indians in the cause of nationalist struggle. Jinnah was disheartened by what he saw as the ephemeral marriage of convenience between the Khilafat Muslims and Gandhi's Hindu following, which he saw displacing the reasoned moderation of his own secular nationalism as sanctified in compromises like the Lucknow Pact. By 1929 he had moved back to London, wondering whether his delicate balancing act between open defiance of British authority and engagement with colonial authority on its own terms as an articulate barrister had alienated the Indian Muslim masses. Jinnah's legal practice and personal investments had by this time secured him a handsome income, and he lived a life of opulence in London despite a thrifty practicality that governed his personal habits. But after a series of visits by Indian Muslims beseeching him to return and take direction of the Muslim League, he moved back to India in 1935.[12]

The same year marked the passage of a new Government of India Act. Facing pressures from Indian nationalists to devolve power, Britain's Conservative government had drafted a white paper on the future administrative structure of India that was reviewed by a parliamentary committee chaired by Lord Linlithgow. The bill that emerged from the committee's recommendations extended the provisions of the 1919 Government of India

Act, which had established the principle of a "diarchy" that divided power among appointed British and elected Indian ministers—although the Indian ministers were entrusted only with technocratic portfolios such as public health and agriculture to limit their political influence. The complex piece of legislation granted considerable responsibility for self-government to India's provinces, outlined the concept of a "federation of India" that would subsume the princely states along with the provinces (though it ultimately never came into existence), extended franchise through the principle of direct elections in lieu of the existing parliamentary assembly, and increased Indian membership in provincial assemblies to the point where they could elect majorities and form their own governments. Nevertheless a series of "safeguards" preserved the viceroy's ultimate authority should crises lock the wheels of representative government.[13]

Jinnah accepted the League's reins again and participated in the first elections held under the provisions of the Government of India Act in 1937, the year most of the Act's provisions entered into force. His basic strategy was to rally the Muslim-majority provinces "under the League's banner" as his political center while enlisting the simultaneous support of Muslims in minority provinces. The plan failed; the League fared poorly in the electoral results, and the resurgent Congress Party swept it aside throughout most of India. Three years later, and two years before the Jewish Agency adopted its Biltmore Program in Palestine, the League issued the Lahore Resolution calling for a Muslim homeland within India.[14]

The war years saw relations between the Muslim League and British colonial authorities improve and deepen. Jinnah offered the colonial state his cooperation in the war effort, in a strategic bargain that again validated his wily aptitude for navigating middle courses between opposition and cooptation. His entreaties forged a new closeness with the British government that would influence how his ultimate negotiating positions on a demand for Pakistan would be viewed. The deepening ties between the League and the India Office paralleled Britain's widening fissure with the Congress Party.[15]

As British allegiances turned toward Jinnah and his Muslim base, the war's outbreak helped solidify a sense of the impending inevitability of Indian self-rule. Anxious to forestall a revolt in the course of the war, in which Britain had declared India a belligerent on the side of the Allies, Prime Minister Churchill and Secretary of State for India and Burma Leo Amery dispatched Sir Stafford Cripps to India in March 1942 to negotiate a plan of self-government. On his arrival in March, Cripps proposed dominion status for India upon the war's end and the option to secede and seek full independence thereafter, but the specific arrangements for decentralization were unclear; while Cripps's offer included an enlargement of the viceroy's Executive Council, he presented no firm plans for its conversion into a body overseeing an independent India. Moreover Congress Party leaders were unsure as to what the British government had authorized the mission to propose. As a result of both concerns and Cripps's failure to close the gap between the Congress Party and the League, the mission failed. Congress launched its Quit India movement, which mobilized a mass uprising against British rule and led to the imprisonment of the party's leadership. Jinnah denounced the movement and maintained cooperation with the British, encouraging Indian Muslims to fight on behalf of the Allied cause. Amity with the British during the later war years helped the League rise to a position of prominence after the hostilities ended and discussions on the transfer of power began in earnest by providing a window for strengthening the party and extending its reach. Jinnah had at last regained some of the momentum he had lost over a decade earlier to the political forces that had threatened to rip away wide swaths of his Muslim constituency.[16]

Notwithstanding the failure of the Cripps mission to unify the positions of India's principal Hindu and Muslim parties, Jinnah shared with Nehru an opposition to the basic premises underlying the proposals for different sets of grievances. While the Congress Party's agitation for full independence and the launch of the Quit India movement was bolder, Jinnah objected to the idea of discussing token changes to the composition of the viceroy's Executive Council and other meager reforms that ignored the separate trajectory of India's Muslims. At the League's 1942 annual session in Allahabad, shortly after the arrival of the Cripps mission, he again pressed the demand for immediate self-determination for Indian Muslims. "Evading the real issues and by overemphasizing the territorial entity of the provinces which are mere accidents of British policy and administrative divisions is fundamentally wrong," he told the gathered delegates.[17] At a press conference in Delhi shortly thereafter, Jinnah was more qualified in his rejection of the offer. "Pakistan was not conceded unequivocally and the right of Muslim self-determination was denied," terms that left the League no choice but to reject the proposals on the table. But the League also "recognized that the same may constitute the foundations of British policy as a historic document," and "the recognition given to the principle of partition... was very much appreciated by Muslim India." The basis for this satisfaction was clear, for in Jinnah's mind, aspects of the plans reflected British acknowledgment of his *idea* of Pakistan.[18]

Colonial authorities in India had long been aware of the attractive force of Islamic identity for India's Muslim nationalists, as the backlash against Abdullah's secularism and the recrudescence of the All Jammu and Kashmir Muslim Conference had shown. The end of the First World War and the activism of Muslim nationalists like Maulana Abul Kalam Azad and the Khilafat movement revealed an expanding core within the anticolonial movement that was rooted among India's Muslims, many of whom had felt politically disenfranchised since the end of Mughal rule. Still, in British India's case, it was true that many Muslim leaders espoused a secular brand of Indian nationalism that preached unity with their coreligionists. But by the close of the war the India Office began to sense that the respective trajectories of India's Hindus and Muslims, growing more divergent as Jinnah clung to his maximalist aims, were leading them away from a common vision and possibly toward a cataclysmic confrontation. Despite the ties that Abdullah had forged with leaders like Nehru and parties like Congress, Jinnah's resurgence underscored the potency of a recast Muslim nationalism in India that, while secular, still threatened Hindu-Muslim unity with the prospect of territorial sovereignty for Muslims and potentially incompatible visions of their respective postcolonial destinies.[19]

As Richard Casey, the governor of Bengal, put it to Viceroy Lord Wavell, "I believe that the demands of Hindus and Muslims have crystallized into irreconcilability—an All-India unitary Government on the one hand and the two-nation theory on the other—centripetal and centrifugal."[20] While Casey believed a viable independent state of "Pakistan," as distinct from a "Hindustan," was "nonsense," he also remained soberly aware of the limits of British policy in shaping the final settlement, arguing that some kind of Muslim state might have to be acknowledged, even if only as an "inevitable stage on the journey" toward more permanent entities. "We can give the Indians independence, but we cannot give them unity," he observed. As such, he suggested that British colonial authorities convey to Muslim leaders "that if the Muslims want Pakistan, they can have it, so far as we are concerned."[21]

For his part, Lord Wavell shared the sense that a Pakistani state might indeed serve as a temporary construct anticipating an eventual federative structure for postindependence India. But he harbored doubts of Indian Muslims' readiness to "abandon Pakistan in its crude form" in the near future.[22] Some historians have argued that Jinnah himself was much less sanguine about temporary measures on the way to a more permanent arrangement, as part of an Indian federation or otherwise. In this view Jinnah held that the emergence of a separate Muslim state was a direct corollary of the historical processes within the empire leading to the pivotal postwar moment of Indian independence and was fully consonant with the international norms that characterized the era in which Indian nationalism had developed and matured.[23]

Nehru and Abdullah's Congress Party and Jinnah's Muslim League thus embodied two different choices facing Indian Muslims in princely states like Jammu and Kashmir. But a prerequisite for understanding what the Muslim demands consisted of was defining *exactly what the abstract notion of "Pakistan" actually connoted in territorial terms*, even in the maximalist variant of Jinnah's vision. In the Lahore Resolution of 1940 the Muslim League had declared that "no constitution or plan would be workable in this country" and that the resulting Pakistan accordingly "shall be autonomous and sovereign." But was it to consist simply of the sum total of India's Muslim-majority provinces, jumbled haphazardly into an unwieldy union of discontinuous territories, of the sort that Casey feared might crumble upon independence? Or did it connote something more clearly articulated in terms of both territorial geography and demographics, an abstract idea that corresponded to tangible outlines on the map of British India? How adamant was Jinnah about his rhetorical references to sovereignty, given its charged nature and obvious resonance with the masses?

As late as 1942 there still seemed to be room for compromise for what the League would accept. A British informant recalled an interview with Jinnah in which he had "again made it clear that, within the framework of the present constitution, he was prepared to cooperate in the formation of a 'so-called' national Government 'on an equal footing.'" Yet before withdrawing his demands about the function of any future provisional government under the auspices of the current constitution, he insisted that "the principle of self-determination was first recognized and Pakistan conceded after the war." The provisional answer seemed to be that Jinnah would allow India's Muslims to decide for themselves. In Lord Linlithgow's words, "His position was this: Did Muslims want separation or not? If they did not, the problem was simple. He could today go to the Congress leaders and tell them that all that Muslims ask for was separate electorates, special weightage and similar safeguards. . . . But if Muslims really wanted Pakistan—and he believed they did—then it was impossible for him to take any line other than he had taken."[24]

But what did it mean precisely for the British to "concede Pakistan"? Jinnah had been accused of refusing to define the bounds of Pakistan. But "the fact was that everyone knew perfectly well what was meant by Pakistan and what the words 'northwestern and eastern zones' signified. The exact delineation of the boundaries of these zones, when separately constituted, and the fiscal and other adjustments which must follow the separation were matters to be decided by special commissions to be set up for the purpose." This did not satisfy Linlithgow, who maintained that "Jinnah has been at great pains not to define exactly what he means by that blessed word."[25] Exactly what Jinnah conceived of had been left unclear. While he had spoken of self-determination for the Muslims of India, the scope or extent of autonomy that he sought remained ill-defined—to his advantage, in the opinion of British colonial officials.[26]

"As far as I know," Glancy (now British lieutenant-governor in the Punjab) wrote in August 1945, "Jinnah has only once given any explanation of this definition." In a September 1944 letter to Gandhi, Jinnah had pinpointed as one of his principal differences with the Indian leader the contention "that Pakistan is composed of two zones, north-west and northeast, comprising six provinces namely Sind, Baluchistan, the North-West Frontier Province, the Punjab, Bengal, and Assam subject to territorial adjustments that may be agreed upon as indicated in the Lahore resolution." Here, then, was an intriguing clue to the precise nature of the elusive notion of "Pakistan" to which Jinnah and the Muslim League clung. What was interesting about this definition was the balance it struck between specificity and flexibility, one that would prove critical for the future question of Kashmir's accession. For the inclusion of predominantly Muslim provinces constituted a basic core for the eventual state of Pakistan that was rooted firmly in the realities of northern India's demographics. But by adding the caveat of "territorial adjustments that may be agreed upon," Jinnah had cleverly preserved freedom of maneuver to resolve individual territorial issues that would have to be settled to effect a separation of the two states as might be necessary at the moment of independence. Interestingly British colonial authorities did engage in contacts with Muslim League officials in provinces like NWFP and Punjab that left them believing that the idea of Pakistan might connote something that fell far short of

Jinnah's ill-articulated vision of a Muslim state. This suggested that there might indeed be wiggle room between outright separation and the relegation of Muslim-majority provinces to domination by the political center. But there was a sense that the pressure of electoral politics might itself *force* the delineation of a territorial notion of Pakistan, purely as a politically charged, maximalist aim that, once expressed in explicit form, could then be contested.[27]

As time wore on, British authorities in India felt that Jinnah and the League increasingly reveled in their oppositionist stance. Moreover the governor in Punjab worried that the League might employ the defense of Islam to stoke forces of extremism in the course of defining its opposition to Congress and the Unionist government there: "The uninformed Muslim will be told that the question he is called on to answer at the polls is—Are you a true believer or a[n] infidel and a traitor? Against this slogan the Unionists have no spectacular battle-cry; they can point no doubt to their consistent support of the war effort, to the various reforms they have introduced, such as the vast reduction of agricultural indebtedness, and to their extensive post-war programme for the benefit of the Province. But all this may carry little weight against the false and fanatical scream that Islam is in danger."[28]

By the end of the war this meant that "party attitudes have hardened since 1942," the India Office concluded.[29] Moreover, worryingly, from the British standpoint, an intercepted letter from Maulana Azad to Gandhi seemed to suggest that the former's personal views might be gravitating toward those of Jinnah and his call for self-determination for India's Muslims.[30] Such a convergence of the disparate possible trajectories for Indian Muslims in the direction of an independent Pakistan enabled Jinnah to stick to his guns and adopt increasingly uncompromising rhetoric in the last years before independence, despite expressions of the British government's willingness to examine the constitutional questions that loomed for India. At the time India Office officials were still pondering how best to proceed with modifications that would adapt the existing constitutional structure to the postindependence era. One of the suggestions under consideration was discussion with provincial governments with a view toward the establishment of an institutional body entrusted with drafting a new constitution.[31]

But for Jinnah, prospective reforms were moot if they did not address the core issue of independence. "No attempt will succeed except on the basis of Pakistan and that is the major issue to be declared by all who are well-wishers of India and who are really in earnest to achieve real freedom and independence."³² In a planned radio address the viceroy contemplated pouring cold water on Jinnah's call for a separate, India-wide plebiscite on the future of the Muslim-majority provinces. After all, Lord Wavell reasoned, no doubt taking into consideration the plight of the Hindu and Sikh populations peppered across India's Muslim-majority provinces, "His Majesty's Government cannot agree to the future of any Province being decided by the vote of a single community." The precedent would be a symbolic one for the future of Jammu and Kashmir and its own plebiscite, which was never to materialize.³³

Jinnah shared his sentiments directly with British authorities early on during the constitutional reform process. "Muslim India will never accept any method of framing the Constitution of India by means of one Constitution-making body for all India, in which the Mussalmans will be in a hopeless minority, and the conclusions are foregone in such an assembly," he wrote Frederick Pethick-Lawrence, secretary of state for India and Burma, in December 1945. "Nor will they agree to any united India Constitution, federal or otherwise, with one Centre, in which, again, they will be in a hopeless minority, and will be at the mercy of the perennial Hindu majority domination."³⁴ Soon thereafter he fired salvos into the continuing debate over interim arrangements borne of the war. In stark contrast to Wavell's notions of transitional administrations, Jinnah sought only a clean break. "There is no reason or ground for talking about interim arrangement, now that the war is over," he told the India Office in February 1946. Jinnah held that the British government had not only recognized the inevitability of the League's refusing consent to "any arrangement which postulates an all-India government whether interim or permanent," but that its statements had even shown a willingness to respect that position.³⁵ His defiance was now unmistakably evident in both his public and private statements, posing a challenge even for officials fully aware of the domestic political rationale behind them in rallying Indian Muslims behind the League. Jinnah may have been pandering to his base, but that hardly made it easy to contend with the League's demands, especially given the growth in its relative strength in the wake of the Cripps mission's failure and the hints of converging Muslim aims, as suggested by the intercepted Azad letter. Still, there were those in the India Office who believed that "HMG [His Majesty's government] may in the end be obliged to impose a solution on India." Despite his maximalist demands, Jinnah had to realize "that HMG could not possibly accept his entire plan and that he must compromise."[36]

THE FINAL ROAD TO PARTITION

As the war effort exhausted Britain, so the drive for Indian self-government accelerated. Wavell had addressed both houses of the Indian Legislature with his first major speech about the plans for postwar India in February 1944, explaining that the British government hoped for a timely withdrawal and that the Cripps offer was not the only route to a new constitution. But a constitution was still a prerequisite for Indian self-government, and it was incumbent on Congress Party and Muslim League leaders to agree on how to progress. Although maintaining that "you cannot alter geography . . . India is a natural unit," Wavell told India's lawmakers that they themselves would have to fashion a structure in which India's various communal groups could coexist.[37] He folded his basic ideas for a settlement into the Wavell Plan, a proposal for eventual Indian self-government. In the months after its presentation, Wavell hosted India's principal political leaders—Hindu, Muslim, and Sikh—to discuss its terms at a conference opening on 25 June in the secluded Viceregal Lodge overlooking a valley in Simla, India's summer capital. But after two days the conference deadlocked on the critical issue of who would be entitled to nominate Muslim ministers in the new proposed Indian government's Cabinet. When Nehru demanded that the Congress Party, given its Muslim representation, should be allowed to nominate at least one minister, Jinnah adamantly refused. At a press conference Jinnah reasoned that "we cannot accept the Congress party's right to choose the Moslem ministers either on principle or on the facts before us," given that India's Untouchables and Sikhs, who would likely vote with the Hindus in a single bloc on most issues, would render the Muslims a permanent minority.[38]

The choice Wavell confronted was thus one of failing to form a government that included both Muslim League and Congress Party representation or going ahead with the formation of a government in which the vast majority of India's Muslims would lack representation. The reverberations of the failed negotiations were considerable; even in predominantly Muslim NWFP, Governor George Cunningham reported, the disappointment of Simla "has made people think and talk more about the Pakistan issue," reinforcing his sense that "not many people here believe in Pakistan in the sense of dismemberment from the rest of India."[39]

This, then, was the deadlock that confronted British officials as they looked to Indian independence: pitting the Congress Party against the Muslim League, not unlike the rift between the Jewish Agency and the Arab Higher Committee. As was the case with the Anglo-American Committee in Palestine, the British government mounted a final effort to try to bridge the gap, through the efforts of the 1946 Cabinet mission, a last-ditch diplomatic appeal by the Labour government to save Indian unity.

In assessing the defense requirements of postindependence India, the Cabinet mission saw the defense of any partitioned successor states of "Pakistan" and "Hindustan" as inextricably linked. Its deliberations unearthed the core considerations for British strategy on Kashmir and toward the wider issues surrounding British India's partition: the nether reaches of what would constitute Western Pakistan, including Baluchistan, Sind, NWFP, and Punjab west of the Sutlej River, were essential for the defense of the subcontinent, the mission concluded. But if any separate defense force for a newly created Pakistan could not adequately address the requirements there, it would be "suicidal" for a Hindustan government to refuse assistance to its beleaguered neighbor's western flanks. Here was the fundamental challenge for Foreign and India Office officials seeking to broker an accord between the Congress Party and the Muslim League: How could a viable Pakistan be constructed so as not to endanger the defense of both newly independent states from foreign invasion from the north and west?[40]

Moreover the situation was inseparable from developments at the opposite tip of the arc of crisis spanning Southwest Asia. The impending publication of the Anglo-American Committee of Inquiry's report drastically complicated the situation. The Cabinet mission remained cognizant of the reality that any proposed solution that did not adequately address Muslim demands could ignite unrest not only in India but northward and westward through the Islamic belt that stretched toward the Middle East. The resulting agitation could even threaten Bevin's postwar Middle East security plans. Wavell himself admitted that the Anglo-American Committee's recommendation to admit additional Jewish immigrations to Palestine might lead to a hardening of Jinnah's demands. Indeed a former member of Labour's International Sub-Committee on Imperial Questions had even written Attlee begging His Majesty's government to refrain from adopting the

Anglo-American Committee's suggestion to admit an additional 100,000 Jewish émigrés on the grounds of its potential effects on India's Muslims, an effect that, in his view, might give rise to Islamic unrest that would "endanger the life-line of the British Empire."[41]

Constrained by these realities of geopolitics and demographics, the Cabinet mission first proposed a postindependence India whose central government would manage defense and foreign affairs and that balanced the Muslim-majority provinces with offsetting Hindu-majority provinces in the national legislature. Lord Pethick-Lawrence's broadcast announcing the plan on 16 May specifically cited the issue of the common defense of India as a rationale for shunning the Muslim League's demand for a separate Pakistan: "The complete separation of Pakistan from the rest of India would in our view gravely endanger the defence of the whole country by splitting the army into two and by preventing that defence in depth which is essential in modern war."[42] Jinnah rejected the proposal on 22 May because of its failure to recognize the League's "demand for the establishment of a complete sovereign state of Pakistan, which we still hold is the only solution to the constitutional problem of India and which alone can secure stable governments and lead to the happiness and welfare, not only of the two major communities, but of all the peoples of the sub-continent."[43] But the Congress Party also lodged reservations to the scheme, declaring that its Working Committee examining the proposals needed a fuller picture of the Cabinet mission recommendations with regard to such issues as the putative process for election of representatives to the Constituent Assembly and the degree of provincial autonomy that India would retain against vague references to provincial groups to determine if "Group Constitutions" would be formed.[44]

To break the deadlock, the mission proposed a second plan on 16 June, which entailed the division of India into a Hindustan and Pakistan that comprised Punjab, Sind, NWFP, Baluchistan, and portions of Eastern Bengal, with opportunities for the princely states to accede to either principal successor state. The Muslim League accepted the latter plan, but the Congress Party rejected it, just as it had the former incarnation, fearing the plan would entail the balkanization of India. When League and Congress leaders failed to participate effectively in the viceroy's Executive Council, to which the League had been grudgingly admitted despite significant Congress Party objections, the path to partition became irreversible. Ultimately the Cabinet mission failed because of the gap between the bargaining positions of the

Congress Party and the League. While the former insisted on the emergence of a single India with a single constitution before dealing with communal issues, Jinnah had by then firmly dug in his heels on a separatist solution as a prerequisite for crossing the threshold of independence.[45]

In the aftermath of the Cabinet mission, a sense of inevitability drove Wavell to push for a fixed date for Britain's departure. He likely sensed the need to move ahead swiftly and agree to a deadline for withdrawal as the only solution in the face of the Muslim League's refusal to enter the Constituent Assembly. After consultations with the Cabinet at a London conference in December 1946, it became apparent that the Cabinet did not share Wavell's commitment to a fixed date for withdrawal, which Attlee dubbed a "defeatist" attitude. The disagreement led the prime minister to confide to Bevin that he was contemplating Wavell's replacement by early January 1947.[46] Yet perhaps not surprisingly, Wavell's successor, Lord Mountbatten, assumed a similar stance almost immediately upon assuming the post of viceroy. He confided to Attlee even before the formal announcement of his appointment as Wavell's successor, "It makes all the difference to me to know that you propose to make a statement in the House, terminating the British 'Raj' on a definite and specified date; or earlier than this date."[47]

That Mountbatten shared Wavell's frustrations even before succeeding him was a testament to the intractability of the situation Britain confronted. As the viceroyalty changed hands, a defeated Wavell confessed to King George that despite British efforts to broker a compromise on the interpretation of the terms of the Cabinet mission provisions, the Muslim League dithered during December and January before its Working Committee announced that it would maintain its policy of non-cooperation with the Constituent Assembly. But the eventual government decision to announce an end to the British Empire in India materialized at last—a pyrrhic victory of sorts for the departing viceroy. Wavell reported, "The Cabinet at home has now taken a definite decision to declare that our control of India will be ended by middle of 1948; and I hope that they have given my successor, whose name I was delighted to hear, either a definite plan for the withdrawal or a free hand."[48]

In the ensuing months Mountbatten and Reforms Commissioner V. P. Menon hastily drew up plans for the transfer of power two provisional governments, each of which was responsible to two constituent assemblies of representatives of the new Hindu- and Muslim-majority states.[49] Without disrupting the continued operation of the existing Constituent Assembly, Mountbatten proposed that the wishes of the people in provinces where a majority of the apportioned representatives were not participating in the assembly should be gauged as to whether they wanted a constitution framed in the existing Constituent Assembly or in a "new and separate" body that included their representatives. "When this has been done, it will be possible to determine the authority to whom power should be transferred," he maintained. This draft plan became the basis for the eventual solution that divided India, crushed Nehru's dream of unity, and awarded Jinnah his separate Pakistan at last.[50]

Abdullah and Jinnah had come to represent distinct conceptions of Muslim identity, with characteristic implications for the political future of their followers in the Congress Party and the League. But the power struggle between the two parties foreclosed any hope of reconciliation before the moment of truth. Abdullah's reformist struggles and Jinnah's crusade for the creation of Pakistan thus constituted forces at the provincial and national levels that contextualized British policy in the Kashmir dispute. That policy, it turned out, would be driven predominantly by British perceptions of the geopolitics of the subcontinent and the attendant defense requirements that the India Office—and the East India Company— had grappled with for decades.

POSTWAR BRITISH STRATEGY ON THE SUBCONTINENT

Even after a series of diplomatic agreements leading up to the 1907 Anglo-Russian Convention curtailed the scope of the "Great Game" played by Russia and Britain for control of Central Asia, the British Empire continued to treat the entire region of northern India, including what became the provinces of Punjab, NWFP, and Jammu and Kashmir, as a belt of territory that afforded India the strategic depth so essential for the subcontinent's defense. The seminal importance of this northern tier along which Jammu and Kashmir lay would prove the single most important consideration affecting British policy on Kashmir throughout the eventful years leading up to partition and beyond.[51]

British strategic thinkers realized that the wider region surrounding Jammu and Kashmir could not be allowed to succumb to the perils of an inadequate defensive presence that invited Afghan tribal invasion or Russian territorial encroachments, given that it bordered Afghanistan to the northwest, the Soviet Union to the north, and China to the northeast. But a separate defense problem arose in the aftermath of partition, which left behind an impoverished Pakistan unable to defend its borders, whose gaze was fixated eastward, preoccupied from birth with the perception of an existential military threat emanating from New Delhi. Compounding this additional concern was Pakistan's inability to support the military infrastructure it had inherited from a united India with its own resources or economic dynamism. About one-third of the Indian army had joined Pakistan's in the massive military transition overseen by Field Marshal Claude Auchinleck, along with two-fifths of its navy and a fifth of the air force. Thus the combination of a panoply of security concerns and a woefully limited defense establishment and defense expenditures meant that a pervasive insecurity crippled the new state of Pakistan from the very outset.[52]

Officials recognized that Kashmir's strategic value emanated from its centrality to *both* of the primary security concerns on the subcontinent: defending it from land invasions from the north, and the internal military imbalance within it that tipped heavily in India's favor. They also grasped the complications for postcolonial British policy that this inherent power asymmetry between the two new dominions posed. At the moment of partition the Commonwealth Relations Office wondered whether a policy of impartiality by Britain might not cripple Pakistan by virtue of the fact that India did not require the military assistance that Pakistan would desperately seek in the case of an escalating confrontation over Kashmir.[53]

The Chiefs of Staff shared this view, laying out the military rationale for aid to Pakistan in a March 1947 report on India's defense. In their view Pakistan was the key to the subcontinent's western defenses and had to receive British military assistance to meet that responsibility, "since the provision of equipment and munitions come mainly from Hindu India."[54] Adhering to these basic geopolitical assumptions, many British officials shared the outlook that Jammu and Kashmir's majority-Muslim population constituted the eastern tip of the Southwest Asian hinterlands of Islam that stretched through Central Asia, Persia, and Anatolia toward the Arabian Peninsula, Iraq, and the Levant. But as with the Arab-Jewish dispute in Palestine, cleavages within the bureaucracy soon became evident. On one side stood a group of senior India hands sympathetic to Nehru, who believed that control of Kashmir was best left to India. Foremost among this group was Lord Mountbatten himself, who remained in the office of governor-general of India, though it was recast after independence as the senior British civilian representative in the country. A certain degree of sympathy for Kashmir on Mountbatten's part was perhaps inevitable. It came by extension from his deep friendship with Nehru and the Indian leader's personal ties to and affinity for the state of Jammu and Kashmir, the plight of whose oppressed Muslims affected him profoundly.[55]

Shortly after assuming his new position, Mountbatten shared with the Cabinet's India and Burma Committee the concerns pertaining to the creation of a "Pakistan" that Glancy had flagged from his posting in the Punjab: both Indians and Europeans with whom Glancy had discussed the issue were convinced violence would explode if and when non-Muslims, especially Sikhs, confronted the prospect of citizenship in an Islamic successor state to British India. These minority populations could hardly acquiesce to rule by a "Mohammedan Raj," he had assured Mountbatten.[56]

While Glancy had only assumed the putative Muslim character of any such government, an assumption that was open to question given the varied flavors of Muslim nationalism, ranging from Abdullah's secularism to the Kashmir Muslim Conference's religious conservatism, Mountbatten was eager to share his subordinate's observations with the Committee and highlight the potential dangers that a partition of individual Hindu- and Muslim-majority provinces might portend. A corollary of this assumption was that control of these potentially restive Muslim areas with minority populations was better left with the government in New Delhi, where the Congress Party stood for all Indians, be they Hindu, Muslim, Sikh, or other. Mountbatten's sympathies for India and minority unrest in Muslim areas were shared by other officials, who ended up sympathizing with Indian claims to Kashmir. His basic assumptions were more or less common to his private secretary, General Hastings Ismay, along with Sir Terence Shone, the high commissioner in New Delhi, and Stafford Cripps.

But on the other side of the complex and bitter dispute stood a different group for whom strategic considerations about the defense of the subcontinent were also paramount, but who concluded that Pakistan's role was central to the discharge of those security responsibilities. These officials, moreover, believed that the necessary requirements could best be met through British agreements with a Muslim state that included the relevant northern and western provinces. Critically for the future of Kashmir policy, Attlee and Bevin, despite their differences over the prolongation of the British presence in the Middle East, both found themselves squarely in this camp. They were joined by Laurence Grafftey-Smith, Olaf Caroe in NWFP, and other midlevel officials involved with India's administration, many of whom had served in Near East posts and developed an acute sense of the challenges that Central Asian Islam posed for British policy at both ends of the plateaus and mountainous highlands that stretched from the Indus to the Bosporus.[57]

Indeed it seems that both sets of British officials, whether adherents of a strong Pakistan or not, saw the linkage between the defense of Pakistan and territories that lay eastward to be critical. But it was the issue of how integrated Pakistan was to that which lay to the *west* of the subcontinent, along the arc of crisis, that divided British strategists. Those officials favoring a strategic relationship between Britain and the new state of Pakistan clearly ascribed far greater importance to the linkage between Pakistan and the rest of the Arab Muslim world than did their counterparts (such as Mountbatten) who emphasized the centrality of Anglo-Indian ties. Importantly from the standpoint of the analysis here, both Jinnah and Nehru shared the assumptions about the centrality of any viable Pakistan's defense for the security of the Middle East, transcending specific political objectives as an underlying geographical reality. Jinnah saw Pakistan and the boundary region of NWFP as a critical bulwark against Afghan, and possibly even Soviet, invasion, as he confided to Hastings Ismay: "It was amazing that the Government of India did not realize that the North West Frontier was their frontier just as much as it was Pakistan's. If the Afghan Army and Air Force, backed up by the tribes, were to smash through the Pakistan Forces, India would be in the gravest peril." Jinnah struck Ismay as oblivious to the fact that American and British assistance would doubtless reinforce Indian defenses in such an eventuality, but Jinnah's position is more likely attributable to the seasoned barrister's preoccupation with making as strong a case as possible for Pakistan to be entrusted with responsibility for the defense of the border regions—which would warrant significant military assistance—rather than a genuine skepticism that international assistance of some sort would rally to the aid of the subcontinent.[58]

Curiously, Nehru too saw the relevance of Pakistan for security requirements farther north and west. During deliberations on mutual defense schemes that might be implemented as part of a partition arrangement, he noted, "The question of Pakistan or separation cannot be considered apart from the question of defence and allied subjects. At any time this could not be ignored. In today's context with trouble brewing in the Middle East, this becomes a paramount consideration."[59]

The strategic rationale that both leaders subscribed to echoed the broader outlines of how much of the British Official Mind conceived of the region, a conception that linked Kashmir to the arcing swath of Muslim lands between India's Northern Frontier and the Mediterranean. No clearer picture of that mental map of this linkage existed than the August 1946 report of the Chiefs of Staff Committee prepared for the prime minister, titled "Strategic Importance of India," akin to the corresponding documents that assessed British defense requirements in the Middle East that were produced during the same years. In explicating that importance, Ismay cited three principal sources: India's "great man-power resources from which we have, in the past, maintained a reservoir of trained personnel for the Armed Forces to assist us in meeting our Defence commitments in the Commonwealth"; airfields that constituted "the nearest bases for attack on the industrial areas of the Urals and Western Siberia, and are essential for the maintenance of our communications to the Far East"; and base access in India "important to our command of the Indian Ocean, in particular to the maintenance of our communications to South East Asia and the Persian Gulf." One of the corollaries of Ismay's analysis was that "the defence of India, both by land, sea and air, should be assured."[60] And the centrality of the state of Jammu and Kashmir along land and air routes into northern India from Central Asia thus meant that its future disposition impinged heavily on British defense requirements for the subcontinent.

From the standpoint of British strategic planning, the political-military implications of partition placed huge strains on the ability of the two new dominions to meet British needs as outlined in Ismay's assessment. As Auchinleck oversaw the division of the Indian armed forces between the two successor states, the Chiefs of Staff noted that "the withdrawal of British troops will seriously weaken the security of the Indian Continent and disorganise the navies and air forces of both Dominions." In expressing their concerns, they pointed specifically to the issue of the Northern Tier: "As the division of the Indian Army is now in progress, the possibility of protecting India from outside aggression has been seriously jeopardised for the time being to the dangerous point where surrounding nations may be encouraged to impose on her security. The weakness is exemplified by the recent Afghan demand for Indian territory adjoining the North West Frontier." Since neither the United Nations nor the Commonwealth had provided robust mechanisms for defense coordination and collective security, the Chiefs of Staff reasoned, Britain had instead "to set up some looser system of coordination" consisting of military-to-military liaison between Britain and the military staffs of each dominion, despite the difficulties of establishing such a mode of operation.[61] India and Pakistan may not have the slightest desire to play nice, the Chiefs surmised, but a degree of defense cooperation was essential if postindependence arrangements were to preserve the integrity of the Northern Tier's defenses.

Such geostrategic logic, and the paramountcy it ascribed to land power and potential land routes for invading armies, bound the question of Kashmir inescapably with the defense of the subcontinent and British military strategy toward the two new dominions in at least two ways. First, Kashmir was central for the defense of northern India from Afghan or Soviet incursions, as Ismay's analysis showed incontrovertibly. Second, an interdominion conflict over its status threatened the system of Commonwealth defense that the Chiefs of Staff envisioned by the time of partition, one reliant on the willing cooperation of the dominions of India and Pakistan. That danger, and the need to bring *both* Pakistan and India along together with regard to the final approach that was adopted, was a principal concern for Mountbatten in the spring before partition was effected.[62] Upon his return to India, Ismay briefed India and Pakistan's Joint Defence Council on his discussions with the Chiefs of Staff, conveying their sense of the subcontinent's "dominating geographical position from the point of defence." Ismay warned that "India's security affects all the countries in S.E. Asia, and all the countries which are dependent on sea communications through the Indian Ocean." As a result, time was of the essence in fashioning arrangements to safeguard subcontinental defenses as the new dominions achieved independence.[63]

As summer turned to fall and the transfer of power was effected, that strategy of subcontinental defense now rested on the conclusion of British defense agreements with both dominions. But the seminal importance of Pakistan because of the co-location of its western border along the Northern Tier led the British Chiefs of Staff to consider whether a defense agreement with India was even necessary. While Indo-Pakistani defense cooperation may have had a bearing on the ability of both dominions to work together to defend the subcontinent, the press of events led British military strategists to wonder whether a defense agreement with Pakistan alone might meet "the majority of our strategic requirements."[64] The Commonwealth Relations Office likewise echoed this rationale when it considered the prospect of the Kashmir dispute consuming Pakistan in tribal conflict, and the potential consequences in the Arab world.[65]

THE BRITISH RESPONSE TO THE KASHMIR CRISIS

Fueled by speculation about the maharaja's intentions and intercommunal incitement through sensationalistic accounts of atrocity, a wave of violence consumed Jammu and Kashmir even before its legally contestable accession to India. The fall of 1947 saw British officials scramble to formulate a strategy to halt the course of events on the ground as the postpartition subcontinent descended into violence that, importantly, extended well beyond the politics and territorial confines of Kashmir. As bands of irregular tribal groups and other Muslim fighters streamed into the princely state, the prospect of Indian reprisal against Pakistan raised the problem of the latter's inadequate defenses. But one of the most fundamental strategic questions for British policy was how to address that inadequacy satisfactorily. Any reinforcement of Pakistani defenses meant breaking with existing policy, which "has been one of strict impartiality towards each of the new Dominions," the Commonwealth Relations Office warned. It also would mean the provision of financial and military support to Pakistan despite the fact that the British government could "not accept an unlimited commitment to Pakistan."[66] The outbreak of violence thus posed an immediate question whose answer was hardly obvious: Did the geographic centrality of the newly delineated borders of Pakistan entitle that dominion to a sort of privileged status in terms of British policy, even at the expense of Anglo-Indian diplomatic amity? And if so, did it warrant British reinforcement of Pakistani defenses even if Pakistan was complicit in the invasion of militants into Kashmir? At the purely strategic level, the answer hinged on the Labour government's policy of linking Pakistan with both the defense of India and the security of the Middle East. But the reality of partition meant that a host of political considerations overlay the core geopolitical logic underpinning British policy.[67]

The commonalities between the views of Jinnah and Nehru on the strategic importance of Kashmir penetrated deep below the level of general musings about the subcontinent's security. In the throes of conflict, while lodging his justification of intervention on behalf of the beleaguered maharaja, Nehru specifically cited the strategic importance of Kashmir's northern borders with Afghanistan, China, and the Soviet Union as a reality that compelled him to act. Given that India shared a border along the southern edge of Kashmir, the net implications of these geographic realities were unavoidable. "Helping Kashmir, therefore is an obligation of national interest to India," he flatly told Attlee. However credible the claim, Nehru assured his British counterpart that India's decision to come to the aid of the princely state was "not designed in any way to influence the state to accede to India."[68]

Moreover Indian representatives highlighted the importance of aiding in the defense of Kashmir to prevent its subversion by communism. "There was a very real danger of Russian infiltration through Gilgit," Secretary of the Ministry of the States V. P. Menon asserted to Alexander Symon, the high commissioner in Karachi. This claim was perhaps as dubious as Jinnah's nonrecognition of the prospect of international assistance to defend the subcontinent from invasion. Menon cited questionable evidence in support of his claim, alleging only that an unusual volume of "foreign 'traders'" carrying gold through the region were "portents" of this contingency arising.[69] Thus Indian officials were sufficiently aware of British strategic calculations to attempt to affect them in the early weeks of the conflict through targeted appeals trained on perceived sensitivities and concerns. Despite general skepticism of assertions like Menon's, some British diplomatic reporting from NWFP in late October validated those concerns, citing the problems that could arise from calls for a "Pathanistan" that might cut into Pakistani territory. But that did not necessarily mean that the optimal course was to give a free hand to Indian intervention, as the likes of Mountbatten and Ismay might have if they had their way. British officials on the ground warned that direct Indian outreach to the tribal areas could even *exacerbate* the problem by disrupting intra-Muslim ties between the tribes and Pakistani government authorities that served to paper over Pakistan's defensive weaknesses and acute overstretch through precarious political compromises that held a tenuous defensive equilibrium north and west of Punjab. In Grafftey-Smith's view, "[The] Indian government's acceptation of accession of Kashmir [was] the heaviest blow yet sustained by Pakistan in her struggle for existence. Strategically, Pakistan's frontiers have been greatly extended as a hostile India gains access to NWFP. This will lead to a redefinition of the Afghan policy for worse.

Second, Russian interests will be aroused in Gilgit and NWFP which creates a new international situation which HMG and the U.S. government can not overlook."[70] Nehru's appeal in defense of India's actions resonated with the pro-Indian cohort in Whitehall, but the Cabinet Commonwealth Affairs Committee observed in November 1947, as the fighting spread in Kashmir, that both sides were at fault to some extent: while "there can be no doubt that Pakistan has connived at the incursion into Kashmir—casual raiders do not travel in lorries with 3.7 artillery," the Committee also admitted that "at the same time Nehru (who is after all a Kashmir Brahmin) has been far too ready to rush in with troops; and his sudden indisposition just before the vital meeting at Lahore with Earl Mountbatten and Mr. Jinnah is suspicious." Irrespective of their individual views, the central importance of this analysis consists in the fact that senior Cabinet officials put the strategic considerations ahead of all others in their response to the Kashmir dispute. Irrespective of the assignment of blame, it was the defense challenges confronting Pakistan that ultimately proved vital for Britain. "The danger is that Pakistan will be unable to control the Pathan tribes of the North and North-West; Afghanistan will be drawn in, North India and by degrees the whole continent will 'slide into chaos.' Russia is waiting." That much was clear no matter who was at fault. But where the Committee's division of blame *was* implicated was in formulating its refusal to come to Jinnah's aid in response to a call for Commonwealth assistance for Pakistan. It was unclear what, if any, effect an answer to Jinnah would have, and there were concerns that it might even "provoke the appeal to the United [N]ations which he has been threatening if the Commonwealth let him down."[71]

The refusal of the Commonwealth to rally to Pakistan's side dealt Pakistani leaders a crushing blow and badly strained their ties with the Commonwealth. But one of the specific sources of the acrimony was rooted in assertions by some in Pakistan that racism was somehow a motivation behind the crown's nonresponse, and that perhaps similar conflict between two dominions populated by white subjects might have engaged the Commonwealth more closely.[72] Whatever the reason, Commonwealth inaction left few options but last-ditch efforts to promote negotiations between India and Pakistan before the issue was raised before the international community.

FOUR

Keystone of the Strategic Arch

When violence gripped Kashmir in the winter of 1947, the first task at hand for the Foreign Office was to determine precisely the situation on the ground. Shortly after the disturbances began to spread, the deputy high commissioner in Lahore traveled to the city of Abbottabad, in the Orash Valley, surrounded by the Sarban hills, which bestrode areas that saw some of the most intense unrest. He painted a picture of a complex insurgency comprising three largely distinct groups of approximately two thousand tribesmen in total. They spanned a wide range of clans, including Pashtun Mehsuds, Waziris, and smaller bands of fighters from Swat and Dir, who came and went on foot. Hardly any of them were loyal to Abdullah, whose influence appeared largely to be limited to the Vale of Kashmir.[1] Though provincial officials had regarded the influx of tribesmen as a nuisance at first, it appeared that they had subsequently found little recourse than to lend assistance and join them in their resistance to the accession. The violence was swelling to such acute levels that it led British officials to the view that "India faces murder on a scale that may put Buchenwald in the shade" and that no less than "the whole of British policy in the East [was] at stake."[2] But it was more than just Eastern policy at stake: British *prestige* in departing the subcontinent by means of a peaceful, managed transition was also on the line. The rationale behind this view, reflective of the dominant line of thinking among the concerned officials, of course warranted urgent conflict-resolution efforts—efforts that somehow would also have to be reconciled with the geographically critical region's strategic implications. Though Mountbatten had predicated Kashmir's accession to India on the organization of a plebiscite, Jinnah had resisted going ahead with the necessary arrangements, charging that Kashmiris would refuse to vote in support of joining Pakistan in the face of an Indian military presence on the ground. British authorities now rushed to bring the parties together to negotiate a cease-fire, with Auchinleck persuading Jinnah to invite Mountbatten and Nehru to Lahore to discuss the situation (despite Nehru's military response before the talks). Though Nehru assented to the visit, and despite his 3 November offer of a plebiscite, the Indian Cabinet became enraged at the situation. The immediate British effort to broker bilateral negotiations quickly failed.[3]

Throughout the end of December, Mountbatten continued futilely to press Nehru to seek a cessation of hostilities as soon as possible, citing the disastrous consequences of a full-scale conflict whose containment would be impossible. The sincere appeals reflected an awareness of and preoccupation with regional dynamics beyond Indian-Pakistani relations, including the potential spillover of the conflict north and west into tribal areas that could ignite Russian or Chinese interest. "The idea that a war between India and Pakistan could be confined to the subcontinent or finished off quickly in favour of India without further complication is to my mind a fatal illusion."[4] But a letter to Nehru from Pakistani prime minister Liaquat Ali Khan five days after Mountbatten's foreclosed any prospect of bilateral diplomacy. Liaquat refused to acknowledge Kashmir's accession and refuted his Indian counterpart's charges that Pakistan was aiding tribal fighters who had streamed into Kashmir with transport and other material assistance. This rebuttal set the stage for India's presentation of the Kashmir issue, like the Palestine dispute that preceded it, before the United Nations Security Council. Still, optimism soared at the Commonwealth Relations Office, which remained confident that a quick end to the fighting could be arranged and harbored a cautious hope that Russian interference or support for either party against the other might be avoided.[5]

In raising the issue of Kashmir before the Security Council, India alleged Pakistani aggression in violation of Articles 34 and 35 of the UN Charter.[6] Foreign and Commonwealth Relations Office officials met almost immediately to consider courses of action that the United Nations could take to end the violence. Both agencies noted that the employment of international armed forces had been considered with regard to prior events in Palestine and that the option should be revisited. Any such international forces would encounter a number of difficulties in Kashmir, the meeting participants concluded. First, there was the question of the acquiescence of India and Pakistan. (There was hardly any discussion of enforcement action against the will of both combatants; officials in London felt that the need to obtain the consent of both governments was a prerequisite to international action of any sort.) Then there was the separate matter of the irregular forces in Kashmir, tribesmen who officials surmised could be controlled only through the payment of bribes and the direction of the mullahs to whom they owed allegiance. An additional complication was the danger that Russian participation in any such international force could not be precluded easily. Finally, there was the practical issue of transporting the troops into the region. Recruited Gurkha troops were unavailable for deployment as part of a U.K. contingent as they had already been earmarked for service in the Far East. This presented a problem for the expedient dispatch of a force of suitable composition that could respond to any forthcoming UN operation forged in the Security Council.[7]

While various uncertainties swirled around the idea of an international force, one thing was certain from the standpoint of the Foreign Office, which ultimately charted the British course in Kashmir: events in Palestine and Kashmir were linked. The former mandate's descent into civil strife and ethnic cleansing meant that the Kashmir proceedings in the Council could not be allowed to lead the United Kingdom into a position, real or apparent, in which it sided against Pakistan. On this point Bevin himself was "most anxious that the Prime Minister should be warned as from him about the obvious dangers of allowing ourselves to be manoeuvered by Nehru into siding against, or appearing to side against, Pakistan. With the Palestine position so critical we simply could not afford to put Pakistan against us and so have the whole of Islam against us."[8]

Here lay the key to British strategy in the resolution of the Kashmir dispute at the United Nations: while that strategy entailed a robust conflict-resolution effort calling on both sides to refrain from actions that could exacerbate the situation on the ground, the overarching concern driving Foreign Office thinking was the need to preserve the harmony of the belt of territory between Palestine and Kashmir so as not to alienate "the whole of Islam" that extended across the arc of crisis and beyond into the wider Muslim world. Attlee himself weighed in on the matter in direct instructions to Permanent Undersecretary Sir Alec Cadogan, who had been dispatched to the United Nations, in a message that revealed the prime minister's preoccupation with the consequences in the Near East of Kashmir policy at the Council. "Any action taken by [the] Security Council should not prejudice our strategic requirements," he admonished his subordinates in New York.[9]

The British response at the United Nations congealed over the following two weeks, and it would consist of a synergy of three basic courses of action. The Foreign Office considered the first order of business to "call on both parties to avoid action which might make the dispute more difficult pending its consideration by the Council." A second step entailed the dispatch of a small commission to India and Pakistan to negotiate arrangements for a fair plebiscite for the state of Jammu and Kashmir. A third step entailed exploring the "dispatch to Kashmir of [a] neutral force of say brigade strength." In light of the difficulties that were noted in the 31 December meeting, the Foreign Office wondered whether the force could be provided by a neutral country such as Belgium on behalf of the United Nations.[10] This idea was developed further at a second meeting between Foreign and Commonwealth Relations Office personnel, on 3 January. Perhaps the officer in charge of an international brigade could also assume command of Indian and Pakistani forces in the region, officials surmised. Still, "there was no indication that either India or Pakistan would be likely to accept any of these proposals," nor was there a "realistic suggestion of any kind as to where the international brigade would come from."[11]

Cadogan was pessimistic about the idea of a neutral force as the Foreign Office conceived of it. But he deferred to the judgment of the chiefs of staff as to the feasibility of such a force.[12] The historical record is unclear as to the official British military assessment of the prospects for such a force. But the option appears to have been considered by General Sir Geoffrey Scoones, the principal officer at the Commonwealth Relations Office, and subsequently dismissed because of a number of considerations. One of the problems was the availability of sufficient numbers of military officers, much less experts familiar with the particular complexities of the Kashmir situation and its historical background. A way around this problem was of course the dispatch of British troops—but such a deployment could open the door to Russian participation and the transformation of the force into a new vehicle for geopolitical confrontation in Kashmir. And the prospect of forces from a neutral power adequately policing the mountainous regions in and around Gilgit seemed highly unrealistic.[13]

The idea of an international force to police Jammu and Kashmir also seems to have been considered briefly, then rejected. By the time the Foreign Office finally sent instructions on a specific course of action the following week, it had discounted the notion of the neutral force that had been discussed since the start of the conflict. "The more we think about [the] proposal for [a] neutral military force . . . the less we like it," the Foreign Office now concluded.[14] Three days later the assessment arrived from the Chiefs of Staff. The summary that the Foreign Office relayed to New York illustrated the practical difficulties at hand. It would be impossible to support a neutral force in Kashmir for three months, the chiefs concluded, which foreclosed the option of a quick response. Other concerns echoed Terence Shone's observations from New Delhi about the difficulty of finding subject matter experts and the prospect of American or Russian involvement in the force.[15] Attlee eventually weighed in himself, judging that the demands associated with deploying such a force were too onerous.[16]

As British strategy at the Council took shape and the idea of mounting an international force faded, Secretary of State for Commonwealth Relations Philip Noel-Baker and Hastings Ismay traveled to New York and Washington for meetings with Indian and Pakistani UN delegations and the State Department. In his sessions with Indian representatives, Noel-Baker expressed concerns about the ability of the Pakistani government to control the Afghan tribesmen and other "insurgents" in Kashmir. Given the inadequacies of the Pakistani military to control the irregular elements that had joined the fighting, a "joint system of defence was required against the tribesmen." Ismay added that both civilian and military forces would have to be introduced to handle the situation. Thus even one of the military officials most sympathetic to India's plight came to focus squarely on the security of the western border regions through which the subcontinent was most vulnerable to invasion.[17] Meetings with the Pakistani delegation to the United Nations revealed the same strategic outlook. Ismay expressed skepticism about the delegation's proposal that Pakistani military forces pacify the Muslim-majority areas of Kashmir.[18] Again the security of the region and its adjoining areas from an invasion from the west trumped other British considerations. What emerges from the records of both encounters is not a clear dependence of the British recommendations on positions in support of either Pakistani or Indian contentions; the responses of Ismay and Noel-Baker, whose basic sympathies for the Indian case are widely recognized, suggest that they were motivated instead by a fundamental lack of faith in Pakistan's ability to independently secure a region of strategic importance.

AMERICA AND KASHMIR AT THE UNITED NATIONS

Anglo-American diplomatic cooperation remained close from the very outset of multilateral negotiations on Kashmir at the Security Council. In relaying instructions to Warren Austin, the American permanent representative at the United Nations, the State Department's Division of United Nations Affairs expressed the official Department view that the only solution that all of the affected parties to the Kashmir dispute would find favorable would likely be based on a plebiscite, even one that might involve the partition of the former princely state into constituent subentities. But the Department instructed Austin to defer to British interests during the negotiations, which seemed in any case to conform with those of the United States.[19] The history of Great Britain's imperial involvement in South Asia naturally led the Truman administration to place great weight on consultations with the British government in formulating South Asia policy.[20] And despite their preoccupation with a Kashmir settlement amenable to Pakistan-Afghan relations, and therefore one that preserved harmony across the Islamic lands stretching north and west toward Palestine, many within the British government saw the Kashmir dispute through the cold war prism that refracted a specific image of the dispute back to Foggy Bottom. Noel-Baker's 27 December telegram to Shone clearly betrayed a concern, however mild, with the danger of Russian involvement in the dispute. But if Russian interference was a new cold war concern for the United States, it was an old Great Game era worry for Great Britain. The Dominions Office seemed to concur with the view that the stakes of a diplomatic settlement in Kashmir were elevated by the prospect of regional instability that might attract unwanted Soviet intervention.[21]

But despite the congruence of American and British concerns in the dispute, London and Washington seemed to rely on different strategic maps of the region in their framing of the problem. Britain's "main objective, if we are to prevent the Russians from causing mischief on the frontier, is to heal the breach between Pakistan and India, and to achieve good relations between Pakistan and Afghanistan," as Permanent Undersecretary for Foreign Affairs Sir Orme Sargent put it.[22] In other words, Britain's first orders of business were solving the twin problems of Indo-Pakistani defense coordination and the pacification of the Northern Tier through which the land routes into India wound. These policy goals reflected the thinking of Attlee, Bevin, and many senior Pakistan hands in the Dominions Office by the late 1940s and were fully consistent with the Kashmir policy that the United Kingdom ultimately pursued at the United Nations. It was a view that contrasted with the State Department's more global concerns that the growing cold war divide would expand into the Kashmir crisis.

Historians have long recognized the globalizing effect of the cold war rivalry on U.S. foreign policy in the early postwar years under the Truman administration. Indeed cold war historiography has delved into the contested origins of that globalization of American national security interests during the years between the end of the Second World War, through the creation of NATO, and up to the U.S. involvement in the Korean War. Its effects were palpably evident on the South Asian subcontinent, posing major consequences and constraints for the U.S. role in resolving the Kashmir dispute.[23] From the standpoint of the Foreign Office, "the direct intervention of the United States in any dispute tended inevitably to inject an additional element of contention inasmuch as that dispute at once became a factor in the United States–Soviet duel."[24] It seemed that at least Indian representatives had latched onto this sense of a U.S. policy "entirely conditioned by the general line-up of the Big Powers and the United States['] intense fear of Communism."[25] This assumption was generally valid in terms of the weight it ascribed to cold war calculations in shaping U.S. policy decisions with regard to South Asia. But the analysis in this study diverges from the interpretation of scholars like Robert McMahon, who hold that U.S. strategy in South Asia recognized Pakistan as vaguely central to the defense of the Middle East, even if senior Truman administration officials had not articulated precisely why, which led to an American deference to a British policy lead.

While the argument that an inchoate and undefined U.S. policy of falling in behind Britain seems to explain the Anglo-American congruence in the Kashmir dispute, the argument here seeks to penetrate deeper into the interdependent but distinct forces driving American and British policies, even if they happened to converge in the form of nearly identical policy objectives in Kashmir.[26] The evidence shows that unlike the British linkage of South Asia with the defense of the Middle East, despite the obvious U.S. concerns with any global threats to the critical oil supplies in the Middle East, U.S. policy in South Asia was more often seen through a different geopolitical lens, one that framed Pakistan and India together as a distant secondary theater of global competition with the Soviet Union, whose quiescence was a significant but not vital American national security concern. Critically, though, unlike in the case of Palestine, those American and British strategic "maps" of Kashmir were not irreconcilable. Moreover the American view of the conflict's geographical location—in a peripheral cold war theater—even provided a rationale for taking less of a leading role in the direct negotiations. That diplomatic deference in turn provided the freedom of maneuver for a developing British policy on Kashmir that Washington would eventually back. Commonwealth Relations Office officials accordingly instructed British diplomats in both India and Pakistan to work closely with their American counterparts so as to enlist U.S. support for British proposals and dispel the impression that Britain was managing the crisis alone.[27]

American diplomatic reporting (like that of the British) during the early weeks of the Kashmir crisis assessed that Pakistan faced grave disadvantages in the military confrontation, disadvantages so daunting they might even threaten the new state's territorial integrity. If anything, that sense of concern led U.S. officials to align with British counterparts on a policy that kept Pakistan's vulnerability in mind. Importantly, though, the documentary record shows a rationale for that policy that was distinct from the British concerns with the defense of the subcontinent and Pakistan's relevance for the stability of the Arab world. While U.S. planning considerations took account of those factors, they existed within the context of a much wider—and geographically broader—set of global considerations, including Pakistan's role in *the Islamic world as a whole,* as opposed to a crescent of Islamic states in South and Southwest Asia; its potential role in the defense of the Indian Ocean; and its viability as a base for air operations given its proximity to the southern flanks of the Soviet Union.[28] For Washington, it was these wider considerations that came to bear most prominently on shaping policy in the subcontinent, whose stability hinged precariously on the Kashmir dispute as 1947 drew to a close, and whose regional dynamics belied distant, second-order geopolitical repercussions. And though U.S. policy on the Kashmir dispute had yet to concretize, the State Department had begun to consider the bigger strategic questions prompted by the partition of the subcontinent.[29]

The United States had taken a deliberately cautious approach prior to the formal consideration of the Kashmir issue by the United Nations. In October, when the government of India had beseeched the Truman administration for air transport to assist with the removal of refugees, Washington's response was that it could consider such assistance only in response to a joint Indo-Pakistani appeal. When Pakistan refused to lodge such a request, the bid failed, despite intense pressure from the American ambassador in New Delhi, Henry Grady. Evenhandedness in the initial response was thus a key characteristic of American involvement. The United States was not going to insert itself in a manner that might lead either or both of the new states to quickly turn against it because of any hasty diplomatic or humanitarian overtures.[30] Nor were U.S. officials ready to contemplate robust military cooperation with either of the two new dominions.[31] From the outset the British representatives on the Security Council found the U.S. approach to the issue "on the whole satisfactory as far as it goes." That approach had been laid out in a State Department position paper advising that U.S. policy at the Council seek to prepare the ground for the arrangements for a plebiscite in accordance with Mountbatten's original plan to enable the inhabitants of Kashmir to decide their future. It was an international approach that sought to legitimize any settlement, in a manner consistent with the liberal international underpinnings of American globalism, which had reached an apogee at the culmination of the war. And there was no more visible symbol of that globalism than the American-sponsored United Nations Organization and the institutional experiment it represented in the wake of the failed League of Nations.[32]

As the case of Palestine had shown, the Truman administration's desire to continue its predecessor's campaign for the United Nations imbued official policy with at least a verbal commitment to develop UN capacity to maintain international security, despite skepticism on the part of individual officials, including Kennan and many other cold war hawks. Manifold historical and strategic factors likely contributed to that official rhetoric—from the untrammeled aggression of Nazi Germany and its associated human costs in Europe, to the intransigence of Soviet Russia in withdrawing its military forces from the Near East in the early postwar period and the expansionary instincts that it betrayed. The State Department's Policy Planning Staff would even consider whether a resolution might be introduced at the UN General Assembly's fourth General Session in 1949 that would have allowed special sessions of the Assembly to be invoked to "make appropriate findings" to determine whether "members of the United Nations would take appropriate action to restore international peace and security" in alleged cases of armed attack.[33] U.S. policymakers had expressed full willingness to participate in the new UN system, including the provisions of Chapter VII of the Charter on "Action with Respect to Threats to the Peace, Breaches of the Peace, and Acts of Aggression." Article

43 of Chapter VII concerned the establishment of special agreements on the disposition of national military forces to be placed under UN command, and the U.S. Senate had passed the so-called Vandenberg Resolution with the hopes of ensuring "maximum efforts to obtain agreements to provide the UN with armed forces as provided by the Charter."[34] The State Department also admitted, publicly at least, that "the United States is deeply committed to press to the limit for the implementation of Article 43."[35] Yet despite the language of Chapter VII, and as the Kashmir dispute would prove, the Truman administration had evolved an acute awareness of the limits on the sort of collective action envisioned by the United Nations. And the intellectual core of officials suspicious of UN capacity to manage the complex security demands of the postwar world was rooted in the State Department itself. It was perhaps this awareness that tempered the U.S. proposals at the Council, however lofty, and directed the central line of the American diplomatic effort at the organization of a plebiscite under UN auspices. That palpable caution was sufficient to trigger the wrath of Jawaharlal Nehru, who interpreted it as American concern that India was "pro-Russian" in its foreign policy outlook.[36]

The Truman administration's reluctance to espouse the deployment of UN military forces in Kashmir may have derived in part, of course, from the fact that UN member states had yet to contribute armed forces to the new organization by entering into any "special agreements" as stipulated by Article 43 of the Charter. But a more pressing factor was the State Department's preoccupation with international communism. The extent of the paranoia in this thinking seems almost absurd in retrospect but appears to have been a core motivation underpinning State Department recommendations. In allowing the UN Security Council to authorize any action, Department officials surmised, even if the Soviet Union did *not* exercise its veto against a U.S.-led or -supported action, it likely refrained from doing so only because the Soviet leadership had deemed that action reconcilable with its objectives to further the international communist movement. In that regard, this logic suggested, any resulting UN undertaking could only be at odds with U.S. strategic interests in confronting international communism and Soviet expansionism.[37]

Such interpretations of guiding sine qua non principles underpinning all Soviet policy toward UN action, especially in world regions of secondary strategic importance, seem exceedingly narrow. Nonetheless they are illustrative of the global conception of security interests that informed

America's early UN policy in Kashmir and the degree to which the cold war rivalry penetrated American policy in South Asia.

Those concerns, as previously noted, had come to light in the earliest informal discussions that U.S. representatives had held with their British counterparts soon after the UN took up the Kashmir dispute.[38] Cadogan's staff had broached the issue of the deployment of international troops to Kashmir in the same meeting with U.S. officials, as part of a suggestion to pursue a UN-sponsored settlement in Kashmir (before the assessment from the British chiefs of staff finally arrived in mid-January). The State Department shared the suggestion with Austin, including the possibility of employing a peacekeeping force, but expressed reservations about such a strategy, recognizing the "obvious complications of [the U.K.] proposal for use of international troops."[39] In reaching the same eventual conclusions as those of the Foreign Office, albeit sooner and for different reasons, the Department had conceived of a more limited fact-finding effort on the part of the United Nations, one that the Division of United Nations Affairs considered a "less complicated suggestion" than the British proposal and "something to be considered by [the] U.K. as perhaps more palatable to the parties and other SC members and more in harmony with [the] realities of SC capabilities" than the prospect of any international force, consisting of the armed forces of the two parties themselves or outside powers.[40] Capabilities on the ground thus seemed to be a concern for U.S. officials, as they had been for Scoones in London. But the real sticking point for U.S. officials was what they considered the inherent danger of sanctioning the presence of Pakistani troops in India—and the implications of such a deployment for other, more critical theaters of the cold war, such as the oil-rich Near East, on which Soviet military presences in Iran and beyond were bearing down menacingly. That cold war mind-set revealed the principal consideration guiding U.S. thought: a geostrategic globalism in which developments in Kashmir came to be associated with other distant regions—not unlike the Truman administration's linkage of the problems of displaced European Jews and the future of Palestine. While British officials like Ernest Bevin, Philip Noel-Baker, and Hastings Ismay preoccupied themselves with Kashmir's impact on India's northern defenses and its effects on territorially contiguous areas, Secretary of State George Marshall worried instead about the precedent that troops in Kashmir could set for other potential global flashpoints—in the Muslim world and beyond—that could implicate UN involvement and imperil the credibility of both the United Nations and its principal patron, the United States. At a minimum, though, there was Anglo-American consensus on the need for a fact-finding mission: no one disputed that more information on the ground had to be collected before sound decisions could be reached.

Deliberations on Kashmir began at last on 15 January, when the Indian representative, Gopalaswami Ayyangar, presented Delhi's case before the gathered representatives of the world's great powers. Kashmir presented a "threat to international peace and security" if not addressed without delay, he maintained, making clear that the question was not one of a dispute over the territory (which ostensibly belonged legally to India) but one of the Pakistani provision of assistance to the tribesmen that had invaded Kashmir. Pakistan, in lengthy written and oral rebuttals of the Indian charges, denied supporting the rebels in Kashmir and lodged counter-charges of its own: of Indian genocide against Muslims in Kashmir, of forcing the Hindu-majority state of Junagadh's accession to India, and of the dispatch of Indian forces to Kashmir, whose accession to India Pakistan refused to acknowledge.[41] Deliberations began in earnest as the claims and counterclaims flew with vicious acrimony, with much of the real diplomacy occurring behind the scenes as the American and British delegations sought to bring the two sides together in accordance with their views of a limited UN presence to monitor and observe. Driven largely by the British approach developed in early January, three days after the Security Council's Belgian president presented a draft resolution on Kashmir on 17 January, the Council passed Resolution 39, establishing a three-person Commission on India and Pakistan (UNCIP) to investigate the circumstances concerning the dispute. Addressing the Security Council, Austin informally suggested that the body oversee the interim arrangement of the proposed plebiscite for Kashmir: "I ask if it is not worthwhile for the parties involved, in their search for peace and for a real, true settlement of a very complex situation, to conduct all these proceedings—the plebiscite especially—under the aegis of the Security Council."[42]

Austin also shared reflections on the futility of military force as a tool to stop the violence in Kashmir. These observations shed light on the Truman administration's general attitude toward the future development of the practice of UN peacekeeping.[43] Commenting on two draft resolutions before the Security Council, Austin suggested that military pressure "could be employed to drive out the trespassers in Kashmir and Jammu, and to force the battle line off this ground, but that might not end the military character of this problem."[44] In other words, even if the dispatch of a peacekeeping force could put out the brush fire, the need to organize a fair plebiscite would still remain. Austin's reasoning attested to some of the basic shortcomings of peacekeeping that later handicapped the ability of later missions to help secure lasting settlements in conflicts like Kashmir's. But despite the administration's public praise for the United Nations, his comments belied a wider skepticism in the efficacy of the new body and its conflict-resolution capabilities that was rooted in global concerns about the introduction of foreign armed forces into hitherto localized conflicts.

For his part, Mountbatten was enraged by Resolution 39 and wrote Attlee charging that British and American policy had turned against India, a betrayal that might very well drive it "into the arms of Russia." Importantly he suspected that an interest in ensuring that British policy did not alienate the Muslim countries of the Arab world had led it to pursue a line so favorable to Pakistan at the Council.[45] Perhaps Mountbatten was especially unnerved by the policy because of the precise moment at which it was adopted: just as sensitive deliberations got under way to determine whether India could be persuaded to remain within the Commonwealth and as Indian officials began to fear that the Truman administration's support for the partition of Palestine would lead to a new policy sympathetic to Pakistan to placate the Muslims of South Asia. Attlee was outraged by the insubordination from Mountbatten, who was not even formally in a position to circumvent Nehru and write the British prime minister. He nonetheless fired back that a Council resolution whose findings were consistent with India's charges would have internationally legitimized an Indian declaration of war against Pakistan.[46]

When British and American officials convened again in February for an "exchange of views," U.S. officials presented a set of principles that could serve as the basis for discussion of the Kashmir issue and reiterated their concerns about the existing presence of Pakistani troops in Kashmir. The root of the matter was critical to the administration's evolving conception of UN peacekeeping and the roles it might take on in other conflict situations. Precepts informed by globalism unmistakably came to bear on the discussions. In light of the U.S. view recognizing Indian claims to Kashmir, the Americans asked, would the implications of a Security Council resolution sanctioning even the interim involvement of Pakistani forces send a wider message legitimizing the presence of "foreign troops from one party to a dispute in the territory of another party to the dispute"? If so, they argued, the ramifications could be felt in countries like Turkey, Iran, Greece, and China. And Soviet leaders could cite the precedent and allege a need for international "peacekeeping" forces to justify Soviet forward military presences and even outright occupation in regions like Eastern Europe and the Middle East. Again, the worldview that this rationale revealed was a more global one than that behind British arguments. It held that the Kashmir dispute, which implicated few direct U.S. interests, could instead pose distant, unforeseen consequences if mishandled. Nevertheless, having by this time abandoned plans for an international force for their own reasons and subscribing to a drastically different conception of the geographic consequences of a future settlement, British Foreign Office officials continued to assert that the introduction of Pakistani troops into Kashmir had to be an essential component of any settlement. British representatives also opposed what they perceived as the unhelpful State Department suggestion to establish an international coalition administration of Kashmir that could oversee a plebiscite (one of the few areas of discord in Anglo-American policy coordination on Kashmir). After all, such an administration would also, of course, be contingent on the establishment of security, the provision of which by the United Nations had now been discounted by both governments.[47]

A coherent U.S. stance in the Kashmir negotiations had not really congealed as of early spring 1948, but the guiding principles of State Department thinking were fairly well established. Considerations stemming from the cold war rivalry with the Soviet Union now resonated—throughout an implicitly global sphere of interactions—in the minds of U.S. strategists. It was what the British deemed a constant "necessity of considering [the] Kashmir issue against [the] background of other problems which have already come or may in [the] future come before the Security Council," or Kashmir's importance as a precedent-setting example rather than as a specific case, that most tangibly impacted American assessments.[48] Pakistan possessed only limited strategic significance for the United States, despite the admission by intelligence analysts that it could "contribute, nonetheless, to U.S. offensive capabilities in the early phase of hostilities" of a global war.[49] But even in a region removed from the cold war's center stage, the presence of foreign Pakistani troops in India was a risk that might implicitly sanction the Soviet military presences or advances in the Near and Far East.

Still, by the end of February British diplomats in New York noted that American policy was converging toward British proposals on five separate points of concurrence. First, there was at least grudging U.S. support for the presence of Pakistani troops in Kashmir, despite American skepticism about the prospects of securing Indian concurrence on the notion. Second, there seemed to be Anglo-American consensus on the interim administration of Kashmir by the key political actors in addition to "an outsider of eminence" to ensure the continuing rule of law. Third, there was agreement on the conversion of UNCIP into a plebiscite commission. Fourth, and hand in hand with the commission was the idea of appointing a senior plebiscite administrator. Fifth, both Washington and London agreed on the need for a concurrent withdrawal of Indian troops and intruders from Kashmir in parallel with the other conflict mitigation efforts. British lobbying was bringing the United States in line gradually, it seemed, perhaps because of the inchoate nature of America's dispersed global concerns. These basic elements would constitute the basis for the Anglo-American policy shaping the evolution of UNCIP throughout the coming months.[50]

The contours of a U.S. policy started to take shape at last in subsequent weeks. On 22 March 1948 the State Department sent Austin its assessment of the text of a draft resolution on Kashmir introduced by the Chinese, outlining four basic points that had arisen from the U.S. mission's deliberations with the British and other UN delegations. First, UNCIP's role in the observation of the termination of fighting and the holding of a plebiscite had to be defined more clearly. Without more precise instructions, it would not even be apparent what the Commission was to do in the field after observers had been deployed. Second, provisions concerning the maintenance of law and order in areas from which Indian and Pakistani military forces were to be pulled back needed to be elaborated further. Third, the plebiscite director and his staff needed judicial powers to maintain law and order while the plebiscite was held. Fourth, the plebiscite director needed to be empowered with the capacity to report back to the Security Council through UNCIP on his findings. These added capabilities would enable the mission to perform the role that the United States envisioned for it, while stopping short of the robust military capabilities that Washington had written off, along with London, as impractical and impossible.[51]

Security Council Resolution 47, passed on 21 April, was based in part on the original Chinese draft but incorporated input from six Security Council members. It enlarged the size of UNCIP to five members and called on both sides to do their part to curb the violence. The resolution urged Pakistan to take steps to remove the presence of nonresidents of the region engaged in the fighting, the so-called irregulars whose autonomous and fluid presence in Kashmir posed vexing problems, while India was to reduce its military presence to the minimum level necessary to ensure peaceful civil administration. The resolution also proposed the creation of a coalition of representatives that would reflect the wishes of the people of the state and called for the plebiscite that American and British officials hoped would determine the state's eventual political fate. Interestingly, after the resolution's passage, the State Department proved increasingly willing to take on a more direct role in the Commission's work while shedding some of its prior hesitations. One key step was the appointment of a U.S. representative to the Commission, J. Klahr Huddle.[52] The cautious foray represented perhaps a slight American concession in the direction of British appeals to take a more active stance. But the mild nature of actions taken at the Council suggested continuing American reluctance to engage too boldly and visibly, for fear of eliciting a sharp Soviet reaction.

If the United States had moved closer to British views in the course of the spring, it seemed that the British might also have become more sensitive to American concerns about communist penetration of Kashmir that could occur if even a quasi-independent Kashmir was recognized as a "separate international entity." As the British high commissioner in New Delhi told his counterpart in Karachi, "It seems important that Kashmir should be part of either India or Pakistan so that one or the other would have undoubted right to intervene without delay or argument to stop any Communist coup d'état." Moreover an "independent Kashmir might also open [the] way for China to pursue her claims in Gilgit Agency."[53] British strategy on the separate issue of the unavailability of international forces to police the dispute also seemed to have migrated closer to U.S. views during this phase. While Attlee himself had weighed in on the issue a few months earlier in the wake of the assessment of the initial suggestion by the Chiefs of Staff, British *reasoning* for why the idea was unsound now seemed to more closely mirror Kennanite, State Department logic, citing the difficulties of obtaining troops from suitable smaller nations that could contribute them (as opposed to the distinct challenges of rapid deployment, supply, and availability of Commonwealth troops cited earlier).[54] In this sense, it is evident that U.S. and British policies on Kashmir exerted a mutual gravitational pull on one another, rather than the former developing in cautious deference to the latter.

THE CEASE-FIRE RESOLUTION

By late summer the Foreign Office's predilection for a Kashmir adjoined to Pakistan seemed to have become the guiding principle for British policy. In the ultimate triumph of Attlee's pro-Pakistani faction, whose "regionalism" linked Kashmir with the Islamic Near East, the Foreign Office elected to call for the withdrawal of both Indian and Pakistani forces from Kashmir. Its concerns about the unlawful Pakistani presence now partially allayed, the United States too fell in line with the approach, a final blow to Mountbatten and the pro-India camp. On 13 August UNCIP passed a resolution calling on both sides to accept a cease-fire, on local tribesmen and Pakistani military personnel to pull back from Kashmir, and on Indian forces to likewise leave the region under reciprocal obligations. But Pakistan conditioned its acceptance of the resolution's terms on a complex set of clarifications. Despite the achievements to date, accord remained elusive, with divergent interpretations of the cease-fire provisions that the two sides failed to reconcile. It would later fall upon a Canadian military officer, General A. G. McNaughton, to devise a plan to implement the cease-fire. But even McNaughton's proposals failed to break the deadlock between Indian demands for the demobilization of the forces of the Azad Kashmir and Pakistani calls for a UN-sponsored plebiscite.

After a summer of energetic diplomacy from London and Washington, Jinnah's death in September cast a pall over Pakistan and its efforts to maintain its pressure on India. But the Pakistan army's commander-in-chief, General Douglas Gracey, reported that all was not as bleak as it might seem from the vantage point of London. "There is a good deal to laugh at," he pointed out, despite the "real tragedy" of Jinnah's death. His successor, Liaquat Ali Khan, struck Gracey as "the calmest, most reasonable man I have ever met and as good as anyone there is to cope with crises of which there has been one after another." Indeed an almost palpable air of optimism surrounded Secretary Marshall's meeting with Nehru on 15 October in Paris, which coincided with the UNCIP meeting scheduled to take place there.[55]

UNCIP had planned to meet in Paris to consider a draft of its interim report, and according to the *Times of London* informal deliberations between Nehru and Liaquat may have begun at a dinner meeting with Attlee in London prior to the report's release.[56] British government hopes for a comprehensive resolution of the dispute between the two Commonwealth countries soared at the Paris talks. The British minister of state Hector McNeil alluded as much to Marshall on the day of his meeting with the Indian prime minister. Moreover the State Department's take on the eve of the event seemed to anticipate such a bilateral announcement that would absolve the United States of "further embarrassment arising from our association with [the] matter through membership in UNCIP."[57] In Marshall's recollection of the meeting, Nehru came across as sincere, seemingly aware of the gravity of the threat posed by the Soviet Union. However, the Indian leader held firm to his country's legal, political, and moral claims to Kashmir and strongly denounced the activities of the "tribesmen" in Kashmir that he believed were being "aided by gangsters from Pakistan."[58] Smoothing over the remaining differences with Pakistan proved more problematic. Marshall found little room for compromise after his 28 October meeting with Liaquat, despite the fact that the Pakistani leader agreed with Marshall on the need to settle the parallel issues in Palestine and that support for UN initiatives had to be universal to be effective—a key consideration given the precedents that the hitherto unproven, abstract idea of peacekeeping could set for a truly global postwar American security policy. When the talks failed, British officials suggested to Marshall that a prominent American be appointed administrator of the plebiscite, whose provisions were outlined in the April Security Council Resolution. But despite Huddle's appointment to the Commission, the State Department balked at the idea of a senior American official occupying such a prominent post as that of plebiscite administrator. That bold an act, the State Department feared, could entrust the United States with the primary responsibility to bring about a peace settlement between India and Pakistan—the dim prospects of which now threatened to impugn American credibility as a key benefactor of UNCIP.[59]

In protest against an alleged new offensive by Indian forces in Jammu and Kashmir, Pakistan's minister of foreign affairs Zafarullah Khan submitted a letter to the president of the Security Council on 20 November. But Nehru denied any such Indian military operation, informing the American ambassador, Loy Henderson, that it was only a case of Indian reinforcements arriving in Kashmir, partly to defend against invading troops headed for Leh.[60] The implications for the role of the United Nations, and whether it would intervene to maintain the peace, were unavoidably at issue in light of the new allegations. While the United States sought a prompt report from UNCIP on the situation, the British Foreign Office raised the possibility of further action under Chapter VII of the United Nations Charter.[61]

But given that both sides of the Atlantic had ruled out an international force, how could the Council's will be enforced? In the absence of such authorities, State Department officials wanted neither to initiate Security Council action to impose a fragile peace on the two sides nor to provoke an unfavorable Soviet response from the appearance of overzealous American resolve to bring India and Pakistan together. By 11 December UNCIP had tabled modified plebiscite proposals to the governments of India and Pakistan, which the United States considered a "more balanced approach" with a higher likelihood of acceptance by the two sides.[62] It was a prognosis that proved correct. Despite its earlier qualms about specific terms of implementation, Pakistan accepted the new agreement, and a cease-fire went into effect in Jammu and Kashmir on 1 January 1949. The reasons for this policy shift on the part of Pakistan are not altogether clear, although diplomatic pressures and Jinnah's sudden death surely played a part. However, the subsequent intransigence on the part of both India and Pakistan throughout the first half of 1949 and beyond would render UNCIP's diplomatic victory of December largely hollow.[63]

THE ELUSIVE SETTLEMENT

Per the terms of the new UNCIP proposals, the cease-fire came into being along with a provisional truce between India and Pakistan, in accordance with the plebiscite terms in Security Council Resolution 47. On 5 January the Council adopted a new resolution whose provisions would govern that plebiscite. But the deadlock had not been fully broken, as subsequent debates at the United Nations would reveal. The sequencing of Indian and Pakistani actions in withdrawing military forces and calling back the invaders had to be coordinated. In a sense, U.S. freedom of action had increased: given at least the nominal acceptance of the cease-fire by the two sides, the State Department dropped its earlier qualms about the appointment of a senior U.S. official to the post of plebiscite administrator, allowing the UN secretary-general to nominate Fleet Admiral Chester Nimitz for that role. The Truman administration's actions also echoed its approach to economic and military assistance to the two countries, which now also came to be seen as diplomatic tools. There was now a sense on the part of American analysts of South Asia of the need to promote regional cooperation on the subcontinent through more direct U.S. involvement and assistance, given that the "continuing internal and inter-regional conflicts" meant that "the combined power potential of South Asia may never develop in the foreseeable future if the individual countries are left to their own devices." Thus "any plan for U.S. assistance should be used as far as practicable as an instrument to effect cooperation within the region," melding diplomacy and economic leverage to achieve a sustainable peace.[64]

Less than a month later UNCIP presented proposals to the governments of India and Pakistan for the implementation of the cease-fire agreement. The basic provisions were threefold. First, Pakistan would withdraw its forces from the region within seven weeks. Second, India would withdraw its own forces within three months. Third, the cease-fire line would be based on the de facto line of control and exclude the Indian occupation of northern Kashmir. The government of Pakistan took issue with the maintenance of Indian troops for the defense of the northern region and the schedule of the pullout. The Indian reservations to the terms were manifold and included the lack of references to Azad Kashmiri forces that New Delhi still accused of running rampant in and destabilizing Kashmir. Despite the appointment of Nimitz, the terms proved irreconcilable for both sides, whose inability to reach common ground reimposed the deadlock of the previous year. In mid-May the State Department considered the few remaining options to break the new impasse, including referral of the matter back to the Security Council. But the British Commonwealth Relations Office suggested Nimitz take on the responsibility for negotiating the truce. Ultimately the State Department opposed both courses. Nimitz's appointment as plebiscite administrator was enough of a responsibility to bear; responsibility for negotiating agreements on behalf of both parties to comply with the cease-fire was a bridge too far. As for Security Council action, the logic of the U.S. reaction to the newly intensified hostilities from the previous November still applied: the forceful pursuit of a Security Council solution was simply too provocative a measure given the constraints in place.[65]

In June Truman's new secretary of state, Dean Acheson, conveyed to Loy Henderson that should the UNCIP negotiations over the implementation of the truce agreement fail, the State Department believed that the matter should be referred to international arbitration. After the U.S. delegation presented a plan to the United Nations envisioning such an approach, Truman and Atlee issued a joint appeal on 25 August calling for the governments of India and Pakistan to accept the UN-sponsored arbitration of the disputed terms of the UNCIP cease-fire. But India refused. In his reply to Truman, Nehru pointed out that while India did not oppose the arbitration of the truce terms in principle, it raised specific objections on two grounds. First, the Indian government refused to acknowledge the authority of the independent arbitrator to determine the scope of issues that would be decided by arbitration. Second, deeming it a basic prerequisite for guaranteeing the safety of displaced refugees and ensuring the conditions of a fair plebiscite, Nehru refused to relegate the disarmament of Azad Kashmiri forces to arbitration. With the Indian government's de facto rejection of the Truman-Atlee appeal, United Nations efforts had extended about as far as they could to bring India and Pakistan together to resolve their conflicting claims to Kashmir. But the limitations on the UNCIP mandate were clear: the Commission was there to mediate the dispute at the consent of the parties. Despite the rhetoric of Chapter VII of the UN Charter, and irrespective of the importance of South Asian security for the maintenance of international peace, the UNCIP mission was crippled by the lack of both procedural protocols and historical precedents in the deployment of UN peacekeeping troops to quell interstate violence. Moreover the onset of the cold war clearly factored into U.S. strategic calculations, as cognizant as American policymakers were of the need to avoid too conspicuous and strident a role in brokering peace in Kashmir.[66]

Given these inherent constraints, the Kashmir dispute had reached a watershed moment.[67] Despite continued calls for a more active American role in the process of conflict resolution, U.S. policymakers consciously sought to avoid asserting a robust presence in the implementation of UNCIP's plans for a cease-fire, truce, and plebiscite over the future of Kashmir. Importantly this reluctance reflected an acknowledgment of the significance and limits of rudimentary UN peace monitoring and observation as an international tool for a rapidly globalizing American foreign policy with diffused security interests embedded in various corners of the world. As acting Secretary of State Robert A. Lovett explained, "I was concerned with the way in which we were constantly being pressured from all directions to take leading parts in virtually all spheres of UN activity and made reference in this connection to Palestine, Indonesia, and Kashmir."[68] In July 1949 India and Pakistan agreed on a cease-fire line that could be monitored by the United Nations Military Observer Group in India and Pakistan, a mission that was to replace UNCIP as a result of talks in Pakistan that produced the Karachi Agreement. But when the positive vibes from Karachi failed to congeal in the form of an Indian commitment to implement specific truce terms, the prospect of the Kashmir issue's reversion back to the Security Council arose again in the fall. Interestingly joint Anglo-American diplomatic discussions on this prospect revealed concerns about the ability of the UN to force a decision on India. What if the Security Council imposed binding measures on India, officials present at the meeting wondered, and India simply refused to carry out the order? After all, India might not readily succumb to the UN pressure that forced the Netherlands to accept the independence of Indonesia. As international peacekeeping had its limits, so did the will of the international community in forcing India and Pakistan to resolve their dispute over Kashmir.[69]

ANGLO-AMERICAN POLICY IN KASHMIR

During the proceedings at the United Nations, Nehru, according to Lord Mountbatten, confided "that he was shocked to find that power politics and not ethics were ruling the United Nations Organisation and was convinced that the United [N]ations Organisation was being completely run by the Americans."[70] Was American control over the Security Council proceedings commensurate with the degree of leverage that the Indian prime minister attributed to the U.S. delegation? The reality was that a coincidence of American and British policies, albeit driven by different conceptions of the geography of the Kashmir dispute, worked to promote the half-hearted conflict-resolution campaign on which Washington and London finally chose to embark.

Scholars like Robert Wirsing have argued that U.S. interests in Kashmir, "largely derivative of the global strategic struggle between the superpowers," were insufficient to justify pushing for a complete settlement.[71] Others, including historian Robert McMahon, have suggested the seminal importance of U.S. adherence to British interests in the minds of American policymakers. It is hard to dispute that a global American policy of containment formed part of the basis of U.S. policy at the Security Council. For Washington, South Asia was essentially a secondary strategic asset in the cold war, after Europe, given its proximity to the Middle East, its large pool of labor, its mineral resources, and its role as a market for the United Kingdom and Europe that could stimulate their postwar economic rehabilitation. But the global geographic scope of American policy and paranoia about international communism revealed an American geography of the Kashmir dispute in which the reverberations of UN involvement could produce ripples felt around the world.[72] International troops on the Indian subcontinent could have created a dangerous precedent for Soviet intervention along its borders. Plus Afghan-Pakistani discord over tribal groups threatened the stability of the subcontinent given the challenges for states like theirs to defend themselves alone. Should the two states fail to live in amity, it would open the subcontinent to Soviet influence through what the Afghan ambassador-designate to Pakistan called "the door of danger."[73]

That sense of the international ramifications of the conflict contrasted sharply with strategic thought on Kashmir as framed by Britain's Foreign Office, Commonwealth Relations Office, and military chiefs of staff. Unlike America's preoccupation with Kashmir's consequences for the spread of Soviet communism and for other conflicts "internationalized" by UN involvement, market access for European economic output, and human and natural resources to power another global war effort, Britain contextualized the Kashmir conflict within a wider region that it deemed both geographically contiguous and central to British postwar planning. That region consisted of the predominantly Muslim populations extending from the Eastern Mediterranean to Central Asia, and spanned areas such as Egypt, where a direct British military presence was retreating in the face of acute financial and military pressures on the imperial footprint. Given that the same region along the arc of crisis saw the nearly simultaneous eruption of conflict in Palestine at its western tip, and in Kashmir at the opposite end, it was inevitable that British policy in the Kashmir dispute had to remain ever mindful of its impact on the Arab Muslim world—and vice versa. For as Viceroy Wavell had observed to the secretary of state for India with regard to British plans for Palestine, "If the short-term decision goes seriously against the Arabs, we may have a good deal of unrest among the Indian Muslims."[74]

But the demographics of Kashmir, contiguous as it was with the Muslim populations of Southwest Asia stretching to the Middle East, were overlaid onto the sprawling princely state's territory and the natural features of forbidding mountain ranges and perilous passages connecting Central Asia with the subcontinent that proved formidable forces of both historical change and continuity dating back to the Great Game. As one of Mountbatten's military subordinates, A. E. G. Davy, put it in a report sent on to the prime minister, "If one looks upon this area as a strategic wall the five most important bricks in the wall are: Turkey, Iran, Iraq, Afghanistan and Pakistan. If the British Commonwealth and the United States of America are to be in a position to defend their vital interests in the Middle East, then the best and most stable area from which to conduct this defence is from Pakistan['s] territory." In Davy's words, Pakistan was nothing less than "the keystone of the strategic arch of the wide and vulnerable waters of the Indian Ocean."[75]

The strategic significance of Pakistani territory bordering Afghanistan was paramount, and Russia remained an ever-present adversary in contesting British influence there. As an Indian diplomat quoting Benjamin Disraeli told his British interlocutor, "Russia was a pillow. If you pushed it back in one place, it bulged in another. If we held Russia in the West by our firmness, it would not fight, but would immediately reopen its pressure in the Far and Middle East." Given long-standing Russian interest in territories bordering the Indian Ocean, the Indo-Soviet border acquired a transcendent significance rooted in geography that stretched back a century and that neither British nor Indian officials could ignore. It meant, in essence, that "in the long run India and Pakistan had a common interest in Kashmir because they had a common frontier to defend there."[76] But given Pakistan's pervasive defense woes, the only solution was its reinforcement from without—especially given that "a [military] guarantee to Pakistan would have a favourable effect on the Muslim countries in the Middle East."[77]

But critically, unlike in the case of Palestine, where the superimposition of American globalism onto British regionalism produced an explosive clash between their respective policies, the Kashmir conflict saw these disparate geographies produce a neat convergence across the agendas in Washington and London. The State Department's preoccupation with the containment of Soviet communism on the subcontinent and the Foreign Office's effort to limit Soviet, Chinese, and Afghan influence in Pakistan's border regions that might threaten British interests led to the same policy objectives: the cautious promotion of conflict-resolution efforts between the two new British dominions. For Britain, such a policy served defense requirements bound up in the mountains of Kashmir and the wider need for a face-saving retreat from the subcontinent. For the United States, it embodied hopes for a pacific Indian subcontinent whose stability was a bulwark against communist expansion that also protected potential assets given the possible recurrence of global war.

FIVE

Imperial Residues

Framed in terms of Bevin's imperial strategy, the British withdrawals from mandatory Palestine and the princely state of Jammu and Kashmir were domestic policy responses to a changed world order—decisions taken by the British government to cede power where the war had exhausted British capacity to exercise it. Palestine's abandonment before the United Nations and the hastily drafted plan to quit India amounted to an acquiescence to geopolitical pressures to curtail forward imperial defenses after the war.[1] As the empire contracted under those military and economic pressures, reliance on cooperation with British dominions and treaty relationships with newly independent states of the postcolonial world would have to substitute for formal imperial structures to safeguard British interests.

Importantly this downsizing of the British overseas military presence also hastened the decolonization process in both the French and Dutch empires. Temporary occupation during the closing stages of the war, and the subsequent demobilization of British troops as operations wound down, acted as a sort of corrosive agent that ushered in the end of French control over Syria and Lebanon and Dutch rule in Indonesia. As the global expansion of American interests eclipsed the Pax Britannica, the balance of European colonial authority that remained throughout the world found itself caught in a geopolitical vise between the forces of self-determination promoted by the United Nations and espoused by the United States, and the ominous precedent of a British admonition of the end of the colonial era before France and the Netherlands were themselves willing to countenance that postwar reality and accordingly rethink the geographical footprints of their empires.

The full sweep of the relevant developments in the Francophone Levant and the Dutch East Indies, though they paralleled events in Palestine and Kashmir, exceed the scope of this work. But a broad overview of the British and American roles in dislodging French and Dutch colonial power in those territories reveals how imperial powers like France and Holland occupied unique positions in the world at the close of the Second World War. Both found themselves caught between two global forces that hastened the end of the colonial era. One was the expanding push of American power projection and the anticolonial ideals of self-determination that Washington had championed since the age of Wilson. The second was the retracting pull of a British Empire willingly in retreat, whose temporary authority helped wash away footholds to which they clung in futility because of their outdated conceptions of their imperial territories.

BRITAIN, FRANCE, AND THE LEVANT

Syria and the Mount Lebanon (the Levant states) came under formal French jurisdiction in 1919 in the wake of the Ottoman collapse. France immediately secured League of Nations mandates over the two new territories to stamp them with the imprimatur of international legitimacy, as Britain had done in the cases of Palestine, Iraq, and Transjordan.[2] But the complex mélange of Sunni, Shia, and Christian Arabs that inhabited the area resisted the imposition of French colonial authority from the very start. That opposition prompted the French to rule largely by the employment of armed force, as it had grown accustomed to on the African continent, beginning with the 1920 expulsion from Damascus of Arab tribal leaders like Faisal bin Hussein bin Ali al-Hashemi, who had allied with T. E. Lawrence to help organize the Arab revolt against the Ottoman Empire. Faisal and Chaim Weizmann had signed a pact the prior year in which the Arab leader offered to recognize Palestine as "the enclave of the 'Zionist Jews,'" an early basis for Arab-Jewish cooperation in the region. But that cooperation soon collapsed when Faisal's appeals to Weizmann to stand up to French assertion of control over Syria went unheeded by the Zionist leader. Abandoned by their erstwhile allies, Faisal and the tribal sheikhs loosely allied with him found Ottoman rule supplanted by new colonial masters imposed on them. Forced out of the state administration, Faisal and his Hashemite brethren turned their attentions to Palestine. The redirection of Hashemite efforts to curry favor from the colonial authorities itself exacerbated Arab-Jewish unrest in the British mandate. For there, the Arabs realized, the Zionists represented weaker rivals than their French and British colonial oppressors in the region.[3]

France had successfully crushed native opposition to its recolonization of the Levant. French military power was likewise brought to bear in the suppression of the Syrian revolt of 1925–1926. Driven by the fervor of its *mission civilisatrice*, French authorities both consolidated political control over the Levant to the extent that they could and attempted to transform the region into an extension of the Francophone empire through institutionalized means of forced cultural and linguistic conversion. The trappings of that cultural imperialism were varied and extensive, as committed as French colonial administration was to appropriating the full complex comprising Levantine identities, societies, *and* political authority. That administration took the form of a network of French-language schools, hospitals, and cultural centers and a patronizing bureaucracy that treated Syria's Arabs with contempt and racist condescension. Disproportionately high Maronite Christian representation in the colonial state created out of Greater Lebanon further exacerbated the unrest that this invasive cultural and ideological project had already triggered. The onerous colonial apparatus thus sowed some of the seeds of its own demise within a quarter century of troubled rule.[4] It also contrasted sharply with Britain's official prioritization of the needs of strategic geography over cultural indoctrination, reliance on local elites to preserve crown interests in its colonial possessions, and Foreign Office careerists' deep knowledge and abiding respect for Semitic peoples and cultures.[5]

The discrepancy between the British and French approaches to colonial administration widened over the decades leading up to the war. Britain, mindful of the limits of its strategic reach, recast its mandatory relationship with Iraq into an alliance between nominally sovereign states with the conclusion of the Anglo-Iraqi Treaty as early as 1930, fifteen years before Bevin's assumption of the reins at the Foreign Office and sweeping surveys of imperial defense requirements. London later entered a similar compact with Egypt in 1936. Yet France grudgingly relented on colonial reforms, seemingly oblivious to the Ottoman Empire's own struggles with the Young Turk movement and reformist pressures from below. One consequence of that callousness in the face of a call to liberalize was the failure to deliver on the promises of Leon Blum's Popular Front government to pursue reforms in the Levant. Though Blum had forged treaty relationships with Syria and Lebanon, the subsequent collapse of his government and right-wing agitation undermined their ratification within the required two-year period.[6] Instead Paris indefinitely suspended the Syrian and Lebanese constitutions upon its entry into the Second World War. The Arabs had little recourse in the face of French duplicity in failing to ratify the treaties, mainly because of their own weakness, as Faisal had realized decades earlier. The fact was not lost on Ben-Gurion as he contemplated his own designs for Palestine. As he confided to his son Amos, "Syria could not survive for a day in the face of Turkey, if it wasn't for France."[7]

The Vichy regime's negotiation of an armistice with Germany inaugurated a period of confusion as two French governments—one of Nazi collaborators, the other an underground resistance—lay claim to the decapitated French Empire. Nominal Vichy rule meant the Francophone Levant observed a policy of neutrality toward Great Britain, setting the stage for Free French reoccupation. When the Vichy regime permitted the Axis use of airfields in Syria and Lebanon, the Allies launched an invasion that landed British troops alongside De Gaulle's Free French forces on the Eastern Mediterranean shores to wrest control of Syria and Lebanon. On 8 June 1941 Australian troops filed into Lebanon, engaging Vichy forces on the road to Damascus and its eventual reoccupation. The same day, Free French troops supported by Indian army units entered Syria. Caught between the parallel British/Free French and Australian advances from the east and south, the Vichy commander appealed to his British counterpart, Field Marshal Henry Maitland Wilson, for an armistice on 12 July.[8] Soon a predicament not unlike that which would confront Mountbatten in the East Indies arose when most of the French troops in the Levant opted for repatriation in lieu of joining De Gaulle's newly arrived Free French units. Acceding to their request rather than continuing hostilities against their own countrymen, the Free French found themselves outnumbered by British troops that now constituted the bulk of the military presence in the reoccupied Levant. That military reality posed a challenge to London's official policy of deference to Free French civil administration of both Syria and Lebanon. For Churchill had expressed Britain's nominal intent to acknowledge French primacy in Syria and Lebanon in Parliament that September. Moreover De Gaulle had chimed in that British forces in the

Levant should not seek the "displacement of authority to the detriment of France."[9]

As William Roger Louis framed the problem, the British faced three courses of action in Syria after its assumption of control of the Levant: assistance to France's effort to reconsolidate its colonial rule after the war; strict nonintervention that would allow Syrians and Lebanese nationalists to wage an independence struggle against France; and direct military involvement to expel the French presence from the Levant.[10] As the war progressed, a key British worry was that growing Syrian discontent with oppressive French rule would elicit an excessive counterreaction by the French. The shortcomings of French colonial administration as perceived by the British, who themselves had always relied on a less invasive occupation presence, led to concerns in London that sheer ineptitude would trigger violence against the Christian populations of the region. As civil disturbances grew and spread, the question now for the Eastern Department of the Foreign Office was whether the concerns about a heavy French footprint and the backlash it could trigger was enough to warrant preemptive British action.[11]

De Gaulle's government issued initial promises of independence for both colonial possessions, and on 27 September 1941 the Free French military commander in charge, General Georges Catroux, had even proclaimed conditional Syrian independence subject to certain wartime expediencies to ease the reassumption of French colonial administration after the defeat of Vichy forces. But the Free French authorities dragged their heels on their pledges, while insisting that the French mandatory rights to Syria and Lebanon remained valid. That claim bred further nationalist agitation on the parts of Syrian and Lebanese anticolonial leaders, and the dissolution of political parties in the spring of 1942. Syria's Muslim and Christian Arab populations were not likely to content themselves with the dim prospect of unilateral French occupation after the war. The situation thus posed a dilemma for British policy in requiring a balance between disastrous inaction and too overt an intervention against a rival European colonial power as the war wrought other sweeping political transitions worldwide. The most impassioned stirrings for a bid to displace French authority in Syria came from the first British minister to the Levant, the enterprising Major General Edward Louis Spears.[12]

As new interim governments in Lebanon and Syria awaited the potentially volatile prospect of elections, Spears pounced on the occasion of worsening French relations with Levantine nationalists to mount nothing less than a personal crusade against Anthony Eden and what he considered a half-hearted Foreign Office policy of French appeasement. In an act of blatant insubordination, Spears circulated to senior officials an analysis of British and French policies in Syria and Lebanon he had prepared for the Eastern Department over the head of Eden and without the formal approval of the Foreign Office. Churchill was struck by the extent of Syria's obtuseness in meeting Arab demands for political decentralization and self-rule in Lebanon.[13] The Spears memorandum was a wake-up call for British policy during the pivotal election year of 1943. It was echoed by others, for the fulfillment of Arab nationalist demands in Syria (and Palestine) were now issuing forth from all quarters, even India, where Muhammad Ali Jinnah's All-India Muslim League called on the British to avoid harming the Arab nationalists.[14] Still, the British government refused to answer any of them in a manner that could be construed as an open challenge to French authority.

That authority seemed shakier than ever after the sweeping electoral victory for Lebanese nationalists in the fall of 1943. Lebanon's new prime minister, Riad al-Solh, immediately demanded sovereignty for the independent state of Lebanon, abolished references to the mandate in the Lebanese constitution, and adopted Arabic as the country's official language in the immediate postelectoral phase, after the convincing referendum on French colonial rule.[15] Lebanon's Free French administrators now faced an unpalatable choice between capitulation and repression. In keeping with precedents of French colonial history, they opted for the latter, imprisoning Lebanese and Syrian Cabinet officials in a short but brutal crackdown that elicited international condemnation. The swift response saw the imprisonment of President Bishara El-Khoury, Prime Minister al-Solh, and other Cabinet ministers. Eventually the French caved to international pressure and released the imprisoned leaders on 22 November 1943. But while French intransigence hardened, the press of events accelerated after the elections. Iraq recognized Syrian independence in August and Lebanon's in October. August also saw the Egyptian government express its intention to extend diplomatic ties to both states.

Spears's indignation toward French policy in the Levant eventually began to exceed the limits of even Churchill's tolerance. The following year Spears attempted to singlehandedly forge a renegade policy of reassuring Syrian and Lebanese leaders that the British government would come to the aid of both states' beleaguered gendarmerie forces, the French-trained Troupes Spéciales du Levant, after France's own refusal to do so. The decision by France was designed to undercut the security forces of both states in the face of their continuing struggles to assert greater autonomy against the Free French colonial administration, and ignored the internal security threats to Lebanon and Syria posed by tribal groups in the Levant. By taking the drastic step of scrambling to offer British assistance to the Syrian and Lebanese governments without authorization, Spears effectively ensured his dismissal from the Foreign Office. Concerned as the Foreign Office may have been about French colonial policy, it was not about to countenance a blatant act of interference in a region where official British policy recognized the preeminence of French interests over those of other colonial powers. In November 1944, after a prolonged silence on the matter, Churchill implored Sears to submit his resignation.

But by the end of the year the Foreign Office realized the full extent of the intractability of the Franco-Arab dispute. The Arab states gathered at a September 1944 conference in Egypt reiterated their support for Lebanese independence in the Alexandria Protocol, which also announced the establishment of the League of Arab States. The French considered the statements on Lebanon a new complication precluding a treaty relationship with the Lebanese state that Paris sought, mainly to preserve its special interests in the Levant. The Free French government promptly retracted Catroux's November 1941 declaration and its attendant accommodations.[16] The breakdown of the Franco-Lebanese negotiations led the Foreign Office Eastern Department's Robert Hankey to conclude that negotiations were unlikely to produce a lasting settlement. "The French will be lucky to get half what we have in Iraq," he observed.[17] One of the structural impediments to a solution lay in the apparent irreconcilability of French policy with both Syrian and Lebanese demands for an end to political and cultural imperialism. But neither was overt support for Lebanese independence an obvious recourse, given its likely effects on the Muslim population of a Levant region teetering on the edge of instability because of the parallel course of events in Palestine. The British Joint Planning Staff in February 1945 had expressed concern about the disturbances that could arise in Syria and Lebanon in response to a Palestine settlement unfavorable to the Arabs as a whole. As the British High Commission observed, Levantine Arabs harbored deep suspicions that the establishment of a Christian state of Lebanon in tandem with the Zionist settlement of Palestine would serve to build a non-Muslim buffer zone to cut off the Arab world from the Eastern Mediterranean and all of its major seaports, with the objective of strangling Arab maritime commerce. Those concerns could spiral out of control even if French authority was ejected from the region as officials like Spears advocated, a consideration that constrained policy options even further.[18]

The Foreign Office instead proposed the establishment of an international trusteeship over Syria and Lebanon. On its face the suggestion seems to have been driven by intra-European political rivalries, especially given the adamant British opposition to even the mildest American suggestions of international trusteeship arrangements that might affect their own imperial possessions. But the justification proffered by the Foreign Office held that such a solution could amount to a clever compromise that balanced a complex set of countervailing pressures. In a single stroke Syrian concerns about French domination would be placated; the restoration of French control would be achieved, with its attendant implications for France's standing; British control of French bases would be secured as part of the agreement, serving the need for radar stations and airbase facilities; and even the anticolonial concerns of the United States would be met by virtue of the establishment of an international arrangement, as opposed to a mandate placed solely under British or French control. Here was a perfect example of British geographic "regionalism" shaping Levant policy. Perceiving France as a strategic colonial competitor in a region where vital British interests remained bound up in neighboring Iraq, Transjordan, and Palestine, the Foreign Office embarked on an approach that would prevent the reemergence of French rule over the Levant while preserving an air of international legitimacy over the entire scheme. In the face of the challenges confronting British strategic thought about the Middle East with the looming end of occupation in Egypt, a trusteeship in Syria represented just the sort of inventive, parsimonious solution that the Eastern Department's policy would require.[19]

But well before any trusteeship scheme could even be afforded proper consideration, crisis consumed the region in the spring of 1945. The agitations of Syrian Arabs, growing increasingly restless with French occupation, were exceeding the capacity of French colonial authorities to maintain order. The conclusion of the Arab League Pact in Cairo that March, with its reference to the League's association with nonindependent Arab states, elicited greater French resentment toward what Paris perceived to be the nuisance of Arab nationalism. But French authorities in Lebanon concerned with the perpetuation of Franco-Lebanese ties were mostly satisfied with new prime minister Abdul Hamid Karami's spirited defense of Lebanese independence against a more centralized organization arrangement within the League, including the preservation of the right of League members to conduct independent foreign relations outside of the League's auspices. But continued Free French pressure to conclude a treaty protecting French economic and other interests only amplified the friction that had arisen over the reinforcement of and future control over the Troupes Spéciales, whose plight had all but cost Spears his position. The French Air Force had now begun to bomb Syria with munitions provided through Lend-Lease. When fighting broke out in Damascus between the French and Syrian nationalists in May, given the presence of British troops in the Levant, Whitehall was left with no other recourse but to take action. A reluctant Churchill ordered British forces to intervene and restore order by brokering a cease-fire.[20]

When order was quickly restored, the immediate security problem had been addressed—but the question of long-term responsibility remained. With British authority substituted for that of the French, the prospect of British troops facing the effects of Arab disaffection with the state of affairs in Palestine became a new concern. A particular worry was that extremists would provoke attacks that the Syrian government would not be able to control, which would allow the French to exploit the situation in a quixotic reversal of the roles those colonial rivals occupied in early 1945. The British Chiefs of Staff candidly observed, "The French, moreover, would do anything they could to cause us trouble. They have always been jealous of our position in the Middle East and have in the past endeavoured to undermine it whenever possible. Their policy in this respect has not changed."[21]

Eventually British and French forces withdrew from both Syria and Lebanon in the spring of 1946, after a protracted campaign to pacify the unrest. France learned a harsh lesson about the realities of the emerging postcolonial order ushered in by the Second World War through its experience with the British military intervention that helped dislodge it after twenty-five years of colonial rule in Syria and Lebanon. Meanwhile Arab impressions of British intentions improved in the wake of Churchill's ultimately decisive intervention, however late in coming. But Foreign Office officials wondered how far that boost in goodwill could be leveraged to

British advantage in shaping Palestine policy as the war drew to a close. Meanwhile they contemplated the costs of having assumed a new security burden in two former French colonial states along the Eastern Mediterranean, whose fates, thanks to their geographical linkages, remained intimately intertwined with the futures of both Palestine and Muslim India to the East.[22]

FOUR FREEDOMS AND FOUR FEARS: AMERICA, SYRIA, AND LEBANON

The United States blamed France alone for the predicament that the Free French faced in Syria and Lebanon after their reassertion of civilian administrative control over both mandates. As Roosevelt told Stalin at Yalta, the backlash against French rule evidenced by the results of the 1943 election and the ensuing violence over constitutional changes "had been entirely due to the attitude of the [Free] French Committee and General De Gaulle." Stalin assented with the American president's view, suggesting that Vichy France had to pay for its collusion with the Germans and hardly deserved Allied assistance with winning back control of its League-mandated territories.[23] But the fact that it was the Free French (not Vichy) forces that had been restored to power over the Levant posed a dilemma for U.S. policy. One key question that arose concerned precisely how much leverage Britain had to wrest French political concessions in the Levant.

Catroux had grudgingly acceded to the demands of both the Syrian and Lebanese governments for the elections of 1943, but French intentions vis-à-vis independence—which Britain deemed equally essential in the near term—were far murkier. The State Department's Bureau of Near Eastern Affairs assured a visiting British official in early 1943 that the United States supported British aims in that regard; Anglo-American policy was fixated firmly on the eventual emergence of both Syria and Lebanon from colonial rule. But Churchill's recognition of the primacy of French interests in both states was a problem for Washington. U.S. officials clarified that the United States "contemplated equality of opportunity for all rather than recognition of a special privileged position for any country, including the mandatory power."[24] The caveat was an important indicator of U.S. thinking on the Levant, one whose diplomatic language belied other intentions.

American officials were unmistakably taking issue with Britain's recognition of predominant French influence in Syria and Lebanon. In doing so, they registered their aversion to any special colonial rights that might stain America's vision for a tabula rasa that swept aside all postmandatory claims to colonial authority in the new global order that the Roosevelt administration envisioned, one founded on self-determination and the principle of sovereign equality. But that aim also had to be reconciled with the concerns of Syrian and Lebanese leaders.

"We have based policy on the Atlantic Charter and talked of the four freedoms," the consul general in Beirut cabled the Department, "while Arab leaders here continued to nurse four fears—of French imperialism, British insincerity, American isolationism, and Zionist expansion."[25] One of the problems of recognizing Lebanese and Syrian sovereignty was the de facto exercise of French control over various elements of the governments of both those states, U.S. officials confided to their British Embassy counterparts in Washington. The extension of formal diplomatic recognition thus hinged on the key question of the nature of the national governments that came to power after the forthcoming elections in both states and the extent to which they would be free of French control. By June, French authorities were assuring American representatives in Beirut of smooth progress toward the elections that U.S. officials firmly supported.[26] When those elections were held in Syria, it seemed to the U.S. consul general in Beirut that "Syria had at long last taken [the] first vital step on [the] road to independence."[27] But State Department officials in Washington still adopted a wait-and-see attitude to assess whether the functions of government would really devolve to local Syrian authorities before deciding on the extension of diplomatic recognition. Word arrived soon thereafter of successful parliamentary elections in Lebanon despite allegations of heavy French pressure to sway results in favor of pro-colonial candidates.[28] At the end of September the Department instructed the consul general in Beirut to inform the Syrian and Lebanese governments that the United States "welcome[d] the successful reestablishment of constitutional governments" with a view toward achieving independence under UN auspices.[29]

In response to a British aide-memoire on Syria and Lebanon, the United States expressed its formal policy views on the issue, including the justification for its delay in extending diplomatic recognition, to British Embassy representatives in a response dated 25 October 1943. The memorandum underscored that while U.S. policy was informed by sympathy for Syrian and Lebanese national aspirations, its policy was also to defer recognition of sovereignty until authorities were in possession of "the machinery of the state" and that U.S. views were "in substantial agreement" with the British with regard to possible French diplomatic entreaties toward the contested successor governments in the new states.[30]

This formulation expressed a clear American intent to recognize the sovereignty of Syria and Lebanon, albeit at the right moment, balancing between an acknowledgment of the forces of self-determination sweeping the Levant and a provocative diplomatic affront to France. But U.S. intentions to displace French authority now unmistakably mirrored that of Foreign Office officials like Spears and perhaps even Churchill himself. In November 1943, as the postelection crisis engulfed Lebanon after the Chamber of Deputies unilaterally amended the country's constitution and abolished references to the mandate, the nettlesome problem of de facto French control over Lebanon continued to complicate the development of U.S. ties to the new Lebanese state. Still, the United States refrained from recognition of the Emile Eddé government that France decreed to be the successor regime.

Back in Paris, the issue of France's *own* government posed perhaps the more significant problem for American policy in the Levant. Irrespective of the State Department's desire to extend cautious diplomatic entreaties to the new Syrian and Lebanese states, U.S. officials again confronted the problem of the provisional nature of the French government and the Free French occupation of the Levant (at the expense of the displacement of Vichy authority) during the wartime Anglo-American consultations in London on the future of dependent territories. But Foggy Bottom's exasperation with Catroux aside, the upcoming San Francisco Conference mandated that U.S. officials handle Franco-American questions about the Levant with extreme delicacy. "Since France as a nation is not in being at the moment, we cannot ask her to subscribe to a decision respecting the Mandated Territories," the visiting undersecretary of state's delegation told its British hosts in London on their April 1944 visit.[31]

Still, that gentle approach did not preclude general explorations of the preliminary legal questions that would arise concerning the postwar future of mandated territories. One of the most important characteristics of that future was the extent to which it would be shaped by America's globalist designs as embodied in the rhetoric of the Atlantic and UN Charters. Those documents, such universal bases of support for Lebanese and Syrian independence, codified the principles on which State Department officials relied in framing their advocacy on behalf of Syria and Lebanon. That unflinching policy commitment was especially important given the possible unrest that American policy in Palestine threatened to generate in states like Syria and Lebanon. As continuing Jewish immigration into Palestine enraged Arab opposition throughout the war years, reactions in both Syria and Lebanon reflected shock and disillusionment with America's apparent disregard for Palestinians' right to self-determination.[32] Embracing Syrian and Lebanese rights to self-determination instead thus provided a palliative with which to at least partly placate mounting Arab opposition to U.S. support for the Zionist project. The benefits of burnishing America's Arabist credentials in the face of the Palestine problem then constituted yet another reason for steadfast U.S. support for Lebanese and Syrian independence within all reasonable limits. In the course of the year the Syrian government assumed control of fourteen government departments responsible for such functions as customs, tribal affairs, taxation, and the Troupes Spéciales. That September, after having "observed with friendly and sympathetic interest the accelerated transfer of governmental powers to the Syrian and Lebanese Governments since November 1943," the United States granted Syria and Lebanon unconditional recognition as sovereign states.[33] Understandably this policy aroused the ire of Zionist leaders, who beseeched the United States to withhold any concessions to Arab demands like support for Syrian and Lebanese sovereignty from French interference as a quid pro quo for their recognition of a Jewish state.[34]

Roosevelt himself delineated the scope of that U.S. support in his now famous meeting with Saudi king Abdul Aziz Al Saud in February 1945 aboard the USS *Quincy* as the situation deteriorated in the Levant and the denouement for France fast approached. The meeting at sea is best remembered for the assurances that Roosevelt gave Saud about consultations with the Arab states before endorsing future positions on the Arab-Jewish dispute in Palestine. But the two leaders also discussed the worsening situation in Syria and Lebanon, which the Saudi king characterized as of "deep concern to him." Specifically Saud asked Roosevelt what the U.S. position would be should France "continue to press intolerable demands upon Syria and Lebanon." Roosevelt told his interlocutor that he had secured in writing French guarantees of Syrian and Lebanese independence, commitments to which he would hold the French government through "all possible support short of the use of force."[35]

As the situation worsened in 1945, the French aerial bombardment prompted Syrian president Shukri al-Quwatli to lambaste American diplomats and call them out on their commitments to the Atlantic Charter as manifested in tangible support for actual Syrian independence from French control. How could the United States stand aside, he demanded to know, while France so blatantly defied basic principles uniting the Atlantic powers?[36] Fortunately for Quwatli, despite a reluctance to irritate the French through bold and conspicuous action, the United States had hardly pursued a policy of neutrality toward the reassertion of French control over the Levant, despite wider U.S. concerns about the dissolution of imperial power in the region as a precursor to Soviet penetration. Indeed the United States had already recognized Syria and Lebanon as independent states. And Washington was not exactly favorably disposed toward the return of those former French possessions to colonial stewardship in the postwar period in blatant violation of the principles of the Atlantic Charter, as Department officials had told their British Embassy colleagues. "We regard our policy towards the independent Levant States as entirely distinct and separate from our policy toward France and the French Empire," the State Department's director for Near Eastern Affairs, Loy Henderson, wrote in May 1945.[37]

Reinforcing British interests to hasten a French exit from the region, the selective application of American anticolonial policy favored the continued independence of both Levantine states in defiance of Free French colonial designs—designs that elicited only the most visceral mistrust on the part of the State Department. That a modicum of caution tempered the eventual American policy response hardly disguised the anti-French instincts driving it. French fears mounted that Quwatli's appeals would echo not only in Washington but also in San Francisco, where the United Nations Conference sessions were held that summer. The simultaneous start of the conference just as a cloud of uncertainty engulfed French authority in Syria and Lebanon had threatened to preclude French participation outright. Fearing the ultimate bearing that arrangements on trusteeship adopted at the Conference might have on the future of the Francophone Levant, French officials threatened to refrain from attendance pending "satisfactory information about its aims and the agenda." Not only did the term *trusteeship* not even translate directly into French, the Ministry of External Affairs told the U.S. ambassador in Paris, but there were the separate concerns of U.S. designs on strategic regions and French claims to the Rhineland. These French suspicions were, of course, remarkably prescient, given at least provisional British Foreign Office plans to pursue some form of international trusteeship for Syria and Lebanon before the crisis of 1945 sidelined the formulation of a thoughtful Levant policy in Whitehall. In the end State Department officials echoed the sensitivities they had expressed in the 1944 London talks to ensure the participation of a major European Allied power in San Francisco. Washington instructed its ambassador to assure Foreign Minister Georges Bidault and De Gaulle that it would only be the proposed institutional machinery, and not the future disposition of any specific territories, that would be discussed at the founding conference for the new world organization.[38]

Despite that act of accommodation, America had already cast its die against the perpetuation of French colonial authority in Syria and Lebanon by recognizing both states as independent nations despite French protests. That diplomatic pressure helped pry the Free French authorities from Lebanon at last in 1946. Thus American power also had a hand in forcing France to devolve power to the newly elected governments and evacuate sooner than it had desired. What was perhaps another important and underexamined factor was the antipathy with which American representatives in the Levant viewed French colonial authority. It was not only the British Foreign Office Arabists who viewed heavy-handed French colonial officials with such disdain. That sentiment was shared by American official and private quarters alike—by Protestant missionaries challenging the French colonial narrative in Syrian and Lebanese religious communities, by institutions of higher learning like the American University in Beirut, and by the Lebanese and Syrian immigrants who mounted campaigns from abroad to wage an independence struggle against the French mandate.[39]

French officials had considered the role played by British occupation forces in the war's Near Eastern theater as motivated by pure British duplicity in a moment of acute strain on the projection of French imperial power. But in a sense France was the victim of larger geostrategic shifts beyond merely a calculated British effort to thwart a colonial rival. French rule in the Levant was instead caught between the "pull" of a controlled British withdrawal from the region associated with Britain's shrinking geographical interests, a withdrawal that dragged French colonial administration out of the Levant along with it, and the "push" of an outwardly expanding American globalism actively working to dislodge France from two states whose sovereignty America had recognized well before the war's end.

BRITAIN, THE NETHERLANDS, AND THE EAST INDIES

As the French were pushed out of the Levant in the last year of the war, the Dutch began a similar experience with "hydraulic" diplomacy that saw the synergy between a global American anticolonialism and a calculated British military withdrawal squeeze them out of the East Indies. By the end of the war in the Pacific, Indonesian nationalism had overwhelmed the limits of Dutch colonial rule. Indeed wartime Japanese occupation had helped incubate that nationalist movement and a functioning local government eager to assert its international sovereignty. That in turn fueled Anglo-Dutch tensions over the British handover of the occupied archipelago to the Netherlands on terms favorable to The Hague and raised the question of the use of British force to quell Indonesian nationalist militancy. After the Japanese surrender in the wake of the bombing of Hiroshima and Nagasaki, the question of the fate of the East Indies had come to the fore in debates about the termination of the war in the Pacific. As had been the case with French colonial rule in the Levant, intermediary occupation by British forces to help liberate the East Indies helped turn conditions on the ground against an unproblematic restoration of Dutch colonial rule. The Allies had entrusted Great Britain with the task of working jointly with the government of the Netherlands to broker an agreement between the leaders of the Indonesian nationalist movement and Dutch authorities to end Japanese occupation. But Dutch officials, having contributed materially to Britain's war effort, expected London to return the diplomatic favor with a simple handover of authority back to The Hague.

The postwar realities had shifted dramatically during the war years, but the struggle was still on for the Netherlands to come to terms with an East Indies policy founded on an outmoded geography of empire. Some of the similarities between the two anticolonial struggles were glaring. Like Syria's Quwatli, Indonesian nationalist leader Sukarno's deputy, Mohammed Hatta, had appealed to American references to the Atlantic Charter principles of self-determination to support the rights of the Indonesian people to self-rule. Both Hatta and Sukarno had cooperated with Japanese occupation forces in the past but now disavowed those ties as they welcomed

Allied liberation and boldly declared Indonesia's independence on 17 August 1945. Refusing to negotiate with Dutch authorities, they offered to meet only with the major Allied powers. An American officer who had landed in Batavia reported Sukarno's terms for cooperating with the Allies as he had expressed them personally to the U.S. serviceman: foreign forces were not to interfere with Indonesian politics; the Japanese were to be promptly disarmed and their POWs and internees evacuated; and absolutely no Dutch troops or officials were to land. Meanwhile U.S. State Department officials observed that Dutch policymakers lacked a clear sense of initiative in advancing their East Indies policy.[40] Compounding the Dutch predicament was the fact that Japanese disarmament, though orderly and in accordance with international norms in most cases, had left some arms caches in the hands of People's Army forces. The upshot was that, as in the Levant, British intervention would play the principal external role in shaping Dutch-nationalist negotiations in the wake of the Japanese retreat. And the side that Britain chose to support would again help tip the balance away from colonial rule.[41]

A week after the Indonesians declared independence, Allied authority for the war effort in the East Indies transferred from American command under General Douglas MacArthur to its British ally, a boundary change in the administration of the war in the Pacific for which the British Chiefs of Staff had lobbied for months, including at Potsdam.[42] Once control had been transferred, the British faced a situation analogous to the choice it contemplated in the Levant vis-à-vis the restoration of French rule. But unlike in the Levant, the awkward position of British occupation forces under the Southeast Asia Command (SEAC) meant that they faced a trilateral strategic dilemma comprising the competing problems of a complex local insurgency, strained Anglo-Dutch relations, and Britain's own discussions on the devolution of power in India, which were about to commence. Some senior British military leaders were incensed by the situation, deeming it an injustice that Mountbatten, having worked to help defeat the Japanese, now had to deal with what were essentially the side effects of Dutch colonial misrule in the East Indies.[43] Like the French, the Dutch were highly suspicious of British intentions from the early days after the transfer of responsibility. The Dutch ambassador to the United States confided to Secretary Acheson that he "regretted the change in the delineation of the commands" given his belief that "the British did not have the forces, or apparently the will, to do anything about the Indies or to help the Dutch do anything." Given preexisting British commitments in Burma, Indochina, and Malaya, the Indonesian archipelago was "a bad last" for Britain, in the Dutch official's view. The result, he told his American interlocutor, was "that the Dutch people felt that they had been abandoned by their allies after having behaved well and with sacrifice to themselves in the Far East."[44]

It was perhaps fitting that the British commander was none other than Louis Mountbatten, an assignment away from staking his claim to fame overseeing the transfer of power in India. Mountbatten's SEAC, keen to limit its involvement in internal political affairs in Java, sought only to secure strategic points like Batavia and Surabaya, assume control over the local Japanese headquarters, disarm Japanese forces, and locate POWs. The Dutch government wanted its allies to assume full responsibility for law and order in the East Indies in anticipation of an eventual transfer of authority back to the Netherlands after Dutch forces were able to land in any significant numbers. Approximately 2,000 Dutch troops in Australia were available for deployment to the East Indies, with another 2,000 in Antwerp awaiting transport to the region; 5,000 more Dutch marines in Quantico, Virginia, also waited to be transported to the region pending an order by the U.S. Joint Chiefs of Staff. The Dutch government thus considered reliance on surrogate British reoccupation (with American logistical support) as a necessary intermediate step before sufficient Dutch troops could arrive to pacify the incipient insurgency.

Mountbatten drew a distinction between the restoration of law and order in the East Indies and assistance to help restore Dutch colonial administration over the territories in the wake of the liberation of the islands from Japanese occupation. He cited the former as justification for beseeching Dutch officials to meet with the nationalist movement. But responsibility for law and order aside, another principal British concern stemmed from the particularly sensitive issue of the involvement of Indian troops deployed in the East Indies against their fellow Asian nationalists.[45]

Mountbatten had been warned by his predecessor in India, Lord Wavell, of "the serious repercussions likely to arise here if Indian troops are used to suppress [the] Indonesian movement and reinstate the Dutch."[46] The British military likewise shared Wavell's sense that all necessary measures should be taken to prevent the deployment of additional Indian troops to the East Indies. By October, prodded by the security situation, the Foreign

Office had opted to increase its military strength to two divisions in Java and one in Sumatra in areas near internment camps and where Japanese presences lingered, while still relying on Indonesian authorities to handle the bulk of responsibility for the maintenance of law and order. But Mountbatten was concerned about even formal acknowledgments of and expressions of gratitude to authorities like the government of Bengal for the employment of Indian troops in the East Indies—which could embarrass the viceroy by drawing attention to the controversial use of those troops against fellow Asian nationalists.[47]

After a period of contemplation akin to the tortuous deliberations on how to manage anticolonial struggle in Syria, the Foreign Office came in line with SEAC thinking. Mindful of both the risk of British involvement in internal Indonesian politics as well as the prospect of creeping Indian troop commitments, the Foreign Office increasingly pressured the Netherlands to negotiate with Indonesian nationalist leaders as agreed at a joint meeting hosted by the British in December 1945 at the prime ministerial residence, Chequers. While SEAC had requested increases in troop levels, the Dutch refusal to negotiate with Sukarno led British officials to conclude that large disturbances could soon break out and challenge the ability of even a reinforced British presence to preserve order. In this regard the differences between the British and Dutch perceptions of the geographies of their respective empires became clear: the former a newly curtailed empire, mindful of its limitations; the latter an outdated one that refused to acknowledge the momentum of a nationalist struggle that had eclipsed its power projection capabilities. The British had negotiated with Aung San in Burma despite his employment of armed force against His Majesty's government—why could the Dutch not realize that the time had come for them to do the same in the East Indies?

Ominously, by this time the presence of native Indian troops in the East Indies had also sparked protests in India, of precisely the sort that Wavell had feared. Britain's worst nightmare was on the verge of materializing in the winter of 1945–1946—but relief arrived at the last moment. A Dutch statement of policy on 6 November opened a crack in the door to comprehensive Dutch-nationalist talks. Fortunately, in February 1946 the Dutch agreed to open formal negotiations with the nationalist forces, precluding the need for augmenting the Indian force levels to a point where it would trigger uncontrollable unrest throughout British India.[48]

It seemed that a settlement allowing Britain to deftly extricate itself might be achieved after all. British officials soon announced their intention to withdraw their small and increasingly embattled military presence in the archipelago by the end of the year. Dutch-nationalist tensions were preventing the drawdown and termination of SEAC in the aftermath of the war, and British forces could not continue to hold the line indefinitely while the future of Indonesia remained unsettled. The danger of entangling British forces in a war of independence for the East Indies coupled with the prospect of growing unrest in India over the troops deployed to the archipelago ultimately prompted the decision out of necessity. Mountbatten beseeched the British ambassador in The Hague to convince the acting Dutch governor-general Hubertus van Mook and newly appointed Indonesian prime minister Sutan Sjahrir to close the negotiating distance soon, before the British and Indian troop presences were withdrawn.[49]

Perhaps Britain felt no need to thwart the Dutch as colonial competitors in the way they had responded to the French in the Levant. But the consequences of an unsustainable presence in the East Indies were evident given the separate British military force entanglements in the Middle East. The very announcement of a British withdrawal in accordance with a timeline increased the pressure on the Dutch and the Indonesian nationalists to conclude a successful agreement in the course of the negotiations agreed to at Chequers in February. Over the course of seven tense months, the two sides hammered out the Linggadjati (Cheribon) Agreement of November 1946. After British and Dutch forces jointly repelled an Indonesian People's Army assault in key territories, the pact ended the immediate fighting and, after the Indonesian rejection of a Dutch offer of autonomy in October, led to the conclusion of a compromise to establish a United States of Indonesia (USI). The agreement served as only a temporary stopgap before the restart of hostilities between the two sides the following year, given ultimately existential disagreements over its implementation: while the Indonesian nationalists demanded sovereignty during the interim phase until the creation of the USI, the Netherlands demanded that Dutch authority persist until the formal cession of sovereignty at the end of that transitional period.[50]

British policy had achieved its desired short-term ends: self-extrication from its military commitments without the outbreak of major hostilities. Moreover the withdrawal left behind a reluctant Dutch Empire that had yet to come to grips with the new geographic reality "that the East ha[d] changed and changed radically as a result of the war."[51] As the Indonesian conflict endured its final months of Anglo-Dutch diplomatic efforts before its discussion at the United Nations, British energies were succumbing to the intransigence of Dutch policy, despite concessions by The Hague that arrived in fits and starts. But solidarity across the nationalist struggles in India and the East Indies also loomed ominously over Foreign Office deliberations. One form it took was the September 1947 proposal by the government of India's Board of Trade to help convince the Indonesian government to transfer their dollar credits to the United Kingdom in sterling, thereby boosting British exports to the Indies at the expense of American goods, in exchange for support for the Indonesian independence struggle. The Foreign Office was not only skeptical of Indian leverage over Indonesian monetary policy but deemed the entire scheme "wild and rather sinister."[52] There were also inklings on the part of the Foreign Office that newly independent Pakistan would side strongly with the Indonesian nationalists—inklings, it turns out, its State Department counterparts shared. It was becoming clear that, as in the case of its own experiences with decolonization in Palestine and Kashmir, the United Kingdom could benefit from the solidarity and leverage that Anglo-American cooperation on the issue of Indonesian independence might afford the Foreign Office's increasingly embattled South East Asia Department.[53]

AMERICA AND THE INDONESIAN INDEPENDENCE STRUGGLE

In transferring responsibility for the East Indies to British command, the United States had endorsed what was essentially a policy of nonintervention in Dutch colonial policy over the islands. Uninterested in the region strategically, and unwilling to damage relations with a Marshall Plan recipient and wartime ally, the Roosevelt administration's policy tilted in favor of the State Department's Europeanists in deferring to Britain and the Netherlands for shaping arrangements for the postwar administration of the islands without complicating international considerations. Notably that policy of deference aroused the protests of State Department officials compelled to honor America's Atlantic Charter commitments to self-determination in the Far East. But those sensitivities to regional political aspirations dissolved into wider U.S. security concerns that evolved out of the postwar requirements of a global military conflict and the need to preserve stability in the far corners of the earth where fragile transitions in the wake of collapsing empires were giving way to uncertain destinies. As the American ambassador to the Netherlands observed during the few months after the end of the war, the dissolution of Dutch authority without Anglo-American assistance to fill the "vacuum" could give rise to Chinese, Japanese, or even Soviet gains.[54]

After the departure of Secretary of State Cordell Hull, who took with him with his sympathies toward the Asian nationalist struggles, the Department approved a civil affairs agreement with the Netherlands accommodating Dutch colonial policy that set the initial stage for U.S. policy toward the East Indies.[55] But it was stability, not accommodation of Dutch colonial interests, that constituted the principal U.S. interest in the region, a goal that did not mean blind adherence to Dutch policy and consistent support of colonial authority against nationalist agitation. As was the case with the prolonged wait before the American recognition of Syrian and Lebanese independence, a balance had to be struck between the aspirations of the anticolonial movement and diplomatic relations with wartime European allies. But America's motivations differed sharply from Britain's, even though both Atlantic powers opted to pursue measured policies. In contrast to British regional interests in South and Southeast Asia and the potential repercussions of developments in the East Indies on unrest in India, America's focus on a managed transfer of authority was the corollary of a wider interest in global stability.[56]

Fortunately those differing views led to policy convergence in the East Indies, as it did in the Levant and on the Indian subcontinent, and not an acrimonious clash, as it did over the question of the partition of post-mandate Palestine. The Truman administration had adopted a policy of guarded optimism and encouragement of the British efforts to bring together Indonesian nationalists and Dutch officials, resulting in the Chequers talks. U.S. policy was equally supportive of the conclusion of the November 1946 Linggadjati Agreement as the last British troops left the islands because the Agreement's provisions largely served the interests of U.S. policy in Southeast Asia. In the preceding negotiations, U.S. policy had amounted to formal acknowledgment of Dutch authority over the islands, tempered by a favorable disposition toward progress toward an increasing degree of self-rule. But Washington's role behind the scenes as British diplomacy and military power played a primary role enabled it to avoid confronting the principal contradiction in U.S. aims between opposing colonialism and supporting European allies. The diplomatic cooperation of America's European allies was essential for the preservation of peace and even for the stability of colonial territories like the East Indies liberated from Axis occupation. Warm Anglo-Dutch relations would thus be essential for the United States to contend with the menacing presence of Soviet armies in Europe and the Near East, managing postwar reconstruction, and other concerns. But America's signed commitment to the anticolonial spirit of the Atlantic Charter—whose words Quwatli and Hatta had invoked so fervently in the service of their national liberation struggles—also loomed above the gritty reality of postwar occupation needs. And the goodwill of the colonial peoples of Asia would be essential for the growth of the American economy through new trade opportunities and raw materials that would become available with the dissolution of imperial blocs—goodwill that rested on the position the United States took on the national liberation struggles under way in India, Indochina, and Indonesia. The transfer of military responsibility to the SEAC and, later, the British assumption of the role of third party at the start of Dutch-Indonesian negotiations, thus fortuitously enabled the United States to absolve itself from taking sides on the wider colonial question that had been such a source of controversy at the United Nations Conference in San Francisco in 1945. In so doing, America's globalism enabled it to rely on its Atlantic partner to pursue its aims in managing the end of Dutch occupation of the East Indies the following year. But as had been the case with the Kashmir dispute, when direct U.S. involvement did come, it was before the United Nations Security Council.[57]

On one hand, the violence that accompanied Indonesian independence was a quintessential example of the threats to international peace that the new United Nations Organization was meant to address. Here was a regionally localized conflict on the periphery of European postwar questions and an opportunity for the great powers to enforce a UN-sanctioned peace through the deployment of international troops in accordance with the will of the Security Council and backed by the legitimacy of the organization's fifty-one founding members. On the other hand, the specific nature of the conflict involving the secession struggle of a Dutch colonial territory against imperial rule posed the question of the very legitimacy of the UN system of sovereign states—and its corollary legal protections against external interference in the internal affairs of UN members. Moreover the great powers were suddenly confronted with the novel implications of the global scope of the new organization's formal mandate, leading U.S. diplomats to question the wisdom of American involvement in a region dominated by British imperial rule and, if anything, squarely within the sphere of China's regional geopolitical influence. In the end, despite the apparent simplicity of the crux of the issue concerning the Dutch East Indies that arose before the Security Council in 1947, the resolution of the dispute through the intended UN enforcement mechanisms proved a challenge impossible to overcome.

On 17 April 1947 a number of countries, including the United States, recognized the de facto existence of the Republic of Indonesia after the Dutch had extended recognition of the sovereignty of Indonesia in accordance with the relevant provisions of the Cheribon Agreement, which was only signed in March (four full months after it was drafted). The United States demarched the government of the Netherlands to implement the full terms of the Agreement. In instructions to the U.S. Embassy in The Hague, the Department flagged the importance of taking a consistent policy toward anticolonial struggles, an approach that revealed its global perspective, viewing cases like Indonesia as one of many that could arise.[58] But the appeal was to no avail: when repeated difficulties arose in efforts to implement the Agreement's terms, the situation gradually intensified. On 25 May the government of the Netherlands outlined its own proposals for the implementation of the Cheribon Agreement, proposals that the United States deemed "a basis for continued negotiations with the possibility of achieving a prompt and workable agreement."[59] The Dutch plan would have permitted the republican government to return to the city of Yogyakarta provided that the nationalist military forces did not return, that no demarcation lines were fixed, that no separate Indonesian currency was established, and that there was no victimization of persons as retribution. However, the proposals also demanded that the republican delegation to the spring talks agreed at Chequers forcibly enlist the Indonesian nationalists to accept the agreement on Dutch terms without the adoption of any additional conditions—which alarmed both Washington *and* London. While U.S. officials envisioned an interim Indonesian government as the best way for the Dutch to implement the agreement, the new Dutch demands precipitated an impasse. Failing to achieve a resolution, the Dutch mounted the first of the so-called police actions on 20 July, launching a widespread crackdown on nationalist activities and military action against the People's Army.[60]

After a frantic Indonesian diplomatic appeal to India's Jawaharlal Nehru, the Indian government announced that it would raise the matter at the United Nations. India and Australia both jointly brought the Indonesia issue before the Security Council. The Indian delegation sought a peaceful resolution of the matter in accordance with Chapter VI of the UN Charter. The Australians considered the Dutch action to constitute a "breach of the peace" and sought more robust Chapter VII action by the Council to restore international peace.[61]

Just before the matter was taken up by the United Nations, State Department officials wary of the Indian proposal to raise the Indonesian issue contemplated potential policy responses. To Henry Villard of the Office of Near Eastern and African Affairs, one alarming prospect was the potential propaganda value of the Indonesian cause to a like-minded bloc of predominantly Muslim countries. Seeming to echo the regionalism of his British counterparts sensitive to the integrity of the global Islamic *ummah* (community of believers), Villard realized the potential reaction from Muslim countries, such as the new state of Pakistan that was to be carved out of British India in a matter of weeks; Jinnah had already told the press that Muslims in India would consider Dutch military action in Indonesia an act against their coreligionists. And the tensions extended beyond South Asia: State Department officials also knew that Arab Muslims had been receptive to the appeals of the Indonesian foreign minister, who had visited a number of capitals seeking their support for a potential appeal to the United Nations. Given that resonance with a wider Muslim population, Villard surmised that the United States could be forced to take the uncomfortable position of siding against Indonesia in the dispute, which in turn "could do immeasurable damage to American prestige in the Near, Middle and Far East."[62]

Villard's inclinations seemed to be confirmed by the sentiments of King Farouk of Egypt, who informed the U.S. chargé Jefferson Patterson that considerations of the human cost of the Indonesian conflict, the Muslim population of Indonesia, and the Egyptian-Indonesian Treaty of Friendship all led Egypt to sympathize with the plight of the nationalists. If the United States didn't assume a more assertive posture to intervene on behalf of the Indonesians, King Farouk warned, Egypt would assume that the United States was treating Indonesia merely as an "eastern country" and that America itself lacked devotion to the principles of the UN Charter it helped frame.[63]

But there was a distinction between the roots of British and American concerns. At first glance Villard's preoccupation with a wider backlash seemed to echo British concerns about linkages between the populations of the Middle East and South Asia's predominantly Muslim regions. But he did not express specific concerns for the strategic and security ramifications of Muslim uprisings that could spread through a geographically delimited area like the crescent of Islam that stretched from the Levant to Afghanistan akin to the kind of reaction that British regionalism would predict. Instead Villard's was a more diffuse worry about wider potential repercussions *throughout the world* that could threaten American interests, even if the Truman administration officials just beginning to grapple with a global national security policy did not know how or exactly where those repercussions would occur.

As an early test case for the proper function of the Security Council, some in the State Department deemed firm U.S. action essential to address the Indonesian dispute. From New York, Warren Austin agreed that it was incumbent on the United States to uphold the provisions of the UN Charter and the will of the Council in its policy toward the Indonesian crisis. Any impulse to shirk that responsibility could validate, against King Farouk's admonitions, that the United States valued its allegiance to the Netherlands above the very principles of the United Nations Organization and set an unhelpful precedent that other states could follow in the pivotal early years of UN function. This signaled a looming danger that the Charter's provisions could forever be relegated to the partisan passions of the very political conflicts that the United Nations had been created to resolve, and that the leadership role of the United States, which relied on its moral authority within the United Nations, would likewise be degraded considerably.[64]

At around the same time that talk arose of the Indian government's disposition to raise the Indonesian matter before the Security Council, the British government floated the prospect of a joint Anglo-American appeal to both sides to resolve the dispute peacefully. U.S. Secretary of State George Marshall immediately recognized the offer's value, as it could preemptively avert lengthy Security Council proceedings on the Indonesian question—proceedings that might stray in directions that ran afoul of American interests in Southeast Asia. The proceedings commenced on 31 July and produced a cease-fire agreement by 1 August, but the agreement did little to curb the ongoing violence. As a result, on 25 August the Council set up a Good Offices Committee consisting of the diplomatic consuls of the Security Council member states in Indonesia, per the suggestion of a Belgian proposal to employ the United Nations machinery for settling disputes. The following day the United Nations reissued its call for a cease-fire.[65]

Within five months of its inception the Committee's diligent efforts had brokered the Renville Agreement, to which both parties consented on 17 January 1948; it was a victory of multilateral diplomacy both welcome and critical. Not only did the British Foreign Office see little else it could do, vested as it was in conflicts like Kashmir and the Greek Civil War, but Lovett himself had admitted that the United States was likewise "'spread very thin' over the face of the globe and that it was therefore wise and prudent in them to reflect very carefully before entering hastily into any new commitments."[66] But even as early as February the U.S. consul in Batavia had expressed his suspicion that, despite the warmer reception the Renville Agreement seemed to have garnered as compared to its predecessor, the Cheribon Agreement, the actual truce that existed on the ground was worryingly unsound. Those premonitions would be proven correct by the subsequent deterioration of talks between the republic and the government of the Netherlands. As a hastily drafted agreement designed to ward off another Dutch "police action" in Indonesia and maintain the fragile peace that remained, the Renville Agreement codified a vague and fragile truce whose precise terms were never clear. The republic acceded to the terms of the new accord, including stipulations that it withdraw guerrilla forces from territory occupied by the Netherlands. It met some of those pledges by withdrawing some 35,000 guerrilla fighters back from behind Dutch lines by the end of February. But compliance with the Renville terms was hardly as strict on the Dutch side, which employed stalling tactics to mire the negotiations while it created new Indonesian states subservient to its own interests in East Sumatra, Madura, and West Java.[67]

Partly as a result of the Dutch intransigence, the parties failed to reach a final settlement, despite the work of the Committee to reopen talks between the two sides by early March. On 16 June the Netherlands broke off negotiations with Indonesia. The Dutch decision was likely motivated by the leak to the international press of a joint Australian-American plan to recognize Indonesia. In return for Australian recognition at the United Nations, it was reported, the republic would designate Australia as its representative on the Good Offices Committee.

A complex course of events ensued in the summer and fall of 1948 that further impaired Dutch-Indonesian relations, and a communist insurgency erupted in Madiun on Java. The subsequent suppression of the communists by the new republican government doubtless helped to endear the nationalist cause to U.S. policymakers.[68]

Perhaps partly as the result of intensified U.S.-Soviet tensions by mid-1948 (not least due to the standoff between Soviet occupation forces in East Germany and the Western allies in Berlin, which had reached crisis proportions after the Soviets blockaded the city in June), officials in Washington became all the more inclined to recognize the inevitability of Indonesian independence. Fearing Soviet infiltration of the republican government, the State Department recognized the need to take a more active role in courting the Indonesian nationalists. Confident that the United States could win over moderate, pro-Western elements within the nationalist movement, the U.S. consul general in Batavia called for firm American support to suppress the communist infiltration of Indonesia. That newfound enthusiasm to embrace the republicans was now also influenced by the Soviet recognition of the republican government, which in the eyes of U.S. strategists represented the early signs of a Soviet effort to absorb newly independent Indonesia into the international communist bloc. These fears helped trigger a U.S. response to fill what it saw as a dangerous new vacuum instead of dragging its heels any longer on the recognition of the republic. The apparent bad faith on the part of the Dutch colonial authorities and the validation of the noncommunist nature of the nationalist government merely provided the final two assurances before the U.S. abandonment of its erstwhile policy of reliance on Dutch-nationalist negotiations toward a settlement. The Dutch relinquishment of the East Indies was now inevitable, in the eyes of American diplomats, and a "hump" that the Netherlands needed to "speedily get over."[69]

The September 1948 Madiun incident marked the critical turning point after which U.S. policy unflinchingly sided with the republic. The American position on the Indonesian question had now reversed course fully since the Potsdam Conference. Washington's policy toward the East Indies had assumed a fairly passive posture since the summer of 1945, primarily because of the assumption that British and Chinese forces would maintain order throughout the region in the aftermath of the war. It had also relied on the putative efficacy of Dutch colonial administration to manage problems with which the United States did not wish to concern itself as the war in the Pacific drew down. But after Madiun, the failure of Dutch policy and the specter of communist penetration of the archipelago spurred the Truman administration to reassess its strategy in Southeast Asia. The costs of allowing the Dutch to carry out their paramilitary operations against the republic now outweighed the benefits of granting a free hand to a European ally to reimpose its repressive authority in its colonial dominions in the East. Now, through the act of recognition of the republic, U.S. planners hoped that in one fell swoop they could both safeguard the rights to import Indonesia's resources and secure a newly independent outpost against Soviet communist influence in Southeast Asia.

As was the case in Syria and Lebanon, the United States wanted to ensure that institutional structures and processes were in place before the formal conferral of recognition. The fall of 1948 saw the United States table the Cochran Plan for Indonesian elections and the establishment of an interim government that would eventually give way to the constitution of a United States of Indonesia. But the Dutch government rejected the proposals, effectively sealing the fate of the Good Offices Committee's negotiations. When even direct talks between the republican prime minister, Mohammad Hatta, and the Dutch foreign minister failed in December, hopes of implementing the Renville Agreement all but collapsed. There was little that could be done, it seemed, aside from pursuing sanctions against the Netherlands at the UN Security Council.[70]

In mid-December the Dutch military launched the second of its "police" actions in Indonesia, arresting the key leaders of the independence movement, including both Sukarno and Hatta. As Dutch troops forcibly occupied towns in Java and Sumatra, the Good Offices Committee condemned the act as a violation of the terms of the truce.[71] This time the United States wholly condemned the Dutch actions, having abandoned its past aversion to reprimanding a European ally and recipient of Marshall Plan aid. The gravity of the security situation in Indonesia had increased sharply since the immediate aftermath of the war, and the harshness of the Dutch reprisals elicited strong international condemnation the world over. The United States thus found itself unable to dissociate from the international support for the cause of Indonesian independence that resulted.

Within the State Department the situation was clear after the events of December 1948. The excesses of the second Dutch military action constituted a brutal crackdown and the exercise of incredibly poor judgment in the eyes of U.S. diplomats, who accordingly considered it indefensible.

Nevertheless the United States could still not seek sanctions against the Netherlands unilaterally unless the remaining UN Security Council members were willing to act, which they decidedly were not. Indeed the cold war entailed a careful balancing act in the American pursuit of its new East Indies policy. For American globalism now meant securing a stable foothold in the East Indies without fully alienating Western powers whose alliances would be essential in the looming geopolitical and ideological confrontation with the Soviet Union. Some historians have argued that the resulting UN response to the second Dutch military operation in Indonesia was consonant with U.S. interests, because the subsequent Security Council resolutions of 24 and 28 December 1948 enabled Washington to formally condemn the Dutch action while refraining from the imposition of sanctions against the Netherlands that might split the solidarity of the Western European alliance. The resolutions also happened to put the United States on the side of the Muslim countries showing solidarity with the Indonesian nationalist struggle at that moment.[72] The approach revealed a concern with wider factors beyond just South or Southeast Asia that factored into American calculations requisite for the navigation of that middle course—factors that reflected the precepts of globalism and diffuse, inchoate American geographic perceptions of new and decidedly global interests to promote self-determination in a postcolonial world threatened by the looming specter of Soviet communism.

ANGLO-AMERICAN OPPOSITION TO FRENCH AND DUTCH COLONIAL RULE

As British troops left Indonesia, Dutch colonial authorities did not have to contemplate a hasty retreat akin to the forced French evacuation of the Levant. But the events of autumn 1946 showed that the Netherlands were caught in the same vortex of international forces that had mandated a French reassessment of colonial policy in the Near East the previous summer. Both continental European powers found themselves horribly overstretched, locked in struggles to reassert control over colonial territories liberated by Allied forces in a changed international environment. In both Syria and Lebanon and the East Indies, British reoccupation had stoked nationalist sentiments during a window of vulnerability that hastened the end of colonial rule. Leaders of national movements in Syria, Lebanon, and the East Indies all appealed to the Allied commitments in the Atlantic Charter and its promise of self-determination for colonial peoples to generate momentum for their independence efforts. France and the Netherlands were caught in the tight space between an American globalism that applied varying degrees of pressure on the grip of their colonial authorities and a British regionalism that shaped the realities in their colonial possessions very directly, including through military presences on the ground. Their shared plight revealed the transformative significance of the war for the future of the colonial world and the undeniable force of a new wave of decolonization sweeping both the Near and the Far East.

In the cases of both Atlantic powers, there were perceptible shifts in policy that led them to the difficult positions they finally adopted. The sudden surrender of Japanese forces in Indonesia had left British forces ill-prepared to deal with civil affairs across the islands. Lord Pethick-Lawrence and his counterpart at the Foreign Office were initially preoccupied with these challenges and the effects of Britain's East Indies policy on Anglo-Dutch relations before the security ramifications of Indian troops on the archipelago trumped all other considerations. Even then the decision was a tortuous one, especially given the widespread evidence that anticolonial nationalists were seeking to strengthen their cause by forging international ties with their brethren abroad. That evidence was widespread in statements at the United Nations, events like Jinnah's "Palestine Day," and reports of Indian diplomatic entreaties to Asian governments shortly after independence. Opposing French and Dutch colonial rule inevitably meant strengthening these causes and the ominous prospect of unforeseen future challenges to British imperial policy.[73]

Similarly, early U.S. policy toward Indonesia at the close of the war entailed some repudiation of Atlantic Charter anticolonialism before the Madiun incident forced the Truman administration's hand.[74] By the time Liaquat Ali Khan came to visit Washington as Pakistan's prime minister, the State Department had concluded that "he will probably need no argument to convince him that the United States is not imperialistic and is not colonial-minded. The strong stand we took in favor of independence for Indonesia made its impression in Pakistan."[75]

It was not as if the balances were easily struck from the standpoint of either country's foreign policy. As a CIA report in January 1949 later made clear, the problem of accommodating the nationalist sentiments of anticolonial struggles would likely continue to challenge U.S. policymakers. But the decisions taken in Washington and London, however difficult, had the undeniable effect of acting as external corrosives on the residue of French and Dutch colonial authority. Seemingly overtaken by the forces of nationalism and allies unwilling to back them unconditionally, France and Holland suddenly confronted the geography of a new postwar landscape for the European colonial powers, one where rapidly expanding American military power, ideas, and trade were fast displacing imperial outposts that they, unlike their British counterparts, refused to abandon willingly until confronted by crises of acute overstretch.[76]

FIGURES

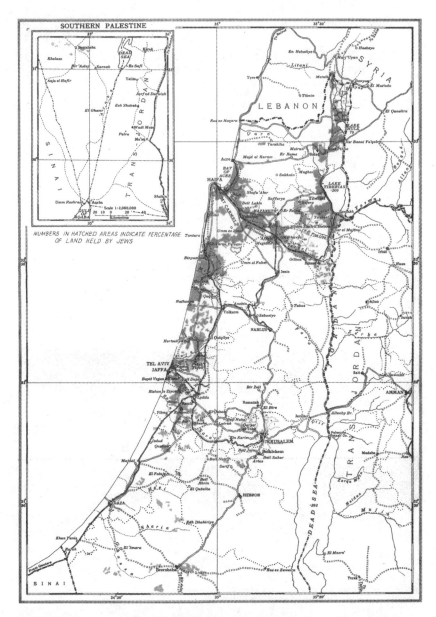

FIGURE 1. A map of Jewish landholdings in Palestine shows the areas in which settlers had acquired territory as of 1937. The map was based on data gathered by the government of Palestine for the massive *A Survey of Palestine* produced in 1945–1946. MS 58, Papers of Isaiah Bowman, Special Collections, Sheridan Libraries, Johns Hopkins University.

FIGURE 2. The Information Branch of the U.S. Army produced maps on specific subjects, such as the flow of oil in the Middle East, to help planners contend with postwar challenges. This map, centered on northwestern Iran and Iraq, includes much of the Eastern Mediterranean region, including Crete and Greece. Library of Congress.

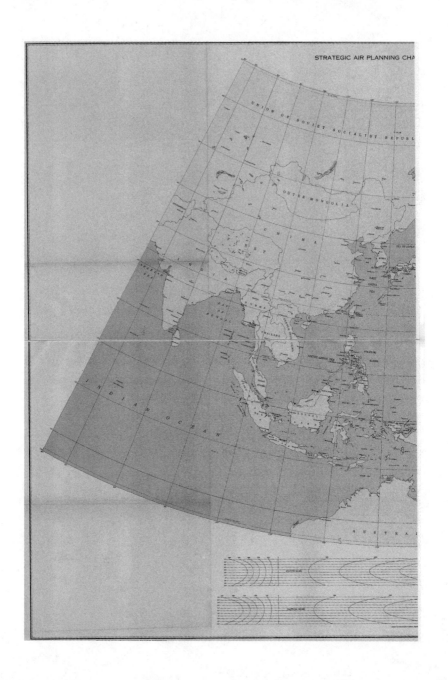

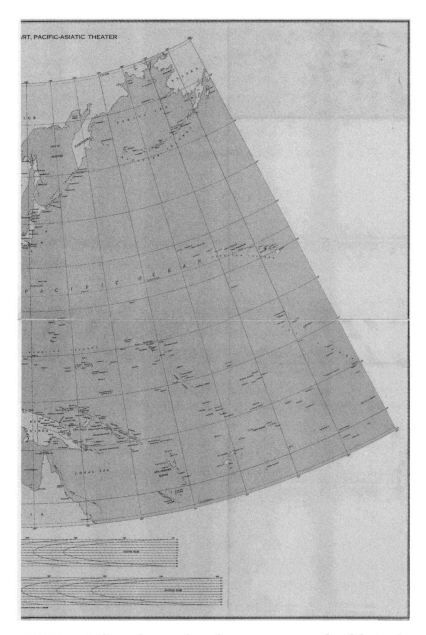

FIGURE 3. Military planning charts for air operations produced during the war after the attack on Pearl Harbor revealed the global scope of intended U.S. power projection in the postwar period. Library of Congress.

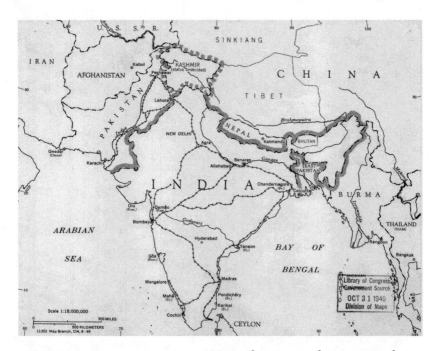

FIGURE 4. U.S. government perceptions of wartime and postwar South Asia were significantly impacted by the intelligence community, which also produced maps on the Indian subcontinent, such as this CIA map. Library of Congress.

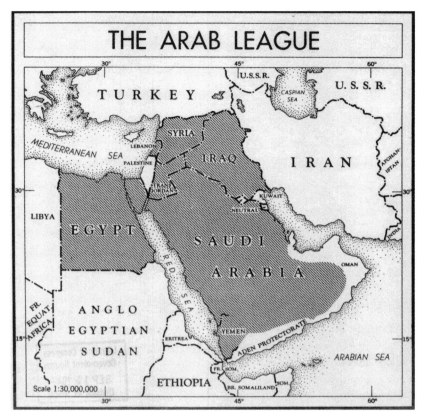

FIGURE 5. The U.S. Department of State's Map Division produced regional maps of the postwar world like this map, depicting members of the Arab League. Library of Congress.

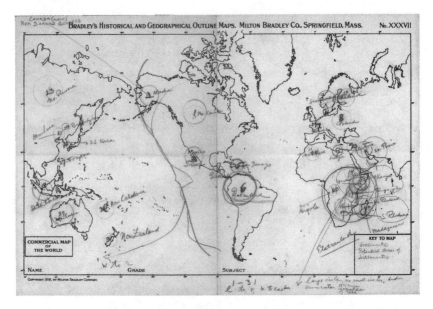

FIGURE 6. The "M Project" explored options for European refugee resettlement throughout the world after the war. The U.S. State Department's Near East Division opposed plans to relocate European Jews to Palestine, which were tabled by the Territorial Subcommittee of the Advisory Committee for Postwar Foreign Policy. MS 58, Papers of Isaiah Bowman, Special Collections, Sheridan Libraries, Johns Hopkins University.

SIX

Two Visions of the Postwar World

Joint British and American diplomatic initiatives on Palestine and Kashmir in the late 1940s belied two fundamentally distinct lenses of analysis focused on the Middle East and Southwest Asia that underlay the respective policy-strategy processes in Washington and London. It was a distinction evident in the Anglo-American diplomacy that helped dislodge the French from the Levant and hastened the end of Dutch rule in the Netherlands East Indies. The American vision for a global national security policy predicated on a global military basing presence, the United Nations Security Council, and civil aviation routes contrasted with the more regionally delimited British view of the postwar world that largely saw the Muslim states of the Near East and South Asia as a single territorial unit and through which the Foreign Office came to view the process of imperial retreat. But these distinct perceptions of the world, and their underlying assumptions, developed from very different national and international circumstances in London and Washington.

FROM MAPS TO WORLDVIEWS

Geographers and political scientists have shown how imagined mental maps, or cognitive representations of physical geography, can frame how individuals conceive of spatial distance and landscapes.[1] These mental maps can be central to the thinking of foreign policymakers entrusted with responsibility for issues or countries confined to a particular region.[2] Once stored in the memories of government officials, these virtual maps may share enough common-denominator perceptions about a region and its peoples—despite obvious variations arising from individual blind spots, prejudices, and other differences in each individual's conceptualization—to amount to a collective body of knowledge. In Weberian terms, it may be argued that these mental maps constitute forms of "tacit knowledge" or metaknowledge: implied knowledge stemming from basic assumptions that frame ideas, policies, and how policymakers conceptualize a region, as opposed to more explicit, substantive "distal knowledge" about a region's particular landscape, natural resource endowments, or historical past.[3]

If aggregated individual knowledge—collective tacit knowledge, so to speak—can reside within organizations like government bureaucracies as knowledge capital, then so may mental maps, as a kind of geographical tacit knowledge, exist in the same form.[4] But that knowledge capital, though it can be difficult to transmit (especially such tacit forms of knowledge as ways of seeing the world), would also be reflected in the massive volume of documentary output produced by government agencies. Government maps for use by civilian and military officials drawn within certain specific boundaries and from specific vantage points, and using certain techniques (e.g., Mercator projection), are one example of this output. (For examples of U.S. Army Information Branch, State Department, and CIA maps from the postwar period, see figures 2–5.) Another consists of policy documents that include certain geographical areas and exclude others, often employing specific expressions and terminology. Both types of documentary records allow for the storage and transmission of the key assumptions and worldviews in mental maps between individuals and across time periods by projecting mental maps onto printed, documentary form and subsequently imprinting the minds of officials rotating in to handle new portfolios. In this way the reproduction and dissemination of mental maps—or at least visual cues that trigger certain elements of mental maps—can allow aggregated conceptions of territory based on large amounts of documentary records and spread across a number of individuals to accumulate as a form of organizational knowledge in a group of military chiefs of staff, the U.S. State Department, or the British Foreign Office. Bureaucratic politics models of foreign policymaking have shown how such embedded knowledge capital, once codified in the form of organizational beliefs, assumptions, and logics, can shape foreign policies.[5] That being the case, even diffuse and distinct conceptions of geography spread between individuals and across organizations, if they share at least some assumptions and commonalties, can and should impinge on the assumptions and worldviews of civilian and military officials.

If key segments of the American and British foreign policymaking establishments adhered to certain conceptions of territory at the end of the Second World War, and if these respective conceptions differed in significant ways, these differences may provide clues as to the underlying ideas and beliefs that shaped the course of national foreign policies. Examining the diffuse origins of American globalism and British regionalism provides insights into how they affected Anglo-American policies during the height of postwar decolonization.

THE WARTIME ORIGINS OF AMERICAN GLOBALISM

U.S. officials and leading intellectuals had begun to contemplate the structure of the postwar world as early as the 1939 launch of the secretive Council on Foreign Relations War and Peace Studies (WPS) project, an effort by leading foreign policy intellectuals on the Council comprising four research groups to separately study the questions of security and armaments and political, economic and financial, and territorial matters pertaining to the war. Over the next two years, with funding from the Rockefeller Foundation, the project produced a multitude of studies and reports on postwar scenarios and U.S. policy options to address them. In so doing, the WPS project served the mutual interests of both an overworked State Department reacting continually to breaking news from the front lines and the pressures of wartime negotiations as well as prominent Council luminaries—titans of industry, lawyers, academics, and other professionals—who had long dreamed of extending that organization's reach directly into the State Department's policy-formulation processes.[6]

In October 1941 Undersecretary of State Sumner Welles asked President Roosevelt to convene secret committees to begin work on all aspects of postwar planning, including deliberations on the design of a truly global postwar international organization that the cunning and managerially efficient Welles himself hoped to lead, undermining the influence of his nemesis, Secretary of State Cordell Hull. Roosevelt consented to the proposal some months later, after the Japanese attack on Pearl Harbor.[7] Soon thereafter the Department began planning efforts in earnest on the broad outlines of a postwar security organization primarily under Welles's aegis. The January 1942 "Declaration by the United Nations," including the United States, Great Britain, the Soviet Union, China, and twenty-two other states, stating that they would not seek a separate peace agreement with the Axis powers, encouraged U.S. hopes for the construction of a formal institutional architecture with which to anchor the postwar order.[8] In Washington the start of the war had led in February to the establishment within the State Department of an Advisory Committee on Postwar Foreign Policy chaired by Secretary Hull and including other Department officials, members of the Council on Foreign Relations, journalists, and other professionals, many of whom had worked directly on the WPS project. Critically, owing to Welles's concern that the new organization not go the way of the defunct League of Nations, he included on the Committee Senators Tom Connally, a Democrat from Texas, and Warren Austin, a Republican from Vermont, member of the Senate Foreign Relations Committee, and later the U.S. ambassador to the United Nations during many of the early test cases for UN enforcement action.

Soon thereafter Hull subsumed the work of the WPS project into the Department's bureaucracy as part of the Advisory Committee, helping the Council realize its dreams of direct influence on policy discussions in Foggy Bottom.[9] Four appointed research secretaries from each of the WPS study groups were now tasked to report to four corresponding Advisory Committee subcommittees meeting on a weekly basis to examine the same issues. Hull and Welles had thus not only created a strategic planning structure within the Department that could examine broad, long-range policy concerns; they had also taken full advantage of the voluminous research of the WPS by incorporating its knowledge into the Department as precious organizational capital. It now constituted a substantial foundation of knowledge on which to base administration thinking on postwar issues and in which to ground the massive planning effort that would be required to formulate positions on key questions that would have to be addressed.

From the outset the work of the Committee was global in scope, reflective of the geographical range American foreign policy interests would have to span. The Committee's discussions led first to a plan espoused by Welles for an interim United Nations Authority—featuring an executive council on which the Big Four would be members, presiding over regional councils with considerable autonomy to discuss specific issues within the geographic scope of their respective mandates. The regional council system was meant to allow for a subordinate dispute-settlement mechanism to deal with localized conflicts within specific regions (or specific great power spheres of influence). The regional councils, the Advisory Committee's early thinking held, would be able to appeal to the executive council if their own efforts failed to produce satisfactory settlements or if disputes arose that spanned separate regions, rendering the decentralized subunits of the system answerable to an integrated superstructure worldwide in its scope. The plan represented one of the earliest concrete U.S. government blueprints for postwar international organization on a global scale.

Hull firmly opposed the Authority as an interim organizational design, citing among his qualms uncertainties about the employment of U.S. military forces in the organization, as well as the representation of various regions whose disparate international agendas spanned little common ground necessary for coordination. Roosevelt likewise was cool on the proposal, deeming it too premature to formalize interwar arrangements into an institutional structure.[10] In the face of Hull's and Roosevelt's discomfiture with the idea, Welles's earliest vision of a two-tiered international organization balancing regional interests but with a global reach thus failed to become a blueprint for the eventual postwar United Nations system. In the spring of 1942 Hull dissolved the full Advisory Committee, leaving the work of the subcommittees to progress independently. Thus the planning efforts continued, with Welles heading up the newly created Subcommittee on International Organization (IO) that assumed a central position in the design effort for the UN system and as a focal point of planning for the postwar peace. Meanwhile the body's Subcommittee on Security evolved closer ties to the military than it had ever enjoyed, especially after the sobering experience of Allied military conferences like the Anglo-American encounter in Casablanca in 1943, where the degree of unity and cooperation on the British side surprised and undercut the negotiating positions of U.S. planners.[11]

Chairman of the Joint Chiefs of Staff William Leahy harbored serious concerns about JCS involvement in postwar political questions. While valid, those concerns were soon allayed by the determination of his subordinates to achieve the requisite levels of civil-military coordination to synchronize U.S. defense needs with international security prerogatives and integrate defense planning with diplomacy. They began working in lock step with the State Department subcommittee on security, whose meetings JCS representatives began to attend. Roosevelt, a former assistant secretary of the navy who was keenly aware of the need for coordinated civilian and military planning for the postwar period, evolved a close and trusting relationship with the Joint Chiefs, at the expense of Hull and what the president perceived to be a feckless State Department both overwhelmed with and sidelined by the frenetic pressures of war planning. Though famously suspicious of overcommitment to fixed strategies that limited options, Roosevelt tasked the military to examine key strategic concerns that would loom as America planned for the end of major hostilities. Specifically he instructed the JCS to examine air basing requirements for the international police force that might be maintained by the eventual successor to the United Nations Authority. This directive triggered furious planning efforts by the JCS and the navy predicated on the assumption that the United States needed to establish a network of overseas bases encircling the globe whose usage could be assured in case of the recurrence of global war and that might later be entrusted to the authority of the proposed international police force. These efforts soon unearthed the full extent of the political-military coordination that would be necessary in the postwar period.[12]

In January 1943, after his public statement on the war effort commemorating the one-year anniversary of the United Nations Declaration by the Allies, Roosevelt addressed Congress and publicly articulated his vision of a role for those same United Nations who "can and must remain united for the maintenance of peace by preventing any attempt to rearm in Germany, in Japan, in Italy, or in any other nation which seeks to violate the Tenth Commandment, 'Thou shall not covet.'"[13] That continuing unity could be preserved only through a formal multilateral structure. At Roosevelt's request, Welles's IO subcommittee produced a new draft constitution for a world organization in March. The structure laid out in the document somewhat corresponded with the regional system Welles had sketched out before, with an eleven-member executive council with the Big Four and regional representatives (two each from Europe and Latin America, and one each from the Middle East, the Far East, and the British dominions).[14] With the president's endorsement of the need for a formal mechanism for Allied postwar coordination, Welles's original ideas began to gain traction.

Roosevelt presented a version of the same plan to visiting British foreign secretary Anthony Eden the following day, endorsing its basic regionalist design—but the president now added a twist. While the final draft charter adopted aspects of the regional councils concept, an idea that Churchill had hitherto steadfastly supported, it now reflected Roosevelt's desire to render the organization's substructure fully accountable to a central administrative council representing the Big Four. But the president also contended that Churchill's suggestion of a system of regional councils acting independently was unacceptable, a point that Eden himself had conceded, reflecting Foreign Office views that were out of touch with Churchill's exaggerated estimates of Britain's influence in the postwar international system.[15] The global executive body atop the structure would have to oversee *all* of the organization's constituent elements, Roosevelt insisted.

Roosevelt's own thinking would mature significantly that critical year, shifting away from the approach favored by Welles and reflected in the plan briefed to Eden, which aligned closely with British aspirations for a connected system of regional peace councils (in which British imperial possessions could assert considerable political weight). As his proposed changes to the IO subcommittee's draft charter suggested, Roosevelt's vision turned now toward the decidedly more globalist blueprint that Hull had favored throughout—with an executive council run by the Big Four that would have to answer neither to the community of nations at large nor to great powers' regional interests when it came to decisions on peace and security. The realization of that vision would ultimately progress until a Security Council bereft of regional subdivisions emerged intact as the sole guarantor of peace and security in the new world order.

Soon after the Anglo-American discussions of March 1943, Roosevelt abandoned the idea of regional councils outright. On the one hand, this change in American strategic thought paved the way for the creation of a neo-Wilsonian United Nations Organization global in its scope, in the face of British and Soviet appeals for an interlocking security architecture that perpetuated regional power balances rooted in the principles of quintessential nineteenth-century Realpolitik into the postwar era. But questions remained: What would be the role of the great powers in that new architecture, and how far would the shift tilt away from regional hegemonies and toward a universal great power concert to preserve peace and security? The final balance of those pressures, once they had resolved themselves, would determine not only whether power politics or liberal internationalism would more profoundly shape the postwar organization but the extent to which the geographic assumptions in America's turn toward globalism would be reflected in its final design.

Later in 1943 the State Department framed its preliminary thoughts on a wartime declaration by the four major allies (the United States, Britain, Russia, and China), committing, inter alia, to the creation of an international organization to preserve the postwar peace. The development heralded the first formal agreement by the world's four major military powers on the need for a permanent institutionalized structure for postwar peace and security, irrespective of its specific details. Understandably, much of the preparatory work leading to these conceptual developments came not from the work of the IO subcommittee but from a tighter, more secretive group consisting of Hull and his advisors, convened in January 1943, known as the Informal Agenda Group. Created partly to subvert the sprawl of the Advisory Committee's increasingly unwieldy bureaucratic expansion, the Informal Agenda Group cemented State Department policy in Hull's conservative globalism and served as a counterweight to the more regionally dispersed designs of the likes of Welles. Comprising Welles, Leo Pasvolsky, Isaiah Bowman, and Council on Foreign Relations president Norman Davis, among others, it was to become the single postwar planning body that stamped its imprimatur on the new UN organization more prominently than any other.[16]

One of the Group's early achievements was the "Tentative Draft of a Joint Four-Power Declaration," produced for Roosevelt in August before his departure for the first Quebec Conference with Churchill. Article 4 of the draft declaration established that the governments of the United States, Great Britain, the Soviet Union, and China "recognize the necessity of establishing at the earliest practicable date a general international organization, based on the principle of sovereign equality of all nations, and open to membership by all nations, large and small, for the maintenance of international peace and security." Article 5 went on to state, "For the purpose of maintaining international peace and security pending the reestablishment of law and order and the inauguration of a general system of security, they will consult and act jointly in behalf of the community of nations."[17] The State Department had shared a version of the declaration with Eden at Quebec, and subsequently cabled a variant of the text to Moscow on 18 September. The British and Soviet reactions to the draft declaration were both lukewarm and mixed. The Foreign Office, mindful of the reaction in the British dominions that a public declaration might arouse, raised concerns that Article 4's reference to "sovereign equality" might embolden smaller powers to become needlessly assertive on issues pertaining to the maintenance of international peace and security. "We should like to temper the doctrine of sovereign equality to the extent of adding the words 'in which all peace-loving nations, great and small, may play their part,'" London argued in its response. It likewise suggested that the Article 5 stipulation that the four powers would "consult and act jointly in behalf of the community of nations" seemed, as the Foreign Office bluntly put it, to be "inaugurating a sort of four-power dictatorship." The compromise language that the Foreign Office proposed instead was "consult one another and as occasion requires with other members of the United Nations, with a view to joint action on behalf of the community of nations."[18] The Soviets' response was more tepid, suggesting that discussions of a Four Power declaration were premature; they urged the United States to consider instead measures to shorten the war in Europe by opening a second front led by an Anglo-American invasion of Western Europe.[19]

The British response met with steadfast opposition from Roosevelt. As the chief of the State Department's Division of European Affairs noted, Secretary Hull had apparently consulted Roosevelt on London's suggestions for revising the draft text, which the president felt "smacked too much [of] 'spheres of influence' policies, the very thing which it was supposedly designed to prevent."[20] Now undeterred in his determination to construct a global organization charged with responsibility for postwar peace, Roosevelt reacted skeptically to Stalin's designs on Soviet occupation of Poland, the Baltics, and the Southeast European states lining Russia's southern frontiers, as well as unambiguous British aspirations to prolong the crumbling empire in the Near East and Asia. By outlining the contours of a global vision for the new organization in his instructions to Hull to revise the draft constitution, Roosevelt had delineated the limits on the accretion of regional power that the United States would tolerate in the new postwar organization. After Welles's departure, the U.S. consensus on that approach consolidated further, teeing up a showdown with the remaining allies that would culminate in the compromises at San Francisco. Still, the governments of the United States, Britain, Russia, and China issued a Joint Four-Nation Declaration at the October 1943 foreign ministers conference in Moscow. The contentious Article 5 of the final declaration, incorporating some of the suggested British language hoping to prevent exclusive Big Four authority over all matters concerning peace and security, now read that the allies would "consult with one another and as occasion requires with other members of the United Nations, with a view to joint action on behalf of the community of nations."[21]

Roosevelt's thinking had fundamentally altered the course of Allied postwar planning in the prelude to the Tehran Conference, edging away from his original institutional concept of a power-sharing compact between the great powers policing their respective spheres of influence, akin to the U.S. role in the Western Hemisphere outlined in the Monroe Doctrine, and gradually embracing the idea of a more universalistic executive body of Four Policemen assuming responsibility for a legitimately global postwar peace. Such was the pull of globalism. Still, Soviet Foreign Minister Vyacheslav Molotov had won an important concession from Hull at Moscow, with regard to limiting the requirements for great power consultations prior to exercising the right to use military force. While Hull had sought such a degree of coordination in the Four Power Declaration from the outset, Molotov insisted that such a requirement could impinge on existing diplomatic commitments that the Four Powers owed other states. A turning point had been reached in the sense that Soviet and British opposition, while unable to mold Roosevelt's template for a postwar international organization into the structure of the regional councils those governments (and certainly both Stalin and Churchill, whatever the Foreign Office's qualms) had sought, had nonetheless altered the character of the Four Power alliance that would form the inner core of its executive body. For the freedom of maneuver that Molotov secured in the form of the "consult with one another" language, preserving a Soviet right to act in Eastern Europe without Four Power consensus, would remain a principal element of the Allied compact through the end of the war and up until the Security Council finally materialized in San Francisco.[22]

On 29 November, in his second day of meetings with Stalin at the Tehran Conference, Roosevelt outlined his plans for a postwar international organization. At the time, Stalin was consumed with the war effort in Europe and the distribution of the military burden among the Allies. Unveiling the cornerstone of his vision of postwar American globalism—a permanent international organization uniting the Allied powers—Roosevelt opened discussion of the subject by noting that the Allies had yet to concretely address the issue of postwar international organization for the preservation of peace. He went on to highlight the basic contours of his ambitious plan. At its core would be "a large organization composed of some 35 members of the United Nations." This body would in turn make recommendations to a smaller "executive committee" consisting of the United States, the Soviet Union, the United Kingdom, China, and six other states (two from Europe, one each from South America, the Near East, and the Far East, and one British dominion) that would deal with "all nonmilitary questions such as agriculture, food, health and economic questions." Atop the three-tiered structure would sit "the Four Policemen," who Roosevelt identified as the United States, the Soviet Union, Great Britain, and China. "This organization would have the power to deal immediately with any threat to the peace and any sudden emergency which requires action." Here, in outline form, was the principal multilateral architecture of globalism laid bare. Its streamlined, centralized character was unmistakable. Gone were the regional councils that continually reappeared in Welles's draft proposals and in Churchill's appeals. Roosevelt's "Great Design" rested instead on a much more tangible, material foundation: the amassed military capabilities of the four most powerful Allied nations.[23]

Stalin met the proposal with initial skepticism and betrayed his doubts as to whether any international organization could check the kinds of aggression of which fascist Germany and Japan were culpable. He was cool toward the idea of Chinese participation. And like Churchill, Stalin expressed a preference for a regional committee structure. Dismissive of the idealistic liberalism behind the new United Nations Organization as framed by Roosevelt, Stalin suggested instead a collection of Allied military bases that could serve as strategic points of pressure with which to contain German and Japanese expansionism, echoing the exploration of basing needs that Roosevelt had of course already tasked the JCS to examine. But by the last day of the conference, whatever his qualms, Stalin nonetheless signed off (in a private session with Roosevelt) on at least the idea of a global international organization with possible Chinese participation cemented by a Four Power concert to keep the peace. Stalin also insisted that French colonial possessions be dismembered from the grip of the "rotten" French regime. Roosevelt agreed that Indochina and other areas of strategic geopolitical importance ought to be wrested from French control. But unlike Stalin, he also envisioned at least temporary administration of these territories by the United Nations, with a view toward the fulfillment of the self-determination rights of their subject populations.[24] These proposals would be considered further within the State Department over the subsequent year, although consensus on the most divisive issues eluded the parties as they prepared for a ministerial meeting on the structure of the United Nations Organization that the United States offered to host.

The 1944 Dumbarton Oaks Conference, in a leafy, secluded estate in the heart of Washington, D.C., lasted over a scorching summer month of tortuous negotiations and notorious press leaks.[25] But the conference soon ran aground on the issue of great power consensus in the new postwar international organization, failing to either produce agreement on the voting procedures for that body's executive "Security Council" or help answer the question of precisely how the veto function wielded by the Big Four would work. The Soviet Union's delegate, Andrei Gromyko, fearing that future Soviet representatives at the Security Council would face encirclement by a coterie of liberal democratic counterparts in deliberations on key strategic and security issues, maintained steadfastly that all Council decisions had to be subject to an absolute veto by other members of the Big Four, essentially demanding a constraint on freedom of speech in the Council among its principal members.

The United States was not as certain about its position after the months between Tehran and Dumbarton Oaks had failed to smooth out differences of opinion within the administration. To some extent the July 1944 preparatory document entitled "United States Tentative Proposals for a General International Organization" clearly reflected the convergence of Anglo-American perspectives on how the Security Council veto would function on matters of peace and security. But American representatives were themselves split on the problematic issue of the voting rights of permanent Council members who were parties to a dispute that other members of the Council wished to raise before that body. When the same debate had unfolded in the months preceding the conference, various U.S. draft position papers reflected that lack of consensus in failing to adopt a particular stance on the issue. The British delegation meanwhile professed its support for taking a position midway between the Soviet and U.S. stances, that of a nonabsolute veto system in accordance with which members of the Big Four party to a dispute that arose before the Council would recuse themselves from voting on matters pertaining to that dispute. After considerable infighting within the administration and State Department on the issue, the United States announced to the joint steering committee of U.S., British, and Soviet representatives on 28 August its accession to the British view and, essentially, its support of a principle of equality of the great powers. But Gromyko adamantly refused to consent to that interpretation, and on 18 September he notified Stettinius that the Russian stance "would never be departed from." Moreover he suddenly insisted that all sixteen Soviet republics be admitted to the General Assembly as individual members, stunning the other members of the joint committee. The voting issue was thus left for resolution at a later date, while remaining elements of the new organization continued to materialize.[26]

What did emerge from the drawn-out discussions was a set of proposals constituting a basic outline of the world organization that would convene in San Francisco the following year. It consisted of a main assembly of all member nations, an eleven-member executive Security Council with five permanent members, an Economic and Social Council, and an International Court of Justice. Member nations would enter into special agreements with the body to contribute armed force contingents to a standby UN force commanded by a Military Staff Committee comprising officers from the permanent Security Council member nations. The unanswered question of how voting procedures in the Council would shape up remained enigmatically missing.[27]

Eventually, in December 1944, the United States proposed a compromise between the Anglo-American and Soviet views to address the question of the Council veto. The proposal became the basis for discussion of voting procedures at the February 1945 Yalta Conference, the first of two summit meetings on postwar questions such as the partition of Germany and the future of Poland. The terms of the agreement entailed a considerable retreat from the prior Soviet insistence on absolute veto rights: while permanent Council members would maintain the right to veto enforcement action in the form of sanctions or military action, the new proposal ensured, they would also forgo the right to prevent the Council from taking up discussions on issues that concerned them. At Yalta the Soviet representatives acceded to this proposal cast in general terms, despite Stalin's initial suspicions about the intent behind it, essentially resolving the dispute over the formal structure of the Council and procedures for the exercise of the veto for the moment, at least until the proceedings at San Francisco the following year. Historian Robert Sherwood characterized the Russian retreat from Gromyko's adamancy at Dumbarton Oaks as "a considerable relaxing of the rigid position" the Soviet Union had hitherto maintained.[28] The Soviet accession cleared the Allied path to San Francisco and resolved the last major obstacle to the inauguration of the new world organization pertaining to the great powers' management of the postwar peace, with Churchill and Stalin having agreed to the admission of two Soviet republics to the General Assembly alongside two additional seats from the Americas. Globalism had won a hard-fought victory leading into the pivotal final year of the war—or so it seemed.

The fall of 1944 saw sweeping changes at the Department of State after Roosevelt's reelection on 7 November. The resignation of Cordell Hull as secretary of state just over three weeks later led Roosevelt to appoint Edward Stettinius, known more for his managerial acumen than his experience with substantive policy, as Hull's successor. Stettinius promptly ushered in a new cohort of senior officials for what was to be Roosevelt's abbreviated final term. The president collapsed and died after a hemorrhage on 12 April 1945 in Warm Springs, Georgia, cutting short his tenure presiding over the consolidation of peace after the most catastrophic global war in human history. His death weighed heavily over the proceedings at the San Francisco Conference.

But the future of the gathering itself was never in doubt. President Truman clarified immediately after he was sworn in that the conference was to continue as planned, that Roosevelt and Hull's vision of a new postwar international organization might be realized, avoiding another failure to engage the United States internationally, as occurred when the Senate failed to ratify the League of Nations charter a quarter century earlier. And so 282 delegates from the charter members of the new organization converged on San Francisco in April 1945.[29] Meanwhile a State Department–led campaign to publicize the proposals for the formal structure and functions of the new international organization laid out the previous summer involving the media, prominent public officials, community leaders, and nongovernmental organizations culminated in a weeklong event called "Dumbarton Oaks Week," in which the hitherto divided American Association for the United Nations and Americans United joined hands to promote the new international body. Myriad national and local organizations, such as the League of Women voters, the YMCA, and church groups, helped distribute pamphlets, generate awareness, and even pray for the conference's successful conclusion. The U.S. delegation took over the regal Fairmont Hotel, whose penthouse suite was reserved for Stettinius and would serve as a nightly gathering place for delegates from the Big Four nations to decide informally on the structure of the Security Council and other substantive issues. The world watched and waited through the long months of negotiations to see whether a new international organization along the lines of the Dumbarton Oaks proposals would finally emerge and just how the great powers conceived that it would contain the recurrence of armed aggression after the defunct League had failed so catastrophically to prevent a new global war.[30]

The conference's formal proceedings were structured by a steering committee, comprising the chairmen of each national delegation, and a fourteen-member executive committee overseeing four commissions and twelve subject-specific committees. But this hierarchy ended up deciding on only procedural and technical issues, while the great powers decided issues of central concern in their informal consultations, often in Stettinius's hotel suite. Soon after the conference began, the first contentious issue manifested itself in the form of a dispute over membership. The Soviet Union pressed for the representation at the conference of its Polish puppet government candidates, the Lublin Poles, and for the admission of Ukraine and Belorussia to the new body. Stettinius and the U.S. delegation opposed the admission of the Polish government without representation by the London-based Polish government-in-exile but acceded to the request to admit the two republics per the compromise fashioned at Yalta under Roosevelt. They also pressed for the admission of Argentina as a counterproposal to admit an additional member from the Americas, underscoring the regionalist tensions that simmered just beneath formal discussions of membership.

But a month and a half into the proceedings, the issue of the Council veto reentered the conference debates in a difference of interpretation on the parts of the Soviet delegation and its U.S. and British counterparts. In what struck the Anglo-American bloc as a sudden reversal of his position at Yalta, Gromyko again held that the Soviet interpretation of the veto extended even to the introduction of issues before the Council for debate, beyond its confinement solely to blocking enforcement action that could otherwise be levied against a permanent member. Stettinius resisted accepting that interpretation, reminding the Soviet representative that the 24 March U.S. interpretive statement from Yalta, agreed upon by Britain and China, and which was issued unopposed by the Soviet Union, limited the veto authority in the Council to enforcement actions and limited it from blocking issues for discussion by the Council. But Gromyko refused to accede to Stettinius's interpretation. The issue dragged on in the proceedings, unresolved, until Stettinius cabled the U.S. Embassy in Moscow and instructed it to seek Stalin's direct personal involvement in the matter.

Stettinius conveyed the message through U.S. Ambassador Averell Harriman to one of Roosevelt's closest advisers, Harry Hopkins, who was already in Moscow to deal with Poland matters, to raise the veto issue with the Soviet leader himself. When confronted by Hopkins, Stalin purported to be unaware of any Soviet-American discord over the issue and dismissed it as insignificant. His decision was relayed back to the American delegation at San Francisco before Gromyko himself had been made aware of the Soviet leader's take on the issue. And with that clarification, the veto issue was finally resolved, enabling the Security Council to assume a final form at last, after years of negotiations among the Allies helped shape its evolution from Roosevelt's inchoate conception of Four Policemen to five permanent members on the Council with a quasi-judicial authority to pass judgment on challenges to international peace.[31]

With Hopkins's clarification of Stalin's view, American globalism crossed a new threshold at San Francisco. Emerging from its origins in U.S. war strategy and the work of the Council on Foreign Relations and the Advisory Committee for Postwar Foreign Policy, that conception of U.S. security interests in the postwar world now came to be enshrined in the institutional structure of the principal postwar international organization through which the great powers would work to solve postwar questions like the disposition of colonial territories and the settlement of interstate disputes. Roosevelt and Truman had succeeded in imprinting a distinctly American vision of the postwar world on the UN Charter.

Importantly that vision came to bear directly on the fate of the postcolonial world. American globalism impacted the situation in Palestine profoundly in the years after the war, as the displaced Jews throughout liberated Europe faced increasingly dire circumstances. The resettlement of European Jews in Palestine seemed completely consistent with the Truman administration's worldview.[32] The linkage between continental Europe and Palestine drawn by American globalism was not arbitrary, as were the proposals to resettle Jews in Africa or Latin America. For in a Braudelian sense, a true geographical proximity *did* underlie the link between Europe and the Middle East in the minds of those who supported the Zionists. Located where the southeastern cusp of Europe met Central Asia, their ancestral homeland of Palestine across the shores of the Mediterranean was the most sensible place for these European refugees to return—as they had begun to do throughout the first half of the century.[33] Indeed the Truman administration had even authorized the U.S. Army to fly Jewish teachers and tons of educational material on military aircraft from Palestine to makeshift camps for displaced European Jews in Germany.[34] Thus a searching desire for truly global postwar settlements only reinforced White House officials' sense of Palestine's *actual* proximity to Europe, thereby linking the plight of displaced European Jews on that continent to the Yishuv through these cognitive connections between liberated Europe and Palestine. The Truman administration's concerns for European Jewry can be attributed in part to the influence of White House officials like David Niles and Clark Clifford, citing the domestic pressures to alleviate the suffering of displaced Jews seeking entry into Palestine and the Jewish vote in the prelude to the 1948 U.S. presidential election. But a balanced historical analysis of the administration's Palestine policy must also acknowledge that the postwar globalism of the U.S. national security establishment as a whole had drawn an implicit geographical connection between the displaced European Jews and the situation in Palestine in the aftermath of a war spread across three continents. Addressing the plight of European displaced persons with assistance from relief services fit squarely within the bounds of that global vision. So did the relocation of displaced persons across the war's various theaters—a realization that had set in even at the State Department, it is worth noting, and well before the end of the Roosevelt administration. As Welles's Advisory Committee for Foreign Policy's subcommittee on Political Problems put it, "Transfers of peoples would be carried out on a voluntary basis when possible and otherwise compulsorily. The definition of self-determination which emerged was 'the freedom of the self to transport himself to the land where he wants to live'; and it was accepted that assistance must be given to the individual so transported. It was determined that territorial questions should be settled prior to action on the transference of populations."[35] That policy view, reflective of the American globalism that had evolved from wartime and postwar planning, came to bear heavily on the Truman administration's subsequent efforts to press for increased Jewish emigration to Palestine, despite British protests.[36]

Having developed during the war under FDR, and perhaps reached its apogee in the U.S. support of the 100,000 additional Jewish migrants to Palestine recommended by the Anglo-American Committee of Inquiry, the globalism projected onto the Middle East persisted after the outbreak of interstate Arab-Israeli conflict in May 1948. While the Near East experts at the State Department had vehemently opposed the specific policy of continued Jewish emigration to Palestine, the minutes of Welles's Subcommittee on Political Problems revealed a willingness to contemplate free migration by refugees to places of their choosing in the course of postwar settlements. The Department also echoed aspects of globalism in its recognition of the worldwide consequences of the outbreak of the conflict in Palestine beyond just the Eastern Mediterranean or the Levant. At that time the State Department assessed that "continued warfare between Jewish and Arab forces would undermine the gains which have been made in Greece, Turkey and Iran, might permanently alienate the Arab world from western influences, and might impose upon the United States a basic re-examination of its own world security position."[37] It was a powerful worldview also shared by U.S. planners on the military side of Palestine policy: its geographic significance was much wider; so much so, the State-War-Navy Coordinating Committee had warned, that employing U.S. troops to address it might cause the entire Middle East "to fall into anarchy and become a breeding ground for world war."[38] While the Arabists at the State Department and the Joint Chiefs may not have shared the White House's proposed approach to the Arab-Jewish dispute in Palestine, the Advisory Committee saw the virtues of free resettlement to such territories. And despite internal disagreements, much of the U.S. national security establishment recognized the profound ways in which the conflict implicated populations far beyond Palestine's verdant orchards and cobalt waters.

In a similar vein American globalism also left its mark on policy toward the Kashmir dispute when that conflict was laid before the Security Council in early 1948—at a moment in time much further along in the evolution of the cold war, it is worth noting. By that point the growing U.S. preoccupation with the threat of Soviet penetration of the Indian subcontinent became the primary American strategic concern in South Asia, leading to the observation that "marked initiative by the United States in this dispute might attract undesirable Russian attention."[39] As has been shown, that concern came to impinge on the U.S. position in the Security Council as Warren Austin grappled with his British counterparts over deploying international troops in Kashmir, emphasizing the need to address the root of the conflict rather than paper over the bilateral disagreements with superficial measures imposed by the United Nations.[40] Such were the early reactions from Washington as the internationalization of the conflict forced a haphazard American crisis response. Unlike the case with Palestine, a better-formulated U.S. policy toward the dispute took shape only with time, often in reaction to British initiatives and overtures. But when it did, the escalating cold war with the Soviet Union and the implicit assumptions of national security globalism were marked and pervasive. And the strategic geography of the subcontinent as a potential bulwark against the southward and eastward expansion of Sino-Soviet influence became the critical factor shaping U.S. policy toward Pakistan, and by extension, the Kashmir dispute.[41] The upshot was a cautious willingness to facilitate British efforts to negotiate between India and Pakistan that was still bounded by a fear of internationalizing the dispute too broadly by the establishment of international forces or the infiltration of international communist elements. In a sense Washington's globalism grew blurrier as it approached South Asia, far from the cold war's principal battle lines in Europe and the Near East. That was probably generally true of the Truman administration's global conception of national security as a whole, especially in the early years of its conception and development.[42] But when the strategic rationales for American policy were articulated in the years after partition, the globalism latent within it was fully evident. "The geographical position of South Asia is such that, if the economic and military potentials of the area were more fully developed, it could dominate the region of the Indian Ocean and exert a strong influence also on the Middle East, Central Asia, and the Far East," the State-Army-Navy–Air Force Coordinating Committee concluded. Accordingly the economic development of India and Pakistan could spur economic recovery in the Far East and "throughout the world."[43] This consideration of the subcontinent's global geographical importance shaped the Truman administration's initial focus on India as a principal defensive outpost against the spread of communism in Asia, as well as the subsequent policy "tilt" toward Pakistan by 1949–1950.[44]

BRITISH REGIONALISM AND IMPERIAL RETREAT

In its essence the tendency toward regionalism to which many British strategists and policymakers gravitated stemmed from the need to preserve the integrity of the energy supplies and imperial lines of communication that sustained the empire in India and Africa. The Middle East was the central node in the empire's linkage of the home islands with India, the Far East, and Australia. Suez provided the critical seaborne connection between the Mediterranean and the Indian Ocean for commerce and naval defense. Alexandria hosted the principal British naval base in the region. Oil reserves in Iraq and southern Persia and the Abadan refinery near the Iran-Iraq border represented key energy supplies for the British military, while the pipeline from northern Iraq to the Eastern Mediterranean port of Haifa constituted a critical piece of infrastructure for the transshipment of oil. In terms of the direct war effort, the region was a base and logistical hub for the war in the Pacific, where American and British oil supplies had to be protected. There was also the issue of supply lines for some 175,000 POWs, not to mention logistics for British resupply of forces in Southeastern Europe and the Balkans.[45] Finally, the region's strategic airbases provided an increasingly critical air link between Europe and points farther south in Africa and east in South Asia and the Far East.[46]

Foreign Office and Imperial General Staff concerns with the Muslim populations that stretched from the Indus to the Bosporus arose from the geographical collocation of key lines of communication and strategic nodes along a wide swath of Southwest Asian Islam.[47] At least that was the innermost focus of British geopolitical interests in the Middle East and Palestine, Egypt Iraq, Persia, and eventually postindependence Pakistan. In the face of these critical requirements, the only territory over which Britain enjoyed full sovereignty was Cyprus. Palestine and Transjordan were mandates whose futures likely entailed some degree of independence, and Egypt, Iraq, Lebanon, and Syria had all gained independence in the wake of the Anglo-French crisis that led to the withdrawal of British and French troops from the two former French possessions.[48] As a result, the Chiefs of Staff concluded, "protection of our vital interests depends, therefore, upon the collaboration which we can obtain from these independent States."[49] The need for residual influence in these largely independent states so geographically central to British postwar interests formed the basis of Bevin's strategy of noninterference in the Middle East and reliance on bilateral relationships with the region's governments to protect British basing rights, transit routes, supply stores, and other interests. It also gave rise by the close of the war to the suggestion of a "Middle East confederacy" that might constitute multilateral mutual defense agreements with the sovereign governments of the region.[50]

But it is worthwhile to note that regionalism in what some British historians have termed the "Official Mind" also had an "outer" meaning beyond the territorially contiguous confines of the Muslim greater Middle East. In a political sense there was also a regionalism that bound the British Isles to all of the empire, as well as the dominions that made up the Commonwealth. Nautical charts and other official and nonofficial maps of the empire often depicted this imperial geography as a world in which British possessions were marked in red to offset them from what lay beyond. As U.S. officials realized, this recasting of the British territorial state contrasted sharply with Britain's parallel identity as a European power. The binary dichotomy between the Anglophone and non-Anglophone worlds also manifested itself in concrete political discussions in the months leading up to creation of the United Nations. The bulk of those discussions took place in Commonwealth heads of state conferences in London, the last of which before the San Francisco Conference highlighted the deep inward pull that the metropole exerted toward colonies like India and the pseudo-colonies of the Commonwealth.[51]

Consensus on proposed postcolonial policies also reflected this wider regionalism, despite differences of views toward mechanisms like international trusteeship on the part of South Africa, which sought to continue its policies of apartheid without international supervision of areas like South-West Africa, and Australia and New Zealand, which saw trusteeship as a vehicle that could transport dependent territories down the road to independence. Thus the convened Commonwealth heads of state agreed in March–April 1945 "that any form of international administration was inadvisable for practical reasons, . . . that such Mandates as might be created should be allotted to a single Mandatory power," and "that there should be no surrender by the nations of the British Commonwealth of any of their existing Mandates."[52] They also deliberated together on how Commonwealth members could attain adequate representation as nonpermanent members on the newly created United Nations Security Council.[53]

One intriguing aspect of these discussions is the extent to which they demonstrated the limits of regional cooperation imposed by the lack of geographical contiguity of the Commonwealth—also a geographical feature of the seaborne empire—and the extent to which it prevented the Commonwealth countries from lodging a realistic appeal to form regional arrangements under the auspices of the draft UN Charter.[54] The Security Council voting issue was tied to another principal concern for British policy: the future disposition of Egypt, from which the Labour government sought to extricate British forces on its own terms. Discussions of the

Dumbarton Oaks proposals thus also necessitated consideration by the Chiefs of Staff of the issue of potential UN Security Council arbitration of disputes over the terms of the 1936 Anglo-Egyptian Treaty, which had begun to grow increasingly acrimonious as Egyptian nationalists began to demand the departure of British forces from the Suez Canal Zone, a presence the British government deemed essential for the Zone's security. The Chiefs of Staff noted that the ultimate formula on voting adopted by the Security Council would impact the Council's ability to pass a resolution demanding British withdrawal from the Zone.[55] These concerns went on to inform Foreign Office discussions on the veto rights of Security Council permanent members that lasted into 1946—discussions revolving around the potential value of the veto to protect the United Kingdom or the Commonwealth from adverse action supported by a Council majority. The discussions revealed some of the broader British strategic concerns that were implicated by the need to reconcile long-standing Commonwealth diplomatic ties with the new multilateral structure of the United Nations Organization.[56]

However, British strategists also recognized that the UN system could actually be leveraged in the service of national interests, as a multilateral body that extended and multiplied British power even in the face of an imperial recalibration in accordance with shrunken mental maps of recast postwar interests. As dominions representatives had noted in the intra-Commonwealth meetings, any future system of collective security that might be assembled as part of Chapters VII and VIII of the UN Charter would constitute the outermost defenses of a three-tiered system of imperial defense (imperial cooperation on security and national defenses constituting the other two tiers).[57] Indeed retracting British power might *have* to rely on international mechanisms. Military strategists recognized, for instance, that future Middle East defense plans in the wake of a British military withdrawal thus "might have to be fitted into the trusteeship clauses of the World Security Organisation with Great Britain as the predominant partner." Moreover the binding responsibility of UN membership might also sufficiently constrain the Truman administration and force it to pursue a more sensible Palestine policy that did not blatantly set Arab sentiments aflame.[58]

Similarly the Foreign Office's Eastern Department recognized the benefits of forging a consensus on Palestine across the permanent members of the putative Security Council before proceeding with a future policy toward the mandate.⁵⁹ Before long the questions about hypothetical UN mechanisms and their implications gave way to real conundrums over how to deal with the specific challenges in the Levant and South Asia. With the trial of partition approaching, the conclusion that British policy in the Middle East had to be coordinated increasingly closely and framed from the standpoint of a single strategic vision was setting in. George Fielding Eliot, an author and confidante of Secretary of State Marshall, confided to Hastings Ismay in June 1947, "Turkey and Greece, Palestine and Egypt, Iran and Arabian oil are all really wrapped up in the same package." These were British concerns in the Eastern Mediterranean and broader Middle East that Eliot surmised could not be dealt with in "piecemeal" fashion.⁶⁰

Complications arising from the nearly simultaneous UN Security Council consideration of the Palestine and Kashmir issues posed central challenges for Attlee and Bevin, who subscribed fully to the precepts of regionalism. Importantly the viceroy of India, Lord Wavell himself, as well as lower-ranking officials in the Foreign, Colonial, and India Offices, also shared that conception. These officials realized that policy decisions taken in one colonial territory could have repercussions in the other, in a ripple effect felt throughout the Muslim populations that could serve the function of an electrical current transmitting the charge of unrest from one end of the region to the other. As the Colonial Office wrote to Ismay in India in August 1945, "The Viceroy states that any solution of the Palestine problem which could be interpreted as injurious to the interests of the Arabs and a breach of the pledges given by His Majesty's Government in the White Paper would be likely to cause serious unrest in the Punjab and would affect recruiting for the army. There would also immediately be excitement among the Frontier Muslims and, if there were any unfortunate incident in Palestine, such as firing on a large Arab crowd or the destruction of a mosque or other sacred Moslem place, there might be big hostile demonstrations in Peshawar and other towns, in which trans-border elements might join."⁶¹ Diplomatic dispatches from India confirmed Wavell's assessment. India's Muslim League demanded that the Arabs be allowed to form their own government upon the termination of the British mandate in Palestine "unfettered by [any] outside agency" and "without further delay."⁶²

Importantly the Colonial Office recognized that the repercussions of a Palestine settlement could spread throughout the region, not only to the Muslims of India: "Our stand against the French in the Levant would inevitably be held up against us, and the prospects of American sympathy or support for British requests for facilities in Egypt or elsewhere for the defence of the Suez Canal would be greatly prejudiced."[63] Such expressions of concern are significant in that they underscored the British Official Mind's rationale for how unrest might spread throughout the region—not merely because Palestine and Kashmir were two key Muslim flashpoints threatening to explode during Britain's postcolonial moment, but because of the actual geographical contiguity of the subregion, the relative proximity of British interests in Palestine, Syria, Lebanon, Suez, and northern India, and the religious homogeneity of its Muslim population. Diplomatic correspondence between London and Kabul in the wake of the failed British diplomatic effort to resolve the Kashmir crisis provides additional evidence of this preoccupation with not only predominantly Muslim territories per se but with those that lay along the Southwest Asian arc of crisis connecting Palestine with Kashmir. Unwanted Afghan influence constituted a key obstacle from across the mountains north and west of the zone of conflict. In the months after partition Whitehall ominously noted its suspicion that "the Afghans are primarily responsible for the breakdown of the Karachi negotiations, and are seeking to profit from Pakistan's present difficulties."[64]

Formulating a defense policy based on such a regional conception of strategy was another matter, however. The independence of the British dominions meant that carefully cultivated relationships had to be developed and maintained to ensure that the Commonwealth states could act together to form the second ring of imperial security that it was envisioned to be. In that regard, dominion heads of state had agreed that a highly centralized system of defense could prove too restrictive in constraining the freedom of action of individual member states. Instead a more semi-autonomous system of British liaisons in each individual dominion, of the sort Auchinleck hoped to oversee for India and Pakistan through the appointment of British military advisors, was necessary to meet the requisite needs. But an added complication beyond the independent foreign policies of the dominions came from the implications of the transfer of power in India for the Commonwealth—and the subsidiary question of the disposition of the princely states of India. What would become of Commonwealth defense if some of the princely states opted for independence? British strategy by mid-1947 had settled on the idea of persuading the princely states to join one dominion or the other. But "separatist tendencies such as those lately shown by Hyderabad, Travancore, Kashmir and Bhopal" continued to threaten future Commonwealth solidarity and provisions for collective self-defense.[65] Whatever its limitations, British defense planners deemed this proposed system an added layer of defense between the British military and any third, outer ring of security that the United Nations might afford the empire-Commonwealth. For the empire's primary military task in peacetime was "the efficient organization of the forces of the Commonwealth to act together in an emergency."[66]

That need to act in an emergency rose glaringly to the fore in the Kashmir dispute, of course, when Pakistan requested a Commonwealth conference to discuss the situation—a request that threatened to embarrass the body given its degree of removal from the crux of the conflict in the contested accession of the princely state of Jammu and Kashmir by India. Nevertheless Laurence Grafftey-Smith in Karachi suggested that Commonwealth governments might still meet on their own to determine whether bilateral efforts between India and Pakistan were proving sufficient to halt the "murder and migration" triggered by the Kashmir crisis.[67] While no such mediation process emerged, the Commonwealth Relations Office considered whether the outbreak of open war might "bring about the downfall" of the Muslim state, assessing that "the effect of the disappearance of Pakistan on the Middle East would be very considerable."[68] Indeed even Mountbatten himself, though a close confidante of Nehru, who viewed with alarm the gradual westward shift of British focus toward Pakistan and the Middle East, seems to have subscribed at least in part to the logic of regionalism, even if it did not prove the decisive consideration in determining his allegiances in the first Indo-Pakistani War.[69] In the end Bevin's edict that the Foreign Office contemplate no Kashmir policy "siding against, or appearing to side against, Pakistan" that united "the whole of Islam against us" superseded all other official arguments.[70]

Similarly the Official Mind's reliance on regionalism meant that the British reaction to the outbreak of civil war in Palestine also needed to take stock of its impact in regions farther east. Prime Minister Attlee himself noted as much in instructing his government to discuss with American interlocutors the implications of the outbreak of the Arab-Israeli War for not only British imperial defense but also "likely developments arising from the Palestine situation throughout the Middle East, India and Burma."[71] For the demographic composition of Southwest Asia meant that backlash effects could be transmitted in both directions, westward and eastward, through the Muslim populations that acted as its conduits. The consequences of failing to consider the impact could be catastrophic, for a settlement unsatisfactory to the Muslims of Palestine meant that "the Arab States [would] not (repeat not) co-operate and they would probably be supported by all the countries of Asia. The world would be split between east and west with the gravest consequences to the British Commonwealth."[72] As Bevin later confided to the House of Commons in January 1949, the distant territories of Afghanistan and Pakistan now had to be considered part of the Middle East.[73]

SEVEN

Maps, Ideas, and Geopolitics

In a sense the UN system represented a reconciliation of the American and British geographical conceptions of postwar order. More problematically there were civilian and military versions of American globalism that first had to be reconciled with *one another*. While the Allied compromise on the Security Council and its voting mechanisms represented a huge triumph of internationalism—and certainly, to a considerable extent, a reconciliation of American and British blueprints—there remained the quandary of the future of dependent territories, a separate issue that resolved itself on a parallel track between early Allied postwar planning in 1942 and the Yalta Conference of February 1945. Like the Security Council, the fate of what became the UN Trusteeship Council can be traced back to Sumner Welles's earliest drafts of a charter for the postwar organization. In essence, ever since Roosevelt abandoned Welles's and Churchill's ideas for a system of regional councils, at least a partial triumph of American globalism was secured. But complex interests spanning security, colonial development, and international accountability all came into play in discussions on the trusteeship issue.

The American president had long considered the idea of trusteeship as a possible mechanism for promoting the advancement of dependent territories toward self-government and independence. But the fall of 1943 and the conferences in Cairo and Tehran represented the threshold moment when his thinking on the nature and purposes of international trusteeship began to crystallize. After his return to Washington, Roosevelt realized that trusteeship could simultaneously assure U.S. postwar security needs in the Pacific, dispossess the European colonial powers of many of their remaining possessions, and provide a vehicle for the liberation of colonial peoples and dependencies wrested from the defeated Axis powers (for instance, the Japanese Mandated Islands). The State Department's Advisory Committee on Postwar Foreign Policy had been independently exploring the idea of trusteeship through a draft article on the subject for the future charter of the world security organization. The article had been drafted by Welles's Subcommittee on Political Problems. By the end of 1942 the subcommittee's members decided that the plan should be adapted to apply trusteeship to dependent territories.[1] Undiluted by the views of more cautious proponents of the idea, such as Hull, Welles and his principal advisors Bowman, Pasvolsky, the Far Eastern expert Stanley Hornbeck, and others laid out a vision for international accountability for dependent territories that would both subsume existing mandates and provide a vehicle for the recovery of Japanese, Italian, and other territories that had fallen to Axis occupation. But these efforts were largely invisible to Roosevelt, who was engaged in thinking of his own about the postwar disposition of dependent territories—specifically in the context of the future of the South Pacific.[2]

Around the same time, Roosevelt had become acutely aware of the need to safeguard the security of the Pacific in the wake of the Pearl Harbor attack. He also grasped the central role that air forces would have to play in that regard. Secretary of War Henry Stimson, Deputy Secretary of the Navy James Forrestal, and Secretary of State George Marshall firmly supported his view.[3] Roosevelt accordingly tasked the Joint Chiefs of Staff to conduct a study to determine where air basing facilities for an "International Police Force" might be located throughout the world, "without regard to current sovereignty."[4] He later clarified the scope of his query at the February meeting of the Pacific War Council, stipulating that the future United Nations body would need access to key strategic points to "control the Pacific."[5]

Roosevelt's invocation of the United Nations as a justification for the change in the sovereignty of the islands in question was significant: the bases would be required for policing the region under the auspices of the new international organization that would ensure peace and security for the world as a whole, not for the strategic advantage of any single nation. Critically he wanted to underscore to the Allied leaders around the table that his proposals did not merely entail naked American designs to snatch control of key Pacific Islands that straddled strategic air and sea lines of communication whose centrality had been validated by the war in the Pacific.

Unfortunately for American policy coordination, the U.S. Navy had formulated just such designs after the tortuous Pacific theater experiences with recapturing Japanese-held territory. The body entrusted with carrying out the study, the navy's General Board, decided of its own volition to reconceptualize the directive that Roosevelt's naval aide had passed to Navy Secretary Frank Knox as "GB 450," a request for a basing study to define the U.S. naval force posture in the Pacific. In stark contrast to Roosevelt's framing, the navy assumed that international supervision of strategic bases was still years away. The only way to ensure interim security and forward U.S. defenses was to parcel key strategic areas like the Southwest Pacific among the other great powers and ensure U.S. control of the key geographical points under study before their eventual transfer to international sovereignty.[6]

Early U.S. postwar strategy toward the dependent territories was thus informed by two competing strands of thought—strands that Roosevelt's successor would see reconciled at the United Nations Conference in San Francisco just a few months after his death. On one side was the vigorous internationalism of the State Department—championed by Welles and somewhat tempered by Hull—that envisioned an international trusteeship scheme over all dependent territories, including former colonies, in which sovereignty would reside with the participating administering nations. On the other were the views of navy strategists like Knox, who (despite Admiral Leahy's persistent concerns about involvement in civilian affairs) insisted throughout on U.S. sovereignty over the Pacific Mandated Islands as a lowest common denominator for any postwar security system. It made no military sense to the navy and the JCS that the United States would willingly cede territorial rights to the islands in case they might have to be retaken in a future conflict. The tensions between this military view and the State Department's principled internationalism delineated the bounds of the policy options spanned by FDR's vision of American globalism.

Intergovernmental disputes aside, that globalism would also have to reconcile itself with the regionalism that underpinned British Foreign and Colonial Office thought on dependent territories. The daylight between those competing ways of seeing the world was as evident in the meetings of the Pacific War Council as in any private Anglo-American conversations on the sensitive issue of the British Empire. Curiously, in the Council's next meeting after Roosevelt had announced the idea of a transfer in sovereignty, British Foreign Secretary Anthony Eden seemed to side with the U.S. military in suggesting "that the United States should take over the Japanese Mandates." Let the Americans assume control of their most prized strategic bases, the British line of argument seemed to suggest, and perhaps they would leave British imperial outposts unmolested as the Allies fashioned final postwar territorial settlements. But Roosevelt was adamant in his refusal to acquire territory on such transparently imperialistic grounds.[7] That summer the navy reported back with three finished studies in response to GB 450, stemming from Roosevelt's request to examine air bases, having carried them out on the assumption that America would have to simply assert sovereign control over the islands. But Roosevelt relented, dismissing the recommendations with his concern that "the sweeping changes in sovereignty recommended by the [General] Board may not be attainable, and, from an economic point of view, all of the acquisitions recommended may not be desirable." But the president still wanted a deeper exploration of "which individual islands because of their geography and location, promise to be of value as commercial airports in the future."[8] Later in the year Roosevelt also requested new JCS guidance on the specific locations of air facilities that the United States should seek.[9]

Driven by bureaucratic pressure for self-preservation and the aggrandizement of influence and control of policy, the navy again recast Roosevelt's request, assuming that "the President want[ed] a comprehensive survey made of the [P]acific from the standpoint of post-war security and commercial aviation."[10] This broadly reinterpreted request led to the production of JCS 570, "U.S. Requirements for Post-War Air Bases"—a massive six-volume military document that constituted a treatise for the expansion and consolidation of American air and naval power throughout the southern and western Pacific Ocean, and an unmistakable strategic blueprint for globalism. The exhaustive study, sweeping in its scope, envisioned three periods after the end of the war. The end of hostilities would first give rise to "an enforced peace in Europe and war against Japan." The second phase of "world-wide peace enforced by the four great powers" imagined a classic Bismarckian concert of powers probably akin to Roosevelt's own early conception of the Four Policemen. The third and final period would see "peace maintained by a formally established world-wide machinery." But the committee entrusted with the study noted "that there are at present so many unknown factors connected with this third period that the problem cannot be solved on a realistic basis at the present time." Accordingly the study recommended that the State Department "initiate negotiations with the governments concerned to acquire permanent or long-term benefit of the bases, facilities and rights required, at the earliest possible moment." In envisioning the three phases, the JCS had incorporated key assumptions dealing heavily with diplomatic issues like the structure of the future postwar international organization and U.S. agreements with relevant nations in the Far East. Astonishingly Roosevelt approved the recommendation outright, with the caveat that the Marquesas and Tuamotu island groups "should be included in the United States' sphere of influence," a specific request that reflected not only his interest in the matter but the depth of his knowledge of geopolitics as a former assistant secretary of the navy. His decision perhaps reflected an awareness of the true extent of political-military coordination that would be necessary to forge far-reaching postwar national security policies.[11]

Despite their eagerness to involve themselves in political matters impinging on U.S. security, Roosevelt's military advisors allowed little negotiating room on substance in interagency discussions. The JCS came to propose formal guidance for the Pacific War Council discussions: "that no statements, agreements or plans be made by them, and no action be taken by forces under their control, which directly or indirectly might be construed as a basis for any nation other than the United States obtaining sovereignty or any other territorial rights in the Japanese Mandated Islands, during or after the present war." The chairman submitted this guidance for Roosevelt's formal approval. But yet again Roosevelt undercut what he saw as an overtly imperialistic tendency in his joint planning staff, noting that the Pacific War Council meeting that very month should have put to rest any lingering JCS concerns about having to protect American access through the acquisition of sovereign territorial rights. "As you attended the last Pacific War Council meeting, you will see that there is no danger of giving away any Japanese Mandated Islands in the Pacific, except that the question of civil administration is still open," he told Naval Aide Admiral Wilson Brown. But there was no doubt in his mind that "the question of the military control of them will be decided in favor of the United States."[12]

Undeterred, Roosevelt continued to press upon his admirals that outright American annexation was *not* a prerequisite for ensuring U.S. control over the strategically located Japanese Mandated Islands and that a much more diplomatically palatable solution would perfectly suffice. But by early 1944 bridging the gap between the civilian and military views in the U.S. government was not the only concern for U.S. strategy and policy, as looming victory posed new challenges for inter-Allied cooperation. For the very act of the liberation of Japanese-held territories seemed to widen the gap between U.S. and British military objectives in the Pacific theater. More than mere rhetorical differences, these were profound policy divergences that comments like Eden's casual suggestion of American occupation of Japanese Mandated Islands merely glossed over. Leahy noted precisely how British objectives seemed to diverge from those of the United States: "Much of the territory in which military operations in that theater are to be conducted consists of portions of the British Empire now under Japanese occupation. British interests and objectives in that area are, therefore, both military and political, while those of the United States are concerned with the defeat of Japan."[13] Leahy had identified a critical point at issue. As differences across Allied war aims came to the surface in the closing months of the conflict, it was clear that the fate of the British Empire and the military necessity of its preservation would remain one of the principal sticking points for Anglo-American relations. But the wartime transatlantic consensus would have to produce an accord on postcolonial issues after hostilities came to an end if the Allied powers were to cement their unity in a permanent structure—one that doubtless would have to propose an agreed mechanism for replacing the antiquated League of Nations mandate system.

Roosevelt thus decided to dispatch Stettinius to London on a mission in April to meet with Foreign and Colonial Office officials with the hope of forging a compromise on the future of colonial territories and other postwar matters on which London and Washington had yet to agree. Stettinius took with him the renowned geographer Isaiah Bowman, who along with Charles Taussig of the State Department's Dependent Areas Division, had become one of the administration's key experts on colonial issues.[14] Bowman's meeting with Churchill proved unproductive when the prime minister refused to discuss territorial concessions by the British Empire. At the Foreign Office, Minister of State Richard Law beseeched Bowman to drop the State Department's bid for a general "Declaration on National Independence" for colonial peoples. General declarations were abstract and oblivious to the particulars on the ground throughout a heterogeneous entity like the British Empire, Law and his colleagues claimed, and stemmed from American ignorance of and inexperience with such particulars. That skepticism about general principles and abstractions to which the Americans always seemed to cling did not appear to divide Anglo-American thinking on the issue of trusteeship in the meetings at the Foreign Office, where Eden's principal aide involved with the talks, Sir Maurice Peterson, seemed to warm to Bowman's ideas on international trusteeship—in particular its application to the case of Palestine. But that apparent convergence of views failed to survive first contact with the Colonial Office experts on dependent territories. Colonial Secretary Lord Stanley dismissed the idea outright; instead he encouraged Bowman to consider the British counterproposal of the establishment of regional commissions entrusted with responsibility for certain functional issues (such as education and welfare) and to which colonial powers might submit periodic reports. Indeed it was a subject on which the colonial secretary remarked that he had opted to speak to Parliament. Moreover, according to Stanley, international supervision of colonial affairs in dependent territories was a matter to which the British government as a whole could simply not agree.[15] Stettinius ruefully observed in his final mission report, "The disposal of the Mandated Territories of 1919 was discussed apart from the colonial question. The legal position of the Mandates is a troublesome question which may or may not need to be resolved before the World Organization is set up with a section in it to deal with dependent peoples."[16] He also captured the philosophical differences that divided Anglo-American views on the future of dependent peoples: "In exchanges between our Government and the British Government during the past year and a half, we have presented for British consideration a set of principles for the guidance of the United Nations in the administration of dependent peoples. These principles are cast in the most general form, and emphasis was at first upon 'independence,' later changed to 'self-government.' It is the British view that these statements are vague and impractical. They claim that the diversities of life and environment among dependent peoples are so great that it is not possible to make any real improvement in the relations of such peoples to the metropole by setting up what they feel is a vague set of general ideals."[17]

Stettinius and Bowman thus returned from their London mission with little in hand. Lord Stanley's visit to Washington in November of that year for meetings with Roosevelt and Taussig likewise failed to produce

Anglo-American accord. But 1944 proved to be the pivotal year in which progress toward international agreement on trusteeship—and more complete blueprints for postwar American globalism—began in earnest. When the Joint Chiefs again sought Roosevelt's stamp of approval on the idea of outright annexation of the Japanese islands, Roosevelt had had enough. Reiterating that America sought "no additional territory" in the postwar period, he now definitively announced that he was "working on the idea that the United Nations will ask the United States to act as Trustee for the Japanese Mandated Islands."[18] Nor would the president allow the protracted interagency dispute between the State Department and the Joint Chiefs to continue unresolved. Though the JCS had successfully persuaded the State Department to postpone discussions of trusteeship at Dumbarton Oaks, Roosevelt summarily tasked the Department to produce preparatory documents on trusteeship in mid-November—work that of course had already begun under the supervision of members of the Informal Agenda Group such as Pasvolsky and Bowman. Lord Stanley's November visit to Washington failed to produce an agreement on the future of the mandated territories. The president refrained from raising the issue of trusteeship directly (perhaps because he had already determined he would not broach the issue until the upcoming Yalta Conference).[19] But Roosevelt's new sense of initiative to tighten up policy coordination had set the wheels spinning in Foggy Bottom. The omission was perhaps a missed opportunity, given that Stanley only cursorily alluded to work that was under way at the Colonial Office on the future of the mandates and the British Empire.

By the end of the year Hilton Poynton and Kenneth Robinson of the Colonial Office's Defence and General Department had produced a memorandum reflecting considerable thinking on the future of colonial policy in the postwar period. In a sense they represented the opposite numbers to Welles, Bowman, and the Advisory Committee for Postwar Foreign Policy's Political and Territorial subcommittees. In December Poynton and Robinson produced a seminal document titled "International Aspects of Colonial Policy," which represented the current state of Colonial Office thought on the disposition of mandated and colonial territories. Reflective of a brand of regionalism to be applied to the world at large, the plan they envisioned criticized not only the outmoded mandates system but also the principle of trusteeship, which they felt perpetuated an inherent dependency on states serving as trustees. Instead Poynton and Robinson envisaged what they termed "partnership" as the more apt and relevant construct. While the document recognized that international interests in colonial territories would have to be accommodated, the modes for that international involvement consisted of regional commissions that would be consultative in nature and functional agencies that would involve themselves with specific issues (like labor rights) intrinsic to all colonial territories. The idea was to preserve British sovereignty while partially accommodating the maximalist demands of the Americans and the antipodean dominions. After considerable internal discussion and dissent, including from within the Colonial Office, the War Cabinet approved the document, enshrining it as the basic reference on postwar colonial policy. Unfortunately for the Colonial Office, however, the American reaction to the proposals would never be gauged.[20]

At Roosevelt's behest, the State Department planning in the months before Yalta recognized the need for international consensus on the issue of trusteeship, a matter that Stanley had raised during his visit. Pasvolsky now suggested to Stettinius that "a chapter on trusteeship should be included in the Charter of the International Organization." Pasvolsky reasoned that the termination of the League of Nations mandates would in any event require some successor system. There was also the issue of additional territories that could be placed under trusteeship voluntarily. Finally, the future of dependent territories was becoming an issue of domestic concern in the United States.[21] Stimson and the military maintained their opposition to discussion of the subject, principally because of the outstanding question of the status of the Pacific Mandated Islands. "You are proposing to include them under your future principles of 'trusteeship' or 'mandates,'" he wrote Stettinius. But "they do not really belong in such a classification. Acquisition of them by the United States does not represent an attempt at colonization or exploitation. Instead it is merely the acquisition by the United States of the necessary bases for the defense of the security of the Pacific for the future world. . . . It is my conclusion, therefore, that we should not bring up the subject of territorial adjustments, including 'trusteeships' for discussion in any form, at least until the war is much further along and Russian participation in the Pacific war is accomplished."[22] But Stimson's appeal came too late, for Roosevelt had decisively set his course. That decision forced the military to reconsider its position on the idea of international trusteeships. Such a mechanism could be broached in Allied discussions, the JCS now agreed, provided that three conditions were met. First, the development of any relevant American policy proposals would have to involve the Joint Chiefs and the military departments. Second, no existing U.S. possessions could be considered for conversion into trust territories. Third, under no condition would sovereignty over the Mandated Islands by any state other than the United States be contemplated.[23]

Anglo-American resolution on the principle of trusteeship finally came at the Yalta Conference in February 1945, in the course of the proceedings that produced the compromise formula that did not at all correspond with Colonial Office intentions. Roosevelt had integrated State Department planning with that of the remainder of his government, and Benjamin Gerig's Dependent Areas Division supplied a paragraph on trusteeship for FDR's Yalta briefing papers. In contrast, the British delegation did not even include a Colonial Office representative who could rebut American charges and offer ingenious counterproposals such as Poynton and Robinson's "partnership" plan, which at the time had yet to even secure approval by the dominions.[24] The result was that, largely at the insistence of U.S. delegation member Alger Hiss, the trusteeship principle was inserted into the deliberations of the conference proceedings. When Churchill inferred from Stettinius that the provisions of the mechanism would not be applied to the British Empire, he signed off on the notion, and an inter-Allied compromise was struck. American diplomat Charles "Chip" Bohlen's notes of the meeting colorfully captured the clash between globalism and regionalism:

> THE PRIME MINISTER interrupted with great vigor to say that he did not agree with one single word of this report on trusteeships. He said that he had not been consulted nor had he heard of this subject up to now. He said that under no circumstances would he ever consent to forty or fifty nations thrusting interfering fingers into the life's existence of the British Empire. As long as he was Minister, he would never yield one scrap of their heritage. He continued in this vein for some minutes.
>
> MR. STETTINIUS explained that this reference to the creation of machinery was not intended to refer to the British Empire, but that it had in mind particularly dependent areas which would be taken out of enemy control, for example, the Japanese islands in the Pacific. He said that it was felt that provision had to be made for machinery to handle this question of

trusteeship for dependent areas taken from the enemy and he repeated that this was not intended to refer to the British Empire.

THE PRIME MINISTER accepted Mr. Stettinius' explanation but remarked it would be better to say it did not refer to the British Empire.[25]

In that haphazard fashion, the great powers agreed on the principle behind the international mechanism that would succeed the League of Nations mandates system, assume control over Axis-occupied territories, and help implement the ideals of self-determination enshrined in the Atlantic Charter. On 11 February the gathered foreign ministers agreed "that the five Nations which will have permanent seats on the Security Council should consult each other prior to the United Nations Conference on the question of territorial trusteeship." They added the caveat that the new mechanism would apply only to existing League mandates, territories detached from the Axis powers, and any other territories "which might voluntarily be placed under trusteeship." It was further agreed that no specific territories would be proposed as candidates for trusteeship at the San Francisco conference.[26] The outcome represented a victory for American globalism, whose scope and extent would be clarified at the San Francisco Conference.

Still, the State Department view of the trusteeship principle had yet to be reconciled with the Department of War and navy stances on the matter, which remained adamantly committed to the preservation of American sovereignty over the Pacific islands reoccupied at the cost of American lives. The day before the Yalta Conference opened, a new interagency Committee on Dependent Area Aspects of International Organization convened to examine the question of trusteeship. In the weeks leading up to the San Francisco Conference, the Committee met weekly—often for hours on end—to smooth out the differences between the respective government viewpoints on the issue. Battle lines were soon drawn between Leo Pasvolsky, the Committee's chair, and its State Department representatives, including both Taussig and Gerig, and the JCS representatives from the Joint Strategic Survey Committee—Stanley Embick, Russell Willson, and Muir Fairchild. Despite arduous efforts to bridge the gap in views, the military representatives held firm to their hard line on American occupation of strategic areas and the impossibility of their surrender to international trusteeship. As proceedings dragged on, Abe Fortas, the undersecretary of the interior (and a future U.S. Supreme Court justice) proposed a compromise view: a distinction between "open" areas that would be subject to international accountability and "closed" areas whose strategic importance would mean that they would remain shielded from visiting commissions and the scrutiny of their reports. Drawing on his legal background, Fortas proposed the innovative terminology of "strategic trust territories" to designate the closed areas.[27] But still the military representatives refused to compromise.

In the end it was Roosevelt who decided the issue. In a 15 March meeting with Taussig, Roosevelt clarified his intention to adhere to a policy of two types of trusteeship, including open areas subject to international agreements and closed counterparts that would be set aside for the benefit not of any single nation but rather world security as a whole.[28] He reiterated this instruction two days before his death, when he confirmed to Stettinius on 10 April that U.S. policy on the trusteeship question was indeed consistent with a memorandum that Gerig had produced on the subject that made the Department's case.[29] Despite a strange episode in which Stettinius seemingly agreed with Stimson and Forrestal on the need to postpone trusteeship discussions until after San Francisco, the secretary of state abruptly changed his mind, possibly after receiving Roosevelt's instruction that the Gerig memorandum indeed reflected his own sentiments. After the president's sudden death, Stimson and Forrestal, who had until that moment been planning to approach Roosevelt directly with a joint memorandum making their case, now finally gave ground on the issue for the sake of policy consensus.[30]

The capitulation by the military represented the final necessary step for a unified U.S. position on trusteeship to be presented at San Francisco. Concerns persisted on the part of some participants that the American and British positions would be difficult to bridge; nevertheless the conceptual accord struck at Yalta had more or less ensured a harmonious resolution.[31]

The San Francisco deliberations were so extensive, and had to cover so many geographical regions and functional areas, that they were structured into a sprawling interconnected tree of committees and subcommittees. The State Department recommendations signed by Truman in the wake of Stimson and Forrestal's concessions came to form the basis of the U.S. proposal for trusteeship at San Francisco. This draft was taken up for consideration by the specific committee entrusted with responsibility for the matter, the II/4 Committee of technical experts charged with drafting what ultimately became the UN formula for trusteeship: the language that was finalized as UN Charter Articles XII and XIII.

In their haste to prepare for the conference, the Big Five powers had failed to consult on key technical issues, including trusteeship, to forge compromise positions on draft language prior to convening in San Francisco. This meant that basic questions and fundamental principles that would otherwise have been smoothed out by working-level discussions now had to be addressed during the proceedings. Despite the delays this entailed, a number of these issues were dispensed with via informal side sessions outside of the formal proceedings of Committee II/4. Those informal discussions also exhibited a degree of candor that enabled the U.S. representatives to make clear that the American position on trusteeship was an interagency compromise forged after an epic debate between the State Department and the Departments of War and the Navy.

When the American delegation—which included Bowman, Gerig, Taussig, and military advisor Colonel Harold Stassen—unveiled their idea of strategic trust territories, Stanley and the Colonial Office balked, deeming it "unacceptable." Understandably, after the achievement of apparent agreement at Yalta, the British representatives at the conference now felt a degree of betrayal when confronted with what appeared to be an American policy innovation. Moreover it was unclear how divisions between strategic and nonstrategic areas would be drawn, leading the British delegation to lodge concerns about the responsibility for the supervision of the inhabitants of strategic trust territories. In addition, British representatives wondered whether the need might arise for the extraction of natural resources from such areas in the event of mobilization to preserve international peace and security—and what the attendant mechanism might be for ensuring rights to act accordingly if potentially huge swaths of territory were arbitrarily designated as strategic trust territories and so excluded from the international supervision that would apply to ordinary trust territories.[32]

In response the British delegation offered a draft chapter of its own that proposed simply to eliminate the distinction of strategic areas. One rationale for this modification, the representatives suggested, was a bid to simplify the classification of the various territories. The modification would also render moot the problematic requirement of specifying the mechanism through which natural resource extraction would function in these areas—some of which could be contiguous. In a sense both British concerns showed a lingering regionalism predicated on the geographical relationships between the proposed strategic areas. Here again was an example of British preoccupation with specific cases to challenge American rationales formulated in abstract and universal terms.[33] In mild form it was the reappearance of the trusteeship debate in a multilateral context. The British draft also diverged from the American version in other significant ways. In only a thinly veiled bid to further shield imperial possessions from possible unwanted subjection to trusteeship (despite the agreement at Yalta that territories would be voluntarily offered up for trusteeship), the British version was guilty of a conspicuous failure to specify precisely how candidate territories would be considered for trusteeship. The U.S. view had held that trusteeship arrangements would have to be approved by the General Assembly (or the Security Council). That difference in views belied yet another divergence of perspectives stemming from the distinct reference points of globalism and regionalism.[34]

Unfortunately for the British, the international response within the II/4 Committee sided wholeheartedly with the Americans. With the Russians, Chinese, and even the South Africans all surprisingly backing the plan, the British representatives had little recourse. Of the unpalatable options that remained, the antipodean dominions' views proposed by Herbert Evatt of Australia and New Zealand's Peter Fraser were even worse, from Whitehall's standpoint; they called for trusteeship to be applied to *all* colonial areas. Lord Cranborne, who was in charge of handling the trusteeship issue at the Conference, cabled the War Cabinet, lamenting, "So far as we can see we have no redress except refusal to sign Charter which appears unthinkable."[35] Shortly thereafter, in light of the fact that most of the British Commonwealth wanted to see American predominance in the Northern Pacific anyway, Churchill approved acquiescence to the American line, hoping that the "mutual agreement" language in the articles would limit the scope of application of the trusteeship principle, despite valid British concerns that the Arab states would employ it to seize control of the debate on the future status of Palestine. In the end the American draft language prevailed with only minor modifications. It accordingly became the textual basis for the system of international trusteeship that was to succeed the League of Nations mandates system and that finally came into force at the first session of the UN General Assembly in December 1946.[36] By that time, as we have seen, the principal questions on UN structure that remained

RECONCILING DISPARATE VISIONS

The reconciliation of interagency U.S. government and international views on both Security Council voting and the idea of trusteeship represented a partial compromise between American globalism and British regionalism. But Great Britain and the United States each sought to make what they could of the institutional compromises. The Security Council decision prompted inter-Commonwealth discussions on the prospects for the British dominions voting as a bloc in defense of their common interests.[37] Similarly the discussions on trusteeship led Whitehall to forge consensus across the dominions to safeguard, to the extent possible, British regional designs that had formally been defeated. The easiest way to do this, over the short run, was to prolong the League mandates system. Thus in the aftermath of Yalta the dominions sought to continue the system "with respect to existing Mandates and territories taken from the enemy." They would seek single-power administration of mandates, as opposed to international administration, which was "inadvisable for practical reasons." Moreover "it was undesirable" that discussion of the future Mandates Council take place at San Francisco.[38] On the American side, Stettinius, Stimson, and Forrestal assured Truman in a joint memo that the system as devised would serve multiple U.S. strategic interests, including "the maintenance of United States military and strategic rights," American control of the key Pacific and other islands necessary for the postwar forward strategy of defense, and the advancement and development of peoples in dependent territories.[39] Some British officials, it is worth noting, also saw possible ways to reconcile the respective representations of the postwar world in the new UN provisions—and indeed perceived a strong rationale to do so. Cunningham, the high commissioner in Jerusalem, for instance, made this point in lobbying Labour's Colonial Secretary George Hall (whose brief tenure preceded Creech Jones's) to place Palestine before the United Nations.[40] Cunningham's view made sense on the cusp of the new postwar international order. New mechanisms like the Trusteeship Council and the UN Charter prohibitions on the use of force had come into effect—why could they not be invoked to manage the decolonization process, indeed in a

Unanswered revolved around the Security Council and the use of the veto by its permanent members.

manner consonant with and legitimized by the weight of international opinion? Views like Cunningham's (and the Foreign Office's last-ditch trusteeship plan for Palestine) nonetheless represented minority views.

It is true that to some extent the British faced in Palestine after 1945 a strategic dilemma that mirrored the American questions vis-à-vis the Pacific islands in prior years. In an analysis that mirrored the JCS assessments of the need for U.S. sovereignty over the Japanese Mandated Islands, R. G. Howe of the Foreign Office observed in May 1946 that British strategic requirements in Palestine as laid out by the Chiefs of Staff could be ensured *only* if the United Kingdom could remain Palestine's sole trustee.[41]

His assessment is revelatory of how some of the same strategic considerations underlay both regionalism and globalism. Indeed, as has been shown, Eden's own appeals to the State Department to annex key Pacific islands outright were further proof of that partial symmetry across American and British strategic defense needs. But the perceptions of geography were also important, it turned out; they represented distortive lenses through which policymakers viewed problems. As William Roger Louis has observed, British strategists continued to frame problems largely in terms of specific territories and cases, in lieu of the American reliance on universal ideas and overarching principles, which were perhaps understandable crutches to support Washington's less-developed mental maps, which grew muddier with radial distance from Europe. Partly because of this distinction, despite the observations of Cunningham and Howe, globalism and regionalism lived on in the respective foreign policy bureaucracies in which they had taken root—and even were perpetuated over time as officials circulated out to diplomatic posts overseas.[42]

What remained unclear were the final ledger entries on the American and British sides after the documents were signed. Did Yalta and San Francisco represent only partial triumphs of American globalism? To what extent were America's global security designs frustrated? And how much regionalism did the UN security system build in? Legal theorists like Thomas Franck have argued that the UN Security Council represented the second coming of a nineteenth-century balance of power, albeit one cloaked in the rhetoric of a liberal internationalist compact binding the victorious postwar powers with the world community to carry the burden of preserving peace. This interpretation of the UN role in the maintenance of peace and security holds that the permanent members of the Security Council became a fairly close representation of Roosevelt's Four Policemen, enlarged by one due to the inclusion of China. Franck maintains that the resulting body amounted to a consortium of overwhelming power that could be brought to bear on any aggressor state that might threaten other states or international security and repeat the excesses of fascist aggression that rent asunder the international system in the early 1940s. By regulating the use of that power through the principle of consensus, his line of reasoning holds, the five permanent members of the Security Council had arrogated for themselves the right to essentially police the international order as they collectively saw fit.[43] But other accounts have challenged that interpretation. Michael Glennon has maintained that the Security Council was instead meant to function more as a world court presided over by the five major victorious powers, amounting to "a grand attempt to subject the use of force to the rule of law." Glennon's legalistic interpretation of an international order governed by legal restraints on the use of force contrasts with the power-political underpinnings of Franck's conception of a Security Council rooted in Realpolitik.[44] Alternatively John Ruggie suggested that a multilateral institutional rationale rooted in constructivist theory underlay the Security Council's design.[45] Alexander George has subscribed to yet another view of a consortium of power bounded by the national will of its members states, claiming that domestic U.S. political and other constraints worked to give rise to an only partial realization of Roosevelt's Great Design for a postwar world order.[46]

The historical record of the origins of the United Nations Organization suggests a more complex picture than simple great power dominance of respective geographic regions of influence, in which a tidy reconciliation of the postwar aims of the victorious Allies evaded the best efforts of Washington, London, and Moscow to cooperate in good faith and resolve key outstanding questions. Anglo-American policy discord during this period was profound: the likes of Roosevelt and Welles clearly subscribed to completely different views of self-determination than Churchill and other defenders of colonialism in the postwar period. Some historians have even questioned whether a hidden desire to replace the British Empire with an American equivalent really drove American participation in the war effort.[47] But like the divergence across their views on self-government for colonial peoples, the statesmen leading the victorious powers also shared contradictory conceptions of the division of policing responsibilities in the new UN order—and the role an executive body like the Security Council would occupy at its institutional center.

Did UN Security Council members in fact agree to a truly universal new world order, or did they seek merely to utilize the United Nations to expand their postwar geopolitical influence? Geographer and anthropologist Neil Smith has argued that the other great powers frustrated Washington's efforts to extend U.S. influence worldwide through an "anti-geographic" American globalism that would defend U.S. strategic and commercial interests worldwide in the UN system that emerged at San Francisco.[48] Indeed the statesmen gathered at the postwar conferences had yet to even arrive at a consensus view of the geographical scope of the United Nations system. Churchill, for one, resisted Roosevelt's vision of a global organization until the very end, hoping instead to leave in place a system of regional councils that would protect key regions with British geopolitical interests from unwanted interference—a policy reflected in the Foreign Office proposals for a system of regional councils to preserve postwar peace, as well as the Poynton-Robinson proposals for regional and functional oversight of colonial territories through "partnership." For Churchill, the paramount objective was the preservation of Britain's empire and postwar status as a great power, which meant the continuation of British control over its colonial dependencies in the Levant, South Asia, and the Far East. Meanwhile the United States sought to prevent the future agglomeration of destabilizing military power in the European heartland, maintain access to key strategic points on the globe, and facilitate the expansion of U.S. commercial influence to Europe, Africa, and Asia via an integrated system of global trade and open markets.

In their pursuit of those interests, to some extent, the British and American framers of the UN Charter never formally addressed the question of the true character of the UN system that came into existence in San Francisco. For the consortium of power that the veto-wielding Security Council represented was embedded in the text of the UN Charter alongside that document's aspirational references to the world of coequal, sovereign states that the Council was entrusted to protect. All that this achieved was to merely codify the glaring incongruity between the conceptual essence of the Council, grounded firmly in nineteenth-century Realpolitik, and the neo-Wilsonian liberal internationalism of the Charter's rules on state conduct, the use of force, and the principle of trusteeship. What emerged was therefore not the realization of any *one* of the coherent national visions that statesmen had debated during the war but an institutional compromise that amalgamated facets from a number of the proposed schemes. Despite the decidedly American imprint on the UN Charter, the compromise—

certainly with regard to the veto powers of permanent Security Council members to block enforcement action—amounted to outright victory for neither American globalism nor the regionalism inherent in British conceptions of its postwar empire. A glaring (and perhaps avoidable) implication of that compromise was ambiguity among the great powers—about whether UN peace and security functions amounted to what international law scholar Hans Kelsen considered a collective self-defense pact binding the world, or whether it represented instead the enshrinement in international law of a postwar world divided into spheres of influence among the great powers. Perhaps more than the Security Council, the Trusteeship Council bore the imprint of American globalism, given its universal design and potential application to all dependent territories. The caveat of strategic trust territories—a fine-grained technical distinction in the plans pushed by Forrestal, Knox, and others in the U.S. military—was to some extent the most "globalist" element of the final provisions. But to characterize it as the most prominent mark of American influence on the finished product is somewhat misleading, given the interest of Churchill and Eden in selling Americans on the idea of outright territorial annexation and their tacit recognition of (and indeed dependence on) American primacy in the Pacific. In this sense American "globalists" were preaching to a small choir in Whitehall.

What, then, *did* the compromise forged in San Francisco amount to, institutionally, and what were the attendant obligations that member nations assumed? Observers at the time certainly grasped the difficulties that would beset the new organization given the need to reconcile its global scope with the latent appeal of spheres of interest on the part of many signatory nations. Latin American reactions in the run-up to the conference debates on the Security Council were certainly laced with regionalist impulses, while some of the U.S. voices seeking to placate those concerns evoked vestiges of the Monroe Doctrine. But surprisingly, when confronted with the alternative evil of a global blueprint for a UN system of collective security, key Latin American nations in March 1945 signed enthusiastically onto a wartime regional security alliance that would extend into the postwar period. The Act of Chapultepec was a gesture that seemed to *endorse* the Monroe Doctrine.[49] Either way, the tension between hemispheric solidarity and global security was palpable. But the tension extended beyond just the Western Hemisphere, for soon after the conference opened, Molotov proposed a Soviet amendment to the UN Charter that would preclude Security Council authority from impinging on security agreements the

Soviet Union had already entered into with Britain, Czechoslovakia, France, Poland, and Yugoslavia. Soviet intransigence from Dumbarton Oaks to Yalta to San Francisco, of course, had long since revealed Stalin's preoccupation with guaranteeing a belt of security around the Soviet Union. After Senator Arthur Vandenberg sought to insert an explicit reference to the Act of Chapultepec to protect America's corresponding sphere of influence in response to the Soviet proposal, Anthony Eden soon sought the same protections for British interests in the Mediterranean, where he feared the projection of Soviet interest. Soviet arguments thus resonated in British ears eager to formulate robust defenses of regionalism. Britain too harbored fears of encroachment on its geopolitical interests, not least by an expanding American globalism of trade and military basing rights, although American designs surely aroused less concern than expansionistic Soviet foreign policies.

Indeed British resistance to the American conception of self-determination rights had revealed London's nostalgia for preserving what remained of the British Empire and partial influence where only former colonies remained. Having dropped the ball on trusteeship, there was the separate issue of regional organizations subservient to the Security Council. But even there the gains conceded to globalism outweighed the modicum of regionalism reflected in the UN Charter. Ultimately the Charter reference to regional organizations was diluted into generic form so as to avoid specific mention of *any* regional alliances or treaty commitments. But the debate preceding that outcome also revealed the extent to which great power competition over geopolitical influence underlay the lofty global aspirations espoused by American officials—and the daylight separating American and British geographical conceptions of the UN system's intended scope.[50] In the pivotal moment when regionalism and globalism were reconciled, as Neil Smith put it, "the geographical contradiction that Roosevelt had always skated over now writhed on the table."[51] *Time* magazine hardly described the paradox more delicately: "Of the victorious powers, only the Big Three have an industrial plant big enough and varied enough to support modern war. This sharp concentration naturally produced a tendency for other states to group themselves around the three strong ones, and for the three Great Powers to try to run things in their own regions."[52] Thus globalism's partial triumph reflected the realities of the worldwide distribution of postwar military power and industrial capacity. But what is impossible to ignore are the conceptions of geography to which these realities gave rise, and their cataclysmic clash in the cable traffic, meetings, and informal consultations that led to the twin compromises of Yalta and San Francisco.

Historians have devoted great attention to analyses of the balancing act between the Charter's universal designs—very much a reflection of American globalism—and the persistent regionalism espoused by Great Britain all along that underpinned Big Four interests leading up to San Francisco and beyond.[53] The compromises appeared in various forms. The Charter's provisions for Security Council voting, trusteeship, and regional organizations were three formal mechanisms by which those impulses were accommodated. But regionalism also crept in through subtler, more indirect ways, like the unstated policies of the great powers *after* the structure of the Security Council was determined. What may not be immediately apparent from the official documentary records of the proceedings at San Francisco is the extent to which the Big Four nations, including the United States and Great Britain, relied on the institutional mechanisms that they ultimately negotiated to protect their regional designs. Despite the wealth of historical and theoretical works examining the nature, structure, and function of the Security Council, including a great number concluding that the Council represented the latest incarnation of a nineteenth-century concert of great powers, few studies have probed the nontrivial effects of latent, implied mental geographies in shaping Council outcomes. Those effects have likely manifested themselves in various ways, even when no formal disagreements arose in the form of insoluble permanent-member conflicts preventing the requisite consensus to take Chapter VII action. Herein lies a critical consideration for assessing the performance of the Security Council in its early years. For if such latent tensions between globalism and regionalism did temper the actions of permanent Council members, documented instances of such effects could amount to new evidence explaining why those members (and by extension the Council as a whole) refrained from interventions in the cases of early postcolonial conflicts such as the first Arab-Israeli War, the first Indo-Pakistani War over Kashmir, and the Indonesian independence struggle.[54]

The history of early great power deliberations at the United Nations suggests that such tensions may have inhibited Council members from taking collective action. That gridlock reveals that unresolved tensions between competing mental geographies persisted into the UN era, well after the Charter was finalized and the organization had begun to function as a system. The documentary record suggests that U.S. policy toward the plight of émigré Jews fleeing occupied Europe impinged heavily on the Truman administration's stance on Palestine, where the principal Foreign Office concern was the reaction of Arab Muslims and the fear that it might spread to other Muslim populations eastward through Central Asia in India. In South Asia, American concerns about the penetration of communist influence led Washington to frame the Kashmir dispute as a problem for subcontinental security—a secondary theater of potential confrontation with the Soviet Union—in contrast to British interests in preserving order among the tribal areas of Pakistan, Afghanistan, and beyond for both imperial defense and strategic reasons. The significance of the U.S.-Dutch wartime relationship and the flow of Marshall Plan aid loomed large as a consideration shaping U.S. policy toward the Indonesian independence movement, especially in the early stages of that conflict, before the excesses of the second Dutch police action prompted the United States to support British efforts to sweep away Dutch colonial authority. Finally, in the case of the Francophone Levant, steadfast American interests in dislodging Free French influence spurred the recognition of Syrian and Lebanese independence well before the acid of British reoccupation helped corrode French control there as well.[55] The anomalous case of Palestine aside, Anglo-American policy coordination proved largely reconcilable, as decolonization proceeded apace as the war came to a close. Fortunately the complementarity between the geographical expansion of American security interests and a corresponding curtailment of British possessions and presences meant that Anglo-American clashes were few. But the vestiges of two distinct ways of seeing the world on both sides of the Atlantic surviving into the post-1945 international order should come as no surprise.

Explanations of the tension between American globalism and British regionalism in the new UN international order must take account of the unprecedented pace of globalization that was under way during the Second World War. After waging a colossal, multitheater war that spanned two oceans and multiple fronts, the Allied powers realized that the responsibility for maintaining international peace would now become a shared burden that they would have to bear through some form of policy coordination and multilateral cooperation. As other processes of globalization proceeded, including the expansion of air travel, the growth of a global petroleum market, an increase in nongovernmental organizations, and the international financial system put in place at Bretton Woods, so too did the maintenance of international peace become a global concern, especially after the consequences of neglecting armed aggression by the Third Reich were clear. In a sense, a host of new problems ascended to a global level merely by virtue of the unprecedented degree of integration that began to link hitherto national and regional concerns. And differing perceptions of the postwar world would necessarily produce competing solutions for these newly internationalized problems as they confronted overburdened statesmen in real time.

But the impact of certain technological and intellectual changes that accompanied the postwar transition was undeniable. As he noted to the JCS in 1943, Roosevelt recognized that air power would be an absolutely central element in the realization of American globalism through power projection. Indeed he had cited the parallel importance of key Pacific basing sites for civilian air transit nodes, which would be critical for the cultivation of U.S. commercial links in the postwar world.[56] The U.S. Air Transport Command (ATC), which was established in June 1942 to allow the U.S. military to enlist the services of the domestic civilian air fleet to help ferry troops and personnel to the war's front lines, was incapable of meeting the necessary lift requirements. It was simply underequipped to transport large numbers of U.S. personnel and materiel in an expeditionary capacity in the service of a forward hemispheric defense strategy of holding distant bases in the Japanese Mandated Islands and the Azores. Even at its height ATC possessed some 3,090 aircraft. But many of these aircraft suffered from mechanical failures and were converted bombers with limited cargo capacity. Indeed unreliability cost the U.S. Air Force a large number of accidents—some 1,229 over the course of wartime flights over the "Himalayan Hump" route from China to India. ATC had become inoperative by 1945 and completely defunct by 1948, when the U.S. Military Air Transport Service (MATS) came into existence, one month before the start of the Berlin Airlift. Soon thereafter American airlift capabilities began to expand. Despite the creation of MATS, with its Continental, Atlantic, and Pacific divisions, U.S. airlift capacity remained woefully deficient at first, and the massive demobilization of forward-deployed U.S. military personnel from the war's distant theaters heavily cut back the military's capability to deploy units to a hypothetical international armed force on behalf of the United Nations. But the development of MATS and the growth of the postwar U.S. Air Force over the cold war years represented a U.S. response to the challenge of globalism—and the worldwide commitments that it now entailed.[57]

That steady rise of American air power, coupled with its deployment throughout the worldwide network of military bases at strategic points determined by the Joint Chiefs of Staff and the U.S. Navy, displaced the British naval mastery that had presided over the Pax Britannica. British postwar strategy all but necessitated a geographical contraction at the birth of the postwar world order. The three billion pounds of war debt was one economic burden on the imperial treasury that all but mandated the imperial withdrawal that Bevin and Labour oversaw from 1945 onward. The rise of independence movements in Egypt, Palestine, and India constituted separate, political burdens. The cumulative weight of these pressures proved unbearable for postwar British foreign policy, given both the extensiveness of its territorial commitments and the degree of the strain on the cost of the imperial presence. Its displacement by the growing reach of American globalism was inevitable. As political scientist Tony Smith has observed, "The global character of the war and the ensuing retrenchment of America's Western European allies from the Near East to the Orient meant that for the first time United States interests were not regional but virtually worldwide in scope."[58]

Ironically, even as American globalism displaced the regionalism of European imperial enclaves, some leading commentators clamored for the opposite phenomenon, calling for an "escape from a theoretical and ineffective universalism into practical and workable regionalism," as historian E. H. Carr observed at the time.[59] But what was to be the basis for this new regionalism? Hemispheric unity had posed one possibility; now the mixed legacy of the Monroe Doctrine, Russian expansionism, Japanese aggression in the Pacific, and Nazi occupation had sowed the seeds of considerable interhemispheric defensive responsibilities that America could no longer shirk. As the Truman National Security Council would observe some years later in uncharacteristically historical terms, "During the 19th century, British sea power was unchallenged within the approaches to the Americas and the United States relied upon Britain to restrain hostile transoceanic powers. By 1900, however, Britain ceased to rule all the oceans and our concept of static isolation and defense became outmoded. Today United States forces cannot afford to wait at home to repel an attack initiated by a formidable enemy. In the age of air power our new security frontiers extend to those continental and island bases outside the Americas from which hostile attacks can be launched to strike the new world."[60] War and occupation had left most of America's European Allies shattered, debt-ridden, and unable to project meaningful levels of military power to balance American influence as it filled postwar security vacuums. Neither had the East-West divide that persisted throughout much of the cold war fully deepened before the huge military expenditures by the United States and the Soviet Union that militarized that conflict and its expansion into the third world by the Korean War's outbreak in 1950. Thus between 1945 and 1947 the United States was able, through a combination of power projection and the institutional structure of the new UN organization, to assert control over the basic structure of the international political system that had been subject to British domination for a century and a half.[61] American globalism thus knew no realistic bounds, no international competitors, at least in those immediate postwar years in which it shaped national security policy and the redefinition of American security in drastically expanded geographical terms.

Nevertheless the United States did recognize the cost-effectiveness and strategic value of reliance on waning European colonial powers to stabilize regions in which it was costly or premature to project direct U.S. power. In retrospect the nuanced American approach to shaping the UN Security Council and Trusteeship Council emphasized some degree of colonial power co-optation: by securing British *buy-in* rather than the precipitation of an outright confrontation. This approach profoundly shaped the global national security policy framed by the Truman administration, which, despite its reliance on Middle East oil supplies and strategic bases from the Ryukyus to the Azores, sought to limit U.S. costs and entanglements to the maximum extent.[62] But its roots lay in the wartime coalescence of American globalism, under Roosevelt's prescient strategic vision. The JCS, as noted, openly recognized the value of relying on European colonial power in the aftermath of hostilities, despite the widening gap in interests as victory was consolidated. As Hull later recalled, "At no time did we press Britain, France or the Netherlands for an immediate grant of self-government to their colonies. Our thought was that it would come after an adequate period of years, short or long, depending on the state of development of respective colonial peoples, during which these peoples would be trained to govern themselves."[63] Perhaps that patience with decolonization processes was the byproduct of the recognition by strategists like Roosevelt, Bowman, and even Hull that at least minimal reliance on former colonial powers made strategic sense from the standpoint of classical geopolitics—a field of academic study that was exploding in the United States and that would provide the intellectual infrastructure to parallel the bases, aircraft, and trade routes that consolidated globalism.

SPYKMAN, GEOPOLITICS, AND MENTAL MAPS OF GLOBALISM

Geopolitical thought underwent transformative change in the decades prior to the Second World War. A half-century before the birth of the United Nations, Sir Halford Mackinder had posited that control over the vast interior of the European landmass was a critical prerequisite for global domination. The essence of that idea formed the basis of the German *Geopolitik* of Friedrich Ratzel, who coined the term *Lebensraum,* and the work of his contemporary, Karl Haushofer, whose theories of geopolitical expansion rationalized the Third Reich's expansionist military strategy.[64] Partly because of the association of German geopolitical works with Nazi ideology, the entire discipline was stigmatized and largely purged from American academic curricula during the war. But some of these ideas evolved and were reconfigured into the work of American strategist and political scientist Nicholas Spykman. Director of Yale University's Institute for International Studies, Spykman first laid out his basic ideas in two articles in the *American Political Science Review* in the interwar years. Geographic location and size were important bases of state power, he contended. In his view, those salient considerations were ignored in interwar debates on America's role in the world, to the detriment of U.S. security.

In contrast to Mackinder's thesis of heartland control as the key to supremacy over the world system, Spykman believed that, from the American vantage point, power balances in the European heartland and in Asia were the key factors on which the future of the international system hinged. The agglomeration of hegemonic power in either region, he contended, could allow potential aggressors to amass requisite natural resource bases and industrial output capacities to project military power against the United States. The implications of this analysis placed a new focus on the littoral Mediterranean regions of Southeastern Europe, the Persian Gulf, the Red Sea, the Indian Ocean, Southeast Asia, and China. They would be the keys to strategic dominance by virtue of their proximity to sea lanes and both human and natural resources. Because of the importance of sea lines of communication, those resources included the coastal waters surrounding the "Rimland" constituting much of the European colonial powers' key territories of Palestine, Egypt, Iran, and India.[65] Spykman described these bodies of water as "the great circumferential maritime highway of the world."[66]

Spykman's work sounded perhaps the loudest clarion call to embrace the globalism that guided American national security policy into the postwar era and the Truman administration. Despite his contempt for global supranational institutions to preserve peace in the aftermath of the League's collapse, Spykman's *America's Strategy in World Politics* (1942) became one of the most complete and accurate monographic blueprints for globalism as it pervaded the minds of Roosevelt and administration officials like Welles and Forrestal. It certainly resonated with the arguments contained in the JCS memos of 1943 arguing for U.S. sovereignty over the Japanese Mandated Islands. For like the U.S. military, Spykman's thinking was grounded almost entirely in strategic necessities. His analysis of America's geopolitical predicament sprang from the baseline reality of involvement in a worldwide conflict. The immediate upshot was a degree of interdependence between the war's theaters and its host continents.[67]

In addition, like Roosevelt's conclusions as confided to the Joint Chiefs in 1942–1943, Spykman's recognition of the significance of air power provided a powerful rationale for a national security globalism supportive of U.S. control of far-flung forward defenses. It was one that the United States *had* to contemplate, out of necessary modifications of the maxims that guided hemispheric defense doctrines throughout the age of isolationism. This meant that America's relative global power depended on the outcome of the Second World War.[68]

For Spykman, the postwar balance of power thus hinged on the contours of the peace settlement and the disposition of U.S. forces at that threshold. The Berlin-Tokyo axis, he argued, had well-developed goals for that settlement should they achieve victory, goals that included undermining hemispheric solidarity by infiltrating America's historic South American allies: "In the 'New World Order,' the United States would have to rescind the protective policy implied in the Monroe Doctrine and be forced to accept in the sister republics below the American Mediterranean fascist governments controlled from Berlin. The result would be complete encirclement."[69] The German-Japanese alliance could achieve that encirclement, Spykman argued, by strangling exports to the Americas from the European landmass it sought to occupy: "If it can conquer all of the Old World, it will have obtained control of raw materials indispensable to the war industries of the United States and achieved a monopoly in the great export market of the Western Hemisphere."[70] The geopolitical implications of that encirclement led Spykman to see the only possible recourse to be a forward strategy of defense, as opposed to a retreat into hemispheric coastal defense, as America had sought in the age of Wilson. This meant American engagement in both the transatlantic and transpacific buffer zones that separated America from would-be aggressors. It was true that the size of the Pacific Ocean and the distances that had to be traversed were a factor that reduced the threat of naval invasion from the west. But Spykman nonetheless cited the Aleutian and Hawaiian Islands as principal bases from which to assure naval mastery over the Pacific and as strategic points to anchor a defense in depth of the West Coast of the United States.[71] These academic arguments of course melded perfectly with the post–Pearl Harbor thinking of Leahy, Knox, and others in the Roosevelt administration. Far from abstract constructs trapped in ivory towers, geopolitical ideas from the likes of Spykman came to bear directly on American postwar security strategy in the late 1940s, through institutional relationships like the State Department's ties to the Council on Foreign Relations, and through individuals like Bowman, who shared Spykman's concerns about the recrudescence of German and Japanese regional power.

Other scholars involved in policy at the time also espoused Spykman's idea of preserving power balances. Interestingly William Langer, the Harvard historian turned analyst for the Office of Strategic Services, wrote in 1945 that the United States should be wary of dissolving the European empires or "championing schemes of international trusteeship which may provoke unrest and may result in colonial disintegration," as their utility as bulwarks against communist advance loomed ever larger in the developing cold war. While this study has argued that the United States instead opted to *displace* rather than perpetuate European colonial power in regions like the Levant and East Indies, Langer's thought nonetheless still embraced the globalism that had shaped military strategy in its recommendation that America consolidate a "Western European–Mediterranean–American bloc," foreshadowing the birth of NATO and the Euro-Atlantic security consensus that would emerge in coming years.[72] The thinking of academics like Bowman, Spykman, Langer, and others directly or indirectly influenced policy and rationalized U.S. designs for the UN system, internationalized mechanisms for securing key strategic regions, and America's postwar strategy for former European colonies in Asia and Africa with powerful new ideas from developing fields like geopolitics and war and peace studies. Bowman himself went to considerable lengths to distinguish the academic pursuit of political geography from the enlistment of geographical research in the service of national policy and the conduct of war. But the intellectual climate of American academia could hardly remain insulated from developments in the war's principal theaters.[73]

The Second World War's transformative effects extended beyond the American academy; its effects on the home front meant that a new awareness of geopolitics now came to permeate the American public imagination more deeply than ever. It is not surprising that the year 1942—which saw the establishment of the ATC as a precursor to the rise of worldwide U.S airlift capabilities, as well as the first draft of what would become the UN Charter—also saw the publication of Spykman's *America's Strategy in World Politics* and its call to arms for America to devise its own brand of geopolitics for the postwar years. Yet 1942 also marked the start of a new era that saw the rise of cheap, ubiquitous commercial maps throughout the United States. Roosevelt, well versed in geopolitics form his navy experience, called for every American to purchase a world map so they could follow along with his fireside chat updates on the war effort. Commercial mapmakers rushed to fill the demand his request triggered. In many instances they depicted the Earth in new ways, challenging widely held conceptions about circumferential distances and hemispheric separation by emphasizing the spherical shape of the planet, often from aerial vantage points reflective of what some scholars have termed "air-age globalism."[74] The National Geographic Society published some 37 million maps during the war, many of which employed new cartographic techniques, venturing from the ubiquitous but increasingly outmoded Mercator projection format. As a testament to their influence on war planning and operations, General Eisenhower ordered 20,000 copies of one of the Society's maps of Germany for the benefit of American ground forces in 1944. At the other end of the war, another Society map saved soon-to-be Pacific Fleet Commander-in-Chief Admiral Chester Nimitz and his crew when they found themselves lost in the skies above the South Pacific.[75] In a sense this public rediscovery of geography helped embed the globalism of national security planners into the national consciousness, diffusing it beyond government bureaucracies into public discourse and the popular imagination. Feedback effects then retransmitted fragments of those geographic conceptions back into foreign policy as new scholars and public officials came to serve the postwar national security establishment, having graduated from new programs in international studies and other fields that emphasized geopolitics and its ramifications for war and peace.

The cumulative impact as this imagined geography of globalism spread and materialized was the gradual expansion of American overseas power projection—through American bases on strategic trust territories, the UN Security and Trusteeship Councils, a global U.S. airlift capacity, worldwide exports of American economic surpluses, and even a sense among ordinary Americans of the nation's new global reach. That growth of American hard power, economic output, and interest in the wider world hastened the end of the age of European imperialism, especially in dependent territories directly affected by hostilities in the war. Though unmistakable, the displacement was not as abrupt or forced as it might have been had the United States embarked on a more deliberately aggressive and unilateral variant of globalism—as espoused by some strategists within the Department of the Navy like Knox and the Joint Strategic Survey Committee. Given the alignments and respective fortunes of the wartime Allies, American globalism actually came to co-opt British support (and even the fait accompli of temporary military occupation) to dislodge distant footholds of European colonial power. Fortunately for postwar Anglo-American coordination, the strategic logic and geographical realities that led the United States to a global security policy neatly complemented the downsizing of the British overseas presence and the curtailment of the Labour government's geopolitical ambitions after 1945. Unlike the French and Dutch empires that clung defiantly to prewar possessions they could no longer administer, the British became willing collaborators in the postwar displacement of colonial cartographies with the new map of American globalism and the UN world order that reflected its dominant themes. Despite their differences on how far and how fast to proceed, Attlee and Bevin successfully recalibrated the imperial footprint, effectively bringing the Pax Britannica to a close with the policy of nonintervention and the weaker relationships that bound together the "informal empire" of the postwar era.

Palestine and Kashmir were decolonized in this changing world order, caught between a rising American globalism and the regionalism of the British Empire and Commonwealth that it effectively succeeded. These diametrically opposed mental geographies help frame the study of Anglo-American policies toward the power devolution process in both key flashpoints. The last two chapters focus on that process, through which forces of nationalism from below clashed with great power strategic designs imposed from above to territorialize violent self-determination struggles in the crucible of independence.

EIGHT

Joining the Community of Nations

Independence movements from the Arab world to South and Southeast Asia sensed a watershed moment as the Second World War ended. While much of Europe's industrial core lay smoldering in ruins, economic and physical devastation compelled colonial powers like Great Britain, France, and the Netherlands to consider the costs of imperial overstretch and the prospect of withdrawals from dependent territories in regions like the Indian subcontinent, the Levant, and the Indonesian archipelago. Meanwhile the creation of the new United Nations organization and its Security and Trusteeship Councils held out the promise of a new deal for emergent nation-states of the developing world, along with a constitutional framework promising to guarantee and legitimize the fruits of their efforts to achieve international legal parity with the Western industrialized world. But fundamental unanswered questions remained with regard to how successor political entities would evolve from Europe's dissolved developing-world empires and organize themselves in accordance with the principle of sovereign statehood. And though the UN trusteeship provisions could theoretically be extended to former colonial territories, the reluctance of colonial powers like Great Britain to employ them made clear that the process would hardly be an orderly one.

What the world witnessed instead was a haphazard, global scramble to enter the community of nations on the parts of a variety of stateless peoples and movements worldwide. In many cases these movements pursued their political destinies largely independent of direct intervention by great powers like the United States and Great Britain. And a significant yet hitherto neglected rationale for that great power apathy stemmed from the language of the United Nations Charter itself and the ambiguities about international legal claims by anticolonial movements to which that document unwittingly gave rise.

The UN Charter's reference to the notion of "self-determination for peoples" would pose considerable challenges for the fulfillment of the UN mission to preserve a peaceful global equilibrium from the very outset. It became evident in the immediate aftermath of the Second World War that balancing the pursuit of sovereign statehood with self-determination, an evolving international legal principle subject to drastically different regional interpretations, would pose serious obstacles for UN member states. These difficulties of interpretation would profoundly shape the wave of independence movements that got under way during the very same period. Critically both globalism and regionalism too came to shape American and British policies toward certain independence movements, which in turn were motivated by myriad strains of nationalist thought.

THE UN CHARTER AND THE IMPRINTS OF MENTAL GEOGRAPHIES

The implications of the UN Charter's parallel sanctification of the distinct principles of sovereignty and self-determination materialized glaringly in at least two basic forms of postwar conflicts: those pitting anticolonial self-determination struggles against former colonial powers (India's struggle against Britain, Indonesia's struggle against the Dutch; the Syrian and Lebanese struggle against the French) and territorial disputes between rival postcolonial claimants staking novel claims to newly independent territory (Israel's versus Palestine's; Pakistan's versus India's).[1] Sovereignty had long been recognized in customary law as the basic organizing principle of the international order. Its codification as a universal legal status for nations in the UN Charter represented a threshold for the development of the modern state system, but the principle itself, and the corollary notion of the sovereign equality of states, had evolved down a long trajectory leading to the San Francisco Conference. And noninterference in the affairs of states had certainly come into being as a norm of customary international law centuries before Article 2 of the UN Charter was written, however inconsistently it had been respected. Meanwhile the principle of self-determination had also evolved in parallel and claimed a bloody history in Europe rooted deeper in historical memory than the postwar explosion of anticolonial nationalist movements in the twentieth century, dating back to the Wilsonian era of the early years after the First World War. Some of the most notorious evidence of that lineage emerged from the Third Reich's invocation of the German right to national self-determination, rooted in the work of pre-Nazi-era cartographers to justify expansionism in East Central Europe well before the Second World War.[2] Indeed the first article of the program of the National Socialist Party espoused "the unification of all Germans to form a Great Germany on the basis of the right of self-determination enjoyed by nations."[3] Such attempts to map national identity onto fixed territorial spaces relied on boundaries of nation-states yet to be realized and constructed only in collective popular imaginations, providing an interpretive context for self-determination in the postwar period.

But wholly new interpretations of self-determination rights evolved when proto-nationalists enlisted the principle in the service of postcolonial experiments in nationhood. Of key historical significance for the course of international relations was the manner in which many such intractable struggles frequently incapacitated the Security Council during the critical, early postwar years, even when political differences between the Council's permanent members were not, in and of themselves, sufficient to precipitate that paralysis. Had the United Nations simultaneously codified sovereign equality and sowed the very seeds of its demise elsewhere in the same founding document? The answers were not clear, and would not be for decades, leaving an ambiguity that exacerbated the already tangled problems associated with the fragmentation of Europe's overseas empires. Faced with this dilemma, the permanent members of the Security Council such as the United States often found themselves unwilling to intervene robustly under the auspices of the newly created world organization, *especially when postcolonial statehood lay at stake*—neither on the side of former European powers seeking to preserve their colonial territories (like Great Britain in post-Raj India) using what Washington deemed the discredited idea of empire, nor on behalf of the anticolonial self-determination struggles waging war against them (like the Indonesian nationalist movement), nor on the side of individual national movements vying for sovereign control over newly independent territories (like Arabs and Zionists in Palestine).[4]

The United States, Great Britain, and the Security Council's other permanent members could justify their collective apathy in the face of clear acts of aggression by citing manifold challenges besetting the UN Organization at its birth during a moment of profound flux in the structure of the international state system. The lack of standing UN military forces under unified command was certainly one. But equally important was the role that the Charter drafters preserved for the Security Council and the discretion they accorded it by allowing it to convene in what U.S. Secretary of State Edward Stettinius termed a "quasi-judicial" capacity to determine whether individual conflicts violated or threatened international peace.[5] That privilege of passing selective judgment on matters arising before the Council led its permanent members down a path of indeterminacy in the face of certain types of conflict, including those pitting allied European nations against national liberation movements driven by fervent anticolonial ideologies that no government, neither Eastern nor Western, wanted to oppose publicly. The resulting dilemmas that arose over intervention in colonial questions were sufficient to challenge the UN Charter's effectiveness, independent of the distinct issue of the often competing political objectives of individual Council members (along cold war lines or in accordance with intraregional rivalries). Part of the reason for this paralysis was the indeterminate nature of principles like sovereignty and self-determination at midcentury. Did sovereignty trump the rights of national groups to self-determination? What did those rights entail, and were they ever intended by the United Nations to connote rights to secession? Contentious international legal debates on these questions would unfold over decades after the birth of the United Nations. Still, as the legal history of self-determination has shown, interpretations of such principles often varied markedly across the world's regions.[6] In the interim the ambiguity surrounding both principles enabled the great powers present at the birth of the world organization to interpret them as they saw fit to suit their postcolonial, imperial, geopolitical, or other prerogatives.[7]

At least one reason for the indeterminacy at the United Nations, this book argues, was the asymmetry between the American and British conceptions of geography when it came to postcolonial issues arising before the Security Council during its early years. American globalism had rationalized the Jewish emigration to Israel that had so unnerved the Arab states that declared war in May 1948; to some in the Truman administration, the combined Arab "act of aggression" against Israel was incontrovertible. Conversely the Foreign Office's regionalism that so wished to placate Palestinian Arabs could hardly allow Britain to find fault with the acts of the national armies and irregular forces that stormed into Palestine after the declaration of Israeli independence in May 1948. The result was a collective nonresponse when it came to enforcement action to stem the violence. In the case of Kashmir, Anglo-American policy goals did converge, but only coincidentally, because of the overlapping strategic objectives that Washington and London sought through the support of Pakistan. The Truman administration considered the new Muslim heir to united India as a bulwark against the spread of communism to the subcontinent, whereas London deemed it the cornerstone of the region's security—security that would prove essential for the rehabilitation of the postwar British economy and the preservation of British prestige as power was transferred to both new dominions. Yet despite the transatlantic accord on the strategic importance of Pakistan, Washington and London again refrained from the deployment of international forces.[8] The British Chiefs of Staff cited the lack of proper international experts trained in the nuances of the region's languages and cultures that might be assembled as part of a peacekeeping force. Washington meanwhile worried about the precedent that international forces in far-flung South Asia might set, fearing the introduction of Soviet troops into the subcontinent—or even other regions, such as Southeastern Europe or the Middle East. Thus although the reasons for inaction in the Council differed in the cases of Palestine and Kashmir, precisely how Washington and London conceived of both flashpoints, in a territorial sense, shaped the positions adopted in each capital to significant degrees.

One consequence of that inaction was the abandonment of both the conflicts in Palestine and Kashmir as fights to exhaustion or other means of resolution absent the direct Security Council intervention envisioned by the framers of the Charter at the postwar United Nations conferences. When coupled with the discretionary avoidance of the Trusteeship Council, that inaction drastically curtailed the new world organization's ability to manage the decolonization process and seems in part to have contributed to two subsequent developments. One was the activation of the United Nations mechanisms for dispute settlement, including the exercise of the secretary-general's good offices role and the deployment of UN observer missions that later evolved into the innovation of "Chapter 6 1/2" UN peacekeeping as a substitute for peace enforcement along the lines proposed in the Charter.[9] The other appears to have been the achievement of sovereign statehood and UN membership by a collection of postcolonial states severely deficient in adequate governance capacity. Both phenomena accompanied a global surge of regional conflicts whose outbreaks coincided with the end of the Second World War and which ended in a series of outcomes: from the crystallization of a tenuous stalemate in Kashmir to the violent emergence of the state of Israel, seemingly into a postindependence world of perpetual, existential conflict, and the eventual realization of Indonesian independence from Dutch colonial rule. (Syrian and Lebanese independence, of course, had been realized before the creation of the world body in 1945.)

At the root of all of these processes was the reconciliation of the ideal of sovereign statehood with the wide range of self-determination struggles that characterized the age.

THE WESTPHALIAN ORIGINS OF SOVEREIGNTY

The literature on the history of sovereignty is extensive and wide-ranging.[10] Scholars of international law have amply documented how the international legal concept of sovereignty has specifically impacted the decolonization process.[11] These studies offer considerable insights into how respect for the principle of sovereignty may have inadvertently undermined the UN collective security architecture by helping to instill a reluctance on the part of one or more of the permanent members of the Security Council to invoke Charter law in certain cases perceived to be "exceptional": instances of conflict in which those members of the Council, seemingly for no other clearly documented reason, deemed collective security action to be inappropriate.[12] The popularity of the idea of sovereignty as manifest in the intellectual currents and general spirit of the age around 1945 is thus undeniable.

However, at a higher level of abstraction, the concept of sovereignty can be traced at least as far back as the natural law of sixteenth-century French philosopher and jurist Jean Bodin. For Bodin, the central problem was the establishment of order in human societies. For this to occur, Bodin surmised in his basic treatise on the subject, *On Sovereignty* (1576), European states could not remain fragmented between Calvinist Huguenots and Catholics in a state of disorderly division and cyclical internecine warfare. Society instead had to be integrated through subjection to a single system of human law presided over by sovereign authority, what Bodin called *souveraineté*. Importantly Bodin considered this early precursor to the contemporary notion of sovereignty to exist solely within the person of the individual, and not a principle that applied to any collective group.[13] Bodin's notion was bound up closely with the principle of religious freedom within the fiefdoms of seventeenth-century Europe, which soon coalesced into largely independent polities by the 1648 Peace of Westphalia, which scholars often cite as the birth of the modern sovereign states system. Logically this period also coincided with the development of the field of international law, whose earliest precepts emerged in the works of scholars like Hugo Grotius.[14] Westphalia marked the end of foreign intervention in the religious affairs of the formative territorial states that had emerged around the time of that settlement.[15] It represented the consolidation of gains begun with the Protestant Reformation and the circumscription of what in the minds of reformers like Martin Luther represented the hitherto extensive temporal authority of the Church to hold land, tax citizenry, and excommunicate political leaders. With the start of the Westphalian system of territorial states, the freedom from interference in internal affairs that came to exist in practice throughout Western Europe gradually gave rise to the basic normative underpinnings of contemporary sovereignty.

Later the classical realism of Thomas Hobbes refined the notion of "the sovereign" as a basic guarantor of order in human societies, along with the parallel development of the related idea of private property. In his *Leviathan* (1651), Hobbes theorized that a populace willfully entered into contracts to subordinate their personal freedoms to a sovereign abstraction (the "Leviathan") manifested by the authority of the state that governed them. They did so by contracting with the sovereign the surrender (or, as Hobbes put it, the "transfer") of those rights in exchange for the sovereign's protection. The authority vested in the sovereign by the populace through entering this compact, in Hobbesian thought, served to legitimize the terms of that social contract and guarantee its enforcement.[16] Hobbes reasoned that a desire to escape what he termed the "state of nature"—one of pervasive insecurity and recurrent war and instability—would drive the urge to seal such pacts: "The final cause, end or design of men, who naturally love liberty, and dominion over others, in the introduction of that restraint upon themselves, in which we see them live in commonwealths, is the foresight of their own preservation, and of a more contented life thereby; that is to say, of getting themselves out of that miserable condition of war, which is necessarily consequent, as hath been shown in chapter xiii, to the natural passions of men, when there is no visible power to keep them in awe, and tie them by fear of punishment to the performance of their covenants, and observation of those laws of Nature set down in the fourteenth and fifteenth chapters."[17] Hobbes believed that peoples could enter covenants with sovereign authorities out of mutual agreement and a common desire to establish what he called "sovereignty by institution," or when compelled to submit to a conquering force that might wipe them out, which he distinguished as "sovereignty by acquisition." Both forms of covenant were equally legitimate. Because of the need for the legitimacy and enforcement of these covenants, Hobbes (like Bodin) reasoned that the authority of sovereigns had to be absolute; for both thinkers, the supreme authority of sovereigns transcended the sphere of positive law, although both also likely believed the sovereign to be accountable to the natural law of God. But later philosophers questioned whether the principle should be refined to fit within the terrestrial rule of human law.

By the mid-seventeenth century, as the Westphalian system of sovereign states was taking shape, Baruch de Spinoza had rejected the Old Testament notion of the divine Covenant of Sinai between God and man, instead recasting the principle it connoted in the idea of a secular compact *among* humans themselves.[18] Through his writings in the 1660s and 1670s, such as the unfinished *Tractatus Politicus* (1676), Spinoza's secularization of the crude, Hobbesian notion of the social contract represented an important development. The innovation led to accusations of heresy against Spinoza, but it helped frame the intellectual problem of polities with their own authority that inhered in the people, as opposed to an "external" sovereign. Spinoza also alluded to intellectual developments in theories of natural law that would carry forward his ideas about covenantal bonds and the nature of political authority as it pertained to the definition and assertion of sovereignty in the work of contemporaries like the liberal theorist John Locke.

In a sense Locke helped deepen the meaning of sovereignty by both echoing Spinoza and presaging Rousseau's notion of democracy as "popular sovereignty" in his exposition on the most fundamental rights extant in the human condition and rooted in "natural law."[19] In *Two Treatises of Government* (1698) Locke held that all men and women were born free from allegiance to any monarchical rule in the ordinary state of nature absent any imposed, human social orders. The implication of the rule of such natural law echoed Spinoza in rendering any claimants to sovereign authority accountable to the populace (or at least their representatives). Locke held that the state of nature so abhorred by Hobbes was still preferable to absolute monarchical rule. For Locke, the former condition represented not a state of anarchical chaos but a sphere of human relations that, like all others, was still governed by natural law—universal moral rules that applied to all peoples everywhere. Natural law for Locke consisted of a system of rules that could coincide with, yet existed separately from, the divine law revealed in scripture. The most basic premise of Locke's natural law was the preservation of mankind. In this way the law of nature guaranteed mankind the rights to life, liberty, and property. This rights-based philosophy served as the foundation for Locke's conception of sovereignty as it applied across all peoples, and therefore across any single body politic. The Lockean conception of natural law synthetically blended Hobbesian ideas about the need to regulate human self-interestedness and Spinoza's interpretation of human covenants distinct from divine counterparts.[20]

As Spinoza and Locke developed ideas that framed sovereignty, including its basis in law and its constitutive capacity as a popular right, the system of sovereign states that had emerged by the Peace of Westphalia began to spread outward over the next three centuries. Developments during this period were perhaps not as foundational as earlier theoretical developments in the idea of sovereignty. One exception was Emmerich de Vattel's *The Law of Nations* (1758), considered by many to be the first comprehensive text on international law espousing the principle of noninterference and the sovereign equality of states.[21] Vattel's work was also a codification of some of the most important developments in the intellectual history of international law. But recent work has argued that the contemporary system of sovereign states is the product of two "revolutions" in intellectual history that bookended the three centuries between Westphalia and the creation of the United Nations. The first was the Protestant Reformation that swept Europe in the seventeenth century, transforming medieval Christendom into the modern world of independent states that emerged at the 1648 Peace of Westphalia in the wake of the religious wars and shaping the thought of sixteenth- and seventeenth-century thinkers like Bodin, Hobbes, Spinoza, and Locke. The second was the wave of anticolonial nationalism that accompanied the collapse of the Dutch, British, French, and other European empires in the second half of the twentieth century.[22]

One might argue that so innumerable were variants of any single platonic ideal of sovereignty that emerged during the three hundred years between those historical periods that political units reflecting their characteristics defy categorization into single analytic categories like "states."[23] Indeed the occasional deadlocked arguments pitting self-determination rights against sovereign statehood are rooted in the malleability of both terms to suit specific political interests. Having acknowledged the differences distinguishing various interpretations of sovereignty, this study is concerned primarily with the idea of what has been termed "international legal sovereignty."[24] The idea connoted by this specific usage emanates from the notion of "negative liberty," a concept that Isaiah Berlin has explored in depth. As opposed to the active exercise of "positive liberty" through systems of entitlements and rights guaranteed to individuals, permitting them to engage in specific activities, negative liberty connotes freedom of a different sort, a passive freedom from the intrusions and infringements of states and societies on individuals that entitles individuals to partake in any of a range of activities in which participation is not specifically proscribed.[25] In this sense international legal sovereignty connotes negative liberty at the national level through the putative guarantee of freedom from interference by other states and the corresponding recourse to international legal relief in the face of infringements of that right.

By the time the founding members of the United Nations gathered at the San Francisco Conference in 1945, this legalistic notion of sovereignty had evolved to represent the primary assumption on which the entire intellectual edifice of the new Charter system stood.[26] Now sovereign states were to constitute the basic interacting units in the community of nations uniting under the banner of the new world organization; they were accordingly the contracting parties bound into the compact of the Charter, enmeshed in the new body of positive law shaped by its provisions. The moment was a watershed for the development of international law, heralding the start of a new cooperative international system governed by the Charter's framework of rules and norms.[27] But just how it would function and its immediate implications remained unclear for the immediate postwar years. Some scholars have argued that this international legal framework, a new world order of formally coequal entities, served only to perpetuate the plight of the decolonized states after the Second World War. These unequal relationships manifest themselves, this line of reasoning holds, through the twin pillars of (in some cases, pre-independence) agreements between Western colonial powers and dependent territories on the cusp of statehood, and economic dependencies that linked these developing states with advanced industrial powers.[28] But at least as convincing a case can be made for the counterargument that the UN order represented a *milestone* for colonial liberation struggles—in which the Charter provisions on aggression, reference to trusteeship, and other safeguards afforded postcolonial struggles newfound legitimacy and protection against colonial or other external interference—through the legitimization of their claims to sovereignty as rooted in the idea of negative liberty. The final balance, at least, was unclear. Part of the problem lay in the references to the time-sanctified Atlantic Charter principle of self-determination, a hallmark of American globalism that had survived into the final text at San Francisco.

THE PROBLEMATIC PRINCIPLE OF SELF-DETERMINATION FOR PEOPLES

Problematically embedded in a document establishing an order of sovereign states was the distinct but ambiguous notion of self-determination for peoples, a reference to which entered the UN Charter at President Roosevelt's behest despite the reservations of Churchill and his counterparts from the European colonial powers. Given that the historical trajectory of the idea of sovereignty had reached an apogee by 1945, the enshrinement of sovereignty in the UN Charter alongside a principle like the "right" to self-determination for peoples amounted to no less than a quixotic legal compromise between two potentially irreconcilable ideals that drastically compounded the problems of war, peace, and colonial independence. The idea of sovereignty may well have enjoyed a long history of intellectual development before the UN Charter. But like sovereignty, the right of national self-determination had also evolved from historical precedents.

The complex origins of the contemporary idea of self-determination date back to Enlightenment rationalism. The idea probably first emerged from the wider Kantian notion of freedom, before commingling later with strands of political nationalism after the advent of modern political theory.[29] Most scholars attribute its development to the French Revolution and the displacement of the early modern notion of the divine right of kings with the idea of popular sovereignty. In the late nineteenth century the idea came to constitute the rationale for Otto von Bismarck's effort through campaigns like the Franco-Prussian War to unify Prussia with the principalities that in his mind constituted a "greater" Germany.[30] The high-water mark of self-determination, of course, was the aftermath of the First World War, with the dissolution of the multiethnic Ottoman Empire and the issuance of Woodrow Wilson's Fourteen Points, during what Erez Manela termed "the Wilsonian Moment." Importantly Lenin also espoused the idea of self-determination as a vehicle for proletarian emancipation against his bourgeois Russian opponents, recognizing its resonance with Russia's large (57 percent) ethnic minority population and potential appeal if the principle could be co-opted for international communist mobilization.[31]

Despite the failure of the United States to ratify the League, with time, self-determination came to be recognized explicitly in both the Atlantic and UN Charters. Scholars also argued that international legal norms about human rights and the international legal context surrounding self-determination by midcentury meant that European overseas empires could no longer be insulated from the application of the idea.[32] That right, at least as reflected in the idea of decolonization as viewed through the lens of American globalism, represented a bold departure from the shape that the idea of colonial independence assumed in the minds of British thinkers like Lord Stanley and even Bevin. Just as sovereignty came in many forms, self-determination connoted different things for different states and societies. Perhaps most important, its incorporation into the UN Charter framework would immediately proliferate myriad interpretations of exactly what "rights" it conferred.

While the British Foreign Office envisioned a process of "evolutionary decolonization" for the colonies in line with the historical evolution of the idea of "responsible government" for Canada embodied in the Lord Durham Report of 1839, after America's entry into the Second World War President Roosevelt and the U.S. State Department subscribed instead to the goal of "universal decolonization" for all colonial peoples.[33] This discrepancy, most certainly impacted by the philosophical gulf dividing globalism and regionalism, had of course constituted the essence of the strain in Anglo-American relations. While self-determination rights clearly extended beyond the Nazi-occupied territories in the minds of Roosevelt and Sumner Welles, they decidedly did not for Churchill. The abstract phrasing of the ill-defined reference both reflected the difference of opinions and codified that source of further discord. As Roger Louis characterized the compromise that was forged in the Atlantic Charter, it was precisely the "ambiguity of the phrasing" that enabled Churchill to argue that Britain's imperial possessions were insulated from the reach of postwar self-determination aspirations.[34] This, of course, was the basis for the drawn-out dispute over trusteeship explored in Chapter 7. The contentious debates between mutually incompatible interpretations played out not only until Yalta and San Francisco but indeed over subsequent *decades*, during which a more precise definition of self-determination would emerge—and even then only after long legal and scholarly deliberations and momentous developments like the pivotal *Western Sahara* case, which arose before the International Court of Justice.[35] While ambiguities about the scope of self-determination arose immediately, that longer process revealed the full extent to which ideas actually mattered for the shape that the postwar international system assumed—ideas traceable back to the language and *traveaux préparatoires* of the UN Charter and prior decades. For the legitimacy of entire national self-determination movements hinged on the applicability of the self-determination principle to the struggles in which many of those movements were locked. Irrespective of the ambiguous bargain struck at Yalta, statesmen like Churchill and Attlee had to wonder whether the UN Charter had sealed the fate of *all* the European colonial empires by virtue of its seemingly innocuous reference to the rights of peoples to their own political fortunes. In a sense their worst fears proved correct. As discussed, while the British Colonial Office's Poynton-Robinson scheme for a system of regional commissions to manage postcolonial territories languished before the dominions, the Allied powers adopted instead the American blueprint for a system of international mandates under the supervision of a Trusteeship Council, arguably thwarting Churchill's strategy to preserve parts of the British Empire or, at the very least, control the destinies of its former possessions.[36] Instead of Nazi Germany's invocation of self-determination to acquire for the German super-state the Lebensraum to which Hitler claimed entitlement, it was now anticolonial movements that cited the principle after the war to rebel against imperial overlordship in the second great twentieth-century wave of fragmentation that helped dismember European colonialism in the Middle East, Asia, and Africa.

But in 1945 it became evident that the validation of any universal claim to self-determination by minority ethnic or proto-national groups would, in certain cases, immediately and diametrically oppose that notion of a unitary state with inviolable borders so integral to the structure of the UN system and which the Charter had just sanctified. This potential contradiction set the stage for one of the most vexing questions facing UN member states and helped prevent the proper discharge of the Security Council's responsibilities for the enforcement of binding resolutions in the service of international peace and security. It also helps explain the great power bias against the imposition of the collective will of permanent Security Council members (who counted among their ranks more than one colonial European power with dependent territories) to intervene in conflicts tinged with shades of anticolonial ideology, like the Syrian and Lebanese struggles against France, the Indonesian nationalist struggle against Dutch colonial rule, the accession of Kashmir to India and its subsequent contestation by Pakistan, and the first Arab-Israeli War, pitting Palestinian nationalists against resettled European Jews who joined Palestine's native Jewish inhabitants.

If the "Wilsonian Moment" of 1918 ushered in the first era of anticolonial nationalism, the immediate post-1945 period witnessed what was perhaps the movement's second great thrust. Despite the wartime recognition of the right to self-determination in the 1941 Atlantic Charter, it is commonly understood that the references to "self-determination of peoples" in Articles 1 and 55 of the UN Charter proved to be of more central importance for the legal development of the principle.[37] Still, the idea was undergoing a state of conceptual flux in the immediate postwar years in a process that entailed interaction with the parallel evolution of ideas like the inviolability of territorial states. Moreover the Charter's *traveaux préparatoires* suggest deep regional divergences across contemporary interests and the interpretations of the self-determination principle to which the international delegations to the San Francisco Conference subscribed. Notably the French delegation raised the issue of what the right to self-determination would entail and whether it would subsume only "the right of a state to have its own democratic institutions or the right of secession."[38]

THE DIVERSE SOURCES OF ANTICOLONIAL NATIONALISM

Some background on the various national ideologies driving self-determination struggles provides useful insights into the raisons d'être for the postcolonial states that they produced.[39] The intent of this discussion is not to formulate sweeping generalizations about "third world nationalisms" or other such blanket terms that fail to capture the richness of the differences that distinguished nationalist struggles in places as diverse as the Francophone Levant, Palestine, Kashmir, and the Dutch East Indies. Indeed theorists and historians of nationalism have attempted such classification schemes.[40] Instead the focus here is on the narrower claim that, once freed from the geographic boundaries of post-Enlightenment Europe in which it had developed, ideas about nationhood spread to and embedded themselves in the minds of many Asian and African nationalists as an intellectual foundation on which to base domestic political orders. While drawing on modern European intellectual thought, the diverse nationalisms that developed were far more than outright appropriations of Western political philosophy; to varying extents they incorporated local sources of identification and historical particularities in a syncretic mix of ideas. Scholars have argued that one point of origin for such nationalist ideals has been the failure of existing states and large empires to adequately address the needs of the dependent peoples over which they exercised sovereignty.[41]

These nationalisms ranged far and wide in accordance with unique trajectories and historical experiences, as the divergent goals and ideals of Abdullah, Jinnah, Ben-Gurion, Quwatli, and Sukarno showed. The Zionist project that gave rise to outright demands for sovereign statehood in Palestine; the religious nationalism in Pakistan whose ultimate objectives Jinnah was so leery of defining; the Indonesian movement toward indigenous political mobilization under Japanese occupation, even before Mountbatten's arrival; and the staunch Arab nationalism of Quwatli and many Lebanese factions: these were movements driven by diverging concerns and rationales. As the cases of Palestine and Kashmir have shown, the indigenous nationalist movements behind the Jewish Agency and the All-India Muslim League had both matured and risen to prominence by midcentury after stewing for decades among different ideas about nationhood rooted in various sources of identity. Each form of nationalism had developed along a specific evolutionary path and in a particular context; Zionism and the demand for Pakistan both clearly bore the unique marks of their respective histories. But each was also forward-looking as modern ideologies. Settler Zionism and kibbutzim preached the virtues of settling Palestine's fertile land in the cause of economic prosperity, national development, and self-fulfillment. Meanwhile the idea of Pakistan promised a new future for Indian Muslims free of persecution and insecurity as a perpetual minority even after independence. This contradictory duality between history and modernity characterizing both nationalist ideologies is a theme that has attracted attention from scholars of nationalism and postcolonial theorists alike.[42]

Some have proposed various models for political mobilization that help explain these various nationalisms that each ultimately triumphed as the winning formula for their respective followers. In a strict sense Jinnah's call for Pakistan, as urban rank-and-file Muslim Leaguers might characterize it, fit fairly well with the basic definition of secular, modern European nationalism, as Eric Hobsbawm defined it—the idea that political units should be coterminous with nations. The seemingly organic upsurge of Indonesian identity that emerged from Japanese and British occupation was another story, however. As John Breuilly has pointed out, "sub-national identities" in such societies were at least as old (or as new) as the European nationalisms working at cross-purposes to preserve the sovereign grip of colonial orders.[43] Unlike in post-Raj India and Pakistan, where parliaments and governors-general persisted into the era of independence, the very incompatibility of native Indonesian paradigms of local order with Dutch colonial authority structures proved sufficiently disruptive to lead to fragmentation, violence, and near-chaos. Such subnationalist challenges to existing forms of colonial authority imposed from without can be conceived of as an alternative ideology of self-determination distinct from the religious nationalism of a Jinnah. In still other instances, the "statist" self-determination struggles on the part of Syrians, Lebanese, Palestinians and Zionists framed new sovereign states as the *only* means to achieve their desired ends. There is a distinction to be drawn, in this sense, between what this book refers to as "statism" (the ideology that held up the sovereign state as the sole, desired end result of anticolonial struggle) and less territorially oriented nationalisms (or subnationalisms) in the sense of communal identity, or what Benedict Anderson called an "imagined community."[44] Jinnah's carefully chosen early rhetoric, for instance, evaded an explanation of exactly what Pakistan connoted. Similarly the foremost goal of the myriad Indonesian ethnic groups was to expel the Dutch before Indonesians had to confront the choice between communism and Sukarno's engineered nationalism rooted in the artificial language of Bahasa Indonesia. Then there were the statists like Shukri al-Quwatli and David Ben-Gurion, who did not mince words; these revolutionaries always equated self-determination with statehood—and specific territorial demands that accompanied it. Movements with such clear territorial aims suggest at least a third distinct brand of self-determination struggle that emerged from the Second World War.

These various characterizations provide at least limited descriptive utility for characterizing the nationalistic ideas brewing in the British Empire at war's end. But the early postwar period enjoyed a rich and diverse mix of ideas about nationality that enriched intellectual debates of the age about statehood. The rationales for self-determination that Ben-Gurion and Jinnah each came to espouse were, after all, only two of numerous competing alternatives that their contemporaries had to choose from. They were distinct not only from one another but from alternative visions that vied for the allegiance of their own followers. For just as the geographic conceptions to which Great Power strategists subscribed were arbitrary and multiple, these ideologies of struggle were merely individual offerings in the marketplaces of nationalist ideas in prewar Palestine and British India. Each faced intellectual-ideological challenges evolved from assumptions grounded in what, in some instances, proved mutually incompatible ideas of nationhood.

Herzl's *Judenstaat,* reborn as Ben-Gurion's dream of a Jewish homeland, signified a unique historical conceptualization of Jewish nationhood. It was a cosmopolitan blend of religious tradition traceable back to the Old Testament account of the Covenant of Sinai struck between God and the Israelites and a progressive modernism that stressed active complicity in the realization of self-determination, the amelioration of the suffering of Jews in the Diaspora, and the noble labors of nation-building. Its intellectual core consisted of the powerful logic of an obligation to steward and direct the forces of history.[45]

As Ben-Gurion underscored to the youth wing of Mapai, literally the future builders of Israel, in an inspiring September 1944 address, "Exile is one with utter dependence—in material things, in politics and culture, in ethics and intellect, and they must be dependent who are an alien minority, who have no Homeland and are separated from their origins, from the soil and labor, from economic creativity. So we must become the captains of our fortunes, we must become independent—not only in politics and economy but in spirit, feeling and will. From that inward self-determination stem the outward forms of way of life and government, foreign relations and economy, which are shaped by achievements in labor and farming, in speech and erudition, by means of organization and defense, by the opportunity freely to live and create, and, at the last, by attainment of national sovereignty."[46] Ben-Gurion's words evoked the basic outlines of his statist vision of nationalism. He called for an ultimate and irreversible act of liberation from the culture of victimhood bred by waves of pogroms and ultimately the Holocaust, a victimhood he found so pervasive throughout Jewish thought in the Diaspora. His call urged Zionists to assert willful independence over their "utter dependence," to emigrate, settle, and cultivate their homeland, and to wrest control of their own destiny at last. But this rousing message was but one definition of Jewish national liberation. It was then perhaps unavoidable for Ben-Gurion's Zionism to grow and mature without incurring criticism from various quarters of Jewish thought. His appeal to resettle the ancestral homeland of the Jews as a modern nation-state came under fire from not only ultra-Orthodox Jewry, as we have seen, but also from progressive Jewish intellectuals like Hans Kohn and Hannah Arendt.[47]

Kohn, a Czech-born lawyer and theorist of nationalism in the tradition of Jewish intellectuals like Martin Buber, had famously proposed a "dichotomy" between what he characterized as civic Western nationalisms based on individualism and liberal government and the ethnic Eastern nationalisms that rendered the individual subservient to the collective will and bred the destructive totalitarian ideologies of Nazism and fascism. One of the virtues of that former category of what Kohn deemed the more humanistic, enlightened nationalisms was its capacity to assimilate and reflect universal, egalitarian values that he believed stemmed from biblical Jewish teachings, classical Greek thought, and Enlightenment rationalism. Kohn's synthetic Judeo-liberal vision of European nationalism was a model for export to the developing world after the Second World War, a messianic goal that at first glance seemed might be compatible with the Zionist settlement of Palestine. But as they materialized, the very statist aims of Zionism offended the pluralistic principles at the root of Kohn's nationalism. While Judaism's embrace of equality and inclusion could and should pervade nationalist ideologies, a call for statehood on the basis of Jewishness seemed to Kohn to fly in the face of the liberal order that he embraced. This line of philosophical reasoning led him to instead become a proponent of a humanistic cultural Zionism whose aims stopped short of political or territorial claims.[48] It was a component of the wider worldview that Kohn came to adopt, whose three principal tenets consisted of the basic unity of all humankind, the sanctity of individual liberty, and the promise of an idealized, humanistic nationalism simultaneously messianic and progressive in its character.[49]

The German Jewish philosopher Hannah Arendt, one of Kohn's contemporaries, shared the liberal individualism that had morally disqualified Zionism's anchorage of state legitimacy in the persecution of European Jewry in Kohn's eyes. Arendt's critique, rooted in the idea of the inseparability of

Jewishness with individual national identities (German, Polish, Romanian, etc.), assailed the premise that the Jewish race itself should serve as the mobilizing ideology behind a movement for statehood. As her views on Zionism evolved between the years 1940 and 1945, an exclusionary character seemed to her to increasingly tinge Zionism, leading her to associate the movement with the same racial nationalisms that had decimated European Jewry before and during the war. Even as "pariahs" agitating for social justice as they grappled with the problem of modernity, in Arendt's view, outcast émigré Jews could not extricate themselves from their existing nationalities even if they so wished, a postulate that led Arendt to rail against what she perceived to be the unholy compromise that Zionism had struck with that most pernicious of all forces—imperialism—while it remained oblivious to the plight of the Arabs of Palestine who would doubtless be affected by continued waves of emigration.[50]

Moreover the Zionist platform's adoption of the idea of "a free and democratic commonwealth" that by 1944 encompassed "the whole of Palestine, undivided and undiminished," reflected a neglect of the Arab population of Palestine that was impossible to square with the conceptions of civic equality that stemmed from Arendt's political philosophy. Arendt condemned the idea of kibbutzim as sheer utopianism and challenged the uncritical assumption that anti-Semitism was "eternal" and could be countermanded only by an activist political nationalism on the part of Jews themselves. For Arendt, that political nationalism would not only transform the resulting Jewish state intro a proxy agent of foreign powers; it would also sow the seeds of "a new wave of Jew hatred" and doom the Zionists through the self-fulfilling prophecy of the Arab backlash it would provoke.[51]

In the face of such countervailing views, the realization of the Zionist dream was thus first contingent upon the adoption of a single consensus view on nationhood for the Jewish people. Once that view emerged through a process of intellectual "natural selection," its proponents Weizmann and Ben-Gurion, having bridged their tactical differences in the course of an internal power struggle, could move forward in a more coordinated fashion to advance the cause of independence. A similar convergence of intellectual and ideological trajectories catalyzed the drive toward independence at the opposite tip of the arc of crisis.

In a similar vein to opponents of political Zionism like Kohn and Arendt, Nehru and Abdullah projected a powerful countervailing vision to Jinnah's

Pakistan, whatever the exact form it might assume, by claiming the moral virtues of an egalitarian Indian nationalism that was only a logical heir to the British Empire's quasi-liberal ideology. As the Khilafat movement and its flirtations with the Congress Party showed during the interregnum before Jinnah's rise, Muslim nationalism in India, like Zionism, existed in many forms and flavors. The moment of crisis for the Ottoman caliphate in the aftermath of the First World War galvanized the opposition of the Khilafatists to the powers threatening their Muslim brethren in Anatolia. Given the binary theological distinction between those who harmed Muslims and those who did not, Khilafatist leaders justified cooperation with Hindu nationalists to free India from British rule. But they envisioned a postindependence future in which Muslims remained religious minorities in Hindu-dominated India. In accordance with this vision, Islamic *shari'a* law would apply to Muslim communities, dispensed through *qadi*-administered courts and related institutions such as an *ulema* (religious council).[52]

Here was an alternative vision to Jinnah's Pakistan. Leaders like Congress Party member Maulana Azad opposed separation from India or the creation of any kind of new Muslim state. What they imagined instead was continued physical coexistence within India and the institution of only a "mental" partition.[53] The idea represented a fundamental break from traditional conceptions of religious nationhood that eventually framed the ultimate political goal of India's Muslims to be an independent state. The Congress Party imagined an India of Muslims, Hindus, Sikhs, and others. The Khilafat movement imagined instead a deterritorialized Islamic *ummah* that was spiritually unified but geographically dispersed throughout India. While those ties bound Indian Muslims to their coreligionists throughout the Islamic world in a sense of fraternal kinship rooted deep in Islamic history—the idea of a Dar-ul-Islam that was contiguous and bounded by frontiers—it is important to realize that they did not necessarily preclude the development of patriotic nationalist attachments on the part of Indian Muslims. Nevertheless what is significant for the discussion here is that the Muslim nationalism espoused by Khilafatists and leaders like Azad represented an alternative future to the Muslim League's notion of a Pakistan as it was cast in its final form in the demand for a separate territorial state. Its ideological moorings were a complex blend: the appropriation of the Islamic theological doctrine of jihad in the service of anticolonial struggle, one that sanctioned a Hindu-Muslim alliance to rid India of British occupation, but not an intrinsic Muslim nationalist separatism that sought to break with India.[54]

It was only after Jinnah's return to Pakistan in 1935 and the Muslim League's earnest efforts to grow its popular base from provincial to national levels that the idea of "Pakistan" came to displace its rivals as the most compelling vision of Muslim nationalism. Evolved from earlier notions of a Muslim federation that might emerge from British India, the idea of Pakistan assumed a distinct political character that diverged sharply at the most basic philosophical level from some Khilafatists' resignation to political unity with India. Whatever its ultimate territorial shape, here was a doctrine of separation that broke fundamentally with the intellectual assumptions of Muslim nationalists like Azad. As one early theorist of a separate Pakistan, Chaudhury Rahmat Ali, put it, "There can be no peace and tranquility in the land if we, the Muslims, are duped into a Hindu-dominated Federation where we cannot be the masters of our own destiny and the captains of our own souls."[55]

Clearly the vision of Pakistan that Jinnah eventually adopted was distinct from, and came years after, Ali's early formulation. But here was a blueprint for Muslim nationalism that contrasted sharply with the apparent quietism of Congress Party Muslims, including former Khilafatists, who saw their political destinies as intertwined with that of the Hindus in a united, independent India. This was an insufferable fate for both Ali and Jinnah, one that would consign India's Muslims to a perpetual minority status that would inhibit them from charting their own destiny. Jinnah had other plans, and the Muslim League would be his vehicle to deliver those objectives. Indeed some former Khlilafat supporters agreed with that vision. The two Khilafatist brothers Maulanas Mohammad Ali and Shaukat Ali had broken with the Congress Party over its rejection of separate electorates in the 1928 Nehru Report. While Mohammad Ali died in 1931, his brother went on to join the Muslim League in 1936 and became a proponent of the idea of Pakistan that was taking shape among Muslim League intellectuals. Some scholars have suggested that the idea of uniting the Muslims of India was likely a more important consideration for activists and thinkers like the Ali brothers than actual support for the seat of the Ottoman caliphate and its restoration. This is a claim supported by their eventual devotion to inchoate, early notions of what Jinnah had in mind.[56]

In one of its earliest forms, "Pakistan" was characterized in a 1932 pamphlet published by Rahmat Ali as a "federation" separate from Hindu India. Though distinct from later incarnations, such early conceptions echoed Jinnah's prophetic claim to the All-India Muslim Students Federation in 1941: "The Muslim League has given you a goal which in my judgment is going to lead you to the promised land where we shall establish our Pakistan. People may say what they like and talk as they like. Of course he who laughs last, laughs best."[57] As he described the struggle the following year, "Muslim India is fighting and struggling for survival and for its right to self-determination, whereas Congress and other Hindu organizations are speeding to establish supremacy and domination over the Muslims as an All-India minority." The Congress Party's goal was nothing less than "to dominate [and] control even those zones where the Muslims are in solid majority and interfere even in their internal affairs" by controlling national defense, finance, and other state functions.[58]

Jinnah's hand grew ever stronger as that victory was achieved, as evidenced by the national reaction to the Lahore Resolution, the favor he curried from the 1942 Cripps Mission, and the leverage he wielded at Simla in 1945, where his ability to prevent the appointments of non-League Muslims to the viceroy's Executive Council was powerfully evident. By the time partition had become imminent in the form of the Mountbatten-Menon plans, many Indian Muslims—including within the League itself—likely opposed what they found on offer. Still others would surely have preferred the trappings of a true Islamic state to Jinnah's model of a modern, secular Pakistan. But fear of persecution by a Hindu-dominated center likely motivated some of them to throw in their lot with the League rather than remain behind, like the 36 million Muslims in India's Muslim-minority provinces, for whom there *was* no choice.[59]

There was also the simpler issue of whether everyday Indian Muslims even grasped the difference between Jinnah's secular vision of a Pakistan for India's Muslims and the countervailing vision of a religious state whose constitutional bases were Islam and shari'a law. The assumption is hardly a stretch given that Jinnah had long refused to define what he meant by Pakistan, stoking British fears that one day his ideas might confront India's Muslims who wished to remain with India with the prospect of having to cast a vote against Islam. Even Nehru blurred the distinction between the secular and religious notions of Pakistan in his October 1949 meeting with President Truman, accusing Jinnah of embracing a particularist vision of a Muslim state and implying that it represented the opposite of the inclusiveness of "secular" India. The context of Nehru's comment conveyed the idea that a plebiscite campaign for Kashmir on "a religious basis of adherence of provinces [to either dominion]" could be incredibly dangerous. But his obfuscation of the nature of the secular Pakistan that Jinnah envisioned was deliberate and egregious.[60]

The contests between individual models of anticolonial struggle to some extent also affected the non-British cases of decolonization briefly surveyed in this book. In a sense Quwatli and the Levantine Arabs too faced choices of their own between unaligned independence and pan-Arabism at the Cairo Conference and the creation of the Arab League at their very moment of achieving statehood. The expulsion of the French and British occupation presences precipitated for the Syrians and Lebanese (if not for their French hand-picked leadership) an existential dilemma of choosing between various forms of nationhood. The separate independent states of Syria and Lebanon thus represented one such choice among other possible outcomes. Finally, Sukarno's consolidation of Indonesian identity had to confront the competing associative forces of Islam and communism— forces that he deftly co-opted into his utilitarian vision of Nasakom in an act of political survival. For Sukarno and Mohammed Hatta, nationalism, Islam, and communism were all equally just ideological foundations for opposition to Dutch rule, not only because their hierarchical equivalence meant a larger base of support for Indonesia but because once woven together syncretically in such a way, they also represented a preemptive bid to undercut competing sources of national identity. Sukarno's purge of Indonesian communists during the second Truman administration was perhaps the best evidence of the fragility of such tenuous political "alliances."

From the standpoint of comparative study, it is interesting to note that the 1924 dissolution of the Ottoman caliphate and the seat of Islamic power it represented as the last of the Muslim "gunpowder" empires gave rise not to a mosaic of religious theocracies in a wave of pan-Islamism washing over the decolonized world but instead to a litany of new secular postcolonial states. The collapse of the Khilafat movement and the rise of particularistic nationalisms saw Islam invoked only in sporadic, piecemeal fashion in the service of anticolonial struggles, struggles that ultimately produced a world of secular nation-states such as Syria, Lebanon, Israel, Pakistan, and Indonesia.[61]

The reasons that some variants of anticolonial ideology won out over others in the course of historical events are the subjects of wide-ranging debate. But a compelling possible explanation emerges if one looks to the compatibility of triumphant movements like Ben-Gurion's and Jinnah's with the geographic assumptions of great powers like the United States and Great Britain about the territories of Palestine and the Indian subcontinent.

NINE

From Imagined to Real Borders

Decolonization occurred at the contact points between nationalist struggle and great power diplomacy. Once specific nationalist ideologies like Zionism and the drive for Pakistan came to motivate and legitimize the struggles of groups like the Jewish Agency and the All-India Muslim League, having squelched competitor ideologies, they became the principal vehicles through which their supporters sought to deliver the goal of statehood. Those struggles for sovereignty (and the attendant international recognition that it conferred, once achieved) were soon buffeted by the pressures of the diplomatic involvement of powers like Great Britain and the United States. Neither the nascent nationalist struggles that had developed and grown from roots stretching into the nineteenth century nor the postcolonial designs of the two principal Atlantic powers were in and of themselves sufficient to determine the fate of Zionism in Palestine or the struggle to define Pakistan that so implicated the fate of Kashmir. Instead the fates of postcolonial independence struggles were shaped by interactions between great power designs driven by specific geographical perceptions and imposed from above and the strength and complexion of particular nationalist movements bubbling up from below.

Outcomes emerged forcefully in the instances in which the mental maps of anticolonial movements, so to speak, converged with the geographical assumptions of the respective interested great powers.[1] One place where this occurred readily was the Indian subcontinent. There Jinnah's vision of Pakistan was buoyed by the mutual reinforcement of *both* the American and British tendencies toward regionalism and globalism, which, for different reasons, supported policy outlooks that viewed a durable Pakistan favorably. In other instances, as in the case of Palestine, inconsistencies arose between the imperatives of globalism and those of regionalism. Ben-Gurion found the Truman administration's globalism connecting Palestine to the mass suffering of the displaced Jews of Europe reinforced his Zionist project. But the dictates of Britain's regionalism, especially after the Colonial Office's full capitulation to Ernest Bevin and the Foreign Office in February 1947, had other ideas, seeking to block continued emigration, even at the expense of ordering the Royal Navy to intercept and turn back vessels like the *Exodus* and its human cargo of refugees. In the case of Palestine, it was thus the relative weight of the national power behind American globalism that determined Israel's fate, in the repeated demands for continued immigration and at the UN General Assembly vote in November 1947.

It is important to clarify that the allegation here is not that regionalism and globalism were somehow permanently bound to counterpart British and American ideologies about colonialism. Indeed American intelligence analysts during the Truman administration had concluded that the accommodation of anticolonial nationalist struggles could even pose a *challenge* for U.S. policy.[2] Neither is the assertion that anticolonial leaders like Ben-Gurion and Jinnah ultimately manipulated their respective Great Power patrons into delivering their hard-fought achievements for them. As shown by the UN General Assembly vote on the partition of Palestine and the final shape of the "maimed, mutilated, and moth-eaten" Pakistan that Jinnah secured, no settlement reflected the maximalist aims of *any* of the protagonists.[3]

What *was* clear was that certain variants of anticolonial nationalist thought coincided with the strategic designs of the great powers in powerfully reinforcing ways. Globalism and regionalism existed on two levels: that of strategic geopolitics and human populations and demographics. On the geopolitical level, great power calculations inevitably contradicted or reinforced the territorial visions of individual nationalist blueprints. Globalism and regionalism also entailed assumptions about the demographics of subject peoples: the respective populations that inhabited particular regions and the dominant sources of their collective identity.

Assumptions about both the compositions of particular territories and the underlying demographics posed consequences for the compatibility of American or British policy with specific anticolonial nationalist ideologies competing for popular support. A belief that Jews and Arabs could coexist in Palestine, or that Jews could not be resettled in predominantly Muslim lands, inevitably meant consonance with or diametric opposition to Zionism, pan-Arabism, and Pakistani nationalism. This was the contact point where great power diplomacy and history from below met and shaped postcolonial futures.

For instance, Anglo-American views about the geography of northwestern India shared key assumptions that played to Jinnah's advantage. The assumptions of American globalism and British regionalism about geopolitics both happened to frame Pakistan as a key end point of sorts. From the frame of reference of Whitehall's "Official Mind" regionalism, Pakistan's stability impinged on that of the southern borderlands of Afghanistan and Central Asia. Meanwhile American globalism framed Pakistan as a northwestern bulwark against the potential penetration of Soviet communism southward and eastward into the subcontinent and Southeast Asia. The demographic realities undergirding globalism and regionalism also led to the same conclusion: preserving the political viability of the Muslim areas of Punjab and the NWFP—a viability that an intact Pakistan could provide—irrespective of whether the goal was to defend South Asia against Soviet penetration (which so preoccupied Washington) or for the sake of the stability of the uninterrupted tribal Muslim populations that extended westward to the Middle East and Palestine (the principal British considerations).[4] In that way a policy supportive of a viable Pakistan (and one that, no doubt, could be dealt a fatal blow by a negative outcome in the Kashmir dispute) proved consonant with the imperatives of both American and British geographical visions of the region.

The resolution of the geographical assumptions of the two most interested great powers and the respective nationalist struggle in question was far more complex in the case of Palestine. Here globalism and regionalism supported very different conclusions. From the standpoint of strategic geography, its proximity to the oil-rich heart of the Middle East rendered Palestine important from the perspective of the strategic objectives supported by American globalism. In this sense it did not loom as large as it did to the British Chiefs of Staff, certainly. However, that globalism—from its early conceptions in the Roosevelt administration—also favored the resolution of the Jewish Question through the emigration of Jews to Palestine. With regard to its demographic (as opposed to strategic) assumptions, globalism was consistent with the Zionist campaign to increase immigration quotas and continue Jewish settlement of Palestine. Fortunately for Ben-Gurion, this outcome had emerged from studies like the massive, top-secret "M Project" on global refugee resettlement run by anthropologist Henry Field and geographer Isaiah Bowman between 1942 and 1945, which examined the prospects of relocating displaced Europeans as far away as Canada, Brazil, Argentina, Manchuria, and Australia. Looming again on the radar by early 1943 was the possible destination of Palestine. The effects of the Second World War now led Roosevelt himself to begin ruminating on the issue. Despite Bowman's personal incredulity, tempered perhaps by a degree of anti-Semitism, toward the feasibility of Palestine as a Jewish homeland, the president was swayed by the logic of the option—one that was reinforced in his mind by the insistent appeals of Eleanor Roosevelt. The president accordingly expressed his own support for the idea in October 1944, though he failed to mention this to the Saudi king on his return from Yalta, noting merely that the United States would "consult" its Arab partners before taking a firm stand on the issue.[5]

Roosevelt's decision and the M Project's work were watersheds for the Zionist movement. Despite the opposition of Bowman and others in the State and Defense Departments, including the Joint Chiefs of Staff, Roosevelt's commitment (later echoed by Truman and supported by the likes of Undersecretary of State Sumner Welles) to relocate European Jews to Palestine proved the compatibility of American globalism with the Zionist dream. Though Truman later disbanded the M Project and its formal recommendations were shelved, it represented the core intellectual database of wartime American globalism. Here, in more concrete form than anywhere else, were American proposals for relocating war refugees on a global scale—one that mirrored the equally expansive strategic geography of a global network of bases in its scope. And it was perfectly consistent with the dominant Jewish nationalist ideology that had emerged since the Balfour Declaration and that codified in the 1942 Biltmore Program its goal of securing Palestine as its territorial end.

That Zionist goal was of course fundamentally incompatible with London's regionalist designs for the Muslim belt that straddled the heart of the empire's maritime circulatory system, the core areas of Suez, the Levant, and the Arabian peninsula, at the level of geopolitics and demographics alike. In terms of the geopolitical implications of British regionalism, Palestine was as important a location on the map of the British Empire and Commonwealth as one could pinpoint, especially in the wake of the looming withdrawal from Egypt and the prospect of new African interests. From the standpoint of demographics, the occupation of that region by predominantly Muslim populations meant that support for continued Jewish emigration to Palestine was anathema for British strategic requirements, as the War Chiefs of Staff repeatedly noted between 1946 and 1947. Fortunately for Ben-Gurion, however, his vision aligned with the expansive scope of American globalism, backed by the rise of American power, as the territorial bounds of British regionalism correspondingly shrank in accordance with British power projection capabilities. American pressure and humanitarian concerns helped realize the Zionist dream at last three years after Roosevelt's death, despite the countervailing pressure of British regionalist concerns.

This was how American and British mental maps came to impinge on the decolonization process in Palestine and Kashmir. Reinforcing certain ideologies enabled these ways of viewing the world to create an international context in which astute statesmen like Ben-Gurion could capitalize on great power interests to achieve their objectives. Others, like Hannah Arendt and Maulana Azad, saw their own dreams washed away by the almost entropic forces of great power diplomacy that were sweeping away the prewar order. These forces set in motion the wave of decolonization that commenced in 1945—a process that during its early years proved curiously immune to the direct influence of the UN structures that America and Britain had shaped to manage them, and to the growing cold war tensions that had yet to fully spread throughout the postcolonial Middle East and South Asia.

DECOLONIZATION IN PRACTICE

The huge literature on the late British Empire has emphasized a range of factors for its decline and ultimate dissolution. These are most often categorized in accordance with three groups of works stressing domestic factors in Britain, placing the locus of imperial decline in the international relations of the age, or highlighting the importance of the rise of anticolonial nationalism. Scholars such as Robert Holland and A. P. Thornton have stressed the importance of domestic public opinion in the age of the welfare state and an increasingly liberal middle-class consciousness that sought a break with the autocratic past as the principal drivers of a willful

British decision to relinquish the British Empire. This school of thought holds that the rise of an increasingly democratic and fundamentally anti-imperialist British middle class in the twentieth century represented a fundamental social transformation of Britain, one of whose inescapable implications was a retreat from the hollow glory of the overextended postwar empire.[6] A second school of thought has held that the dissolution of the British Empire was concomitant with the changes in the international system wrought by two world wars and that replaced the Eurocentric nineteenth-century concert of power with the bipolar cold war superpower rivalry.[7] In a sense this body of work emerged mainly from the controversial conclusions of Ronald Robinson and John Gallagher's seminal 1953 *Economic History Review* article, "The Imperialism of Free Trade," and their later 1953 monograph, *Africa and the Victorians*.[8] Some of the works in the "internationalist" school that they inaugurated have stressed the relative economic weakness of debt-straddled Britain.[9] Others meanwhile have focused on the rising geopolitical influence of the United States.[10] A third school of historiography has examined the influence of anticolonial nationalism as a catalyst and accelerant of the decolonization process; its proponents have highlighted the role of nationalist struggles in wresting independence from British rule in the postwar period.[11]

In a sense the explanation of the causes of decolonization in Palestine and Kashmir proffered in this book combines elements of arguments from all of these bodies of work. If the American tendency toward globalism was partly a product of American domestic political thought and the academic and public debates feeding into it, then so too was its British counterpart a product of domestic British society. This study has not delved as deeply into the geographical mind-set of the British public and the relevant debates about the scope of the empire during and after the war as sources of British regionalism, as it has examined the work of Spkyman and other American thinkers in the case of globalism and its intellectual development. The reason for that disparity is the deeper impact of geopolitical thought on what was an inchoate American vision of the postwar world grappling for intellectual guiding philosophies and constructs. Instead the argument here has attributed Labour's regionalism more to the exigencies of Britain's postwar crisis and the calculations of the War Chiefs of Staff: regionalism was a prism through which postwar British strategists were *forced* to see the world, given Britain's economic and strategic burdens at war's end.[12] British academics and geopolitical thinkers hardly enjoyed the luxury of bringing their arguments to bear on British perceptions of geography as profoundly as their American colleagues did. That did not mean that geopolitical thinking did not factor into the calculations of the British "Official Mind."[13] It just meant that there was less room for academic ideas to inform debates on strategy during a moment of acute imperial crisis. But however different its origins, and to the extent that regionalism became a way the Foreign Office saw the world, domestic factors certainly can also be said to have impinged on Britain's retreat from empire, as they did on America's expansionary foreign policy.[14] With regard to international concerns, the pull of American globalism and the compromises forged in institutions like the UN Security and Trusteeship Councils can be thought of as reflective of international pressures on British policy to pursue decolonization. However, this study perhaps has underemphasized these factors given the argument that the limited application of trusteeship, the ineffectiveness of the Security Council, and the postponement of a declaration on colonial and dependent peoples curbed the intended influence of the UN system on the process of decolonization. Finally, the discussion of anticolonial nationalist ideologies that happened to align with certain great power assumptions about geography highlights the centrality of colonial voices in the fight for independence. Without the leadership of Ben-Gurion and Jinnah, it is doubtful whether the disparate, competing visions of postcolonial nationalism in Palestine and British India would have been able to rouse themselves in solidarity against the perpetuation of British rule (or in Palestine's case, the mandatory authority).

Instead of more simplistic explanations of British imperial retreat, this work has sought to build on more recent efforts to provide a richer explanation for decolonization in Palestine and Kashmir. Specifically it has examined the empire and Commonwealth from the standpoint of a bureaucratic system of trade routes, bases, high commissions, and other tangible and intangible elements. The focus on geographical perceptions and their codification as human capital means that the bureaucratic assumptions and perceptions of the Official Mind have been placed front and center to support the argument, keeping with the theme of recent work drawing on newly declassified material on the imperial system.[15] In both cases the complex interaction of national struggles with the geographic perceptions of American and British statesmen thus shaped postcolonial struggles during the critical years of 1945–1950. Key bargains had of course been struck, like the Yalta compromise on trusteeship. But the discretionary right of the great powers to place territories under trusteeship meant only the selective invocation of the relevant provisions. The Truman administration's haphazard, eleventh-hour suggestion of trusteeship merely as "an effort to fill the vacuum soon to be created by the termination of the mandate" in Palestine did not exactly amount to strategic great power use of the UN system to manage the decolonization process.[16] Great Britain was hardly more eager to employ the new system. If anything, the Colonial Office considered the new Trusteeship Council and its associated processes to be a defeat for British policy goals, its own views as expressed in the Poynton-Robinson proposals never having factored into the course of the international deliberations. But even the Chiefs of Staff characterized the need to take account of the Trusteeship Council from the earliest stages as a handicap of sorts that bound the Labour government's freedom of maneuver in Palestine. The prospect of a new international body that would shape the future of dependent territories was something that Britain now had to live with, even if it did not have to like it.[17]

Similarly the Security Council's failure to respond with international forces to stop the violence in both Palestine and Kashmir helped shatter other false hopes of the unified, collective might of the great powers stepping forth to halt the ravages of postcolonial strife.[18] Like the Trusteeship Council, the Security Council too was subjected to policy pressures shaped by parochial national interests and the geographic assumptions to which they gave rise. As has been shown, internal British deliberations on the use of the Security Council veto betrayed the influence of regionalism on the prospect of its use to protect "a majority on the Security Council" from harming the strategic interests of the United Kingdom or the Commonwealth, especially in the wake of the withdrawal from Suez.[19] As one official put it, "The governing factor is, I think, that the Security Council has not yet established itself in the eyes of the world as a powerful and respected organisation; and, even more important, it has not at its disposal any troops, and has no means of implementing any decision it may come to. Accordingly it would not be the slightest use for them to produce an ideally perfect solution which would be rejected by one or other, or both the parties to the dispute."[20] The British resentment toward the Security Council's compromise structure, lacking as it did a more decentralized network of regional councils as Churchill, and to a lesser extent Eden, wanted, mirrored the indignation aroused by the trusteeship fiasco in the lead-up to Yalta. But the frustrations with the new organization and its limitations also extended across the Atlantic.

When even the Security Council–approved UNCIP body failed to broker a Kashmir settlement by the middle of 1949, the recourse sought by the United States was still not robust enforcement action approved by the Council but rather international "arbitration by an impartial third party."[21] It reflected a broader American reluctance to reflexively employ the United Nations machinery and take the lead in resolving brushfire conflicts like the postcolonial struggles of the day. As Undersecretary of State Robert Lovett put it in early 1949, "I was concerned with the way in which we were constantly being pressured from all directions to take leading parts in virtually all spheres of UN activity and made reference in this connection to Palestine, Indonesia, and Kashmir."[22]

It was as if having reconciled their respective geographical maxims about the postcolonial world in a new global architecture of multilateral institutions at Dumbarton Oaks, Yalta, Potsdam, and San Francisco, neither the United States nor Great Britain now wanted to exercise their full capabilities in the world organization's earliest trials by fire. The question of the overseas empires of America's European allies was a critical dilemma for American strategy as globalism assumed a tangible shape. And the struggle to preserve NATO alliance ties on the one hand, and promote colonial independence on the other, meant severe, self-imposed constraints on U.S. policy in multilateral postwar contexts.[23] Washington and London now opted to revert back to their respective mental maps of the emerging colonial disorder, which began to guide their policies anew, *even at the meetings of the very multilateral body that was supposed to provide them a common frame of reference from a set of shared Atlantic Charter principles.* American and British officials now resisted each other's designs in the very forum they had built together. That process of reversion is clear in such UN deliberations as the October–November 1947 lobbying efforts for the UNSCOP majority proposal in support of the partition of Palestine into Arab and Jewish states that was led by the United States. It occurred again during the far less divisive (but equally revelatory) Anglo-American debates over the problems of Pakistani forces in Kashmir and the introduction of international armed forces into the disputed areas. It was yet again evident in the various suggestions floated back and forth between American and British counterparts on Kashmir. One case in point was the clear globalism latent in the early American suggestion of "coalition administration" for Kashmir.[24] That influence may be contrasted with the British proposal of an American plebiscite administrator for Kashmir, an act of disentanglement that indulged British regionalist imperatives by refusing to find immediate fault with Pakistani actions and calling for international mediation of the dispute, albeit without further angering the Indian government or putting a British face on the mediation authorities.

One upshot of the failure of multilateral mechanisms like the Trusteeship Council and the Security Council to smooth over acrimonious postcolonial conflicts, whether because of great power apathy or gridlock, was that many post-1945 self-determination struggles raged on, largely independent of external great power interventions, leading to a range of diverse outcomes between the polar extremes of victorious secession and ultimate independence (or annexation) and abject failure and extirpation by repressive state purges. This was certainly true of both Palestine and Kashmir, conflicts in which all the relevant parties found themselves having reaped only partial gains after the dust had settled.

One reason that the immediate decolonization struggles in Palestine and Kashmir may have ended this way, frozen in a state of suspended animation instead of pursued to bitter ends, was that both escaped immediate transformation into proxy wars within the wider cold war. While nascent cold war rivalries in Europe and the Near East prompted key superpower involvements in some civil wars (as in Greece and Korea), the first Arab-Israeli War and the Indo-Pakistani war over Kashmir remained insulated from polarization in strict accordance with the alignments of cold war blocs.

In the case of Palestine, the strategic importance of Middle East oil reserves warranted that both Washington and Moscow exercise considerable caution before introducing military forces into the region, even as part of an international peace force, lest one superpower provoke the other into a spiraling contest for geopolitical influence in the key region. In the case of Kashmir, it was precisely the conflict's removal from the dangerous front lines of cold war confrontation in Europe that isolated that postcolonial war from the messy implications of cold war entanglement. But though polarization did not immediately raise the stakes in Palestine and Kashmir, what was unclear was the net effect of the relative superpower apathy (as compared to the contrasting superpower focus in Greece or Iran, for instance) on the outcomes. It is unclear if a more rapid expansion of the cold war to the Arab-Israeli and Kashmir disputes would have encouraged speedy resolutions of either; given the dynamics of other regional conflicts in which the United States and the Soviet Union locked horns, that seems highly unlikely. But the lack of superpower involvement certainly seems to have perpetuated a violent status quo. Leaving colonial powers and secessionist combatants to fight themselves to exhaustion, the great powers essentially decided, in the words of Edward Luttwak, to "give war a chance" in the cases of these independence struggles or postcolonial rivalries between newly independent neighbors.[25] Free of direct external military involvement, both conflicts raged unabated save for the occasional monitors, mediators, or Good Offices Committee.

The result of the simultaneous legal effects of sovereign equality and the recognition of the right of self-determination seems to have been the triumph, for all intents and purposes, of perhaps a nonabsolute but still preponderant respect for sovereign equality, at least in the eyes of the great powers during the earliest years of the United Nations. While that triumph may not have been recognized and interpreted identically worldwide, it could very well have formed a basis for an unspoken consensus among the permanent members of the UN Security Council as to when and where it would take action to address threats to or breaches of the peace. That normative triumph over secessionist challenges defended with invocations of self-determination rights, at least from the standpoint of punitive UN enforcement action, seems to have affected two important developments that shaped decolonization.

The first was the innovation of Chapter VI regarding UN "peacekeeping," which was devised as a compromise between total nonintervention by the United Nations in the face of intense armed conflicts, which would be morally indefensible and badly discredit the new organization, and robust peace enforcement operations backed by the unanimous will of the Security Council that would have amounted to UN endorsements of secessionist causes and extended well beyond the political realities of the age. The second development was the emergence of what political scientist Robert Jackson called "quasi-states," or entities that were sovereign in international legal terms but were hardly capable of administering government functions throughout their territories in the aftermaths of those secessionist struggles that did happen to succeed. A huge range of factors contributed to both the invention of UN peace operations and the proliferation of weak states. But both developments seem to have been shaped profoundly by the unwillingness of the great powers to intervene decisively in many early postcolonial struggles, like those that broke out in Palestine, Kashmir, and the Dutch East Indies.[26]

THE INNOVATION OF UN PEACEKEEPING

Peacekeeping came into being as an ad hoc practice that lacked any founding UN Security Council resolution or other document citing a specific authority or basis in international law. It was instead a makeshift solution for interposing international armed forces "to help control and resolve armed conflicts," albeit in a manner consistent with the political sensitivities of belligerents, troop contributing nations, and the wider international community. The central premise of peacekeeping is to bring about a cessation of hostilities through the establishment of what one historian called "negative peace." Akin to Isaiah Berlin's notion of negative liberty, negative peace exists not on account of any structural foundation that brings it about but arises from the absence of violence. Thus the principal aim of early peacekeeping was merely to end hostilities even by unsustainable means so as to wedge open paths to more lasting settlements.[27]

The strategic rationale for early peacekeeping missions centered on the separation of combatants, ideally while some conflict-resolution process could start up and bring them to the negotiating table. Most such missions numbered more than a few thousand very lightly armed troops organized as infantry battalions, with little heavy equipment, armored vehicles, artillery, or tactical aircraft.[28] Some have cited potential sources of legitimacy for peacekeeping in the powers of the General Assembly to form subsidiary organs, in the Chapter VI provisions for dispute settlement, and in the provisional measures outlined in Article 40 of the Charter. No single source, however, has consistently been cited as a foundational Charter reference legitimizing peacekeeping operations. Conceived long after 1945, during Norwegian diplomat Trygve Lie's tenure as UN secretary-general, peacekeeping revealed the limits of UN conflict-resolution capabilities in the constraints of the postwar political landscape.[29]

The institutional form that early peacekeeping operations assumed reflected both the novelty of these undertakings and their operational limitations. The tolls exacted first by invading, then liberating military forces sweeping through Europe, North Africa, and the Pacific represented unsavory precedents for the first universally sanctioned deployments of multinational armed forces into conflict zones. The allied experience in the Middle East had glaringly revealed the consternation and unrest that foreign military presences could arouse in traditional societies like Egypt's—so much so that the danger of such a reaction factored into the calculus of U.S. policymakers weighing the merits of an international force to address the Palestine problem. The searing memory of occupation aside, there was the wholly separate issue of the *idea* of standing UN military forces. In this regard the historical moment seemed simultaneously both opportune and inhospitable for different aspects of peacekeeping operations. On the one hand, the postwar upsurge of support for the international ideals of human rights and conflict resolution lent UN dispute settlement efforts credibility as noble endeavors. But the trials of war and mobilization to distant overseas theaters also sapped domestic public enthusiasm for the commitment of national armed forces to the whims of the new world organization. As it happened, the early precursors to true peacekeeping operations like UNCIP and the UN Military Observer Group in India and Pakistan (UNMOGIP) emerged at a moment of rapid geopolitical flux. And while Lie's mediatory efforts helped resolve key international issues concerning the great powers, such as the Soviet Army's withdrawal from Iran, they were unable to bring to an end more heated disputes closer to the cold war's front lines, such as the blockade of Berlin or the postwar presence of Soviet occupation forces in Iran and Turkey. Farther afield than Europe and the Soviet Union's southern flanks, however, UN mediation and the innovation of peacekeeping helped at least initiate discussions between India and Pakistan over Kashmir and massage through the violent ordeals of Israeli independence and the first Indo-Pakistani War with relative speed and a modicum of international coordination.

Through UNCIP, UNMOGIP, and the UN Truce Supervision Organization (UNTSO) the practice of peacekeeping partly entered into existence to help manage the complex local conflicts to which decolonization had given rise. But the participation of current and former colonial powers in early peacekeeping missions in postcolonial conflict zones gave rise to a tension of sorts.[30] As peacekeeping evolved, academic debates arose over whether the practice represented the imposition of a neocolonial order that necessarily imposed value judgments through the act of intervention. Some likened the practice to the reimposition of colonial enforcement mechanisms for policing and regional stability employed by the likes of the French and British empires.[31] Such charges were less serious in the early years of peacekeeping, during which the conflicts in Palestine and Kashmir consumed the rival postcolonial claimants to power in both disputes. But the development of the institution was a novel practice that represented a threshold moment in the global history of international military forces as precursors to more robust peace enforcement operations of the 1960s and beyond.[32]

The Palestine-Israel and Kashmir observer missions were the first of a series of well over sixty UN operations established between 1948 and the present, over the course of which the practice of peacekeeping came to be defined. The earliest missions consisted of observation teams monitoring truces and cease-fire lines, like those in the Levant and Kashmir. But the first major force assembled under the rubric of UN peacekeeping was the UN Emergency Force (UNEF) mission in the Suez in 1956, to observe the withdrawal of foreign militaries from Egypt. UNEF I's rules of engagement also established the principle of the requirement of host-government consent, which became one of the basic assumptions underpinning later UN peace operations reliant on Chapter VI of the UN Charter (as opposed to Chapter VII on peace enforcement). But the distinctions between these new experiments in the use of international armed forces and peace enforcement were clear from the start. As international law scholar Christine Gray noted, "Interestingly, the Secretary-General said that the nature of peacekeeping precluded the employment of UN forces in situations of an essentially internal nature. Nor should such a force enforce any specific political solution; it would require specific authority for offensive action. It should use force only in self-defence. A wide interpretation of this right was not acceptable because it would blur the distinction between these operations and those under Chapter VII."[33] One implication was that, even before peacekeeping had institutionally come into being, UN observer missions proved incapable of serving as neutral arbiters in the sorts of internal conflicts that afflicted newly decolonized successor states like India, Pakistan, Indonesia, Israel, and the Palestinian territory.

Caught between the need to validate the credibility of the new organization's peace and security functions on the one hand, and the challenges of Chapter VII enforcement actions that UN member states had neither the will nor the capacity to conduct on the other, Chapter VI peacekeeping operations emerged as compromise institutions to fill the void. In a sense the new practice embodied as robust a preventative diplomacy role as the United Nations could assume, given the operational and political limits constraining it and the novelty of the idea of UN-led interventions in the intellectual climate of the mid-1940s. As one observer put it, "Peacekeeping brands no state as the aggressor and is *not* designed to influence the military balance in the area. Indeed, consent of the host state is necessary before the peacekeeping unit is deployed. Thus, one side in a dispute does not necessarily benefit from the UN action, and in this respect peacekeeping is less controversial than collective security or any other punitive action."[34]

The principle of state sovereignty clearly circumscribed the space that peace operations came to fill as tightly as any other constraining principle or political reality—well before the cold war's permanent battle lines were drawn on the postwar world map. This is an important point that seems to elude some scholars of early peacekeeping. International missions invited into conflict zones with the consent of the parties on the ground with a view toward monitoring truces and observing cease-fire lines were within reach of UN operational capacity and the political will of nations contributing peacekeepers. However, at that early juncture deployment of multinational peace enforcement units under unified UN command and control structures proved unrealistic, given the reluctance of U.S. (and likely other government) officials to take clear sides in anticolonial struggles, introduce Western armed forces into the Middle East, and fill security vacuums without political settlements in sight in the newly decolonized territories of the Middle East and Asia.[35]

Importantly these political and operational realities are noteworthy and largely unexplored factors shaping the final form of early peacekeeping operations. Past studies have certainly explored theoretical explanations for outcomes of peace operations, such as the effects of spoilers to peace settlements and the disposition of combatants at particular points in a conflict.[36] But hardly any serious empirical work has examined why these operations assumed the form that they did, and why peace enforcement operations never fully came to be realized, save for the corpus of work attributing that failure purely to the zero-sum geopolitics of the cold war. One central source of that weakness in UN capacity to enforce peace was perhaps the normative triumph of the indivisibility of sovereignty over the self-determination rights claimed by subject populations of multiethnic and multireligious states like Israel and Pakistan.[37]

Another source of weakness besetting the early practice of peacekeeping was the fact that, like the Security and Trusteeship Councils, peacekeeping operations embodied a compromise between the American globalism that underlay much of the UN system and the tempering effects of regional interests and authority, manifest in the limitations delineated by early principles of traditional peacekeeping (such as the requisite consent of the relevant host governments before a mission was deployed). Global in its scope—but subject to caveats that could render it adaptable to specific circumstances, just like trusteeship—peacekeeping quickly became yet another imperfect implement in the UN toolkit for applying to intractable conflicts like those that quickly filled postcolonial areas. Developing as a formalized practice only after the UNEF I mission in the Suez, its limited efficacy to mitigate conflict in Israel-Palestine and in Kashmir came to bear in rudimentary and experimental form as pilot observer missions that did little beyond providing reassurances to both sides and monitoring developments on the ground. Yet its precise contributions to the decolonization process remains largely unexplored.[38]

THE POSTWAR ORIGINS OF WEAK STATES

Peacekeeping operations unable to close the "sovereignty gap" between postcolonial states unable to govern themselves and the stark reality of negative sovereignty posed a problem. It was a problem that gave rise to a new world of so-called weak states throughout the developing world. The origins of this trend were rooted in the shift toward internal conflicts that developed after the Second World War but were not recognized until much later in the postwar period.

State failure seemed to become ubiquitous in the first decade after the end of the cold war. From Somalia's implosion to the ethnic cleansing in Kosovo, a litany of collapsed societies violently perforated the fabric of the New World Order. But the origins of the structural deficiencies crippling what political scientists have termed a class of fragile or weak states lay deeper in the historical past, dating back to the aftermath of the Second World War.[39] As scholars examining the history of cold war–era civil strife have concluded, these conflicts increased steadily from 1945 onward, despite the common wisdom holding that their levels held constant throughout the second half of the twentieth century, accelerating sharply after the collapse of the Soviet Union. Even correcting for the increase in the number of states joining the international system, itself an indicator of inherent weaknesses in the structural integrity of the fragmenting predecessor states, the data reveal a steady increase between 1945 and 1995 of the percentage of states in the international system with at least a single conflict within its borders.[40] Moreover, during the cold war years superpower involvement with shoring up structurally unsound regimes supportive of regional superpower interests and a measure of caution vis-à-vis sowing instability overtly in regions under the de facto influence of their adversary may well have masked state weakness and a potential for state failure throughout the postcolonial world.[41]

Part of the reason for the emergence of the new class of weak states was the design flaws that plagued them from the start. Those designs were the result of the reinforcement of the principle of sovereignty after the creation of the United Nations Organization, after surviving, only partly unscathed, the challenge leveled by the assertion of postcolonial self-determination rights—and the subsequent incorporation into the UN order of a series of states with weak or nonexistent national identities and limited administrative capacities.[42] Here was a class of states whose political boundaries were determined by the precarious compromises entailed by maximalist national visions like Ben-Gurion's Jewish homeland and Jinnah's Palestine, and their subsequent territorialization only in truncated, compromised forms through both the exigencies of political bargains and collusion with British imperial authorities and the application of the geographic perceptions of the Anglo-American alliance that largely shaped the fates of both eventual states. As freeloaders, convenient political allies, and forced compromises colored the purity of both original visions in the act of territorializing them, the bases for statehood that each leader had established now shifted. The pure aspirational nationalisms of Zionists and Indian Muslims, however ethnoreligious or secular, as products of twentieth-century Europe that existed in the abstract as platonic ideals, now were recast as nationalisms based on postcolonial territories that mapped onto specific boundaries, often corresponding with the existing colonial administrative units of the British Empire. It was a shift that paralleled what two theorists called a reconceptualization of *national* sovereignty, "which emphasizes a link between sovereign authority and a defined population," as *state* sovereignty, "which stresses the link between sovereign authority and a defined set of exclusive political institutions."[43]

In the creation of Israel and Pakistan, both these transformation also meant that, after statehood, the basis for national identity changed. Whatever ideas of nationhood had existed before in the minds of Zionists and

Muslim Leaguers now became immaterial in the face of the fait accompli of achieving their own state. If some of Jinnah's allies were uncertain about the secular nature of his Pakistan, if Ben-Gurion's fellow Jewish Agency officials had doubts about whether the homeland they coveted would encompass all of Palestine, those myriad, imagined nations now collapsed into a single material reality mapped onto a single set of national borders for each newly independent state.[44] They were now Pakistanis and Israelis, confronting a remapped international order.

While individual conceptions of national identity still remained a subjective experience for each citizen, now there was one Pakistan and one Israel, with only one map each of their national boundaries, specific border disputes aside. With those acts of creation, new state-building enterprises began in earnest, enterprises that inevitably entailed *new* compromises for both states soon after birth. Thus Pakistan obtained de facto control of only portions of Kashmir, while the borders of the Jewish state were determined only after the demarcation of the 1949 armistice line ending the first Arab-Israeli War. Often the only national ideologies that remained to preserve tenuous links between state and society were the founding myths in the narratives of Ben-Gurion and Jinnah—narratives that, as has been shown, were contested by rival conceptions and ideologies from the start. These competing narratives would beset the new nations from their birth and constitute sources of their early weakness as members of the international community.[45]

In many cases antipathy toward former colonial masters had to provide the glue that held these new states together. As historian R. F. Holland put it, Indonesian president Sukarno "needed some external issue to keep alive the emotions of Indonesian anti-colonialism, since there was precious little else binding together a new state constructed from such a patchwork of ethnic, economic, and regional interests."[46] Rather than reinforcing national identities with binding sectarian loyalties or religious allegiances (beyond any superficial level, at least), these states were instead often united under artificial banners of existential struggles against external threats, real or apparent. Measures for state weakness vary, but one of the most commonly consulted indices relies on the concept of degrees of "social control."[47] In those terms, the sources of weakness in governance were manifold across Palestine, Israel, Syria, Lebanon, and Pakistan—from their nascent institutions and colonial legacies to the surfeit of arms inflows that streamed in and external pressures to honor human rights.[48]

In Israel not only did the plight of the Palestinian refugees lead to the immediate declaration of war by the Arab states in opposition to the Jewish state's claim to legitimacy, but armed struggle began within the country's territory at its very birth, culminating in the Arab League's 1964 creation of the Palestine Liberation Organization. The somewhat ad hoc formation of the Muslim state of Pakistan gave rise to a multiethnic postcolonial state whose future leaders would turn to myriad religious and secular sources of national identity that led to periods of dictatorship interspersed with spurts of democratic government, and even civil war in 1971. In Indonesia the consensus of the nationalist movement against Dutch colonial rule quickly frayed, leading to a complex, four-way struggle between Marxists, Islamists, liberal democrats, and proponents of an indigenous, consensus-based parliamentary system. And the problematic emergence of Lebanon and Syria as separate, independent states has left the former state ravaged by war, occupation, and factionalism, with its embattled Maronite Christians competing for control with the country's growing Shia Muslim population.

The historical origins and trajectories of these postcolonial states reveal the roots of state weakness in the key flashpoints of the decolonization process. As Robert Jackson explained, many of the underdeveloped states of the third world were "territorial jurisdictions which were formed under colonial rule and emerged into the light of day by an international legal transaction—decolonization—whereby sovereignty was transferred from European states to indigenous governments."[49] The corresponding lack of durable state authorities (and, in some cases, coherent national identities at the popular level) in these newly independent states meant an absence of legitimacy that the institutional embodiments of positive sovereignty normally confer. Coupled with the dysfunction impeding UN collective security during the early years of its operation, these two deficits at the domestic and international levels thwarted the international community's final attempts to resolve many postcolonial struggles before they erupted into violence—sowing the seeds of regional conflicts like the standoff in Kashmir and the Israeli-Palestinian Second Intifada that remain unresolved today.

A direct consequence of the weakness of these states and their complex internal rivalries was the impediments they posed for the dispensation of UN peace and security functions. After UN inaction and great power restraint had allowed independence struggles to continue unabated, contributing to the emergence of weakly governed successor states, the civil conflict seething within those states in turn severely challenged the limited capacity of those modest UN operations that *could* be mounted, closing a negative feedback loop of largely unmitigated internecine violence. Given both the need for unanimity in the Security Council to conduct Chapter VII operations and the checkered pasts of former colonial powers on the Council like Britain, Russia, and China, achieving consensus on the use of armed forces to resolve postcolonial conflicts became prohibitively difficult. Aware of the potential ramifications of any universal settlements in Palestine or Kashmir for their various regional geopolitical aspirations, the permanent members of the Security Council were gripped by a paralysis that prevented them from sanctioning many expeditionary adventures in the form of UN deployments to conflict zones. Even in the case of historically anticolonial powers like the United States, the dividing line was often blurry between combatants in postcolonial struggles such as Israeli nationalists and bands of Palestinian Arab militants or Pakistani Muslims who streamed into Kashmir and the Indian military authorities that came to the aid of the maharaja's embattled security forces.

Globalism and regionalism provide lenses through which to view such questions fraught with the perils of moral relativism and zero-sum outcomes. They accordingly provide compelling contextual frameworks for explaining how the United States and Great Britain perceived the violent upheavals of decolonization and the birth of a new generation of weak states.

Conclusion

This book has examined how perceptions of geography shaped British decolonization as it occurred on the opposite ends of the greater Middle East. In so doing, it has drawn comparisons between American and British strategies and policies, the corresponding ways of viewing the territorial geography and underlying demographics of specific regions that accompanied them, and the ideologies and goals driving various anticolonial nationalist struggles. Importantly it has shown how key (often implicit) assumptions laden within certain perceptions of the Levant, South Asia, and other regions likely drove foreign policies in Washington and London.

However, the argument presented here acknowledges that perceptions of geography were a part of basic intellectual frameworks of foreign policy-makers and constituted assumptions just like other biases and prejudices surely informed their thinking. It does not seek to argue that the assumptions about lands and peoples bound up in regionalism and globalism always determined policy or shaped outcomes. As policy differences like those that divided Lord Mountbatten and Sir Olaf Caroe about Pakistan showed, even officials who shared some of the same assumptions about geography did not see eye to eye on the best policy courses. But what is clear is the extent to which those policy courses were shaped by assumptions about geography.

The arguments presented here have straddled the three broad themes cited at the outset of this work. First and foremost, the trends toward globalism and regionalism made clear that geography and how it is perceived played a central and largely unexamined role in framing the postwar grand strategies of both the Churchill and Attlee governments and the Roosevelt and Truman administrations. Informed by the academic field of geopolitics in the United States and the deep training of Oxford's Arabists and their ilk in Britain, Anglo-American strategy after the Second World War revealed just how central geography was as a driver of international affairs in the increasingly globalized post-1945 international order. Second, the various experiences of the independence struggles in Palestine, Kashmir, the Levant, and the East Indies revealed that anticolonial ideology drew from myriad intellectual and cultural roots. The ideologies driving these movements were far from simple appropriations of European ideas about revolution and sovereignty; they were syncretic mixes of Enlightenment rationalism and ethnic and religious identity politics. Third, this book has shown how the histories of the early cold war, the origins of the United Nations, and the decolonization of the British and other European colonial empires after 1945 are really interwoven in a single grand narrative of sweeping change.

Within these broad thematic contexts it is insightful to conclude with a handful of additional observations about American and British experiences with postwar decolonization along the arc of crisis. Specifically these concern the nature of mental maps, the origins of contested postcolonial borders, the influence of popular conceptions of geography on foreign policy, and the idea of geographical measures of overstretch.

MENTAL MAPS AND FOREIGN POLICY

Importantly perceptions of geography not only grew from assumptions and perceptions about specific lands and peoples that helped shape policies and outcomes; they were also products of material realities in terms of the geopolitical predicaments of Britain and the United States by the Second World War. Of course British war debt and the burdens of policing the empire with Indian Army units entailed an inevitable contraction as the war years wore on—a contraction that shaped the development of regionalism by the second half of the 1940s. Globalism too was a product of the position in which America found itself on the world stage in the aftermath of the Second World War, which had laid waste to all of Europe's most powerful states. It was a moment of strategic departure for the United States—a break with the historical past and the reliance on the Monroe Doctrine that had carefully stewarded American foreign policy and guided it away from the overseas entanglements that George Washington had warned of at the nation's birth. That sense of a new world order in which American foreign policy interests circumscribed the earth as a whole globalized U.S. national security policy, but only after contentious debates—of the sort that unfolded at Dumbarton Oaks between defenders of the Monroe Doctrine such as Harold Stassen and John Foster Dulles and globalists such as President Franklin Roosevelt, Sumner Welles, and Leo Pasvolsky.[1] But as was the case across the Atlantic, globalism was the product of not just ideas from the field of geopolitics and the pages of *National Geographic* but also of the geopolitical and economic circumstances of the age. American economic expansion and geopolitical necessities associated with a forward strategy of defense after the December 1941 Pearl Harbor attack meant an outward growth of the radius of the postwar American security perimeter and the resulting strategic ideas adopted by the late Roosevelt and Truman administrations.

The perceptions of the wider world bound up in globalism and regionalism thus validate how material power shaped ideas, which then became codified through maps, memoranda, and other documents that reflected distinct conceptions of human and strategic geography. But over time those codified conceptions produced doctrinal anachronisms when strategic balances changed before great power strategists could adapt to changing conditions in timely and responsive ways. Ideas about geography ossified within bureaucracies like the State Department and the British Foreign Office in the form of documents passed down from one group of policymakers to another as official responsibilities changed hands and new officers rotated through assignments. The result was the perpetuation of certain views of specific lands and peoples that remained static while strategic balances shifted, demographics morphed, power disparities grew, and international norms evolved. Where official bureaucracies allowed gaps to widen between rigid policy assumptions and actual power projection capabilities, strategic mismatches led official policies astray from the on-the-ground realities of imperial administration. French and Dutch imperial officials like Georges Catroux and Hubertus van Mook learned this lesson the hard way in the Levant and East Indies. Where the bureaucracy was able to adapt its views in accordance with change in the international system, as was the case for Britain's Labour government under Attlee and Bevin, newly redrawn visions provided the blueprints for novel strategies that had the boldness to break with precedent. The historical evidence cited in this study reveals the impact of globalism and regionalism in influencing Anglo-American policy during the war and postwar years.

American globalism was a rough and ill-defined way of seeing the world during and immediately after the Second World War. Except in regions where U.S. security considerations had become starkly clear, the clarity of its boundaries and labels seemed to blur as radial distance from Washington increased; American interests were broad and ambiguous in distant regions like South and Central Asia. These were parts of the world about which Americans knew very little. But where gaps and blind spots may have cropped up, globalism seems to have borrowed from the past to color in its maps. One part of the world in which this seems to have occurred is the Eastern Mediterranean. There an almost Braudelian sense of a "Mediterranean world" led a number of Roosevelt and Truman administration officials, including Sumner Welles, Clark Clifford, David Niles, and President Truman himself, to the natural solution of resettling European Jews in Palestine—a process that had already begun and rose to the fore because of the dictates of the humanitarian emergency to which it was bound. Viewed through the lens of globalism, the plight of Jewish refugees from Europe was intimately connected with the lands of Palestine across the Mediterranean Sea on the western edge of the Levant. The records of the Field-Bowman "M Project" and the work of the Advisory Committee for Postwar Foreign Policy amount to hard evidence of that cognitive linkage— well before the arrival of the Truman administration, to which American support for Zionism is so completely and unquestioningly attributed.

While the trend toward regionalism led Britain to vastly different conclusions about Palestine, it represented a similar way of viewing a particular region that associated key elements of geopolitics and demographics while excluding others. For Attlee, Bevin, and even Mountbatten, the compelling logic of the need to preserve the sanctity of what was perceived to be an unbroken bloc of Muslim lands from the Levant to South Asia proved irresistible from the standpoint of strategic first principles. It was a concern so vital for the preservation of the empire's lines of communication that it became the paramount concern impinging on the policies that shaped decolonization. The prime minister's January 1948 guidance to the British Mission to the United Nations was unmistakable in that regard: no policy was to be adopted in Kashmir that would prejudice British interests in Palestine. Here was evidence par excellence of the weight of considerations stemming from the assumptions in regionalism: the geography of the regions connecting the two flashpoints preoccupying British imperial defense policy had become the principal consideration affecting policies toward either one, at the highest levels of the Labour government.

Moreover, as the State Department's M Project and the Advisory Committee for Postwar Foreign Policy's global refugee resettlement agendas reflected institutional evidence of globalism, regionalism too came to shape the priorities and institutional structures in the British foreign policy establishment. Perhaps the most obvious example of that bureaucratic impact was the creation of the Middle East Office in Cairo. Granted, the office abjectly failed to tie together British policy in the Near East with the degree of policy coordination and keen awareness of regional implications that planners had hoped the Office would produce. Nonetheless it represented a specific example of how intangible ideas and assumptions came to be reflected in actual structures.

The two ways of perceiving the geography of the Middle East and South Asia also accompanied a fundamental difference in ideological views across the Atlantic—toward the central issue of colonialism—that separated Washington and London. Those ideologies were the products of both the divergent histories of the United States and Great Britain and the geopolitical circumstances in which both powers found themselves after the Second World War: one falling from its perch after a century of global supremacy, while the other ascended to primacy to displace it as a political and cultural heir.

COLONIALISM, ANTICOLONIALISM, AND IMAGINED BOUNDARIES

As John Gallagher once described the process of British decolonization, "The collapse had its origins in small sparks eating their way through long historical fuses before the detonations began."[2] Those detonations can be thought of as the explosive outcomes of a process that various historians have traced back to different chronological periods.[3] But by the historical endpoint of 1945, Britain confronted a new international order in which colonial rule had become an anachronism of sorts. Sumner Welles's later blueprints for the UN Charter, the American negotiating coup at Yalta while the Poynton-Robinson proposals for regional councils fell by the wayside, and the incapacitating quandaries of the retreats from Palestine and Kashmir were all emblematic of that course of events. Still, unlike the rigid persistence of French and Dutch colonial control in the Levant and the East Indies until the bitter end, the inherent willingness to reassess and reexamine was the greatest strategic virtue of British regionalism. That flexibility enabled Whitehall to conceptualize anew Britain's role in a changed postwar world under the stewardship of Labour's policy of colonial development and the substitution of informal relationships for formal imperial connections.

For it was the vision and awareness of statesmen like Clement Attlee and Ernest Bevin that enabled Britain, under extreme economic and strategic duress, to adapt colonial rule to a postcolonial world. They may have disagreed about the pace of the British retreat and the relative importance of factors like strategic competition with the Soviet Union in the Middle East, but both these "regionalists" grasped the need to emphasize the protection of key British footholds straddling imperial lines of communication between the home islands and India and scale back imperial commitments as financial and military strains grew unbearable. These statesmen were also cognizant that the new American role in the world, backed by the primacy of air-age globalism and the arrival of the nuclear era, meant a westward shift of the strategic focal point from which the West's power radiated into the world from London to Washington. Expanding membership in the Commonwealth, which India, Pakistan, and Ceylon had joined by 1949, provided one way to mitigate the strategic consequences of that shift. The conceptual innovation of "informal empire" thus proved a critical means of survival for British influence in the post-1945 order as a new wave of European decolonization began to break.[4] But Labour's ideology of the empire as a progressive force in the world provided an adaptive capacity to adjust and a more palatable ideological justification for the perpetuation of British imperial authority. Both those tools proved invaluable at the critical moment when power devolved in Palestine, Kashmir, and beyond to eager anticolonial leaders clamoring to assert authority against the imperial metropole. British decolonization was thus a process that both shaped and was shaped by Foreign and Colonial Office policies through complex interactions and feedback effects that transformed the meaning of citizenship in the dissolving British Empire.

As that process got under way, given both cold war superpowers' mutual antipathies toward colonial rule and the importance of self-determination as a principle underlying the UN system, the basic thrust of U.S. policy toward postcolonial independence movements in the early years of the

United Nations is not difficult to explain.[5] In both Israel-Palestine and disputed Kashmir, the State Department refrained from strong initial endorsements of any individual claimant to the respective territories. In the case of Palestine, initial U.S. support for the UN recommendation of partition gave way to the Truman administration's eventual embrace of the state of Israel, but only after the outbreak of war and driven largely by domestic political considerations. In Kashmir U.S. policy coincidentally lined up squarely with British efforts to mediate the conflict between India and Pakistan through the United Nations and the appointment of a plebiscite administrator.

Where American power did not displace the Pax Britannica directly, American policies, however cooperative on the surface, were geared fundamentally toward accelerating the dissolution of colonial rule. In the Dutch East Indies, the United States (along with the Soviet Union) eventually endorsed the independence of the new Indonesian state only after the second police action in December 1948 completely discredited Dutch colonialist policy through the perpetration of excessive violence. Similarly the American recognition of Syrian and Lebanese independence after a cautious waiting period to gauge the efficacy of nascent institution-building processes and discredit French-installed candidates like Emile Eddé validated the State Department's intent to discourage the perpetuation of French colonial rule in the Middle East, where energy supplies critical for any future global conflict necessitated an American forward strategy.

But despite the strong Wilsonian tone in U.S. rhetoric in support of these postwar anticolonial struggles, scrutiny of the actual policies suggests that the uncomfortable and uncertain coexistence of the principles of sovereignty and self-determination likely weighed on all of them. By deliberately choosing an inconsistent policy approach toward the decolonization process in the Levant, South Asia, and the East Indies, the United States was able to strip the former European colonial powers of dependent territories from which they could draw critical resources to retain postwar economic competitiveness, while simultaneously exercising caution in its handling of the upsurges of communism in Greece, Turkey, and Italy.

In its initial endorsement of the UN partition plan for Palestine, the United States opted to walk a fine line. Despite British assurances to Palestinian Arabs and the ambiguities inherent in the Balfour Declaration, U.S. policymakers refrained from endorsements of Israeli claims or universal condemnation of the Arab forces that declared war on the state of Israel immediately after its foundation. Nevertheless through undertakings like the M Project, the Roosevelt administration and members of

Welles's Political Subcommittee of the Advisory Committee for Postwar Foreign Policy revealed a humanitarian interest in the resettlement of displaced European Jews in Palestine that was a logical corollary of the maxims that underlay globalism—even within the State Department, an organization normally viewed as opposing Jewish resettlement in Palestine through and through. Despite the efforts of the State Department's Division (later Bureau) of Near Eastern Affairs and others who firmly opposed the partition of Palestine into Arab and Jewish states, the manifestation of that vision of globalism came to be realized only after the Truman administration's reversal of course against the recommendations of the Department and the fateful policy shift of May 1948 that led to U.S. recognition of Israel.

From the start, the United States refrained from embroiling itself in the Kashmir affair, assiduously avoiding a finding of either Indian or Pakistani rights to the territory in question. In a sense the struggle pitted Kashmiri "self-determination," in terms of control over its political destiny, against *both* Indian *and* Pakistani claims of sovereignty when colonial rule expired and as Pakistan's borders took shape. The U.S. response to the conflict reflected an aversion to taking sides in at least the international legal contest. That reluctance is evident in the intelligence analyses at the time, which focused on conditions on the ground in Kashmir and demilitarization rather than legal determinations. And the statements of Ambassador Warren Austin at the Security Council echoed that reluctance, citing the transitory nature of dispute settlement through a UN observer mission that Austin knew would prove unable to supply the requisite long-term solution to the postcolonial aspirations of India and Pakistan.

What emerges from the historical record of U.S. foreign policy toward the early postwar anticolonial nationalist movements is a lack of any overarching guiding principle beyond rhetorical support for the principle of self-determination during the immediate aftermath of the war, before the selective invocation of the principle against the territorial integrity of only certain sovereign states. Part of the problem inhered in the difficulties of defining the terms *sovereignty* and *self-determination,* neat constructs that actually connoted a wide range of meanings in the real world.[6] Significantly the conceptual incoherence of those normative ideals resulted from their unique intellectual origins as well as their selective application worldwide.

The U.S. policy that filled this strategic vacuum was thus one unguided by clear precepts or strategic doctrine: a global policy toward dependent territories that walked a fine line between disavowing anticolonial struggles and defending European colonial possessions at all costs. The upshot was U.S. nonintervention in a number of conflicts that perhaps constituted egregious breaches of the peace or acts of aggression by almost any interpretation of UN Charter law. It was often a cautious deference to more conciliatory UN mechanisms and the interests of the relevant colonial powers themselves that would remain the core of American strategy toward the postcolonial world during the years of flux after the Second World War, before the cold war policy of containment and NSC-68 would provide the vision and the means to subsume the developing world into Washington's binary vision of liberal, democratic allies and revolutionary socialist adversaries.

OFFICIAL AND NONOFFICIAL CONCEPTIONS OF GEOGRAPHY

Such were the ideological outlooks of the two English-speaking powers presiding over the postwar dissolution of key elements of the British colonial system. To some extent their dominant conceptions of geography were products of these ideological differences and the material power realities that shaped them. But globalism and regionalism were also partly constructions of the imaginative thoughts and formulations of the officials that staffed the respective foreign ministries and other relevant agencies. Each confronted the challenge of devising mental pictures of the world regions where their national interests lay that were conditioned by their upbringing and education, the particular age they lived in, and sets of geopolitical opportunities and constraints. To some extent the United States today faces a similar challenge in devising a vision of the world in which transnational armed groups have proliferated and mounted challenges to key U.S. national security interests.

But what of the mental maps of individuals in this wider narrative centered on the views of diplomats and generals? Like the two principal state protagonists in this narrative, the United States and Great Britain, the relevant anticolonial nationalist movements and their leaders in Palestine and Kashmir also viewed the world using mental maps of their own. These were by no means based on universal or uncontested cartographies. The varying degrees of popularity that Ben-Gurion's vision of a Jewish national homeland spanning all of Palestine enjoyed across various circles of Zionist and Jewish political thought reflected the highly contingent nature of his mental map of Palestine. His image of "all of Palestine" for the Jews was one man's vision: it drew adherents from across the international Zionist movement with compelling attractive force, but it also repulsed the likes of Hans Kohn and Hannah Arendt with its exclusivist political and human geography of ethnic nationalism. In this sense Muhammad Ali Jinnah was far more cagey with his imprecise vision of "Pakistan" as a homeland for India's Muslims: an elusive concept that defied delimitation and confirmation until the act of partition. Some of his British interlocutors suspected Jinnah of leveraging this ambiguity to his advantage. In reality its fixation as a specific territorial unit may have been a maximalist aim that the eventual founder of Pakistan avoided until the terrible end and the Sartrean dilemma that accompanied the fait accompli of a partition that circumstances had imposed on him.

Likewise Shukri al-Quwatli's vision of an independent Syria freed of French mandatory control represented a counterpoint to the Arab nationalist urges driving Hashemites who sought a single Arab nation-state from the Mediterranean to the Persian Gulf and from the southernmost tip of the Arabian peninsula to Mosul. Though subjected to less exacting scrutiny, the more problematic notion of Lebanese national identity also sprang from specific ideological roots and challenged the great power politics that had hitherto held sway over the fortunes of the colonial-era Levant. One of the most compelling mental maps of nationhood was probably Sukarno's, given the immense geographical expanse over which the tens of thousands of islands in the Indonesian archipelago was scattered. Though localized in the populated areas of Java, Sumatra, and Papua, the idea of "Nasakom" and its realization as a united states of Indonesia in 1949 represented a bold vision of a post-Dutch future for the East Indies; it was an intellectual construct based on territorial notions that bound together fortunes of local populations that spanned extraordinary ethnic diversity and immense physical distances.

The final boundaries of the postcolonial states of Israel, Syria, Lebanon, Pakistan, and Indonesia would emerge only when the competing territorial blueprints in the minds of different leaders and activists and abstract notions of sovereignty and self-determination that had yet to be articulated in messy, real-world specifics all were reconciled in the often explosive conferral of statehood. Until the end, these boundaries remained indeterminate, as has become glaringly evident today in the decolonized territories of the Muslim world.[7] That indeterminacy was perhaps inevitable given the myriad contingencies as play. As this study has shown, a litany of largely independent forces shaped that process of state formation in both Palestine and Kashmir, from the war plans of generals to the colonial policies of diplomats to the national dreams of founding fathers like Ben-Gurion and Jinnah.

CONCEPTIONS OF GEOGRAPHY AND OVERSTRETCH

The contrast that this book draws between the willing contraction of the British Empire under the postwar Labour government and the almost irrational retrenchment of French and Dutch imperial power during the same postwar years warrants a final observation about the nature of overseas empires. In retrospect European colonial policies during this period may well provide critical insights for U.S. grand strategy in the world today. For one can readily argue that conceptions of geography like globalism and regionalism are useful metrics for assessing whether states are overextended by virtue of the scope of their projected power overseas. Paul Kennedy first suggested this idea of imperial overstretch as a condition in which the far-flung commitments at the peripheries of regional or global powers overtax the military basing, revenue generation, demographic, and other capacities required to sustain that presence.[8] But without a more granular definition, the parsimoniously elegant argument that overstretch leads great powers to expand until they are "crushed under their own weight" suffers from a tautological flaw. For *overstretch* is a term that requires geographical definition of the proper power projection limits a state should be subject to at a given point in history. In certain terms—economic capacity, for instance—it may be possible to locate the "tipping point" at which, say, a state's defense burdens exceed its revenues. Such tipping points enable analysts to determine trajectories of expansion or decline.[9] How can similar measures be devised to help size a great power's ideal global footprint at a specific historical moment?

The findings in this study suggest that the collective official perceptions of geography serve as a powerful and compelling construct for gauging such footprints. Moreover Great Britain's postwar experience with regionalism provides an invaluable case study for examining how redrawn mental maps are essential for reframing the basic geopolitical assumptions that underlie major strategic reassessments at transitional periods in history. The regionalism that informed the strategic thought of Attlee, Bevin, and

British diplomatic and military strategists powered the pragmatic and prescient reconceptualization of British security interests accompanying the retreat from Egypt that formed the doctrinal core of Britain's recast postwar strategy. The British policy in the Near East seeking to defend the Home Islands' lines of communication to India that William Roger Louis summed up in its entirety as a search for alternatives to the massive presence in Egypt was no hasty, ad hoc response to the catastrophic effects of the war and the burdens of imperial policing. The failures of successive plans for power devolution may have led to frantic redrafting of proposals like the Anglo-American Committee of Inquiry's plans for Palestine and the Cabinet Mission plan for India. But Labour's wider strategy was rooted firmly in basic first principles that fundamentally rethought the notion of the empire and the Commonwealth, relying on informal relationships to secure for Britain what formal arrangements had hitherto safeguarded.

Regionalism was also tightly delimited in its geographical focus, as the periodic assessments of the War Chiefs of Staff over 1945–1947 make clear. In offering their various updated reassessments of British strategic requirements in the Near East, the Chiefs continually recognized the greater importance of British influence over specific sea lines of communication like the Suez Canal, transit facilities like the port in Haifa, and air linkages in the Levant that were more critical to preserve British imperial security than the need to maintain a presence in Egypt or Palestine. The contours of this regionalism provided a sensible blueprint for British overseas power projection in the postwar world—one that was commensurate with a war debt that had edged over three billion pounds, the sudden loss of manpower for imperial defense resulting from Indian independence that became jarringly evident in Indonesia, and the other strains that were bending and buckling imperial moorings in Asia.

In stark contrast, the experiences of the French and Dutch empires in the Levant and East Indies, respectively, revealed the catastrophic costs of failing to recalibrate imperial footprints in accordance with a new era of rapid change for colonial powers. By refusing to withdraw from Syria and Lebanon before the Anglo-French crisis of spring 1945, the Free French government revealed a lack of strategic forethought and sensibility despite the travails of war and the stark reality of parallel government in exile during Nazi occupation. That strategic failure seemed inexplicable after the American recognition of Syrian and Lebanese independence, although it was perhaps perpetuated by the public British acquiescence to the idea of

French primacy in the Levant that Churchill had acknowledged until the crisis.

In this sense the Dutch refusal to retreat from the East Indies and concede Indonesian independence, even after the British-sponsored conference at Chequers, mirrored French policy in the Levant. Officials like Hubertus van Mook likely continued to view the Indies through a Dutch imperialist lens that envisaged a global empire scattered across the Indonesian archipelago and other resource-rich colonies. This was an outmoded vision that had yet to be squared with the harsh realities of the liberal anticolonialism that came to pervade the postwar world that the map of American globalism represented more accurately than any other. Like the case of the last years of French rule in the Levant, Dutch retaliation in a series of crises lay bare once and for all the frailty of Dutch authority in the East Indies and The Hague's inability to recognize the extent and durability of the domestic Indonesian institutions that had come into being and begun functioning independently during the brief but fateful interregnum of Japanese occupation.

Perhaps the reluctance of French and Dutch colonial policy to accommodate the necessary structural policy changes can be attributed in large part to organizational dynamics and the inevitable inertia guiding large colonial policy bureaucracies struggling to come to terms with the gradual but inevitable dissolution of the colonial world they were created to manage.

The resistance of the French and Dutch imperial bureaucracies to adapt—the persistence of "Official Minds," so to speak—lends credence to the view that strategies and doctrines, like the geographic assumptions in which they are grounded, evolve slowly and unevenly, down specific trajectories, until they are suddenly and violently shaken by events like Pearl Harbor, the Arab-Israeli War, or the Second Dutch Police Action. The lasting consequences of such events are testaments to the perils of the strategic overstretch that beset the European colonial empires by the middle of the twentieth century.

ABBREVIATIONS

NOTES

ARCHIVES CONSULTED

ACKNOWLEDGMENTS

INDEX

Abbreviations

BL	The British Library, London, United Kingdom
CAB	Cabinet Papers
CIA	Central Intelligence Agency
C.M.	Cabinet Minutes
CO	Colonial Office
C.O.S.	Chiefs of Staff
CRO	Commonwealth Relations Office
DO	Dominions Office
FDRL	Franklin D. Roosevelt Presidential Library, Hyde Park, New York
FO	Foreign Office
FRUS	*Foreign Relations of the United States*
HSTL	Harry S. Truman Presidential Library, Independence, Missouri
IOR	India Office Records, The British Library, London, United Kingdom
JCS	Joint Chiefs of Staff
LEHI	Lohamei Herut Israel [Fighters for the Freedom of Israel]
LHCMA	Liddell Hart Centre for Military Archives, Kings College London, United Kingdom
NSC	National Security Council
ORE	Office of Reports and Estimates
PREM	Records of the Prime Minister's Office
PSF	President's Secretary's Files

SANACC	State-Army-Navy-Air Force Coordinating Committee
SWNCC	State-War-Navy Coordinating Committee
UKNA	United Kingdom National Archives, Kew, Richmond
UN	United Nations
UNCIP	United Nations Commission on India and Pakistan
UNMOGIP	United Nations Military Observer Group in India and Pakistan
UNTSO	United Nations Truce Supervision Organization
USNA	United States National Archives II, College Park, Maryland
WHCF	White House Central Files

Notes

INTRODUCTION

1. See W. K. Hancock and M. M. Gowing, *British War Economy* (London: Her Majesty's Stationery Office, 1949). On the growing importance of Africa, see William Roger Louis, *The British Empire in the Middle East, 1945–1951: Arab Nationalism, the United States, and Postwar Imperialism* (Oxford: Clarendon Press, 1984), 11–12.
2. See, for example, Irvine Anderson, *Aramco, the United States, and Saudi Arabia: A Study in the Dynamics of Foreign Oil Policy, 1933–1950* (Princeton: Princeton University Press, 1981); Alan S. Milward, *The Reconstruction of Western Europe, 1945–51* (Berkeley: University of California Press, 1984); Aaron David Miller, *Search for Security: Saudi Arabian Oil and American Foreign Policy, 1939–1949* (Chapel Hill: University of North Carolina Press, 1980), especially chapter 6.
3. On the expanding postwar American military presence, see Melvyn Leffler, *A Preponderance of Power: National Security, the Truman Administration, and the Cold War* (Stanford: Stanford University Press, 1993). Revisionist cold war historians have argued that capitalist U.S. designs on postwar world markets drove an aggressive American postwar foreign policy, helping precipitate the cold war. See, for instance, William Appleman Williams, *The Tragedy of American Diplomacy* (New York: Norton, 1972); Walter LaFeber, *America, Russia, and the Cold War, 1945–2000* (New York: McGraw-Hill, 2002).
4. One such scheme was the idea of a "Middle East Confederacy." See Memorandum by Commander-in-Chief Middle East Force, A Middle East Confederacy, C.C. (45), 25, CAB 80/100, UKNA; Roger Louis, *The*

British Empire in the Middle East, 22. Another example, of course, was the British effort to mediate the conflict between India and Pakistan through British high commissioners advising the respective military staffs.
5. Hastings Ismay Papers 3/7/67/100, LHCMA.
6. See Alexander George, "Domestic Constraints on Regime Change in U.S. Foreign Policy: The Need for Policy Legitimacy," in G. John Ikenberry, ed., *American Foreign Policy: Theoretical Essays,* 4th edition (New York: Longman, 2002), 328.
7. See Neil Smith, *American Empire: Roosevelt's Geographer and the Prelude to Globalization* (Berkeley: University of California Press, 2003), 326–336, quote on 328.
8. Reprinted from *World Affairs* 115, no. 2 (1952), Truman Papers, PSF, Subject File, 1940–1953, Box 169, HSTL.
9. William Roger Louis, "American Anti-Colonialism and the Dissolution of the British Empire," *International Affairs* 61, no. 3 (1985): 395–420, quote on 397; Annex, Effect of World Organisation's Charter upon Anglo-Egyptian Treaty of Alliance, in so far as it concerns the British position in Egypt, 16 July 1945, C.O.S. (45), 506 (0), CAB 80/100, UKNA; W.P. (45) 205, L/E/9/1527, IOR, BL.
10. The most important works are probably Roger Louis, *The British Empire in the Middle East;* J.C. Hurewitz, *The Struggle for Palestine* (New York: Norton, 1950); Michael J. Cohen, *Palestine and the Great Powers, 1945–1948* (Princeton: Princeton University Press, 1982).
11. Herbert Samuel, "An Analysis of the Palestine Situation," Box 4, File 4, Cunningham Papers, Middle East Centre Archive, Oxford University Library.
12. Bevin, Speech to House of Commons, 26 January 1949; MS Attlee dep 77, Attlee Papers, Bodleian Library, Oxford.
13. See, for example, Peter Hahn, *Caught in the Middle East: U.S. Policy toward the Arab-Israeli Conflict, 1945–1961* (Chapel Hill: University of North Carolina Press, 2004); Bruce J. Evensen, *Truman, Palestine, and the Press: Shaping Conventional Wisdom at the Beginning of the Cold War* (New York: Greenwood Press, 1992); Ritchie Ovendale, *Britain, the United States, and the End of the Palestine Mandate, 1942–1948* (Woodbridge, Suffolk, UK: Boydell Press, 1989); Cohen, *Palestine and the Great Powers.*
14. Report by the Policy Planning Staff on Position of the United States with Respect to Palestine, 19 January 1948, *FRUS,* 1948, vol. 5, *The Near East, South Asia, and Africa,* p. 546; "Problems and Objectives of United States Policy," Leahy Records, Joint Chiefs of Staff, Folder 88, Research and Analysis Branch of OSS, George C. Marshall Library, University of Virginia.

15. Memorandum from Colonel A. J. McFarland to the State-War-Navy Coordinating Committee, 21 June 1946, Documents on the Recognition of the State of Israel, HSTL, available at http://www.trumanlibrary.org/whistlestop/study_collections/israel/large/documents/newPDF/70.pdf.
16. Byrnes to Bevin, 28 October 1945, Truman Papers, PSF, Subject File, 1940–1953, Box 148, HSTL.
17. Truman to Attlee, 10 October 1946, Truman Papers, PSF, Subject File, 1940–1953, Box 148, HSTL.
18. Dening to Bevin, 20 April 1948, FO 371/69721, UKNA. On British policy in Kashmir, see Sumantara Bose, *Kashmir: Roots of Conflict, Paths to Peace* (Cambridge, Mass.: Harvard University Press, 1993); Robert A. Huttenback, *Kashmir and the British Raj, 1847–1947* (Karachi, India: Oxford University Press, 2004); Ian Copland, *The Princes of India in the Endgame of Empire, 1917–1947* (Cambridge, UK: Cambridge University Press, 1997); Robert G. Wirsing, *India, Pakistan and the Kashmir Dispute: On Regional Conflict and Its Resolution* (New York: St. Martin's Press, 1994); Alastair Lamb, *Kashmir: A Disputed Legacy, 1846–1990* (New Delhi: Oxford University Press, 1991).
19. See *Memoirs of Sir Olaf Caroe*, Mss Eur C273, Caroe Papers, IOR, BL, quoted in Peter John Brobst, *The Future of the Great Game: Sir Olaf Caroe, India's Independence, and the Defense of Asia* (Akron, Ohio: University of Akron Press, 2005), 126–127. The expression "arc of crisis" was popularized after its use in a speech by Zbigniew Brzezinski was quoted in *Time* magazine. According to Brzezinski, "An arc of crisis stretches along the shores of the Indian Ocean, with fragile social and political structures in a region of vital importance to us threatened with fragmentation. The resulting political chaos could well be filled by elements hostile to our values and sympathetic to our adversaries" ("The Crescent of Crisis," *Time*, 15 January 1979).
20. CIA Report on India-Pakistan, 16 September 1948, Papers of Harry S. Truman, President's Secretary's Files, HSTL; Wirsing, *India, Pakistan and the Kashmir Dispute*, 237–238. On the United States and the Kashmir question more broadly, see Dennis Kux, *Estranged Democracies: India and the United States, 1941–1991* (Delhi: Sage, 1994); Dennis Kux, *Disenchanted Allies* (Delhi: Oxford University Press, 2001); Josef Korbel, *Danger in Kashmir* (New York: Oxford University Press, 2002); Robert J. McMahon, *The Cold War on the Periphery: The United States, India and Pakistan* (New York: Columbia University Press, 1994).
21. CIA ORE 17–49, Report on the Strategic Importance of the Far East to the U.S. and the USSR, 4 May 1949, Papers of Harry S. Truman, PSF, Intelligence File, Box 256, HSTL.

22. Background Memoranda on Visit to the United States of Liaquat Ali Khan, Prime Minister and Minister of Defense, Government of Pakistan, Truman Papers, PSF, Subject File, 1940–1953, Box 160, HSTL.
23. Roger Louis, *The British Empire in the Middle East*, 148–149.
24. Memorandum by Henderson, 23 May 1945, *FRUS*, 1945, 8: 1093–1095.
25. Robert J. McMahon, *Colonialism and Cold War: The United States and the Struggle for Indonesian Independence, 1945–49* (Ithaca: Cornell University Press, 1981), 118–119.
26. See Robert Divine, *Second Chance: The Triumph of Internationalism in America During WWII* (New York: Atheneum, 1971), 227; Robert Hilderbrand, *Dumbarton Oaks: The Origins of the United Nations and the Search for Postwar Security* (Chapel Hill: University of North Carolina Press, 1990), 245–257.
27. Alfred Thayer Mahan's classic work *The Influence of Sea Power Upon History* (Boston: Little, Brown, 1894) cited sea power as a driving force behind the rise of the British Empire to a position of primacy. See also Halford Mackinder, "The Geographical Pivot of History," in *Democratic Ideals and Reality* (Washington, DC: National Defense University Press, 1996), 175–194; Nicholas Spykman, *America's Strategy in World Politics: The United States and the Balance of Power* (New York: Harcourt, Brace, 1942).
28. See, for example, Jared Diamond's groundbreaking *Guns, Germs, and Steel: The Fates of Human Societies* (New York: Norton, 1997); Kenneth Pomeranz, *The Great Divergence: China, Europe and the Making of the Modern World Economy* (Princeton: Princeton University Press, 2001).
29. See, for instance, Jennifer Van Vleck's *Empire of the Air: Aviation and the American Ascendancy* (Cambridge, Mass.: Harvard University Press, 2013); Alan Henrikson, "The Geographical 'Mental Maps' of American Foreign Policy Makers," *International Political Science Review* 1, no. 4 (1980): 495–530, which looks at the role of mental maps as guides for policymakers. Conversely, Susan Schulten's *The Geographical Imagination in America, 1880–1950* (Chicago: University of Chicago Press, 2001) explores how historical and cultural factors, in turn, influenced American maps—representations of geography that shaped the way America viewed the world—from the late nineteenth century to the early cold war.
30. See Partha Chatterjee, *Nationalist Thought and the Colonial World: A Derivative Discourse* (London: Zed Books, 1986); Erez Manela, *The Wilsonian Moment: Self Determination and the International Origins of Anticolonial Nationalism* (New York: Oxford University Press, 2007).
31. See Ben Halpern, *The Idea of the Jewish State* (Cambridge, Mass.: Harvard University Press, 1961), 27–28. The literature on the origins and

evolution of Zionism is vast. The movement is usually traced to the publication of Theodor Herzl's *Der Judenstaadt* in 1896. See also Walter Laqueur, *A History of Zionism: From the French Revolution to the Establishment of the State of Israel* (New York: Random House, 2003); Howard Sachar, *A History of Israel* (New York: Knopf, 2007). Ben-Gurion himself drew a strong link between the present and the Jewish people's "age-long connexion with Palestine." See David Ben-Gurion, *Rebirth and Destiny of Israel* (New York: Philosophical Library, 1954). On the morality of Jewish collusion with colonial powers to settle Palestine, see Hannah Arendt, *The Jewish Writings* (New York: Schocken Books, 2007).

32. Compare, for example, the discussions in Ayesha Jalal's *The Sole Spokesman: Jinnah, the Muslim League, and the Demand for Pakistan* (Cambridge, UK: Cambridge University Press, 1985) and Stanley Wolpert's *Jinnah of Pakistan* (New York: Oxford University Press, 1984). On the Kashmir dispute specifically, see Alastair Lamb, *Crisis in Kashmir, 1947–1966* (London: Routledge, 1966); Lamb, *Kashmir: A Disputed Legacy*. On Kashmir's more recent history, see Wirsing, *India, Pakistan and the Kashmir Dispute*.

33. The standard work on modern Indonesian nationalism has long been George McT. Kahin, *Nationalism and Revolution in Indonesia* (Ithaca: Cornell University Press, 1952). See also Bernhard Dahm, *Sukarno and the Struggle for Indonesian Independence* (Ithaca: Cornell University Press, 1969); William H. Frederick, *Visions and Heat: The Making of the Indonesian Revolution* (Athens: Ohio University Press, 1989); Richard McMillan, *The British Occupation of Indonesia, 1945–1946: Britain, the Netherlands and the Indonesian Revolution* (London: Routledge, 2005); Adrian Vickers, *A History of Modern Indonesia* (Cambridge, UK: Cambridge University Press, 2005).

34. See Albert Hourani, *Syria and Lebanon* (London: Oxford University Press, 1946); Philip Khoury, *Syria and the French Mandate* (Princeton: Princeton University Press, 1986); A. L. Tibawi, *A Modern History of Syria, Including Lebanon and Palestine* (New York: St. Martin's Press, 1969); Zeine N. Zeine, *The Struggle for Arab Independence* (Delmar, N.Y.: Caravan, 1977). On Lebanon specifically, see Helena Cobban, *The Making of Modern Lebanon* (Boulder, Colo.: Westview Press, 1985); Wade Goria, *Sovereignty and Leadership in Lebanon* (Ithaca: Cornell University Press, 1985); William Harris, *The New Face of Lebanon* (Princeton: Markus Wiener, 2006).

35. William Roger Louis's epic multiarchival study *Imperialism at Bay: The United States and the Decolonization of the British Empire* (New York: Oxford University Press, 1978) remains the most comprehensive account

of how American postwar ambitions, British insecurities, and intra-Commonwealth differences with Australian and New Zealand policies were finally reconciled at the United Nations. See also Robert F. Holland, *European Decolonisation 1918–1991: An Introductory Survey* (London: Macmillan, 1985); John Darwin, *Britain and Decolonisation: The Retreat from Empire in the Post-War World* (London: Palgrave Macmillan, 1988); John Darwin, *The End of the British Empire: The Historical Debate* (Oxford: Oxford University Press, 1991).

36. See John Lewis Gaddis, *The United States and the Origins of the Cold War* (New York: Columbia University Press, 1972); Bruce Kuniholm, *The Origins of the Cold War in the Near East: Great Power Conflict and Diplomacy in Iran, Turkey and Greece* (Princeton: Princeton University Press, 1980); Melvyn Leffler and David Painter, eds., *Origins of the Cold War: An International History* (London: Routledge, 2005), part 2: "Three Cold War Crises: Iran, Turkey, and Greece."

37. Robert E. Sherwood, *Roosevelt and Hopkins: An Intimate History* (New York: Harper Brothers, 1948). The work of Roger Louis, of course, also addresses this issue in considerable depth.

38. See Hilderbrand, *Dumbarton Oaks;* Christopher O'Sullivan, *Sumner Welles, Postwar Planning, and the Quest for a New World Order, 1937–1943* (New York: Columbia University Press, 2008); Townsend Hoopes and Douglas Brinkley, *FDR and the Creation of the UN* (New Haven: Yale University Press, 1997).

1. ALL OF PALESTINE

1. On the great power diplomacy that dissolved Ottoman possessions in the Near East and produced the French and British mandates in Syria, Palestine, and Iraq, see David Fromkin, *A Peace to End All Peace: The Fall of the Ottoman Empire and the Creation of the Modern Middle East* (New York: Owl Books, 2001).

2. On the history of Palestine throughout the dissolution of the Ottoman Empire, see Elie Kedourie, *England and the Middle East: The Destruction of the Ottoman Empire, 1914–1921* (London: Bowes & Bowes, 1956); John Darwin, *Britain, Egypt and the Middle East: Imperial Policy in the Aftermath of War, 1918–1922* (New York: St. Martin's Press, 1981); Ahmed Emin, *Turkey in the World War* (New Haven: Yale University Press, 1930); Isaiah Friedman, *Germany, Turkey, and Zionism: 1897–1918* (Oxford: Clarendon Press, 1977); Albert Hourani, *The Emergence of the Modern Middle East* (Berkeley: University of California Press, 1981); Howard Sachar, *The Emergence of the Middle East, 1914–1924* (New York: Knopf, 1969).

3. See Fromkin, *A Peace to End All Peace*, 276–283.
4. McMahon Letter to Hussein, 24 October 1915, *Correspondence between Sir Henry McMahon and the Sherif Hussein of Mecca,* Parliamentary Papers, CMD 5957 (London: H.M. Stationery Office, 1939). The standard work on this correspondence is Elie Kedourie's *Into the Anglo-Arab Labyrinth: The McMahon-Husayn Correspondence and its Interpreters 1914–1939* (Cambridge, UK: Cambridge University Press, 1976).
5. See Leonard Stein, *The Balfour Declaration* (New York: Simon and Schuster, 1961); Charles Smith, *Palestine and the Arab-Israeli Conflict* (Boston: St. Martin's Press, 2004), chapter 3. There is debate as to whether McMahon specified to Hussein that Palestine would not be included in the territory promised the Arabs. See Mayir Vereté, "The Balfour Declaration and Its Makers," in Norman Rose, ed., *From Palmerston to Balfour: Collected Essays of Mayir Vereté* (London: Frank Cass, 1992); Jehuda Reinharz, "The Balfour Declaration and Its Maker: A Reassessment," *Journal of Modern History* 64, no. 3 (1992): 455–499.
6. The historiography of modern Palestine in the mandatory period includes J. C. Hurewitz, *The Struggle for Palestine* (New York: Norton, 1950), probably still the most authoritative account; Sami Hadawi, *Bitter Harvest: Palestine, 1914–1967* (New York: New World Press, 1967); Ilan Pappé, *A History of Modern Palestine: One Land, Two Peoples* (Cambridge, UK: Cambridge University Press, 2004); Mark A. Tessler, *A History of the Israeli-Palestinian Conflict* (Bloomington: Indiana University Press, 1994); Tom Segev, *One Palestine, Complete: Jews and Arabs Under the British Mandate* (New York: Metropolitan Books, 2000).
7. Howard Sachar, *A History of Israel* (New York: Knopf, 2007), 127–129; Pappé, *A History of Modern Palestine*, 84.
8. Sachar characterized the mandatory language as neither a full victory nor a total setback for the Zionist project (*A History of Israel,* 129).
9. On the Nabi Musa and May Day Riots of 1920–1921, see Gudrun Krämer and Graham Harman, *A History of Palestine: From the Ottoman Conquest to the Founding of the State of Israel* (Princeton: Princeton University Press, 2008). On the 1929 Western Wall "Buraq" Uprising, see Segev, *One Palestine Complete,* 295–313.
10. David Ben-Gurion, *Rebirth and Destiny of Israel,* translated by Mordekhai Nurock (New York: Philosophical Library, 1954).
11. Yossi Katz, "Status and Rights of the Arab Minority in the Nascent Jewish State," *Middle Eastern Studies* 33, no. 3 (1997): 535–569, especially 538.
12. On the revolt of 1936–1939, see Ted Swedenburg, "The Role of the Palestinian Peasantry in the Great Revolt (1936–1939)," in Albert Hourani et al., *The Modern Middle East* (London: I. B. Tauris, 2004), 467–503.

13. *Palestine Royal Commission Report*, CMD 5479 (London: H.M. Stationery Office, 1946), 278–296.
14. See "Section II: Immigration" of the *White Paper*, reproduced in, J.C. Hurewitz, *The Middle East and North Africa in World Politics, 1914–1945* (New Haven: Yale University Press, 1979), 532–538; Michael J. Cohen, "Appeasement in the Middle East: The White Paper on Palestine, May 1939," *Historical Journal* 16, no. 3 (1973): 571–596; Katz, "Status and Rights of the Arab Minority in the Nascent Jewish State," 559. Cohen's standard treatment casts the White Paper as an act of "appeasement" of the Arabs.
15. Chaim Weizmann, *Trial and Error* (New York: Harper and Brothers, 1949), 389, 401.
16. See Ben Halpern, *The Idea of the Jewish State* (Cambridge, Mass.: Harvard University Press, 1961), 178.
17. See Sachar, *A History of Israel*, 9–10.
18. Sachar, *A History of Israel*, 27–28.
19. Sachar, *A History of Israel*, 141. On Jewish immigration to Palestine more generally, see Shulamit Carmi and Henry Rosenfeld, "Immigration, Urbanization and Crisis: The Process of Jewish Colonization in Palestine during the 1920s," *International Journal of Comparative Sociology* 12, no. 1 (1971): 41–56; Yossi Katz, "The Palestinian Mountain Region and Zionist Settlement Policy, 1882–1948," *Middle Eastern Studies* 30, no. 2 (1994): 304–329; Anita Shapira, *Land and Power: The Zionist Resort to Force, 1881–1948* (New York: Oxford University Press, 1992); Ilan Troen, *Imagining Zion: Dreams, Designs, and Realities in a Century of Jewish Settlement* (New Haven: Yale University Press, 2003).
20. Halpern, *The Idea of the Jewish State*, 198; Weizmann, *Trial and Error*, 258.
21. Herzl expressed this notion well before the Zionist settlement of Palestine in his pamphlet *The Jewish State* (1896), which contemplated the financing, colonization, and financing of a Jewish state, perhaps in Argentina or in Palestine.
22. Ben-Gurion, *Rebirth and Destiny of Israel*, 85.
23. Quoted in Sachar, A *History of Israel*, 224.
24. Moshe Pearlman and David Ben Gurion, *Ben Gurion Looks Back in Talks with Moshe Pearlman* (New York: Simon and Schuster, 1965), 64.
25. *Palestine: A Study of Jewish, Arab, and British Policies* (New Haven: Yale University Press, 1947), 1: 41.
26. See, for example, Ilan Troen, *Israel: The First Decade of Independence* (Albany: State University of New York Press, 1995), 173. Ben-Gurion echoed this sentiment later, confiding that "an essential part of my

Zionism—seeking sovereignty for the Jewish people in their land—was reviving the language they had spoken when they last enjoyed sovereignty, the language of the bible, Hebrew" (Ben Gurion and Pearlman, *Ben Gurion Looks Back in Talks with Moshe Pearlman*, 45).

27. The vision was later subjected to harsh postmodern critiques by the likes of Edward Said: "Zionism therefore reclaimed, redeemed, repeated, replanted, realized Palestine, and Jewish hegemony over it. Israel was a return to a previous state of affairs, even if the new facts bore a far greater resemblance to the methods and successes of nineteenth-century European colonialism than to some mysterious first-century forebears." Said, *The Question of Palestine* (London: Routledge and Kegan Paul, 1980), p. 87.

28. See Shabtai Teveth, *Ben-Gurion and the Palestine Arabs: From Peace to War* (New York: Oxford University Press, 1985), 188.

29. Teveth, *Ben-Gurion and the Palestine Arabs*, 188.

30. See Benny Morris, *1948 and After: Israel and the Palestinians* (Oxford: Clarendon Press, 1994), 9.

31. See Smith, *Palestine and the Arab-Israeli Conflict*, 113–115. quote on 168; Noah Lucas, *The Modern History of Israel* (New York: Praeger, 1975), 76–93.

32. Ben Gurion and Pearlman, *Ben Gurion Looks Back in Talks with Moshe Pearlman*, 62.

33. See Ritchie Ovendale, *Britain, the United States, and the End of the Palestine Mandate, 1942–1948* (Woodbridge, Suffolk, UK: Boydell Press, 1989), 8.

34. Weizmann to Churchill, 2 April 1943, *The Letters and Papers of Chaim Weizmann*, vol. 21, series A, *January 1943–May 1945*, (New Brunswick, N.J.: Transaction Books, 1979), 20.

35. Smith, *Palestine and the Arab Israeli Conflict*, 167–171.

36. See Murray to Hull, 6 December 1944, *FRUS*, 1944, vol. 5, *The Near East, South Asia, and Africa, the Far East*, pp. 642–643.

37. Hull to Winant, 14 June 1945, RG 84, 59A543 part 5, Box 1057, USNA, cited in Ovendale, *Britain, the United States, and the Palestine Mandate*, 74.

38. Weizmann to Churchill, 22 May 1945, *The Letters and Papers of Chaim Weizmann*, vol. 21, series A, *January 1943–May 1945*, 11.

39. Weizmann to Churchill, 15 June 1945, *The Letters and Papers of Chaim Weizmann*, vol. 21, series A, *January 1943–May 1945*, 20.

40. The recent work of the New Historians of Israel has meticulously documented the Zionist strategy for territorial acquisition in Palestine. Benny Morris has shown how the Jewish Agency's territorial objectives extended beyond the lands allocated for the Jewish state in the UN partition plan.

See Avi Shlaim, *Collusion across the Jordan* (New York: Oxford University Press, 1980), p. 17.

41. Herbert Samuel, "The Balance of Forces," January 1945, Box 4, File 3, Cunningham Papers, Middle East Centre Archive, Oxford University Library.
42. Herbert Samuel, "'Palestinism," Box 4, File 3, Cunningham Papers, Middle East Centre Archive, Oxford University Library.
43. Minute by Colonel deGaury, 3 June 1945, FO371/45378, UKNA.
44. As Grigg put it, "It would be tragic indeed if, after our splendid war achievement in this region, where the forces of the Empire bore the brunt alone, we should find our future less secure in 1946 than it was in 1939. But this is what will befall us if we do not establish our position in Palestine, which is central to our whole Middle East position, with as little delay as possible." Grigg to Eden, 29 June 1945, FO 371/45378, UKNA.
45. Grigg to Eden, 29 June 1945, FO 371/45378, UKNA.
46. Grigg, Policy towards Palestine, Enclosed comments as requested upon the memo on Palestine Policy, n.d., FO371/45378, UKNA.
47. J. Campbell, "Palestine Policy: Foreign Office Appreciation of International Repercussions," 26 July 1945, FO 371/45378, UKNA.
48. Minute by Jebb, "Palestine Policy: FO Appreciation of International Repercussions," 17 July 1945, FO 371/45378, UKNA. Harold Beeley, the senior Foreign Office Palestine expert, nevertheless doubted whether unrest among Jews in Palestine could rise to the level of the threat to the peace that would be necessary to invoke UN mechanisms. See handwritten notes by H. Beeley on Palestine policy: FO Appreciation of International Repercussions, 17 July 1945, FO 371/45378, UKNA.
49. See Letter from A. L. Zissu, Chairman of the Assembly, Romanian Section of the Jewish World Congress to the British Mission in Roumania, 28 June 1945, FO 371/45405, UKNA; the voluminous correspondence in the folder marked "Jewish Nationalist Activities" in FO 371/45405, UKNA; Killearn to Eden, 12 February 1945, FO371/45405, UKNA; "Voice of Israel: Haganah's clandestine radio station: proposed monitoring and publication of text of broadcasts in United States: approach to the United States Govt. by H.M.R., Washington," FO371/52541, UKNA.
50. Halifax to Eden, 1 July 1945, FO 371/45378, UKNA.
51. Ovendale, *Britain, the United States, and the End of the Palestine Mandate,* 59–60.
52. Prime Minister's Personal Minute, Colonial Secretary, Chiefs of Staff Committee, 6 July 1945, FO 371/45378, UKNA.
53. "Future Control of Palestine," Chiefs of Staff Committee, Joint Planning Staff, J.P. (45) 167 (Final), FO 371/45378, UKNA.

54. Lord Halifax had observed that among non-Jews in the United States, a partition decision would likely be looked upon favorably, but only if "it were freely accepted by both Jews and Arabs." See minute by J. Campbell, Palestine policy: Foreign Office Appreciation of International Repercussions, n.d., FO 371/45378, UKNA.
55. Memorandum by Kohler, 19 April 1944, *FRUS*, 1944, 5: 603–604.
56. Hull to Roosevelt, 13 December 1944, *FRUS*, 1944, 5: 648–649.
57. Hull to Roosevelt, n.d., *FRUS*, 1944, 5: 655–657; Palestine: Jewish Immigration, Briefing Book Paper, n.d., *FRUS*, 1945, vol. 1, *The Conference of Berlin (the Potsdam Conference)*, pp. 972–974.
58. Memorandum by Henderson, 28 June 1945, *FRUS*, 1945, 1: 974–977.
59. Pinkerton to Grew, 10 July 1945, *FRUS*, 1945, 1: 978–979.
60. On the problematic course of U.S. and British attempts at policy coordination in postwar Palestine, see Ovendale, *Britain, the United States, and the End of the Palestine Mandate;* Michael Cohen, *Palestine and the Great Powers* (Princeton: Princeton University Press, 1982); William Roger Louis, *The British Empire in the Middle East, 1945–1951: Arab Nationalism, the United States, and Postwar Imperialism* (New York: Oxford University Press, 1984); Evan Wilson, *Decision on Palestine: How the U.S. Came to Recognize Israel* (Stanford, Calif.: Hoover Institution Press, 1979); Bruce Evensen, *Truman, Palestine, and the Press: Shaping Conventional Wisdom at the Beginning of the Cold War* (New York: Greenwood Press, 1992).
61. Grew to Truman, 16 June 1945, PSF, Subject File, 1940–1953, Box 160, HSTL.
62. See Stettinius to Truman, 18 April 1945; Grew to Truman, 28 May 1945, Truman Papers, PSF, Subject File, 1940–1953, Box 160, HSTL.
63. See, for example, Henderson to Hull, 14 February 1944, *FRUS*, 1944, 5: 565.
64. See Cohen, *Palestine and the Great Powers*, 45–46.
65. See Memorandum of Conversation by Berle, 28 January 1944, *FRUS*, 1944, 5: 561; Abdullah to Roosevelt, 3 March 1944, *FRUS*, 1944, 5: 582; Palestine: Jewish Immigration, Briefing Book Paper, n.d., *FRUS*, 1945, 1: 972–974.
66. See Wilson, *Decision on Palestine*, 57–61; Eliahu Elath, *Zionism at the UN: A Diary of the First Days* (Philadelphia: Jewish Publication Society of America, 1976); David Golding, "U.S. Foreign Policy in Palestine and Israel" (PhD diss., New York University, 1961); the correspondence on the Palestine issue in the *FRUS*, special volume, 1945, vol. 1, *The United Nations;* and Merriam to Henderson, 31 August 1945, Truman Papers, PSF, Subject File, 1940–1953, Box 160, HSTL.

67. "The Military Implications of Palestine Policy," CAB 80/100, UKNA.
68. "Middle East Policy," 30 August 1945, C.O.S. (45), 555 (0), CAB 80/100, UKNA.
69. Harris to Baxter, "Summary of probable Middle East reactions to the five courses mentioned in the memorandum on Palestine Policy" 11 July 1945, FO 371/45378, UKNA.
70. See the Annex, Effect of World Organisation's Charter upon Anglo-Egyptian Treaty of Alliance, in so far as it concerns the British position in Egypt, C.O.S. (45), 506 (0), CAB 80/100, UKNA.
71. Annex, Effect of World Organisation's Charter upon Anglo-Egyptian Treaty of Alliance, in so far as it concerns the British position in Egypt, C.O.S. (45), 506 (0), CAB 80/100, UKNA.
72. See Richard Crossman, *Palestine Mission: A Personal Record* (New York: Harper, 1947). On the membership of the Committee, see Amikam Nachmani, "British Policy in Palestine after World War II: The Anglo-American Committee of Inquiry" (DPhil thesis, University of Oxford, 1980), cited in Roger Louis, *The British Empire in the Middle East*, 397–399.
73. Halifax to Byrnes, 19 October 1945, *FRUS*, 1945, vol. 3, *The Near East and Africa*, p. 772. The 100,000 figure was most likely proposed by Chaim Weizmann to Churchill in November 1944. Cohen, *Palestine and the Great Powers*, 56; Halifax to Foreign Office, 4 December 1945, CO 733/463, UKNA. See also Cohen, *Palestine and the Great Powers*, 60–67.
74. FO Memorandum to the Anglo-American Committee of Inquiry, n.d., FO371/52525, UKNA.
75. Ben-Gurion, *Rebirth and Destiny of Israel*, 190.
76. Report of Meeting with Mr. James F. Byrnes, 22 September 1945, *The Letters and Papers of Chaim Weizmann*, vol. 22, series A, *May 1945–July 1947* (New Brunswick, N.J.: Transaction Books, 1979), 56–57.
77. Report of Meeting with Mr. James F. Byrnes, 22 September 1945, *The Letters and Papers of Chaim Weizmann*, vol. 22, series A, *May 1945–July 1947*, 65, 71–72.
78. *Ibid.* Report of Meeting with Mr. James F. Byrnes, 22 September 1945, *The Letters and Papers of Chaim Weizmann*, vol. 22, series A, *May 1945–July 1947*, 71–72.
79. Bevin to Halifax, 12 October 1945, PREM 8/627, UKNA. See also Roger Louis, *The British Empire in the Middle East*, 18–19.
80. Cabinet Palestine Committee, C.P. (45) 156, 8 September 1945, PREM 8/627, UKNA.
81. Bevin to Halifax, 12 October 1945, PREM 8/627, UKNA.
82. Attlee to Truman, 16 September 1945, PREM 8/89, UKNA. Truman's White House advisors, however, were advising him that the admission of

100,000 additional Jews was not "a change in the basic situation," given that the 1.2 million Arabs in Palestine outnumbered Jews by a factor of two and that Roosevelt's promise to "consult' with Arab and Jewish leaders did not bind the president's hands with regard to "whatever action you wish." See Rosenman to Truman, 17 October 1945, Truman Papers, PSF, Subject File, 1940–1953, Box 160, HSTL.

83. See Annex, Middle East Policy, Copy of a letter dated 18 August from the Colonial Office to General Ismay, C.O.S. (45), 539 (0), CAB 80/100, UKNA.
84. See Truman to Ball (unsent letter), 24 November 1945, Truman Papers, PSF, Subject File, 1940–1953, Box 160, HSTL.
85. See "U.S. Zionist Heads Affirm Demands," *New York Times*, 14 January 1946, copy in FO371/52568, UKNA.
86. Memorandum on the Present State of Jewish Affairs in the United States, A. H. Tandy, First Secretary, British Embassy Washington, 12 March 1946, FO371/52568, UKNA.
87. See Memorandum by Crossman, 22 April 1946, PREM 8/302, UKNA; Wilson, *Decision on Palestine*, chapter 5: "President Truman and the 100,000 Jews," 57–67; Smith, *Palestine and the Arab-Israeli Conflict*, 178–185; Peter Hahn, *Caught in the Middle East: U.S. Policy toward the Arab-Israeli Conflict, 1945–1961* (Chapel Hill: University of North Carolina Press, 2004), 32–35.
88. Joint Chiefs of Staff to the State-War-Navy Coordinating Committee (SWNCC), 21 June 1946, *FRUS*, 1946, vol. 7, *The Near East and Africa*, p. 632.
89. See Joint Chiefs of Staff to SWNCC, 21 June 1946, *FRUS*, 1946, 7: 632; Hahn, *Caught in the Middle East*, 53; and Cohen, *Palestine and the Great Powers*, 367.
90. Cohen, *Palestine and the Great Powers*, 159.
91. See Roger Louis, *The British Empire in the Middle East*, 383–386.
92. See Hall memorandum, 20 June 1946, C.P. (46) 238, CAB 128/5, UKNA; Smith, *Palestine and the Arab-Israeli Conflict*, 171, 182–183; J. Bowyer Bell, *Terror Out of Zion: Irgun Zvai Leumi, LEHI, and the Palestine Underground, 1929–1949* (New York: St. Martin's Press, 1977), 121–136, 168–175; Ovendale, *Britain, the United States, and the End of the Palestine Mandate*, 32–38.
93. Cunningham to Amery, 4 December 1945, Box 1, File 1, Cunningham Papers, Middle East Centre Archive, Oxford University Library.
94. "Military Implications of the Anglo-American Report," C.O.S. (46) 188, PREM 8/627, pt. 3, UKNA.
95. Grafftey-Smith to Cunningham, 27 April 1946, Box 1, File 1, 27 April 1946, Cunningham Papers, Middle East Centre Archive, Oxford University

Library. On Arab reactions to the Report, see Lovett to Truman, Memorandum for the President, Subject: Reaction in Near East to Palestine Report, 26 July 1946, Truman Papers, WHCF, Official File 204, Box 916, HSTL.
96. Ross to Acheson, 30 April 1946, Truman Papers, WHCF, Official File 204, Box 916, HSTL. On the findings of the Committee and their presentation, see Roger Louis, *The British Empire in the Middle East*, 397–414.
97. See Brief for Secretary of State's discussion with Mr. Byrnes on the Anglo-American Committee's Report on Palestine and the Jewish Question, 7 May 1946, PREM 8/627, UKNA. Field Marshal Alanbrooke, the chief of the Imperial General Staff, believed that the publication of the report would probably "provoke some disorder" that British troops could deal with, but that the immigration recommendations would impose additional security burdens for which "more troops would be required than were at present available for use in the Middle East." See Meeting of Prime Ministers of UK, Australia, New Zealand, and South Africa on PALESTINE, Report of Anglo-American Committee of Enquiry, 30 April 1946, PMM (46), 8th Meeting, PREM 8/627, UKNA.
98. Extract from C.M. (46) 38th Conclusions of 29.4.46, 29 April, 1946, C.M. (46), 38th Conclusions, 8th Meeting, PREM 8/627, UKNA.
99. Harriman to Byrnes, 27 June 1946, *FRUS*, 1946, 7: 638n87.
100. See "Adventures in Diplomacy," p. 159, Henry F. Grady Papers, HSTL.
101. Grady to Byrnes, 19 July 1946, *FRUS*, 1946, 7: 646–647.

2. REMAPPING ZION

1. For an account of the conference proceedings, see William Roger Louis, *The British Empire in the Middle East, 1945–1951: Arab Nationalism, the United States, and Postwar Imperialism* (New York: Oxford University Press, 1984), 441–442, 451–452.
2. Cunningham to Hall, 20 September 1946, FO 371/52562, UKNA, cited in Roger Louis, *The British Empire in the Middle East*, 448–449.
3. Clayton to Truman, 12 September 1946, Truman Papers, PSF, Subject File, 1940–1953, Box 160, HSTL.
4. Truman to Attlee, 10 October 1946, Truman Papers, PSF, Subject File, 1940–1953, Box 148, HSTL.
5. Bevin to Attlee, 9 January 1947, P.M. (47) 8, PREM 8/473, UKNA.
6. C.O.S. (47) 5(0) Revise, Middle East Strategic Requirements, 8 January 1947, PREM 8/473, UKNA.
7. Personal Minute by Attlee, 31 May 1946, PREM 8/473, UKNA.

8. Palestine—Strategic Requirements, J.P. (47) 1 Final, 6 January 1947, FO 371/61763, UKNA.
9. Minutes of the Chiefs of Staff Committee meeting to consider the Foreign Secretary's memorandum on provincial autonomy, n.d., FO 371/61763, UKNA; "Palestine, The Present Position," Draft Cabinet Paper, 10 January 1947, FO 371/61763, UKNA; Minutes, C.O.S. (47) 9th Meeting, 13 January 1947, FO 371/61763, UKNA.
10. Note of a meeting between United Kingdom representatives and a delegation representing the Jewish Agency for Palestine held in the Colonial Office on Wednesday, 29 January 1947, at 2.30 P.M., FO371/61873, UKNA.
11. Note of the second meeting between United Kingdom representatives and a delegation representing the Jewish Agency for Palestine held in the Colonial Office on Monday, 3 February 1947, at 3.00 P.M., FO371/61873, UKNA.
12. Note of the third meeting between United Kingdom representatives and a delegation representing the Jewish Agency for Palestine held in the Colonial Office on Thursday, 6 February, 1947, at 5.00 P.M., FO371/61873, UKNA.
13. See the statement by Bevin, 18 February 1947, FO371/61749, UKNA; C.M. (47) 18, 7 February 1947, CAB 128/9, cited in Roger Louis, *The British Empire in the Middle East*, 461.
14. See Michael Cohen, *Palestine and the Great Powers*, (Princeton: Princeton University Press, 1982), 217–221 for a discussion of this episode; and Joint Memorandum, C.P. (47), 49, 6 February 1947, CAB 129/16, UKNA.
15. C.O.S. 161/7 6 February 1947, PREM 8/627, UKNA.
16. See Charles Smith, *Palestine and the Arab-Israeli Conflict* (Boston: St. Martin's Press, 2004), 179–185.
17. *Parliamentary Debates* (House of Commons), 25 February 1947, col. 2007, cited in Roger Louis, *The British Empire in the Middle East*, 462.
18. See "Palestine: The Autumn Session of the General Assembly," 19 August 1947, FO 371/61948, UKNA.
19. Attlee to Truman, 16 September 1945, PREM 8/89, UKNA.
20. Ross to Austin, 23 July 1948, *FRUS*, 1948, vol. 1, *General: The United Nations*, p. 366.
21. Report by the Policy Planning Staff on Position of the United States with Respect to Palestine, 19 January 1948, *FRUS*, 1948, vol. 5, *The Near East, South Asia, and Africa*, p. 546.
22. Harry S. Truman, *Memoirs: Years of Trial and Hope* (New York: Doubleday, 1955), 2: 156–158.

23. See Ilan Pappé, *A History of Palestine: One Land, Two Peoples* (Cambridge, UK: Cambridge University Press, 2004), 123–128; Cohen, *Palestine and the Great Powers*, 276–300.
24. Creech Jones to Cunningham, 1 November 1947; Creech Jones to Cunningham, 13 November 1947; and Message by Jenkins, 17 November 1947, Box 2, File 3, Cunningham Papers, Middle East Centre Archive, Oxford University Library.
25. See Cohen, *Palestine and the Great Powers*, 306–312; Netaniel Lorch, *The Edge of the Sword: Israel's War of Independence, 1947–1949* (New York: Putnam, 1961), 51; CIA study, "Possible Developments in Palestine," *FRUS*, 1948, 5: 666–675.
26. See the transcript of Truman's colorful 15 January 1948 news conference in *Public Papers of the Presidents of the United States: Harry S. Truman, 1948* (Washington, DC: Government Printing Office, 1964), 101, reproduced in *FRUS*, 1948, 5: 542.
27. Rusk to Lovett, 26 January 1948, in *FRUS*, 1948, 5: 558.
28. Rusk to Austin, 3 February 1948, in *FRUS*, 1948, 5: 589.
29. Clifford to Truman, 6 March 1948, Box 13, Clark Clifford Papers, HSTL.
30. Clifford to Truman, 8 March 1948, Box 14, Clark Clifford Papers, HSTL.
31. Kennan to Lovett, 29 January 1948, in *FRUS*, 1948, 5: 577.
32. See Ritchie Ovendale, *Britain, the United States and the End of the Palestine Mandate, 1942–1948* (Woodbridge, Suffolk, UK: Boydell Press, 1989), 249–250; David Tal, *War in Palestine, 1948: Strategy and Diplomacy* (London: Routledge, 2004), 70.
33. Department of State to President Truman, 23 February 1948, *FRUS*, 1948, 5: 639.
34. Statement Made by Ambassador Austin to the Security Council, 24 February 1948, *FRUS*, 1948, 5: 653.
35. "Review of Current Trends, U.S. Foreign Policy," Report by the Policy Planning Staff, 24 February 1948, *FRUS*, 1948, 5: 656. The report concluded, "In the Mediterranean and the Middle East, we have a situation where a vigorous and collective national effort, utilizing both our political and military resources, could probably prevent the area from falling under Soviet influence and preserve it as a highly important factor in our world strategic position. But we are deeply involved, in that same area, in a situation which has no direct relation to our national security, and where the motives of our involvement lie solely in past commitments of dubious wisdom and in our attachment to the U.N. itself."
36. "Possible Developments in Palestine," Report by the Central Intelligence Agency, 28 February 1948, *FRUS*, 1948, 5: 672.
37. JCS Report to Departments of State and Defense, *FRUS*, 1948, 5: 631–633. See also Cohen, *Palestine and the Great Powers*, 348.

38. Draft of "The Position of the United States With Respect to Palestine," 17 February 1948, Subject File, Clifford Papers, HSTL.
39. The Joint Chiefs concluded that the requirements would include 1st Army Corps, consisting of three infantry divisions plus support personnel totaling approximately 100,000, six destroyers, six patrol craft, an air reconnaissance squadron, and over seventy aircraft. The JCS ominously concluded, "It is our considered opinion that a truce between the responsible representatives of the Jewish Agency and the Arab Higher Committee would not assure the termination of violence by irresponsible elements. The extent of that violence cannot be predicted, but based on past history it must be assumed that it will be considerable." Memorandum for the President, Subject: Provision of U.S. Armed Forces in Palestine, 4 April 1948, Truman Papers, PSF, Subject File, 1940–1953, Box 160, HSTL.
40. Memorandum for the President, Subject: Provision of U.S. Armed Forces in Palestine, 4 April 1948, Truman Papers, PSF, Subject File, 1940–1953, Box 160, HSTL.
41. The nonparticipation of U.S. military contingents in such a proposed force is alluded to in a section of the paper enumerating the advantages of the trusteeship/federal status option, one of which is listed as "Lessens probability of use of U.S. military forces in combat in Palestine." See Memorandum for the President, Subject: Provision of U.S. Armed Forces in Palestine, 4 April 1948, Truman Papers, PSF, Subject File, 1940–1953, Box 160, HSTL, p. 14.
42. See statement by Austin, 19 March 1948, *Department of State Bulletin* 18, no. 457 (1948): 407.
43. Statement by President Truman, 25 March 1948, *Department of State Bulletin* 18, no. 457 (1948): 451.
44. See Peter Hahn, *Caught in the Middle East: U.S. Policy toward the Arab-Israeli Conflict, 1945–1961* (Chapel Hill: University of North Carolina Press, 2004), 45–49. See "Editorial Note," *FRUS*, 1948, 5: 744–747, which documents the shift in U.S. policy leading to the endorsement of a temporary UN trusteeship until a permanent solution could be achieved.
45. See UN Security Council Resolution 727, 23 April 1948.
46. For a detailed treatment of Palestinian Arab and Israeli military operations leading up to the Arab invasion of May 1948, see Tal, *War in Palestine*, 86–128.
47. On the Arab Liberation Army's involvement, see British reporting from Palestine in the folder marked E1906, FO 371/68366, UKNA, cited in Cohen, *Palestine and the Great Powers*, 302, 308. For a detailed overview of the political considerations affecting Arab decision making, see Tal,

War in Palestine, 146, 169–170; Benny Morris, *1948 and After: Israel and the Palestinians* (Oxford: Clarendon Press, 1994), 13.

48. See *Yearbook of the United Nations, 1947–48* (1949), 417–422; John Quigley, *The Case for Palestine* (Durham: Duke University Press, 2005), 77–81. Secretary of Defense Forrestal had presented the NSC with the Joint Chiefs' assessment of the possible military implications of the resolution should it entail the introduction of an armed force in Palestine to enforce a cease-fire. Here the JCS cited its concerns about "the entry of Soviet forces into Palestine" and the Soviet gains in the form of footholds in the Near East. Memorandum for the National Security Council, Subject: U.S. Military Point of View for the Eventuality of United Nations Decision to Introduce Military Forces into Palestine, 19 August 1948, Truman Papers, PSF, Subject File, 1940–1953, Box 169, HSTL.

49. See James Brown Scott, "The Two Institutes of International Law," *American Journal of International Law* 23 (1932): 91; Quigley, *The Case for Palestine*, 75.

50. In a sense the Council acknowledged that right by hearing the Jewish Agency's appeal.

51. See Quigley, *The Case for Palestine*, 74; W. Michael Resiman, Comments in "Self-Determination and Settlement of the Arab-Israeli Conflict," *Proceedings of the American Society of International Law* 65 (1971): 50.

52. See Article 51, Charter of the United Nations (1945). The standard treatment of the history of the customary law principle is Yoram Dinstein's *War, Aggression, and Self-defence* (Cambridge, UK: Grotius, 1988).

53. See, for example, Julius Stone, *Israel and Palestine: Assault on the Law of Nations* (Baltimore: Johns Hopkins University Press, 1981), 125; Stanimir Alexandrov, *Self-Defense against the Use of Force in International Law* (Boston: Kluwer Law International, 1996), 125–127. The issue of self-defense aside, the Arab invasion could have been sufficient to trigger a UN response in the form of an enforcement action. Similarly the Israeli response to the Arab military incursion also resulted in counterattacks in the Negev, after which reports emerged of Israeli Defense Force troops entering Egyptian territory. Those reprisals could likewise have been invoked in a Chapter VII–sanctioned response. See Holmes to Lovett, 28 December 1948, *FRUS*, 1948, 5: 1691–1692; Hahn, *Caught in the Middle East*, 60; Itamar Rabinovich, *The Road Not Taken: Early Arab-Israeli Negotiations* (New York: Oxford University Press, 1991), 47–54.

54. This critical tendency to avoid the question of a clear legal determination is manifest in the Council's reluctance to vote on the U.S. draft resolution in May 1948, as well as in the Council's ultimate July decision to lodge a finding of a threat to the peace without assigning responsibility or labeling

any of the parties as "aggressors." It is this tendency to avoid such findings that A. Mark Weisburd surmised was the result of the novelty of some postcolonial boundaries in *Use of Force: The Practice of States since World War II* (University Park: Pennsylvania State University Press, 1997).
55. Lovett to 18 March 1948, *FRUS*, 1948, 5: 740.
56. Austin to Marshall, 17 March 1948, *FRUS*, 1948, 5: 732–734.
57. Statement Made by Ambassador Austin to the Security Council, 19 March 1948, *FRUS*, 1948, 5: 743.
58. Austin to Marshall, 8 May 1948, *FRUS*, 1948, 5: 937–938.
59. Lie to Austin, 16 May 1948, *FRUS*, 1948, 5: 1001.
60. Kennan to Marshall, 21 May 1948, *FRUS*, 1948, 5: 1020–1021.
61. UN General Assembly Resolution 186, 14 May 1948.
62. United Nations Security Council Resolution draft S/749, 17 May 1948.
63. Carter to Connelly, with attached telegraph message, Austin to Marshall, 20 May 1948, President's Secretary's Files, Truman Papers, HSTL, available at http://www.trumanlibrary.org/whistlestop/study_collections/israel/large/documents/newPDF/78.pdf; Quigley, *The Case for Palestine*, 77.
64. NSC 27/1, 19 August 1948, *FRUS*, 1948, 5: 1321.
65. Memorandum for the National Security Council, Subject: U.S. Military Point of View for the Eventuality of United Nations Decision to Introduce Military Forces into Palestine, 19 August 1948, Truman Papers, PSF, Subject File, 1940–1953, Box 169, HSTL.
66. Memorandum for the National Security Council, Subject: U.S. Military Point of View for the Eventuality of United Nations Decision to Introduce Military Forces into Palestine, 19 August 1948, Truman Papers, PSF, Subject File, 1940–1953, Box 169, HSTL. The NSC later specifically explored the wider question of U.S. commitments that could entail the deployment of military force. See NSC 35, Memorandum for the President, Subject: Existing International Commitments Involving the Possible Use of Armed Forces, 17 November 1948, Truman Papers, PSF, Subject File, 1940–1953, Box 169, HSTL.
67. Department of State Comments on NSC 27, undated, NSC 35, Memorandum for the President, Subject: Existing International Commitments Involving the Possible Use of Armed Forces, 17 November 1948, Truman Papers, PSF, Subject File, 1940–1953, Box 169, HSTL, p. 1362.
68. See introduction, n15.
69. See David Painter, *Oil and the American Century: The Political Economy of U.S. Foreign Oil Policy, 1941–1954* (Baltimore: Johns Hopkins University Press, 1986), 96–102; Melvyn Leffler, *A Preponderance of Power:*

National Security, the Truman Administration, and the Cold War (Stanford: Stanford University Press, 1992), 237–238.
70. See, for example, Douglas Little, *American Orientalism: The United States and the Middle East Since 1945* (Chapel Hill: University of North Carolina Press, 2004), chapter 2.
71. Herbert Samuel, "An Analysis of the Palestine Situation," April 1948, Box 4, File 5, Cunningham Papers, Middle East Centre Archive, Oxford University Library.

3. THE CONTESTED VALLEY

1. Ellsworth Huntington, "The Vale of Kashmir," *Bulletin of the American Geographical Society* 38, no. 11 (1906): 657–682, quote on 661. Interestingly Huntington also led the Yale Expedition to Palestine in 1909.
2. Despite the Vale of Kashmir's relative isolation, the greater state of Jammu and Kashmir that did emerge, bordering Afghanistan and China, was central to the defense of the subcontinent—an argument commonly invoked by Pakistan as a basis for its claims to Kashmir. See, for instance, Robert Mayfield, "A Geographic Study of the Kashmir Issue," *Geographical Review* 45, no. 2 (1955): 192. It was also cited by Maharaja Hari Singh in the letter that accompanied his Instrument of Accession to India. See the excerpt quoting from the letter in Sheikh Mohammad Abdullah, "Kashmir, India, and Pakistan," *Foreign Affairs* 43, no. 3 (1965): 525–535.
3. See Paul Bowers, "Kashmir," Research Paper 04/28, 30 March 2004, UK House of Commons Library, accessible at http://www.parliament.uk/briefing-papers/RP04-28.pdf.; Alastair Lamb, *Kashmir: A Disputed Legacy, 1846–1990* (New Delhi: Oxford University Press, 1991), 6–9; Sir Francis Younghusband, *Kashmir* (London: J. Jetley, 1909), 168–169.
4. See Mridu Rai, *Hindu Rulers, Muslim Subjects: Islam, Rights, and the History of Kashmir* (Princeton: Princeton University Press, 2004), 66–79; Younghusband, *Kashmir*, 13. Rai discusses the efforts of British imperial authorities to secure Gulab Singh's authority over Kashmir's Muslims with at least "a veneer of lawfulness" (68).
5. See Sumantara Bose, *Kashmir: Roots of Conflict, Paths to Peace* (Cambridge, Mass.: Harvard University Press, 1993), 19. For a historical analysis of the causes of the riots as a response against not just Hindu rule but the fact that Jammu and Kashmir had become a Hindu *state*, see Rai, *Hindu Rulers, Muslim Subjects*, chapter 5.
6. On the inquiries and findings of the Glancy Commission, see Bose, *Kashmir*, 19–20; Lamb, *Kashmir*, 91–92; Rai, *Hindu Rulers, Muslim Subjects*, 217–219.

7. Abdullah doubtless was also influenced by his deepening ties to Nehru and the Congress Party platform of secular, nonsectarian inclusion. See Lamb, *Kashmir,* 93–94; Rai, *Hindu Rulers, Muslim Subjects,* 274; Ramachandra Guha, "Opening a Window in Kashmir," *World Policy Journal* 21, no. 3 (2004): 79–80.
8. Jinnah, unsurprisingly, disapproved of the National Conference, endorsing instead the reincarnated Muslim Conference in the course of his limited involvement with Kashmiri politics. Alistair Lamb reasons that he maintained this cautious distance on the grounds that the internal affairs of the princely state should be kept legally separate from those of India (*Kashmir,* 97).
9. See Bose, *Kashmir,* 30–36 for a concise synopsis of the outbreak of hostilities.
10. Quoted in Josef Korbel, *Danger in Kashmir* (Princeton: Princeton University Press, 1954), 25. The debate about the plebiscite is addressed in H. V. Hodson, *The Great Divide: Britain—India—Pakistan* (Oxford: Oxford University Press, 1985), 459–466; Victoria Schofield, *Kashmir in the Crossfire,* (London: I. B. Tauris, 1996), 159.
11. See Lawrence Ziring, *Pakistan: At the Crosscurrent of History* (Oxford: Oneworld Publications, 2003), 4–5; Ayesha Jalal, *The Sole Spokesman: Jinnah, the Muslim League, and the Demand for Pakistan* (Cambridge, UK: Cambridge University Press, 1985), 9.
12. See M. Naeem Qureishi, *Pan-Islam in British Indian Politics: A Study of the Khilafat Movement, 1918–1924* (Leiden: Brill, 1999), 1; Gail Minault, *The Khilafat Movement: Religious Symbolism and Political Mobilization in India* (New York: Columbia University Press, 1982), 50–65.
13. See Denis Judd, *Empire: The British Imperial Experience from 1765 to the Present* (New York: Basic Books, 1996), 266–268; Robert L. Hardgrave and Stanley A. Kochanek, *India: Government and Politics in a Developing Nation* (Boston: Thompson, 2008), 52–53.
14. Jalal, *The Sole Spokesman,* 35. For general overviews of the rise of Jinnah, see also Akbar Ahmed, *Jinnah, Pakistan and Islamic Identity: The Search for Saladin* (London: Routledge, 1997), chapter 1; Stanley Wolpert, *Jinnah of Pakistan* (New Delhi: Oxford University Press, 2005).
15. See Ziring, *Pakistan,* 22.
16. See R. J. Moore, *Churchill, Cripps, and India* (Oxford: Clarendon Press, 1979), 145. Moore attributed the failure of the Cripps mission to two principal factors: Britain's low standing with regard to the affairs of the subcontinent in 1942 and the narrow limits on the mission's negotiating position, which was circumscribed by a War Cabinet resolution that Cripps himself helped author. By May 1943 the colonial government had taken

note of the fact that "the stock of Gandhi and Congress is at present so low." See Linlithgow to Amery, 13 May 1943, IOR/L/PO/6/102B, IOR, BL.

17. Presidential Address at the 29th Annual Session of the All India Muslim League, Allahabad, April 4, 1942, in Syed Pirzada, ed., *Foundations of Pakistan—All-India Muslim League Documents: 1906–1947*, vol. 2 (Karachi: National Publishing House, 1970), pp. 386–387.

18. Statement on Cripps's Proposal at Press Conference, New Delhi, 13 April 1942, in Jamal-uddin Ahmed, ed., *Speeches and Writings of Mr. Jinnah* (Lahore: Shaikh Muhammad Ashraf, 1960), p. 379.

19. It is important to note, however, that many Muslim groups came out firmly against Jinnah and his vision of a "Pakistan." Among them were clerics like Maulana Abul Kalam Azad, who was a Congress Party member and confidante of Mahatma Gandhi and an adherent of the Deobandi school of Islamic theology. Gandhi's declared support for the Khilafat movement both distanced and enraged Jinnah. See Ziring, *Pakistan*, 41; Jalal, *The Sole Spokesman*, 8.

20. Casey to Wavell, 6 November 1944, IOR/R/3/1/105, IOR, BL. Casey added, "The Hindus are largely to blame for the Muslim attitude, by their policy in the Congress-governed provinces between 1937 and 1939. In consequence, the Muslims are convinced that no paper safeguards can ensure them a fair deal in an All-India set-up."

21. Casey to Wavell, 6 November 1944, IOR/R/3/1/105, IOR, BL.

22. Wavell to Casey, 13 November 1944, IOL/R/3/1/105, IOR, BL.

23. Lawrence Ziring has discussed the importance of the fact that Jinnah "was born into the age of self-determination, a period wherein peoples long under alien rules would assert their right to administer their own affairs. . . . The twentieth century beckoned the formation of the nation-state, and India could not avoid its destiny as a contemporary member of the family of nations" (*Pakistan*, 2). This view contrasts with those of scholars like Ayesha Jalal who consider Pakistan to be more of an end result of the tortuous negotiated settlement forced on the Congress Party and the Muslim League in the last few years before the transfer of power.

24. Linlithgow to Amery, 16 November 1942, IOR/L/PJ/8/690, IOR, BL.

25. Linlithgow to Amery, 16 November 1942, IOR/L/PJ/8/690, IOR, BL.

26. Without descending to the level of geographic specifics, Jinnah had asked the Muslim League in the wake of the failed Cripps mission to ask themselves, "Whose self-determination do you want to ascertain? Self-determination of the two nations put together or one nation alone? The answer is, of course, of both put together." Muhammad Ali Jinnah, Presidential Address at the 29th Annual Session of the All India Muslim League, Allahabad, 4 April 1942, quoted in *Dawn* (Karachi), April 1942.

27. Glancy to Wavell, 16 August 1945, IOL/R/3/1/105, IOR, BL; Wavell to Pethick-Lawrence, 5 August 1945, IOR/L/3/1/106, IOR, BL.
28. See Cunningham to Wavell, 11 August 1945; and Glancy to Wavell, 11 August 1945, IOR/R/3/1/106, IOR, BL. As Glancy put it, "I must confess that I am gravely perturbed about the situation, because there is a very serious danger of the elections being fought, so far as Muslim [sic] are concerned, on an entirely false issue. Crude Pakistan may be quite illogical, undefinable and ruinous to India and in particular to Muslims, but this does not detract from its potency as a political slogan."
29. Wavell to Pethick-Lawrence, 19 August 1945, IOL/R/3/1/106, IOR, BL.
30. Wavell to Pethick-Lawrence, 25 August 1945, IOL/R/3/1/106, IOR, BL.
31. Menon to Jenkins, 24 October 1945, IOR/R/L/3/105, BL.
32. "Division of India—Only Solution," *Dawn* (Karachi), 21 September 1945, copy in IOL/R/3/105, IOR, BL.
33. Wavell to Pethick-Lawrence, 25 October 1945, IOR/L/R/3/105, IOR, BL.
34. Jinnah to Pethick-Lawrence, 6 December 1945, L/PO/6/115, IOR, BL.
35. Jinnah to Pethick-Lawrence, 9 February 1946, IOR/L/3/1/105, IOR, BL.
36. Acting Viceroy to Wavell, 2 September 1945, IOR/R/3/1/106, IOR, BL.
37. See V. P. Menon, *Transfer of Power in India* (Hyderabad: Orient Longman, 1957), 153–154; Penderel Moon, ed., *Wavell: The Viceroy's Journal* (New York: Oxford University Press, 1997), p. 56.
38. "Simla Conference," *Time,* 9 July 1945.
39. Cunningham to Wavell, 11 August 1945, IOR/R/3/1/106, IOR, BL.
40. The Cabinet mission's authoritative statement of the strategic problems posed by a potential partition appeared in the form of a note by Pethick-Lawrence titled "Viability of Pakistan," 13 February 1946, IOR/L/PJ/10/21, *Transfer of Power*, vol. 6, no. 427, pp. 951–963. See the second section of this lengthy study, entitled "The Defence Problems of Pakistan."
41. Lord Alexander warned that "he would regard widespread trouble with the Muslims in the Middle East and in India together as a very grave threat to the defence system of the Commonwealth. It would completely defeat the Foreign Secretary's plans for a Middle East security system." Record of Meeting of Cabinet Delegation and Field Marshal Viscount Wavell on Wednesday, 24 April 1946 at 4pm, IOR/L/PJ/5/337, *Transfer of Power*, vol. 7, no. 134, pp. 323–326. See also Record of Meeting of Cabinet Delegation and Field Marshal Viscount Wavell on Thursday, 25 April 1946 at 9.30 am, IOR/L/PJ/5/337, *Transfer of Power*, vol. 7, no. 138, pp. 330–334; Wavell to Henderson, 25 April 1946, IOR L/PO/10/26, *Transfer of Power*, vol. 7, no. 143, pp. 341–342; F. Burrows to Attlee, 6 May 1946, *Transfer of Power*, vol. 7, Encl. to no. 205, pp. 444–446. In his

25 April letter Wavell conveyed to Henderson his fear that Palestine "would naturally add fuel to the fire" if the Muslims resisted Cabinet mission proposals for constitutional arrangements.
42. Text of Lord Pethick-Lawrence's Broadcast made on 16 May 1946 at 8.45 PM I.S.T., IOR/L/PJ/5/337, *Transfer of Power*, vol. 7, no. 304, pp. 592–594.
43. Statement made by Mr. Jinnah on 22 May 1946, IOR/L/PJ/5/337, *Transfer of Power*, vol. 7, no. 360, pp. 663–669.
44. Maulana Azad to Pethick-Lawrence, 24 May 1946, IOR/L/PJ/10/43, *Transfer of Power*, vol. 7, no. 370, pp. 663–669.
45. See Jalal, *The Sole Spokesman*, 183.
46. Attlee to Bevin, 2 January 1947, IOR/R/30/1, *Transfer of Power*, vol. 9, no. 243, pp. 445–446.
47. Mountbatten to Attlee, 3 January 1947, Mountbatten Papers, Official Correspondence Files: Viceroy's Staff, Appointments to, *Transfer of Power*, vol. 9, no. 247, pp. 451–452.
48. See Wavell to King George VI, 24 February 1947, Wavell Papers. Private Correspondence: H. M. the King, *Transfer of Power*, vol. 9, no. 460, pp. 801–812.
49. See Viceroy's Conference Paper V.C.P. 40, 1 May 1947, IOR/L/PO/6/123, *Transfer of Power*, vol. 10, no. 273, pp. 525–527.
50. Mountbatten to Ismay, 13 May 1947, Telegram, Mountbatten Papers. Official Correspondence Files: *Transfer of Power*, part 2(a), vol. 10, no. 430, pp. 808–812.
51. A number of scholars have cited the key geographical importance of Jammu and Kashmir, not the least northern Gilgit's borders with a narrow strip of Afghanistan jutting eastward and northwest Baltistan's borders with the Soviet Union. Perhaps less of an issue has been made of Baltistan's and Ladakh's northern and eastern borders with Sinkiang and Tibet, respectively—a region of largely ethnic Tibetans where Pakistan has not contested Indian territorial claims. See Robert G. Wirsing, *India, Pakistan, and the Kashmir Dispute: On Regional Conflict and Its Resolution* (New York: St. Martin's Press, 1994), 86–88; Korbel, *Danger in Kashmir*, 6–9; Lamb, *Kashmir*, 17–75.
52. See Ayesha Jalal, *The State of Martial Rule: The Origins of Pakistan's Political Economy of Defence* (Cambridge, UK: Cambridge University Press, 1990), 64; Wirsing, *India, Pakistan, and the Kashmir Dispute*, 86–88. On the consideration of various options for joint or separate defense of Pakistan as part of a future arrangement, see the Note by Mr. Zinkin on Pakistan, IOR/L/PJ/10/19, *Transfer of Power*, vol. 11, no. 359, pp. 801–805.

Colonial officials were of course aware of the broader structural and economic impediments that would cripple any future state of Pakistan as conceived by most officials (as a hodgepodge combination of India's Muslim-majority provinces). See, for example, Casey to Wavell, 17 December 1944, IOL/R/3/1/105, IOR, BL.
53. See Mudie to Hallett, 11 November 1948, quoted in Raju G. C. Thomas, ed., *Perspectives on Kashmir: The Roots of Conflict in South Asia* (Boulder, Colo.: Westview Press, 1992), 315; Carter to Scoones, 22 October 1947, Mss Eur, F200/103, Mountbatten Papers, IOR, BL.
54. "Copy of a report by the chiefs of staff, concerning defence problems in India," 18 March 1947, MB1/D141/8, Mountbatten Papers Database, Hartley Library, University of Southampton.
55. Mountbatten's closeness to Nehru was known, and he was accused by Pakistani officials of colluding with the government of India in the Kashmir dispute from the start, allegations from which he has been only partly absolved in the work of historians like Alastair Lamb. Soon after the outbreak of hostilities in Kashmir, Mountbatten met with Jinnah and assured him that the response of the Indian army in deploying to Kashmir to come to the aid of Maharaja Hari Singh's government could not have been premeditated. See Shone to Carter, 4 November 1947, DO 133/73, UKNA. On Nehru's growing alarm with the maharaja's brutality and Kashmir Muslim suffering, see Nehru to Wavell, 23 January 1947, IOR/R/1/29, *Transfer of Power*, vol. 9, no. 302, pp. 540–541.
56. Mountbatten to Cabinet India and Burma Committee, 31 August 1945, IOL/R/3/1/105, IOR, BL. Mountbatten flat out told the Committee, "I do not think there is at present any clear scheme of partition which can be announced by His Majesty's Government as their notion of the ultimate safeguard for the Muslims. Nor can such a scheme be prepared immediately and without consultation with Indian opinion."
57. Bevin, for his part, observed in Parliament that the partition plan "would help consolidate Britain in the Middle East." See Narendra Sarila, *The Shadow of the Great Game: The Untold Story of India's Partition* (New York: Basic Books, 2006), 15. Despite Sarila's controversial thesis about British designs to partition the subcontinent to secure access to Middle East oil fields through Pakistan, his recollections about the strategic observations of officials like Bevin are useful for contextualizing how senior Labour government officials thought of the Kashmir dispute.
58. Record of a Conversation between Lord Ismay and Mr. Jinnah at Karachi on 3rd October 1947, Ismay Papers 3/7/68/40, LHCMA, King's College London.

59. Nehru to Cripps, 27 January 1946, IOR/L/PJ/10/59, *Transfer of Power*, vol. 9, no. 384, pp. 851–859, quote on 855.
60. Ismay to Attlee, "Strategic Importance of India," 30 August 1946, PREM 8/467, UKNA.
61. "India—Defence Requirements," Brief for Negotiations by Chiefs of Staff, 24 July 1947, PREM 8/467, UKNA. On the War Staff's assessment of the viability of Pakistan from the standpoint of defense, see Monteath to Pethick-Lawrence, 5 February 1946, IOR, Mss Eur D 714/74, *Transfer of Power*, vol. 9, no. 397, pp. 881–882.

   Before partition became imminent and unavoidable, Auchinleck had always believed that independent India had to emerge united and as a member of the Commonwealth if Britain were to be able to defend her lines of communication along the Indian Ocean rim and therefore throughout the Commonwealth as a whole. His thinking held that British strategic resources would be taxed beyond their limits if they were encumbered with defending a separate "Pakistan" with close ties to Russia against a "Hindustan." Instead a united subcontinent and its combined armed forces could provide the manpower for its *own* defense. See, for instance, "Copy of a note by General Sir C. J. E. Auchinleck, concerning the strategic implications of the inclusion of Pakistan in the British Commonwealth," 11 May 1946, MB1/D130/1, Mountbatten Papers Database, Hartley Library, University of Southampton.
62. Mountbatten's affinities for India aside, this was a separate reason why he did not support the idea of Pakistan joining the Commonwealth without India. He favored the idea of using Pakistan's interest in Commonwealth membership "as a lever to help Congress [Party] 'take the plunge.'" See Extract from the minutes of the Viceroy of India's twenty fourth staff meeting concerning the retention of India within the British Commonwealth, 1 May 1947, MB1/D130/10, Mountbatten Papers Database, Hartley Library, University of Southampton.
63. Statement made by Lord Ismay at the Joint Defence Council Meeting on 6 August 1947, Ismay Papers 3/7/12/4, LHCMA, King's College London.
64. C.O.S. TP (47) 90, 7 September 1947, L/WS/1/1030, UKNA.
65. The consequence was that "we must adopt the policy of assisting Pakistan even at the risk of ruining our present entirely friendly relations with the Indian Government." See Minute by CRO, 14 October 1947, Mss Eur, F200/102, Mountbatten Papers, IOR, BL.
66. "Appreciation of the Situation in India and Pakistan by P.S.O.," Commonwealth Relations Office, Mountbatten Papers, Mss Eur, F200/102, IOR, BL.
67. Indeed some officials in the Commonwealth Relations Office thought so: "We must adopt the policy of assisting Pakistan even at the risk of ruining

our present entirely friendly relations with the Indian Government." See "Assistance to Pakistan," 22 October 1947, Mountbatten Papers, Mss Eur, F200/103, IOR, BL.
68. Nehru to Attlee, 26 October 1947, FO 371/63570, UKNA.
69. Symon to Noel-Baker, 29 October 1947, FO 371/63570, UKNA. Some in the Foreign Office harbored skepticism about the claim that the Soviet Union might take advantage of instability in Kashmir for territorial aggrandizement, if for no other reason than the geographic impediments to such an advance. As one official observed, "The possibility of direct Russian intervention in the Kashmir struggle, though constantly quoted by both sides, is more in the nature of a Red herring than anything else; there is no way into Northern Kashmir from Russia except through China (Kashgar) or through Afghanistan, or over 18,000 foot passes now snow-bound." See Minute by Murray, 25 November 1947, FO 371/63571, UKNA.
70. Grafftey-Smith to Noel-Baker, 29 October 1947, FO 371/63570, UKNA. This issue was of long standing and had arisen the year before, when Nehru's plans to visit the frontier areas had alarmed officials like Caroe in NWFP, who were concerned that tribal leaders would be up in arms in protesting the visit—even to the point where it could interfere with border defense. The October 1946 visit led to hostile League demonstrations and the stoning of Nehru's motorcade. See Caroe to Wavell, 29 September 1946, IOR/R/3/1, *Transfer of Power*, vol. 8, no. 382, p. 626; Caroe to Wavell, 23 October 1946, IOR/R/3/1, *Transfer of Power*, vol. 8, no. 498, pp. 786–792.
71. See Minute by Murray, 10 November 1947, FO 371/63571, UKNA.
72. Grafftey-Smith to Carter, 5 December 1947, Box 1, File 1, Grafftey-Smith Papers, Middle East Centre Archive, Oxford University Library.

4. KEYSTONE OF THE STRATEGIC ARCH

1. Stephenson to Shone, 8 December 1947, FO 371/69705, UKNA.
2. Memorandum by Lord Addison, 3 November 1947, FO 371/63571, UKNA.
3. H. V. Hodson, *The Great Divide: Britain—India—Pakistan* (Oxford: Oxford University Press, 1985), 459–466; Note on the Situation in India on 30 November 1947, Ismay Papers 3/7/66/6a, LHCMA, King's College London.
4. Mountbatten to Nehru, 25 December 1947, DO 133/73, UKNA.
5. *White Paper on Jammu and Kashmir* (New Delhi: Government of India, 1948), 80; Noel-Baker to Shone, 27 December 1947, DO 133/73, UKNA.
6. See Sumit Ganguly, *Conflict Unending: India-Pakistan Tensions Since 1947* (New York: Columbia University Press, 2001), 20–22. See also the

account by Czech diplomat and UNCIP member Joseph Korbel, *Danger in Kashmir* (Princeton: Princeton University Press, 1954).
7. Minute by General Scoones, 31 December 1947, IOR/L/WS/1/1148, IOR, BL.
8. Minute by Dening, 1 January 1948, FO 371/69705, UKNA. Attlee directed that Bevin's warning be circulated to key posts in the dominions. See Attlee to Noel-Baker, 10 January 1948, DO 142/490, UKNA.
9. Attlee to Cadogan, 13 January 1948, FO 371/69705, UKNA. By "prejudice our strategic requirements," Attlee ostensibly meant straining the defense of the subcontinent as well as endangering the British presence in the Near East linking India to the British Isles through air bases and sea lines of communication. For a discussion of the need for continued British engagement with the region to allay Muslim sentiments in India and beyond from the standpoint of imperial strategy, see John Darwin, *End of the British Empire* (Oxford: Basil Blackwell, 1991), 64–65.
10. FO to Cadogan, 3 January 1948, IOR/L/E/9/1523, IOR, BL.
11. Minute by Dening, 3 January 1948, FO 371/69705, UKNA.
12. Cadogan to FO, 5 January 1948, IOR/L/E/9/1523, IOR, BL.
13. Shone to FO, 5 January 1948, FO 371/69705, UKNA.
14. FO to Cadogan, 10 January 1948, IOR/L/E/9/1523, UKNA.
15. FO to Cadogan, 13 January 1948, FO 371/69705, UKNA. A copy of the assessment itself does not appear in the file, and only the summary appears to have been sent forward to Cadogan in New York.
16. Attlee to Noel-Baker, 24 January 1948, DO 133/74, UKNA.
17. Cadogan to FO, 12 January 1948, FO 371/69707, UKNA.
18. Cadogan to FO, 14 January 1948, FO 371/69707, UKNA.
19. Marshall to Austin, 6 January 1948, *FRUS*, 1948, vol. 5, *The Near East, Africa, and South Asia,* part 1, pp. 271–273.
20. On the sources and scope of U.S. deference to British policy in South Asia, see Robert J. McMahon, *The Cold War on the Periphery: The United States, India, and Pakistan* (New York: Columbia University Press, 1996).
21. As the Dominions Office put it, "With the darkening world situation, that corner of the world represented by Persia, Afghanistan, Pakistan, and India is bound to be one of the danger spots in Soviet schemes for expansion. The main bar to unity in this region is the Kashmir dispute, and we can not help feeling that this dispute should be viewed in the light of the wider considerations mentioned above." See DO Minute, 21 December 1948, DO 142/521, UKNA.
22. See Orme Sargent to Cadogan, 28 January 1948, FO371/69706, UKNA. Sir Orme Sargent observed ominously, "Jinnah once said that, now

Pakistan was a separate country, he would have to have friends outside India but that he was too old to learn Russian. Talk of friendship with Russia is thus at the moment, we feel, largely a result of despair and disappointment, combined possibly with a desire to make our flesh creep. But the danger is real enough to be borne in mind."

23. As Robert McMahon has argued, the gradual U.S. alignment with Pakistan in the late 1940s was a key element in the globalization of the U.S. strategy of Soviet containment after the Marshall Plan. See McMahon, "United States Cold War Strategy in South Asia: Making a Military Commitment to Pakistan, 1947–1954," *Journal of American History* 75, no. 3 (1988): 813–814. On the cold war's expansion into South Asia, see Selig S. Harrison, "Case History of a Mistake," *New Republic*, 10 August 1959, 10–17; William J. Barnds, *India, Pakistan, and the Great Powers* (New York, 1972); Selig S. Harrison, *The Widening Gulf Asian Nationalism and American Policy* (New York, 1978); Stanley Wolpert, *Roots of Confrontation in South Asia: Afghanistan, Pakistan, India, and the Superpowers* (New York: Oxford University Press, 1982).

24. Allen to Falla, 15 January 1948, FO 371/69706, UKNA.

25. Shattock to Noel-Baker, 28 January 1948, DO 133/74, UKNA.

26. Nevertheless the analysis here does track with McMahon's sound observation that American "globalism" during these early stages of its formulation was more inchoate and underdeveloped and that "historians should pay more attention to the limitations and inconsistencies of American strategic designs" than rely complacently on overarching geographical blueprints that purport to explain early cold war U.S. foreign policy. See McMahon, "United States Cold War Strategy in South Asia," 815.

27. Noel-Baker to Shone, 30 December 1947, DO 133/73, UKNA. The British Embassy in Washington also met with State Department officials on the following day to coordinate on the desired approach at the United Nations Security Council of asking both parties to refrain from provocative actions. See Cadogan to FO, 31 December 1947, FO 371/69705, UKNA.

28. As American officials told visiting Indian officials in the spring of 1948, U.S.-Indian relations were "the anchor of stability of the whole area from Africa to South East Asia." See MemCon on "U.S. Indian Relations," 2 April 1948, U.S. Embassy, New Delhi, Classified General Records, 1942–1963, Box 64, RG 84, USNA.

29. As of the end of November 1947, for example, the Department's Office of Intelligence and Research had studies under way examining the Muslim League, problems confronting the new state of Pakistan, and India's future policy in Southeast Asia, and had contributed an article to the

Intelligence Digest on the affiliation of the constituent states of postcolonial India. See "Monthly Report of Research Activities and Works in Progress, Office of Intelligence and Research, Division of Research for Near East and Africa," November 1947, U.S. Embassy, Karachi, Classified General Records, 1947–1961, Box 8, RG 84, USNA.

30. See Grady to SecState, 20 September 1947, U.S. Embassy, New Delhi, Classified General Records, 1942–1963, Box 45, RG 84, USNA; Grady to SecState, 25 September 1947, U.S. Embassy, New Delhi, Classified General Records, 1942–1963, Box 45, RG 84, USNA; Lovett to Grady, 21 November 1947, U.S. Embassy, New Delhi, Classified General Records, 1942–1963, Box 40, RG 84, USNA; H. W. Brands, "India and Pakistan in American Strategic Planning, 1947–54: The Commonwealth as Collaborator," *Journal of Imperial and Commonwealth History* 15, no. 1 (1986): 42.

31. Consider the cool American response to an early Indian military request for defense cooperation and intelligence sharing during the Kashmir crisis. See Memcon of conversation between Colonel F. J. Graling and Colonel B. M. Kaul, 27 January 1948, U.S. Embassy, New Delhi, Classified General Records, 1942–1963, Box 64, RG 84, USNA.

32. Cadogan to FO, 5 January 1948, IOR/L/E/9/1523, IOR, BL.

33. Memorandum by Mr. Gordon P. Merriam of the Policy Planning Staff, 13 June 1949, *FRUS*, 1949, vol. 6, *The Near East, South Asia, and Africa,* p. 38.

34. U.S. Senate Resolution 239, Eightieth Congress, Second Session, 11 June 1948.

35. "Armed Forces to Be Furnished under Article 43 of the United Nations Charter," Report by the Policy Planning Staff, 29 June 1948, *FRUS*, 1948, vol. 1, *General: The United Nations,* pp. 359–362.

36. Nehru adamantly denied that India had a more favorable view of the Soviet Union, as he made clear to Parliamentary Undersecretary of State for Commonwealth Affairs Patrick Gordon-Walker: "He said with force that India was not pro-Russian and that if the U.S. State Department read their Ambassador's reports they would know it." See Minute by Gordon-Walker, 31 January 1948, DO 133/74, UKNA.

37. "Armed Forces to Be Furnished under Article 43 of the United Nations Charter," Report by the Policy Planning Staff, 29 June 1948, *FRUS*, 1948, vol. 1, part 1, pp. 359–361.

38. In those discussions U.S. officials admitted that any "marked initiative by the United States in this dispute might attract undesirable Russian attention and make a solution more difficult." India-Pakistan Dispute over Kashmir, Proposed Security Council Action, 10 January 1948, *FRUS*, 1948, vol. 5, part 1, pp. 276–278. For the British take on the American concerns, see Allen to Falla, 15 January 1948, FO 371/69706, UKNA.

39. India-Pakistan Dispute over Kashmir; Proposed Security Council Action, 10 January 1948, *FRUS*, 1948, vol. 5, part 1, pp. 276–278.
40. Marshall to Austin, 14 January 1948, *FRUS*, 1948, vol. 5, part 1, pp. 280–281.
41. By refusing to acknowledge Kashmir's accession to India, and in light of the standstill agreement Pakistan had entered into with Kashmir, the government of Pakistan maintained that the dispatch of Indian armed forces to Kashmir constituted "a direct attack upon and aggression against Pakistan which Pakistan was entitled to repel by force." See Korbel, *Danger in Kashmir*, 97–100 for a narrative summary of the presentation of both sides of the case before the Security Council.
42. *Official Records*, United Nations Security Council, 226th–240th meetings, 6 January–4 February 1948, Lake Success, New York, pp. 260–262.
43. See McMahon, *The Cold War on the Periphery*, chapter 1.
44. *Official Records*, United Nations Security Council, 226th–240th meetings, 6 January–4 February 1948, Lake Success, New York, p. 287.
45. Mountbatten to Attlee, 8 February 1948, DO 142/496, UKNA.
46. See "Copy of a letter from Lord Mountbatten to P. C. Gordon Walker, concerning the constitutional relationship between India and the British Commonwealth," 27 February 1948, MB1/D132/26, Mountbatten Papers Database, Hartley Library, University of Southampton; Attlee to Mountbatten, 10 February 1948, DO 142/496, UKNA. Mountbatten later shared with the prime minister his suspicion that a pro-Pakistan faction led by Noel-Baker had forced the hand of British policy at the United Nations and was threatening to unravel their India policy. See Mountbatten to Attlee, 24 February 1948, IOR/L/WS/1/1141, IOR, BL.
47. Memorandum of Conversation by Asst. Chief of the Division of South Asian Affairs (Thurston), 27 February 1948, *FRUS*, 1948, vol. 5, part 1, pp. 306–307; Minute by Cockram, 16 February 1948, FO 371/69711, UKNA. British officials noted the Anglo-American tension over the issue of Pakistani troops during the early deliberations with the State Department. See Inverchapel to FO, 23 February 1948, FO 371/69710, UKNA. Aside from the issue of Pakistani troops, the United States was also skeptical of British proposals to entrust administration of Kashmir to interim authorities to oversee the plebiscite—skepticism that may explain the initial U.S. interest in international coalition administration. See Cadogan to FO, 23 February 1948, FO 371/69710, UKNA.
48. Cadogan to FO, 23 February 1948, FO 371/69710, UKNA.
49. CIA Report on the Strategic Importance of the Far East to the U.S. and the USSR, 4 May 1949, Papers of Harry S. Truman, PSF, HSTL.
50. Cadogan to FO, 27 February 1948, FO 371/69711, UKNA.

51. Marshall to Austin, 22 March 1948, *FRUS,* 1948, vol. 5, part 1, pp. 312–313.
52. Marshall to Austin, 5 May 1948, *FRUS,* 1948, vol. 5, part 1, pp. 338–339.
53. Shone to Grafftey-Smith, 17 March 1948, IOR/L/WS/1/1141, IOR, BL. Between India and Pakistan, the Foreign Office would strongly have preferred the latter. Considerations stemming from the outbreak of civil war after the partition of Palestine led Foreign Office officials to express concerns the day before the Security Council passed Resolution 47 on Kashmir about how Pakistan's loss of Kashmir might deal British prestige in the Islamic world a terrible blow. See Dening to Bevin, 20 April 1948, FO 371/69721, UKNA.
54. As Joint Permanent Under-Secretary for Commonwealth Relations Archibald Carter put it, "The British Commonwealth is not prepared to burn its fingers by producing troops for reasons that are pretty obvious; and the universal opinion is that it is no good asking one or two other small nations whose troops might perhaps have been employed without danger of international complications." Carter to Grafftey-Smith, 25 March 1948, Box 1, File 1, Grafftey-Smith Papers, Middle East Centre Archive, Oxford University Library.
55. Gracey to Ismay, 23 September 1948, Ismay Papers 3/7/44, LHCMA, King's College London.
56. Marshall to Huddle, 22 October 1948, *FRUS,* 1948, vol. 5, part 1, pp. 433–434.
57. Marshall to Lovett, 15 October 1948, *FRUS,* 1948, vol. 5, part 1, pp. 429–430.
58. Marshall to UK Embassy, 20 October 1948, *FRUS,* 1948, vol. 5, part 1, pp. 431–432.
59. Marshall to Lovett, 29 October 1948, *FRUS,* 1948, vol. 5, part 1, pp. 435–436; Memorandum of Conversation, by the Secretary of State, 10 November 1948, *FRUS,* 1948, vol. 5, part 1, pp. 445–448.
60. Henderson to Marshall, 23 November 1948, *FRUS,* 1948, vol. 5, part 1, p. 458.
61. Dulles to Marshall, 23 November 1948, *FRUS,* 1948, vol. 5, part 1, pp. 459–460.
62. Dulles to Marshall, 7 December 1948, *FRUS,* 1948, vol. 5, part 1, pp. 471–472.
63. Lewis to Marshall, 27 December 1948, *FRUS,* 1948, vol. 5, part 1, pp. 481–484.
64. SANACC 360/14, Appraisal of U.S. National Interests in South Asia, Appendix B, Discussion, Truman Papers, PSF, Subject File, 1940–1953, Box 178, HSTL.

65. See UN Security Council, 4th Special Supplement No. 7 (1949), pp. 102 ff; Henderson to Acheson, 22 April 1949, *FRUS*, 1949, 6: 1700–1701; Memorandum of Conversation by Mr. F. D. Collins of the Division of South Asian Affairs, 10 May 1949, *FRUS*, 1949, 6: 1708–1710.
66. Acheson to Embassy New Delhi, 18 June 1949, *FRUS*, 1949, 6: 1721–1722; Henderson to Acheson, 8 September 1949, *FRUS*, 1949, 6: 1737. Before Acheson's cable to New Delhi, Acting Secretary James Webb had proposed the idea of "arbitration by impartial third party" in his telegram to the Indian Embassy on 2 June 1949. See *FRUS*, 1949, 6: 1715.
67. Alastair Lamb, *Kashmir: A Disputed Legacy, 1846–1990* (New Delhi: Oxford University Press, 1991), 170.
68. Memorandum of Conversation by Lovett, 4 January 1949, *FRUS*, 1949, 6: 1686.
69. Memorandum of Conversation by Mr. F. D. Collins of the Division of South Asian Affairs, *FRUS*, 1949, 6: 1746.
70. Mountbatten, Report of the Governor-General, cited in Hodson, *The Great Divide*, 469–470.
71. Robert G. Wirsing, *India, Pakistan, and the Kashmir Dispute: On Regional Conflict and Its Resolution* (New York: St. Martin's Press, 1994), 237–238.
72. See the chapter "United States Cold War Strategy in South Asia," in McMahon, *The Cold War on the Periphery;* CIA Report on India-Pakistan, 16 September 1948, PSF, HSTL, especially the fifth section of the report, titled "Strategic Considerations Affecting U.S. Security."
73. See Palmer to Marshall, 7 April 1948, U.S. Embassy, Karachi, Classified General Records, 1947–1961, Box 8, RG 84, USNA; Alling to Marshall, 4 May 1948, U.S. Embassy, Karachi, Classified General Records, 1947–1961, Box 8, RG 84, USNA.
74. Wavell to Pethick-Lawrence, 1 October 1945, IOR/L/PO/10/22, *Transfer of Power*, vol. 11, no. 127, pp. 304–309, quote on 307. Wavell's concerns were validated by public shows of support by Indian Muslims. The Muslim League had even organized "Palestine Day" rallies to show support for their coreligionists in the Middle East. See Wavell to Pethick Lawrence, 29 October 1945, *Transfer of Power*, vol. 11, no. 177, pp. 420–425, especially 421.
75. A. E. G. Davy, "The Strategic and Political Importance of Pakistan in the event of War with USSR," 19 May 1948, DO 142/353, UKNA. A copy of the document was also passed to the U.S. Embassy in New Delhi. See Donovan to SecState, U.S. Embassy, New Delhi, Classified General Records, 1942–1963, Box 64, RG 84, USNA.
76. Minute by Gordon Walker, 29 January 1948, DO 133/74, UKNA.

77. Rumbold to Noel-Baker, 28 July 1949, Box 1, File 1, Grafftey-Smith Papers, Middle East Centre Archive, Oxford University Library.

5. IMPERIAL RESIDUES

1. Scholars like R. F. Holland and Miles Kahler have informed debates on decolonization by emphasizing the impact of decisions taken at the metropole to willingly cede colonial territories, as opposed to the relative impact of national, anticolonial movements or changing norms in the international system about colonial rule and human rights. See Holland's *European Decolonisation, 1918–1981: An Introductory Survey* (London: Macmillan, 1985) and Kahler's *Decolonization in Britain and France: the Domestic Consequences of International Relations* (Princeton: Princeton University Press, 1984). Kahler cites "the differing effects that change in a particular set of external relations—those with colonial empires—could produce within the metropolitan societies" (6).
2. The most comprehensive treatment of the history of both mandates may still be Stephen Longrigg's *Syria and Lebanon under French Mandate* (London: Oxford University Press, 1958). See also Meir Zamir, *Lebanon's Quest: The Road to Statehood, 1926–1939* (London: I. B. Tauris, 2000); Elizabeth Thompson, *Colonial Citizens: Republican Rights, Paternal Privilege, and Gender in French Syria and Lebanon* (New York: Columbia University Press, 2000).
3. See Isaiah Friedman, *Palestine, a Twice Promised Land? The British, the Arabs and Zionism, 1915–1920* (New Brunswick, N.J.: Transaction, 2000), 217–238; Howard Sachar, *A History of Israel* (New York: Knopf, 2007), 118–125, 169.
4. See A. B. Gaunson, *The Anglo-French Clash in Lebanon and Syria, 1940–5* (London: Macmillan, 1987), 4–5.
5. That respect was embodied in a litany of British officials such as Lawrence and Lieutenant General Sir John Glubb, whose service in the Middle East helped develop a brain trust of expertise on the region, and in academic institutions like Oxford's St. Antony's College, whose Middle East Centre came to acquire one of the richest collections of official historical documents and personal correspondence on the region. On Anglo-French competition over cultural influence in the Levant as Anglo-American ideals and interest displaced those of the French, see Jennifer Dueck, *The Claims of Culture at Empire's End: Syria and Lebanon under French Rule* (New York: Oxford University Press, 2010), 142–163.
6. For accounts of the Lebanese and Syrian treaty relationships with France, whose bitter legacy fed the profound Arab mistrust in the years between

the 1943 election and the crisis of 1945, see Raghid El-Solh, *Lebanon and Arabism: National Identity and State Formation* (London: I.B. Tauris, 2004), 11–97; and Albert Hourani, *Syria and Lebanon: A Political Essay* (London: Oxford University Press, 1945), 199–229.

7. See Ben-Gurion to Amos Ben-Gurion, 28 July 1937, in David Ben Gurion, *Letters to Paula* (Pittsburgh: University of Pittsburgh Press, 1971), 155; David Ben-Gurion, *Rebirth and Destiny of Israel* (New York: Philosophical Library, 1954), 90.

8. On the military reoccupation of Syria and Lebanon, see Wilson's personal recollections in Henry Maitland Wilson, *Eight Years Overseas* (London: Hutchinson, 1948), 114–118; Gaunson, *Anglo-French Clash in Lebanon and Syria*, 44–45.

9. De Gaulle to Churchill, 29 June 1941, PREM 3/422, UKNA.

10. William Roger Louis, *The British Empire in the Middle East, 1945–1951: Arab Nationalism, the United States, and Postwar Imperialism* (Oxford: Clarendon Press, 1984), 148–149. See also Hourani, *Syria and Lebanon*.

11. Minute by R. M. A. Hankey, 28 February 1945, FO 371/45561, UKNA.

12. See Kais Firro, *Inventing Lebanon: Nationalism and the State under the Mandate* (London: I. B. Tauris, 2003), 186–195.

13. See Spears, "Memorandum on Anglo-French Relations in Syria and the Lebanon," 5 July 1943, and Minute by Churchill, 12 July 1943, FO 371/35178, UKNA, cited in Gaunson, *Anglo-French Clash in Lebanon and Syria*, 110–117.

14. Summary of Press Messages Received from India through Reuters and Other Press Sources for the week ending 29 April 1943, IOR/L/PO/6/102B, IOR, BL.

15. The postelection exchanges between Lebanese and French colonial authorities also included Lebanese demands to convert the office of the French delegate-general into an embassy and the discontinuance of French, even as second language. See K. S. Salibi, *The Modern History of Lebanon* (New York: Praeger, 1965), 188–190.

16. See Cairo to London, 19 October 1944, Box 2, File 6, Edward Spears Papers, Middle East Centre Archive, Oxford University Library; El-Solh, *Lebanon and Arabism*, 245–251.

17. Minute by R. M. A. Hankey, 10 December 1944, FO 371/40307, UKNA.

18. See "Report by the Joint Planning Staff on Internal Security in the Middle East," J.P. (45)32, CO 537/1240, UKNA; Memorandum on "Great Britain and Palestine," n.d., Box 4, File 3, Cunningham Papers, Middle East Centre Archive, Oxford University Library. The latter document is contained in a folder marked "Palestine Memoranda etc 1944–1945." Faris Bey Khouri, the Syrian delegate to the UN General Assembly, had

warned the Foreign Office that Zionists should be convinced to abandon the idea of a state based on religious and racial distinctions. See Ritchie Ovendale, *Britain, the United States, and the End of the Palestine Mandate, 1942–1948* (Woodbridge, Suffolk, UK: Boydell Press, 1989), 192.

19. Minute by R. M. A. Hankey, 3 March 1945, FO 371/45569, UKNA, cited in Roger Louis, *The British Empire in the Middle East*, 154.
20. El-Solh, *Lebanon and Arabism*, 275–276, 279–280; Roger Louis, *The British Empire in the Middle East*, 169–170. Lebanon's staunch defense of its sovereignty and rights to conclude treaties with other governments also pleased the British government. See Killearn to Eden, 3 March 1945, FO 371/45236, UKNA.
21. The Chiefs of Staff noted that such a role reversal in which the French could exploit an embattled Britain "now holding the ring" would pose considerable strains for imperial defense. See "The Military Implications of Palestine Policy," C.O.S. Paper, 16 July 1945, CAB 80/100, UKNA.
22. See Grigg to Eden, "Policy towards Palestine, Enclosed comments as requested upon the memo on Palestine Policy," 29 June 1945, FO 371/45378, UKNA; Wavell to Pethick-Lawrence, 6 November 1945, IOR L/PJ/8/525, *Transfer of Power*, vol. 6, no. 194, pp. 450–454.
23. Roosevelt-Stalin meeting, November 28, 1943, 3 P.M., Roosevelt's Quarters, Soviet Embassy, *FRUS*, 1943, *The Conferences at Cairo and Tehran*, p. 484.
24. Memorandum by the Secretary of State of a Conversation with the British Minister of State for the Middle East (Casey), 5 January 1943, *FRUS*, 1943, 4: 953–955.
25. Wadsworth to Hull, 23 March 1943, *FRUS*, 1943, 4: 963–965.
26. Memorandum of Conversation by Alling, 14 May 1943, *FRUS*, 1943, 4: 969–971; Wadsworth to Hull, 11 June 1943, *FRUS*, 1943, 4: 975–976.
27. Wadsworth to Hull, 18 August 1943, *FRUS*, 1943, 4: 985–987; Firro, *Inventing Lebanon*, 195–208.
28. Welles to Wadsworth, 22 August 1943, *FRUS*, 1943, 4: 987; Wadsworth to Hull, *FRUS*, 1943, 4: 987–989.
29. Hull to Wadsworth, 23 September 1943, *FRUS*, 1943, 4: 993.
30. Memorandum from the Department of State to the British Embassy, 25 October 1943, *FRUS*, 1943, 4: 1000–1001.
31. Report to the Secretary of State by Undersecretary Stettinius on his Mission to London, April 7–29, 1944, 22 May 1944, *FRUS*, 1944, vol. 3, *The British Commonwealth and Europe*, p. 18. Of course, the provisional

nature of the French government also posed much wider problems, including for France's representation at the United Nations Conference as a whole. See Grew to Caffery, 20 February 1945, *FRUS, 1945*, vol. 1, *General: the United Nations,* p. 80.
32. Memorandum by the Director of the Office of Near Eastern and African Affairs (Murray) to the Acting Secretary of State, 8 December 1944, *FRUS, 1944*, vol. 5, *The Near East, South Asia, and Africa, the Far East,* p. 645.
33. Hull to Wadsworth, 5 September 1944, FRUS, 1944, 5: 774–775.
34. See, for example, the records of Undersecretary of State Joseph Grew's meeting with Rabbi Wise, Nahum Goldmann, and other Zionist leaders on 28 June 1945 in Memorandum by the Director of Near Eastern and African Affairs (Henderson), *FRUS, 1945, The Conference of Berlin (the Potsdam Conference),* vol. 1, pp. 974–977.
35. Memorandum of Conversation between his Majesty Abdul Aziz Al Saud, King of Saudi Arabia, and President Roosevelt, February 14, 1945, Aboard the USS *Quincy,* Truman Papers, PSF, Subject File, 1940–1953, Box 160, HSTL.
36. Quwatli to Stettinius, 30 May 1945, *FRUS, 1945,* 8: 1118. See also Roger Louis, *The British Empire in the Middle East,* 162–163.
37. Memorandum by Henderson, 23 May 1945, *FRUS,* 1945, 8: 1093–1095.
38. Grew to Caffery, 20 February 1945, *FRUS,* 1945, 1: 80.
39. See Dueck, *The Claims of Culture at Empire's End,* 164–180. The work of scholars like Dueck show how the American globalism that came to displace French colonial rule in regions like the Levant took the form of both cultural "soft power" and the better-studied economic relationships and more extended military power projection that scholars like Melvyn Leffler and cold war revisionists like William Appelman Williams have documented.
40. Memorandum of Conversation, by the Chief of the Division of Southeast Asian Affairs (Moffat), 6 December 1945, *FRUS,* 1945, vol. 6, *The British Commonwealth, the Far East,* p. 1178.
41. See Mohammed Hatta, *Portrait of a Patriot: Selected Writings by Mohammed Hatta* (The Hague: Mouton, 1972), 501; Robert J. McMahon, *Colonialism and Cold War: The United States and the Struggle for Indonesian Independence, 1945–49* (Ithaca: Cornell University Press, 1981), 42.
42. See Memorandum from British Chiefs of Staff to Combined Chiefs of Staff, *FRUS, 1945, Conference of Berlin (Potsdam),* vol. 2, pp. 313–314; McMahon, *Colonialism and Cold War,* 80–81.

43. "Letter from Lord Birdwood to [Lord Louis] Mountbatten remarking that it seems unfair that Lord Mountbatten has to sort out the problems of the Netherlands East Indies, 24 November 1945," MB1/C35/75, Mountbatten Papers Database, Hartley Library, University of Southampton.
44. Memorandum of Conversation, by the Undersecretary of State (Acheson), 10 October 1945, *FRUS*, 1945, 6: 1163–1164.
45. Cumming to Marshall, 8 October 1945, *FRUS*, 1945, 6: 1158–1163.
46. Wavell to Pethick-Lawrence, 7 November 1945, IOR L/WS/1/727, *Transfer of Power*, vol. 6, no. 198, p. 460. Pethick-Lawrence was already aware of the difficulties, of which Wavell had warned him for months. He suggested a careful balance between addressing the situation on the ground adequately and not inflaming Dutch sensitivities. See Pethick-Lawrence to Wavell, 12 October 1945, IOR L/PO/10/22, *Transfer of Power*, vol. 6, no. 140, p. 337.
47. Wavell to Pethick-Lawrence, 17 October 1945, C.O.S. (45), 625, CAB 80/100, UKNA; Memorandum of Conversation by the Chief of the Division of Southeast Asian Affairs (Moffat), 18 October 1945, *FRUS*, 1945, 6: 1165–1166; "Copy of a letter from [Lord Louis Mountbatten] to R. G. Casey, informing him that he prefers to thank members of the Government of Bengal informally, to avoid highlighting the use of Indian troops against independence movements in Indo-China and Indonesia, 20 November 1945," MB1/C47/42, Mountbatten Papers Database, Hartley Library, University of Southampton.
48. Winant to Byrnes, 7 November 1945, *FRUS*, 1945, 6: 1168–1169; Winant to Byrnes, 1 December 1945, *FRUS*, 1945, 6: 1175; McMahon, *Colonialism and Cold War*, 118–119.
49. "Signal from General Sir H. L. Ismay to Lord Louis Mountbatten concerning the termination date for SACSEA," 12 February 1946, MB1/C145/5, Mountbatten Papers Database, Hartley Library, University of Southampton; "Copy of a letter from [Lord] Louis Mountbatten to the [British] Ambassador to The Hague, about the situation in the Netherlands East Indies," 22 March 1946, MB1/C35/99, Mountbatten Papers Database, Hartley Library, University of Southampton.
50. See "Basic Dutch-Indonesian Issues and the Linggadjati Agreement," ORE 20, Central Intelligence Group, 9 June 1947, Truman Papers, PSF, Intelligence File, 1946–1953, Box 214, HSTL, available at www.foia.cia.gov/sites/default/files/document_conversions/89801/DOC_0000256979.pdf; Alastair M. Taylor, *Indonesian Independence and the United Nations* (Ithaca: Cornell University Press, 1960), 28–29.

51. Dening to FO, 24 October 1945, FO 371/46396, UKNA; McMahon, *Colonialism and Cold War*, 95; Peter Dennis, *Troubled Days of Peace: Mountbatten and the South East Asia command, 1945–46* (Manchester, UK: Manchester University Press, 1987), 138–139.
52. H. S. Allen, "India and Indonesia," 12 September 1947, FO371/63568, UKNA.
53. Note by South East Asia Department before visit by Pakistani UN Delegation leader Muhammad Zafrullah Khan, 12 September 1947, FO371/63568, UKNA.
54. Hornbeck to Byrnes, 1 December 1945, *FRUS*, 1945, 6: 1176–1177.
55. See McMahon, *Colonialism and Cold War*, 72–73.
56. Text of press release contained in Acheson to Foote, 19 December 1945, *FRUS*, 1945, 6: 1182–1183.
57. As one State Department official put it, "We must not put ourselves in a position where we cannot move with the historical stream rather than attempting to block a force which might prove too strong for us" ("American Interests in Southeast Asia," 26 March 1945, Box 5, Lot 54 D 190, RG 59, USNA, quoted in McMahon, *Colonialism and Cold War*, 69).
58. Marshall to Baruch, 16 March 1947, *FRUS*, 1947, vol. 6, *The Far East*, pp. 924–926. The Department wrote, "U.S. has given serious consideration to situation Southeast Asia. Strong nationalist movements throughout area are not isolated phenomena of concern to few colonial powers only. Outcome will have profound effect on future world. Area strategically located athwart Southwest Pacific and of greatest economic importance" (924).
59. See Foote to Marshall, 3 March 1947, Marshall to Foote, 14 June 1947, Truman Papers, PSF, Subject File, 1940–1953, Box 157, HSTL.
60. For a contemporary account of the negotiations in the wake of the Linggadjati Agreement up to the Dutch military action in July 1947, see Rupert Emerson, "Reflections on the Indonesian Case," *World Politics* 1, no. 1 (1948): 59–68.
61. For additional discussion of the Indian and Australian initiatives to bring the matter before the Security Council, see McMahon, *Colonialism and Cold War*, 185; Evan Luard, *A History of the United Nations*, Vol. 1: *The Years of Western Domination, 1945–1955* (New York: St. Martin's Press, 1982), 135–136; W. J. Hudson, "Australia and Indonesian Independence," *Journal of Southeast Asian History* 8 (September 1967): 226–239. The Foreign Office had warned U.S. Embassy officials in London that by raising the Indonesian matter before the Security Council themselves, they could prevent "some other power" from preempting them. See British

Embassy in Washington to the Department of State, 14 July 1947, *FRUS,* 1947, 6: 988.
62. Villard to Bohlen, 29 July 1947, *FRUS,* 1947, 6: 994–995.
63. Patterson to Marshall, 30 July 1947, *FRUS,* 1947, 6: 1000.
64. See Austin to Lovett, 15 October 1947, *FRUS,* 1947, 6: 1055.
65. See the Decision of 26 August 1947 (194th meeting), U.N. Security Council, Second Year, No. 82, S/513.
66. Allen to Falla, 15 January 1948, FO371/69706, UKNA.
67. Livengood to Marshall, 20 February 1948, *FRUS,* 1948, vol. 6, *The Far East and Australasia,* pp. 99–100.
68. See McMahon, *Colonialism and Cold War,* 223, 242–243; George Kahin, *Nationalism and Revolution in Indonesia* (Ithaca: Cornell University Press, 1952), 248; Andrew Roth, "American Flipflop in Indonesia," *Nation* 167, no. 2 (July 10, 1948), pp. 39–40.
69. Livengood to Marshall, 12 June 1948, *FRUS,* 1948, 6: 242.
70. For a discussion of the considerations that shaped early U.S. postwar policy toward Indonesia at Potsdam and beyond, see George Kahin, "The United States and the Anticolonial Revolutions in Southeast Asia, 1945–1950," in Yonosuke Nagai and Akira Iriye, eds., *The Origins of the Cold War in Asia* (New York: Columbia University Press, 1977), 338–386.
71. For an account of the immediate prelude to the second Dutch military operation, see Luard, *A History of the United Nations* 1: 145–151.
72. Rusk to Jessup, 23 December 1948, *FRUS,* 1948, 6: 598. On Arab Muslim solidarity with the Indonesian struggle, see, for example, the statement by the League of Arab States to UN Security Council, 21 December 1948, UN S/1128, during the council discussions of the draft resolution of 24 December.
73. See "Carbon copy of a typescript letter from Lord Killearn to E. Bevin concerning problems faced by the allies following the Japanese surrender, 27 April 1946," MB1/C150/43, Mountbatten Papers Database, Hartley Library, University of Southampton. Indian diplomatic entreaties that alarmed British officials included Nehru's organization of the Asian Conference on Indonesia in January 1949, triggering fears of "expanding Indian ambitions of hegemony." See Grafftey-Smith to Noel-Baker, 16 February 1949, Box 1, File 1, Grafftey-Smith Papers, Middle East Centre Archive, Oxford University Library. For the American take on the conference, see SANACC 360/14, Appraisal of U.S. National Interests in South Asia, Appendix A, Facts Bearing on the Problem, 19 April 1949, Truman Papers, PSF, Subject File, 1940–1953, Box 178, HSTL.
74. See McMahon, *Colonialism and Cold War,* 310. For an elaboration of the argument that dispels the myth of unfailing U.S. support for Indonesian

anticolonial nationalism, see Frances Gouda and Thijs Brocades Zaalberg, *American Visions of the Netherlands East Indies/Indonesia: U.S. Foreign Policy and Indonesian Nationalism, 1900–1949* (Chicago: University of Chicago Press, 2002).

75. Background Memoranda on Visit to the United States of Liaquat Ali Khan, Prime Minister and Minister of Defense, Government of Pakistan, n.d., Truman Papers, PSF, Subject File, 1940–1953, Box 160, HSTL.

76. "Review of the World Situation as It Relates to the Security of the United States," CIA 1–49, 19 January 1949, President's Secretary's File, Intelligence File, Box 250, HSTL.

6. TWO VISIONS OF THE POSTWAR WORLD

1. On the idea of mental geography, see Yi-Fu Tuan, "Images and Mental Maps," *Annals of the Association of American Geographers* 65, no. 2 (1975): 205–213. As Tuan puts it, "A mental map may be the image of a real map, that is, an abstraction of a real map which is itself an abstraction of reality. Maps can of course be created in the mind without recourse to pen and paper" (208). For a discussion of how the environment can shape the views of policymakers, see Harold Sprout and Margaret Sprout, "Geography and International Politics in an Era of Revolutionary Change," *Journal of Conflict Resolution* 4, no. 1 (1960): 145–161.

2. See Alan K. Henrikson, "The Geographical 'Mental Maps' of American Foreign Policy Makers," *International Political Science Review* 1, no. 4 (1980): 495–530.

3. Michael Polanyi elaborated on the idea of tacit knowledge in *The Tacit Dimension* (Chicago: University of Chicago Press, 1966).

4. For the most comprehensive explication of the concept of human capital, see Gary Becker, *Human Capital: A Theoretical and Empirical Analysis, with Special Reference to Education* (Chicago: University of Chicago Press, 1964).

5. See Morton H. Halperin, *Bureaucratic Politics and Foreign Policy* (Washington, DC: Brookings, 1974) and the discussion of organizational "repertoires" in Graham Allison, *Essence of Decision: Explaining the Cuban Missile Crisis* (Boston: Little Brown, 1971).

6. For the most comprehensive overview of this entire effort, see Neil Smith, *American Empire: Roosevelt's Geographer and the Prelude to Globalization* (Berkeley: University of California Press, 2003), 325–332.

7. Welles to Roosevelt, October 18, 1941, Welles Papers, Box 151, FDRL; Christopher O'Sullivan, *Sumner Welles, Postwar Planning, and the Quest*

for a New World Order, 1937–1943 (New York: Columbia University Press, 2003), chapter 4.

8. "Declaration by the United Nations," 1 January 1942, *FRUS*, 1942, 1: 21–22.

9. For records on the establishment of the Advisory Committee and minutes of its earliest Committee meetings, see the contents of Boxes 170–174, Harley Notter Papers, RG 59, USNA. See also Lawrence Shoup and William Minter, *Imperial Brain Trust: The Council on Foreign Relations and United States Foreign Policy* (New York, Monthly Review Press, 1977), 156; Smith, *American Empire*, 325–326, 329–330; William Roger Louis, *Imperialism at Bay: The United States and the Decolonization of the British Empire* (New York: Oxford University Press, 1978), 159–160.

10. See Ruth Russell, *A History of the United Nations Charter: The Role of the United States: 1940–1945* (Washington, DC: Brookings Institution, 1958), 99–100; Townsend Hoopes and Douglas Brinkley, *FDR and the Creation of the U.N.* (New Haven: Yale University Press, 1997), 51.

11. On the Committee's establishment, organization, and representation, see the Records of the Advisory Committee on Postwar Foreign Policy, Harley Notter Files, esp. Boxes 160–164, RG 59, USNA; Hoopes and Brinkley, *FDR and the Creation of the U.N.*, 43–51; Smith, *American Empire*, 325–332.

12. For an in-depth discussion of these interagency rivalries and civil-military coordination challenges, see Mark Stoler, *Allies and Adversaries: The Joint Chiefs of Staff, the Grand Alliance, and U.S. Strategy in World War II* (Chapel Hill: University of North Carolina Press, 2000), especially 106, 138–145.

13. Samuel Rosenman, *Public Papers of Franklin Delano Roosevelt* (New York: Random House, 1950), 2: 30, 32–33; Robert A. Divine, *Second Chance: The Triumph of Internationalism in America During WWII* (New York: Atheneum, 1971), 84.

14. See O'Sullivan, *Sumner Welles, Postwar Planning, and the New World Order*, chapter 4; Divine, *Second Chance*, 114–115. Roosevelt had asked the State Department to prepare such a plan in October 1942, according to Hull. Welles briefed the president personally on the IO Subcommittee's work in January 1943. See Cordell Hull, *The Memoirs of Cordell Hull* (London: Macmillan, 1948), vol. 2, 1639; Hoopes and Brinkley, *FDR and the Creation of the U.N.*, 68–69.

15. Smith, *American Empire*, 382; Divine, *Second Chance*, 114; Hoopes and Brinkley, *FDR and the Creation of the U.N.*, 69–73.

16. See Smith, *American Empire*, 337–338.

17. "Tentative Draft of a Joint Four-Power Declaration," Annex 1 to Memorandum by the Secretary of State to President Roosevelt, 14 September 1943, *FRUS*, 1943, vol. 1, *General*, pp. 522–523.

18. "Observations by the Foreign Office on the British Amendments to the Draft Four-Power Declaration," 28 September 1943, *FRUS*, 1943, 1: 532–533. This was an impression that some in the Department like Isaiah Bowman likewise had begun to share.
19. Molotov to Hamilton, 29 September 1943, *FRUS*, 1943, 1: 534–535.
20. See Comment on the British Aide-Mémoire, 5 October 1943, *FRUS*, 1943, 1: 544.
21. Joint Four-Nation Declaration, Moscow Conference, October 1943, reprinted in Russell, *A History of the United Nations Charter*, 977.
22. See *FRUS*, 1943, 1: 690; Robert Dallek, *FDR and American Foreign Policy, 1932–1945* (New York: Oxford University Press, 1979), 423.
23. *FRUS*, 1943, vol. 3, *The Conferences at Cairo and Tehran*, pp. 530–532.
24. See Dallek, *Franklin D. Roosevelt and American Foreign Policy*, 434–435; Divine, *Second Chance*, 157–159.
25. See Robert Hilderbrand, *Dumbarton Oaks: The Origins of the United Nations and the Search for Postwar Security* (Chapel Hill: University of North Carolina Press, 2001) for a full treatment of the conference and its outcomes.
26. Hoopes and Brinkley, *FDR and the Creation of the U.N.*, 145–147. Russell, *A History of the United Nations Charter*, 445–457; Robert E. Sherwood, *Roosevelt and Hopkins: An Intimate History* (New York: Harper Brothers, 1948), 845; "U.S. Tentative Proposals for a General International Organization," 18 July 1944, *FRUS*, 1944, vol. 1, *General*, pp. 653–654.
27. Divine, *Second Chance*, 227; Hilderbrand, *Dumbarton Oaks*, 245–257. Hilderbrand argues that Dumbarton Oaks marked the turning point on the great powers' march toward true collective security, where the United States, Great Britain, the Soviet Union, and China opted instead to safeguard their own sovereignty at the expense of emasculating the executive powers of the new international organization with regard to the maintenance of peace and security, including enforcement action. While the issue of the veto procedures had not been resolved, the arrangements for special agreements to place national military forces under the command of the five permanent Security Council members on the Military Staff Committee seem to support Hilderbrand's argument. On Stalin's concerns and his linkage of the issue with membership for two Soviet Socialist Republics to the General Assembly, see Dallek, *FDR and American Foreign Policy*, 510–511.
28. Sherwood, *Roosevelt and Hopkins*, 854–855.
29. Numerous historical treatments of the San Francisco Conference have comprehensively documented the proceedings. The most detailed account is probably Stephen Schlesinger's *Act of Creation: The Founding of the*

United Nations. A Story of Superpowers, Secret Agents, Wartime Allies and Enemies, and Their Quest for a Peaceful World (Boulder, Colo.: Westview Press, 2003), 111–265. Schlesinger provides broad coverage of both the American planning for and choreography of the conference, as well as the behind-the-scenes diplomacy between the Big Four. See also Russell, *A History of the United Nations Charter;* Smith, *American Empire,* 401–415; Divine, *Second Chance,* 288–298; Sherwood, *Roosevelt and Hopkins,* 910–912.

30. See Divine, *Second Chance,* 283–287 for an account of the final preparations in the lead-up to the conference.
31. Hopkins's record of the conversation, reprinted in *FRUS,* is reproduced in his final report for Truman. See Hopkins-Stalin Conference Record Moscow, May–June 1945, 6 June 1945, Hopkins Papers, Sherwood Collection, Box 338, FDRL. See also Russell, *A History of the United Nations Charter,* 732–735; Sherwood, *Roosevelt and Hopkins,* 910–915.
32. See David Reynolds, *One World Divisible: A Global History Since 1945* (New York: Norton, 2000), 76–77; William Hitchcock, *The Struggle for Europe* (New York: Doubleday, 2002). As Hitchcock put it, the Truman administration agreed that "the Jews had earned statehood. The world knew it, and the Zionists would fight for it" (60).
33. As Braudel observed, "From the Black Sea to the Straits of Gibraltar, the Mediterranean's northern waters was the shores of Europe. Here again, if he wants to establish boundaries, the historian will have more hesitating than the geographer. 'Europe, a confused concept,' wrote Henry Hauser. It is a twofold or even threefold world, composed of peoples and territories with whom history has dealt very differently. The Mediterranean, by its profound influence over southern Europe, has contributed in no small measure to prevent the unity of that Europe, which it has attracted towards its shores and then divided to its own advantage." Fernand Braudel, *The Mediterranean and the Mediterranean World in the Age of Philip II* (New York: Harper and Row, 1972), 1: 188.
34. Leahy to Truman, 8 March 1946, Box, 10, RG 218, USNA. The military flights were authorized unbeknownst to the War Department in response to UN requests and without the proper British flight clearances. Knowledge of the flights sent War Department planners scurrying to cable its military commands in the European, Mediterranean, and Middle East theaters to obtain more information.
35. As the meeting's summary of conclusions noted, "Migration voluntarily or by imposition was regarded as the best solution for peoples discontented with sovereignty or territorial settlements" (Minutes, P-3, Meeting of 21 March 1942, Welles Papers, Box 190, FDRL).

36. See Chapter 2.
37. See Department of State Comments on NSC 27, *FRUS*, 1948, vol. 5, *The Near East, South Asia, and Africa*, p. 1362.
38. McFarland, A. J., SWNCC 311, Memorandum for the State-War-Navy Coordinating Committee, Subject: British Proposals in Connection with the Report of the Anglo-American Committee of Inquiry on Palestine, Truman Papers, PSF, Subject File, 1940–1953, Box 160, HSTL.
39. See *FRUS*, 1948, vol. 5, part 1, pp. 276–278.
40. Marshall to Austin, 14 January 1948, *FRUS*, 1948, vol. 5, part 1, p. 280.
41. As the State Department noted in a 1949 briefing book for Truman for Nehru's visit to Washington, "India's political stability and economic and military potential, combined with its relative security from overland aggression afforded by the mountain barriers protecting the peninsular land mass shared with Pakistan, make it possible for India, if its leaders so desire, to take a firm position of leadership against Communist expansion in South and Southeast Asia. India and Pakistan are the only remaining countries on the Asian continent so favored" (Background Memoranda on Visit to the United States of Pandit Jawaharlal Nehru, Prime Minister and Foreign Minister, Government of India, October 1949, 3 October 1949, Truman Papers, PSF, Subject File, 1940–1953, Box 157, HSTL).
42. This was a point that Professor John Darwin drew to my attention in a conversation, one echoed by Roger Louis in *Imperialism at Bay*.
43. See SANACC 360/14, "Appraisal of U.S. National Interests in South Asia," 19 April 1949, *FRUS*, 1949, vol. 6, *The Near East, South Asia, and Africa*, pp. 8–31; Robert J. McMahon, *The Cold War on the Periphery: The United States, India and Pakistan* (New York: Columbia University Press, 1994), 11–19; and S. Mahmud Ali, *Cold War in the High Himalayas: The USA, China and South Asia in the 1950s* (New York: St. Martin's Press, 1999), 8–14.
44. Over time the administration came to recognize Pakistan's strategic importance given its proximity to both the southern borders of the Soviet Union and Middle East petroleum reserves. See Memorandum by the JCS, 24 March 1949, *FRUS*, 1949, 6: 29–31.
45. See "The Military Implications of Palestine Policy," 16 July 1945, CAB 80/100. UKNA.
46. For an official statement of these considerations, see, for example, "Great Britain's Position in the Middle East," 8 September 1945, C.P. (45) 156, PREM 8/627, UKNA.
47. As the governor-general of Bengal observed, the military considerations were foremost:

After all, our major interest is to have an India that is as friendly as possible towards us in the post-war world. We do not want in particular to antagonise the Muslims because—

(a) they have been our friends and supporters for a great many years;

(b) the potential N-W and N-E.—Pakistans lie across the track of our major imperial line of communication; and

(c) we do not want to antagonise their Muslim cousins in the Middle East, who also lie across our imperial communications by sea and air." (Casey to Wavell, 6 November 1944, IOL/R/3/1/105, IOR, BL)

48. As Herbert Samuel put it, "On the relinquishment of direct British and French administration of the Middle East, country by country, Great Britain has patiently built up a whole block of Arab states within her sphere of influence" ("An Analysis of the Palestine Situation," April 1948, Box 4, File 5, Cunningham Papers, Middle East Centre Archive, Oxford University Library).

49. Annex, Middle East Policy, Copy of a letter dated 18 August from the Colonial Office to General Ismay, 18 August 1945, C.O.S. (45), 539 (0), CAB 80/100, UKNA.

50. Memorandum by Commander-in-Chief Middle East Force, A Middle East Confederacy, 30 August 1945, C.C. (45), 25, CAB 80/100, UKNA.

51. An academic participant at a conference assembled by the Truman administration observed in late 1949, "The British have the fundamental ties both ways with the Continent and the Commonwealth overseas. They are acutely conscious of that. Whenever they feel that we are trying to press them into integration, closer association with the Continent, they immediately begin talking about their Commonwealth ties" (Record of Round-Table Discussion by Twenty-Four Consultants with the Department of State on "Strengthening International Organizations," 17, 18, 19 November 1949, Truman Papers, WHCF, Confidential File, State Department Correspondence, 1945, Box 40, HSTL.

52. New Zealand prime minister Peter Fraser and his Australian counterpart and attorney general, Dr. H. V. Evatt, were of the mind that parent states should voluntarily place their colonies under trusteeship. But the British secretary of state for dominion affairs, Lord Cranborne, explained that His Majesty's government did not intend to apply the idea to the British colonies. See World Organisation, W.P. (45) 205, 31 March 1945, L/E/9/1527, IOR, BL; Roger Louis, *Imperialism at Bay*, 17–18.

53. B.C.M. (45) 6th Meeting, British Commonwealth Meeting, 9 April 1945, IOR/L/E/9/1527, IOR, BL. The idea of the body voting together in the Council as "a British Commonwealth Group" was abandoned the following day, not least because it "would never result in more than one member

of the British Commonwealth, other than the United Kingdom, securing representation at any one time [on the Council]." Regionalism thus afforded the ability to maintain a degree of informal cohesion despite the dispersal of international political power, enabling Commonwealth members to vote as a bloc in lieu of amassing as a single, sovereign Council member. See B.C.M./G.E.N. British Commonwealth Meeting, Election of Non-Permanent Members of the Security Council, Draft Report of Committee of Experts, 10 April 1945, IOR/L/E/9/1527, IOR, BL.

54. See B.C.M. (45) 9th Meeting, British Commonwealth Meeting, 11 April 1945, IOR/L/E/9/1527, IOR, BL.

55. See Annex, Effect of World Organisation's Charter upon Anglo-Egyptian Treaty of Alliance, in so far as it concerns the British position in Egypt, 16 July 1945, C.O.S. (45), 506 (0), CAB 80/100, UKNA.

56. See "The Right of Veto," Note by the Foreign Office, Cabinet, Steering Committee on International Organisation, 13 October 1946, I.O.C. (46) 85, PREM 8/377, UKNA; Cadogan to FO, 18 November 1946, PREM 8/377, UKNA; Minute by DO, 21 November 1946, IOR L/E/9/1415, IOR, BL.

57. See "Imperial Co-operation in Defence," 17 October 1945, C.O.S. (45), 625, CAB 80/100, UKNA.

58. As the Chiefs of Staff put it, "If the United States were represented upon an International Body which dealt with immigration it would silence that uninformed criticism which might at any time impair Anglo-American relations. Not only would it be a check on Palestine Jewry, who rely to a great extent upon American opinion to attain their ends, but it would also have a great effect on the Arabs who associate America with prosperity and the future development of Middle East countries" ("The Military Implications of Palestine Policy," 16 July 1945, CAB 80/100, UKNA).

59. See Minute by Jebb, 17 July 1945, FO 371/45378, UKNA. In handwritten notes, the Foreign Office's preeminent Palestine expert, Harold Beeley, commented that despite a likely Arab challenge that the jurisdiction of the permanent members of the Council did not extend to an intra-Palestine dispute, and reluctance on the part of the Big Five to decline action, Jebb's proposal was still worthy of consideration.

60. Statement made by Lord Ismay at the Joint Defence Council Meeting, 6 August 1947, Ismay Papers 3/7/67/100, LHCMA, King's College London.

61. See Annex, Middle East Policy, Copy of a letter dated 18 August from the Colonial Office to General Ismay, 18 August 1945, C.O.S. (45), 539 (0), CAB 80/100, UKNA.

62. See Lucknow to FO, 27 March 1946, FO 371/52607, UKNA.

63. Lucknow to FO, 27 March 1946, FO 371/52607, UKNA.
64. FO to Kabul, 7 February 1948, FO 371/69709, UKNA.
65. See Minute by Dening on "Future Position of the Indian States," 28 July 1947, FO 371/63568, UKNA.
66. "India—Defence Requirements," 24 July 1947, PREM 8/467, UKNA.
67. Nehru, whom Attlee had gone to visit on 1 October, had told the British prime minister that he had no interest in a joint Indo-Pakistani appeal for Commonwealth mediation "on any terms whatsoever." See Grafftey-Smith to Noel-Baker, 2 and 13 October 1947, Box 1, File 1, Grafftey-Smith Papers, Middle East Centre Archive, Oxford University Library.
68. Appreciation of the Situation in India and Pakistan By P.S.O. Commonwealth Relations Office, 14 October 1947, Mss Eur F200/102, Mountbatten Papers, IOR, BL.
69. See the discussion on p. 177 of Mountbatten's appeal to Nehru for bilateral talks in the first few months of the crisis given the "fatal illusion" that a subcontinental war could be contained and that Indian army involvement could not fail to provoke charges of communal attacks on Muslims by India. Mountbatten to Nehru, December 25, 1947, DO 133/73, UKNA.
70. Minute by Dening, 1 January 1948, FO 371/69705, UKNA.
71. Attlee to Smuts, 23 April 1948, L/WS/1/1163, IOR, BL.
72. Noel-Baker to PM of New Zealand, 28 May 1948, IOR/L/WS/1/1163, IOR, BL.
73. Bevin Speech to the House of Commons, 26 January 1949, MS Attlee, dep. 77, Attlee Papers, Bodleian Library, Oxford.

7. MAPS, IDEAS, AND GEOPOLITICS

1. P-38, Minutes of Subcommittee on Political Problems, 19 December 1942, Records of the Advisory Committee on Post-War Foreign Policy, Harley A. Notter File, Box 54, RG 59, USNA. Future meetings of Welles's influential political subcommittee decided that "as a general principle the peoples of any Far Eastern country or territory should be liberated after the war, and such possessions should be placed under an international trusteeship to assist the peoples concerned to attain political maturity and to control the raw materials of the area in the interest of all peoples." See Hull to FDR, 12 March 1943, Records of the Advisory Committee on Post-War Foreign Policy, Harley A. Notter File, Box 54, RG 59, USNA.
2. Roger Louis has underscored the point about FDR's (perhaps willful) ignorance of State Department planning efforts.
3. See Melvyn Leffler, *A Preponderance of Power: National Security, the Truman Administration, and the Cold War* (Stanford: Stanford University

Press, 1993), 56–59; Mark Stoler, *Allies and Adversaries: The Joint Chiefs of Staff, the Grand Alliance, and U.S. Strategy in World War II* (Chapel Hill: University of North Carolina Press, 2000), 146–210.
4. See McCrea to Leahy, 28 December 1942, Map Room Files, Box 162, FDRL.
5. Minutes by Wilson Brown, 28th Meeting of Pacific War Council, 17 February 1943, Map Room Files, Box 168, FDRL.
6. Hepburn to Knox, GB 450, "Post-war Employment of International Police Force and Post-war Use of Air Bases," 20 March 1943, Map Room Files, Box 162, FDRL.
7. Roosevelt was clear that the United States did not covet bases in the Japanese Mandated Islands, urging instead that they (and other Pacific islands) be reserved as air bases for the new UN organization. See Minutes by Wilson Brown, 30th Meeting of Pacific War Council, 31 March 1943, Map Room Files, Box 168, FDRL.
8. See Knox to Roosevelt, 19 June 1943, Map Room Files, Box 162, FDRL. The chairman of the Navy Board, Admiral Arthur Hepburn, had argued—unsatisfactorily, in Roosevelt's judgment—that the recommendations were not tantamount to American neo-imperialism and were therefore defensible. See Hepburn to Knox, 6 April 1943, Map Room Files, Box 162, FDRL.
9. See Stoler, *Allies and Adversaries,* 159.
10. See Roosevelt to Knox, 30 June 1943. The study was conducted by Roosevelt confidante Admiral Richard Byrd, who would go on to achieve fame as an aerial surveyor of the South Pole. Byrd's April 1944 report was integrated with naval defense plans for the entirety of the Pacific and included surveys of some 130 islands. See Byrd to Roosevelt, 14 April 1944, Map Room Files, Box 162, FDRL.
11. See F. B. Royal and A. J. McFarland, "JCS 570, U.S. Requirements for Post-War Air Bases," and Roosevelt to Leahy, 23 November 1943, Map Room Files, Box 162, FDRL.
12. See Leahy to Roosevelt, "Policy Regarding Japanese Mandated Islands," 11 January 1944, and Roosevelt to Brown, 14 January 1944, Map Room Files, Box 167, FDRL. The notes of the 12 January War Council meeting to which Roosevelt referred is contained in Map Room Files, Box 168, FDRL.
13. See draft letter from Leahy to Roosevelt, 25 January 1944, RG 218, Box 19, USNA.
14. Reports from Stettinius's mission are contained in Departmental File State: Stettinius, Edward R., Jan.–Nov. 1944 Folder, PSF, Box 75, FDRL. Selected reports were reproduced in *FRUS,* 1944, vol. 1, *General.* See also Neil Smith, *American Empire: Roosevelt's Geographer and the Prelude to*

Globalization (Berkeley: University of California Press, 2003), 360–370; Roger Louis, *Imperialism at Bay: The United States and the Decolonization of the British Empire* (New York: Oxford University Press, 1978), 327–336.

15. See Memorandum by Stanley, 18 April 1944, CO 323/1877, UKNA; Memorandum by Kohler, 19 April 1944, *FRUS*, 1944, vol. 5, *The Near East, South Asia, and Africa, the Far East*, pp. 600–603.
16. Stettinius to Hull, 22 May 1944, *FRUS*, 1944, 2: 18, 20–22.
17. Stettinius to Hull, 22 May 1944, *FRUS*, 1944, 2: 20–22.
18. See Leahy to Roosevelt, 4 July 1944, and Roosevelt to Leahy, 10 July 1944, Map Room Files, Box 167, FDRL.
19. See Roger Louis, *Imperialism at Bay*, 436–440.
20. The final draft of the document is "International Aspects of Colonial Policy," 16 December 1944, W.P. (44) 738, CAB 66/59; Roger Louis, *Imperialism at Bay*, 392–397.
21. Pasvolsky to Stettinius, 25 January 1945, *FRUS*, 1945, *The Conferences at Malta and Yalta*, pp. 83–84.
22. Stimson to Stettinius, 23 January 1945, *FRUS*, 1945, vol. 1, *General: the United Nations*, pp. 23–25.
23. See JCS 973/4, "International Trusteeships," 9 January 1945, ABC 093 (7–28–44), RG 165, USNA, cited in Stoler, *Allies and Adversaries*, 208; Memorandum of Conversation between Pasvolsky and Willson, 25 January 1945, Pasvolsky Papers, Box 3, Library of Congress.
24. See *FRUS*, 1945, *The Conferences at Malta and Yalta*, p. 92; Roger Louis, *Imperialism at Bay*, 450.
25. *FRUS*, 1945, *The Conferences at Malta and Yalta*, p. 844.
26. Working Draft of the Protocol of Proceedings Revised by the Foreign Ministers, 11 February 1945, *FRUS*, 1945, *The Conferences at Malta and Yalta*, pp. 934–935.
27. Minutes, D-2, Meeting of February 8, 1945, Notter Files, Box 189, RG 59, USNA; Roger Louis, *Imperialism at Bay*, 475–482.
28. Memorandum by Taussig, 15 March 1945, *FRUS*, 1945, 1: 121–124; Roger Louis, *Imperialism at Bay*, 484–487.
29. *FRUS*, 1945, 1: 211–213.
30. For a treatment of this convoluted, apparent reversal of course, see Roger Louis, *Imperialism at Bay*, 490–496.
31. As Herbert Samuel recounted for Harry Hopkins, trusteeship was a bit of a sticking point for Anglo-American agreement at San Francisco. But on principle the British and American differences had been smoothed out. See Samuel to Hopkins, 4 May 1945, Hopkins Papers, Sherwood Collection, Box 338, FDRL.
32. See "An explanatory note on the draft chapter submitted by the United Kingdom delegation," UNCIO, *Documents*, 3: 618–619; Stanley to

Cranborne, 2 May 1945, FO 371/50808, UKNA; Roger Louis, *Imperialism at Bay*, 521–524.
33. See James N. Murray, Jr., *The United Nations Trusteeship System* (Urbana: University of Illinois Press, 1957), 35–36; and Charmian Toussaint, *The Trusteeship System of the United Nations* (New York: Praeger, 1956), 26.
34. See Toussaint, *The Trusteeship System of the United Nations*, 22.
35. See Cranborne to Stanley, 14 May 1945, FO 371/50809, UKNA; Roger Louis, *Imperialism at Bay*, 528–529.
36. Roger Louis, *Imperialism at Bay*, 33–36.
37. Attlee himself backed the idea of securing adequate representation for the British Commonwealth on the Security Council via nonpermanent rotating seats based on their geographical distribution. See B.C.M. (45) 6th Meeting, British Commonwealth Meeting, 9 April 1945, L/E/9/1527, IOR, BL.
38. World Organisation, W.P. (45) 205, 31 March 1945, IOR/L/E/9/1527, IOR, BL. As noted previously, the antipodean dominions continued to press for the idea of colonial powers voluntarily opting to place their territories under mandates, including in accordance with the new principle of trusteeship.
39. State-War-Navy Joint Memo to Truman, 13 April 1945, Truman Papers, WHCF, Confidential File, State Department Correspondence, 1945, Box 36, HSTL.
40. Cunningham to Hall, 4 December 1945, Box 1, File 1, Cunningham Papers, Middle East Centre Archive, Oxford University Library.
41. Memorandum by R. G. Howe, 25 May 1946, FO 371/52527, UKNA.
42. A good case in point is Stanley Hornbeck's subsequent appointment as ambassador to the Netherlands after his work on problems of dependent territories in the Far East in Foggy Bottom.
43. See Thomas Franck, *Recourse to Force: State Action against Threats and Armed Attacks* (Cambridge, UK: Cambridge University Press, 2002).
44. See Michael Glennon, "Why the Security Council Failed," *Foreign Affairs* 82, no. 3 (2003): 16–35.
45. See John Ruggie, "Contingencies, Constraints, and Collective Security: Perspectives on UN Involvement in International Disputes," *International Organization* 28, no. 3 (1974): 493–495.
46. See Alexander George, "Domestic Constraints on Regime Change in U.S. Foreign Policy: The Need for Policy Legitimacy," in G. John Ikenberry, ed., *American Foreign Policy: Theoretical Essays*, 4th edition (New York: Longman, 2002).
47. See Roger Louis, *Imperialism at Bay*, 20–23.
48. See Smith, *American Empire*, chapter 14.

49. See Arnold Offner, *Another Such Victory: President Truman and the Cold War, 1945–1953* (Stanford: Stanford University Press, 2002), 36–37. Alternatively it is perhaps also possible to interpret the Act as an assertion of regional influence to subject the unilateral U.S. right of intervention embodied in the Doctrine to collective Latin American consensus.
50. See Smith, *American Empire*, 405–409.
51. Smith, *American Empire*, 406.
52. See "Why It Is So Tough," *Time*, 4 June, 1945.
53. See, for example, Alan Henrikson, "Regionalism and the United Nations," in Louise Fawcett and Andrew Hurrell, eds., *Regionalism in World Politics: Regional Organization and International Order* (Oxford: Oxford University Press, 1995), especially 125–128.
54. The United Nations had of course yet to exist during the spring 1945 Anglo-French crisis in the Levant.
55. See Robert J. McMahon, *Colonialism and Cold War: The United States and the Struggle for Indonesian Independence, 1945–49* (Ithaca: Cornell University Press, 1981), 177–178; Peter Hahn, *Caught in the Middle East: U.S. Policy toward the Arab-Israeli Conflict, 1945–1961* (Chapel Hill: University of North Carolina Press, 2004), 52–53. As the conflict progressed, a debate ensued over the continuation of European Recovery Program funding to the Netherlands (McMahon, *Colonialism and Cold War*, 255–257).
56. American interest in civilian air transit was manifest in Roosevelt's later endorsement of the November 1944 International Civil Aviation Conference in Chicago. The State Department footed the bill for the Conference as an appropriation under "International Conferences (Emergency)" in the 1945 State Department Appropriation Act—perhaps the most incontrovertible piece of evidence that civil aviation constituted an arm of U.S. globalism. See the records of the 1944 International Civil Aviation Conference, Official File, Of5594, FDRL.
57. See Walter Boyne, *Beyond the Wild Blue: A History of the United States Air Force: 1947–2007* (New York: St. Martin's Press, 1997), 194–195; Stanley Ulanoff, *MATS: The Story of the Military Air Transport Service* (New York: Franklin Watts, 1964).
58. Anthony Smith, *The Pattern of Imperialism: The United States, Great Britain, and the Late-industrializing World since 1815* (Cambridge, UK: Cambridge University Press, 1981), 165.
59. See E. H. Carr, *Nationalism and After* (London: Macmillan, 1945), 45.
60. NSC 35, Memorandum for the President, Subject: Existing International Commitments Involving the Possible Use of Armed Force, 17 November 1948, Truman Papers, PSF, Subject File, 1940–1953, Box 169, HSTL.

61. See Smith, *The Pattern of Imperialism,* 183–184; Walter LaFeber, *The American Age: United States Foreign Policy at Home and Abroad since 1750* (New York: Norton, 1989), chapter 13; P. Eric Louw, *Roots of the Pax Americana: Decolonization, Development, Democratization and Trade* (Manchester, UK: Manchester University Press, 2010), 89–169.
62. See Leffler, *A Preponderance of Power,* 97–98.
63. Cordell Hull, *The Memoirs of Cordell Hull* (London: Macmillan, 1948), 2: 1599.
64. See Harriet Wanklyn, *Friedrich Ratzel: A Biographical Memoir and Bibliography* (Cambridge, UK: Cambridge University Press: 1961); Andreas Dorpalen, *The World of General Haushofer* (New York: Farrar & Rinehart, 1984). Haushofer adamantly denied active complicity in imparting his geopolitical ideas toward the development of Nazi ideology.
65. See Nicholas Spykman, *America's Strategy in World Politics: The United States and the Balance of Power* (New York: Harcourt, Brace and Company, 1942).
66. Spykman, *America's Strategy in World Politics,* 181.
67. Spykman, *America's Strategy in World Politics,* 165.
68. Spykman, *America's Strategy in World Politics,* 195.
69. Spykman, *America's Strategy in World Politics,* 197.
70. Spykman, *America's Strategy in World Politics,* 291.
71. Spykman, *America's Strategy in World Politics,* 413–417.
72. See William Langer and Geroid Robinson, "Problems and Objectives of United States Policy," 2 April 1945, ASW 336 Russia, RG 107, USNA, cited in Stoler, *Allies and Adversaries,* 234.
73. For discussions of the rise of geopolitics as a subdiscipline and the growth of geographical awareness in the American public consciousness during the war years, see Susan Schulten, *The Geographical Imagination in America, 1880–1950* (Chicago: University of Chicago Press, 2001), chapter 9; Smith, *American Empire,* chapter 10.
74. See Alan Henrikson, "The Map as an 'Idea': The Role of Cartographic Imagery During the Second World War," *Cartography and Geographic Information Science* 2, no. 1 (1975): 19–53; Jennifer Van Vleck, *Empire of the Air: Aviation and the American Ascendancy* (Cambridge, Mass.: Harvard University Press, 2013).
75. See Schulten, *The Geographical Imagination in America,* 204–212; Michael Hunt, *The American Ascendancy* (Chapel Hill: University of North Carolina Press, 2007), 119. Schulten notes that the president obtained his personal maps from the Society. See FDR to National Geographic Society, 24 December 1941, Grosvenor Papers, Part I, Box 170, Manuscript Division, Library of Congress.

8. JOINING THE COMMUNITY OF NATIONS

1. For a thorough analysis of the gradual codification of the ideas of sovereignty, the "nation-state," and self-determination, as well as notable omissions (such as the lack of references to self-determination rights in both the European and American human rights conventions), see Hurst Hannum, *Autonomy, Sovereignty, and Self-Determination: The Accommodation of Conflicting Rights* (Philadelphia: University of Pennsylvania Press, 1990), chapters 2–3.
2. See Guntram Henrik Herb, *Under the Map of Germany: Nationalism and Propaganda, 1918–1945* (New York: Routledge, 1997) for a discussion of how state cartography shaped ideas about "Greater Germany" and built ideological support for territorial expansionism in the Third Reich.
3. See Adolf Hitler, *Mein Kampf* (1935 edition), 1, cited in Alfred Cobban, *The Nation State and National Self-Determination* (New York: Thomas Crowell, 1969), 93–97.
4. A distinction is drawn here between American support for the UNSCOP majority proposal and the lack of aggressive American support at the Security Council on behalf of either side after the start of hostilities.
5. Explanatory Statement by Secretary of State Edward R. Stettinius Jr., "State Department Announcement of the Proposed Voting Procedures in the International Security Organization," *New York Times*, March 5, 1945.
6. Compare, for example, the divergence of views between Yoram Dinstein's chapter in defense of Israel's right to self determination, "Self-Determination and the Middle East Conflict," with Robert Friedlander's chapter challenging the existence of such a right, "Self-Determination: A Legal-Political Inquiry," both in Yonah Alexander and Robert A. Friedlander, eds., *Self-Determination: National, Regional, and Global Dimensions* (Boulder, Colo.: Westview Press, 1980).
7. See, for example, Hurst Hannum, "Self-Determination in the Post-Colonial Era," in Donald Clark and Robert Williamson, eds., *Self-Determination: International Perspectives* (New York: St. Martin's Press, 1997), 12–44.
8. The absence of more robust multilateral great power intervention in postcolonial conflicts like Palestine and Kashmir has been subjected to study, but few scholars have proposed systematic explanations. See, for example, the chapter entitled "Postimperial Wars," in A. Mark Weisburd, *Use of Force: The Practice of States since World War II* (University Park: Pennsylvania State University Press, 1997), 97–118.
9. On the international legal legitimacy of the practice of peacekeeping, see Thomas Franck, *Recourse to Force: State Action against Threats and*

Armed Attacks (Cambridge, UK: Cambridge University Press, 2002), 20–44.

10. The literature on the history of the idea of sovereignty is understandably vast. On the modern conception of sovereignty, see F. H. Hinsley, *Sovereignty* (New York: Basic Books, 1966); Hendrik Spruyt, *The Sovereign State and Its Competitors: An Analysis of Systems Change* (Princeton: Princeton University Press, 1994); Daniel Philpott, *Revolutions in Sovereignty: How Ideas Shaped Modern International Revolutions* (Princeton: Princeton University Press, 2001).

11. On the specific issue of the application of sovereignty to European colonial empires, see Lauren Benton, *A Search for Sovereignty: Law and Geography in European Empires, 1400–1900* (Cambridge, UK: Cambridge University Press, 2010); Hendrik Spruyt, *Ending Empire: Contested Sovereignty and Territorial Partition* (Ithaca: Cornell University Press, 2005); Jane Burbank and Frederick Cooper, *Empires in World History: Power and the Politics of Difference* (Princeton: Princeton University Press, 2010), especially chapters 11–14. For a radical treatment suspicious of the utility of the concept of sovereignty in the third world, see Mark E. Denham and Mark Owen Lombardi, eds., *Perspectives on Third World Sovereignty: The Postmodern Paradox* (Basingstoke, UK: Macmillan, 1996).

12. See Hans Kelsen, "Collective Security and Collective Self-Defense under the Charter of the United Nations," *American Journal of International Law* 42, no. 4 (1948): 783–796.

13. See Jean Bodin, *On Sovereignty: Four Chapters from the Six Books of the Commonwealth* (Cambridge, UK: Cambridge University Press, 1992).

14. Hugo Grotius, *The Law of War and Peace*, translated by Francis W. Kelsey (Oxford: Clarendon, 1925).

15. The Peace of Westphalia helped consolidate the system of territorial control by a series of German princes that had been nominally established at the 1555 Peace of Augsburg but that had proven insufficiently stable to guarantee religious freedoms across those principalities and degenerated into the religious wars and ultimately, the Thirty Years War.

16. Thomas Hobbes, *Leviathan: Or the Matter, Form and Power of a Commonwealth, Ecclesiastical and Civil* (London: Routledge, 1886), 84–89.

17. Hobbes, *Leviathan*, 82.

18. On Spinoza's notion of a covenant among peoples, see Aviel Roshwald, *The Endurance of Nationalism* (Cambridge, UK: Cambridge University Press, 2006), 167–174; David Novak, *The Election of Israel: The Idea of the Chosen People* (Cambridge, UK: Cambridge University Press, 1995),

32; Nancy Levene, *Spinoza's Revelation: Religion, Democracy, and Reason* (Cambridge, UK: Cambridge University Press, 2004), 219–221.

19. While seminal in its importance, Rousseau's theory of a social contract is probably of greater significance for the development of theories of democracy than for sovereign statehood in the international system.
20. See John Locke, *Two Treatises of Government* (Cambridge, UK: Cambridge University Press, 1988).
21. See Emmerich de Vattel, *The Law of Nations* (London: G. G and J. Robinson, 1797).
22. This is the primary constructivist premise of Philpott's *Revolutions in Sovereignty*.
23. Competing definitions of the state abound, but as one scholar put it, "there is at least a 'cluster' of characteristic ideas, institutions, and practices around which many commentators isolate their working definitions of the modern state." See Christopher Pierson, *The Modern State* (London: Routledge, 1994), 2.
24. See Stephen D. Krasner, *Sovereignty: Organized Hypocrisy* (Princeton: Princeton University Press, 1999).
25. See the chapter "Two Concepts of Liberty," in Isaiah Berlin's *Four Essays on Liberty* (London: Oxford University Press, 1969), 118–172.
26. On the history of the United Nations' legal order, as it evolved from the treaties of Westphalia (1648) and Utrecht (1713) through nineteenth-century power balances and the failed League of Nations to San Francisco, see Clive Archer, *International Organizations* (New York: Routledge, 2001); Margaret P. Karns and Karen A. Mingst, *International Organizations: The Politics and Processes of Global Governance* (Boulder, Colo.: Lynne Rienner, 2004), chapters 3–5.
27. For basic overviews of the UN international legal order as established by the Charter, see Ruth Russell's massive study *A History of the United Nations Charter: The Role of the United States: 1940–1945* (Washington, DC: Brookings Institution, 1958); Oscar Schachter and Christopher Joyner, eds., *United Nations Legal Order* (Cambridge, UK: Cambridge University Press, 1995); Thomas Weiss, David Forsythe, and Roger Coate, *The United Nations and Changing World Politics* (Boulder, Colo.: Westview Press, 2009).
28. See, for example, Anthony Anghie, *Imperialism, Sovereignty, and the Making of International Law* (New York: Cambridge University Press, 2005).
29. See Elie Kedourie, *Nationalism* (Oxford: Blackwell, 1993).
30. On the development of the international legal theory and practice of self-determination from the French Revolution up through the ideas of

Vladimir Lenin and Woodrow Wilson to codification in the UN Charter, see Antonio Cassesse, *Self-Determination of Peoples* (Cambridge, UK: Cambridge University Press, 2005), 1–66; Cobban, *The Nation State and National Self-Determination*, 39–93; A. Rigo Sureda, *The Evolution of Self-Determination* (Leiden: A. W. Sijthoff, 1973), 352–356. As Cobban put it, "The revolutionary theory that a people had the right to form its own constitution and choose its own government for itself easily passed into the claim that it had a right to decide whether to attach itself to one state or another, or constitute an independent state by itself" (41).

31. See Ilya Levkov, "Self-Determination in Soviet Politics," in Alexander and Friedlander, *Self-Determination*, 137–139.
32. See chapter 8, "Self-Determination," in Christopher O. Quaye, *Liberation Struggles in International Law* (Philadelphia: Temple University Press, 1990), 212–242.
33. See Robert H. Jackson, *Quasi-States: Sovereignty, International Relations, and the Third World* (Cambridge, UK: Cambridge University Press, 1990), 87–88.
34. See William Roger Louis, "American Anti-Colonialism and the Dissolution of the British Empire," *International Affairs* 61, no. 3 (1985): 399–400.
35. The 16 October 1975 verdict by the Court acknowledged the right of Western Sahara's indigenous Sahrawi people to self-determination. Importantly this interpretation identified self-determination rights as international legal protections afforded to populations and not states. See 1975 *I.C.J.* 12, 31.
36. This was at least William Roger Louis's interpretation. See *Imperialism at Bay: The United States and the Decolonization of the British Empire* (New York: Oxford University Press, 1978), 463–496.
37. See Ian Brownlie, *Principles of Public International Law* (Oxford: Clarendon Press, 1979), 594.
38. *Documents of the UN Conference on International Organization*, vol. 10VII, p. 143, See the useful discussion of competing interpretations of the right of self-determination debated at San Francisco in 1945 in Helen Qane, "The United Nations and the Evolving Right to Self-Determination," *International and Comparative Law Quarterly* 47, no. 3 (1998): 537–572, especially 541–544. Qane concludes, "The *traveaux préparatoires* seem to confirm the interpretation of self-determination arrived at on the basis of the ordinary meaning of the term, construed in context and in the light of the Charter's object and purpose. The term 'peoples' can refer to States, in which case self-determination means sovereign equality. To the extent that self-determination refers to sovereign equality it is possible to speak of a legal right to self-determination in

the Charter. The term 'peoples' can also refer to the inhabitants of NSGTs [non-self-governing territories] and Trust Territories. In this context, self-determination refers to the right of self-government or independence. The Charter envisages the progressive development of the territories until self-government or independence is attained. This indicates that in 1945 there was no immediate legal right to self-determination for the inhabitants of these territories" (544).

39. One broad, useful overview is Walter C. Opello, Jr., and Stephen J. Rosow, *Nation-States and Global Order: A Historical Introduction to Contemporary Politics* (Boulder, Colo.: Lynne Rienner, 2004).

40. These include Hans Kohn's dichotomy between Western and Eastern nationalisms, Carlton Hayes's six ideological strands of nationalism, and other typologies. See Anthony Smith, *Theories of Nationalism* (New York: Holmes and Meier, 1983), 192–199.

41. See, for example, Hinsley, *Sovereignty*, 45–158; Hannum, *Autonomy, Sovereignty, and Self-Determination*, 23–245.

42. In *Imagined Communities*, Anderson described the predicament of the nation-state as continually looking back to history but also forward, into the future. In the specific context of postcolonial nationalism, Partha Chatterjee accounted for the contradiction by distinguishing between the "spiritual" realm of colonial life in which religion and language provided historical bases of national identity, and British ideas about modernity and development that shaped the "material" realm of technological progress and democratic politics. See Chatterjee, *The Nation and Its Fragments* (Princeton: Princeton University Press, 1993).

43. See John Breuilly, *Nationalism and the State* (New York: St. Martin's Press, 1982).

44. See Hannum's differentiation between nationalism and statism in *Autonomy, Sovereignty, and Self-Determination*, 23–25. From the standpoint of this study, statism has been treated as a class of nationalism preoccupied with the establishment of sovereign, territorial nation-states.

45. For a discussion of the idea of a blend of religious and liturgical messianism coexistent with the imperatives of modern nation-building inherent in the Zionist movement as it developed from the nineteenth century, see Roshwald, *The Endurance of Nationalism*, 60–62.

46. David Ben-Gurion, *Rebirth and Destiny of Israel* (New York: Philosophical Library, 1954), 137.

47. These competing ideologies are the subject of Noam Pianko's *Zionism and the Roads Not Taken: Rawidowicz, Kaplan, Kohn* (Bloomington: Indian University Press, 2010).

48. On Kohn's dichotomy, see his *The Idea of Nationalism: A Study in Its Origins and Background* (New Brunswick, N.J.: Transaction, 2008). Kohn, like Martin Buber and other cultural Zionists, believed that the contemporary Zionist movement should concern itself not with statist nationalism of the sort Ben-Gurion espoused but with the internal renewal of the Jewish people. The cultural Zionists accordingly supported the idea of the creation of a binational state in Palestine. See Ken Wolf, "Hans Kohn's Liberal Nationalism," *Journal of the History of Ideas* 37, no. 4 (1976): 651–672, especially 652–656. Wolf argues that, "like Buber, Kohn feared that other Zionists were more devoted to the Jewish state than to the interior renewal of Judaism that he and Buber sought." As Buber himself framed the essence of the matter, "We should never consider the nation an end in itself" (653).
49. In this regard Kohn's messianic aspirations for nationalism tracked nicely with the idea of American "manifest destiny." See Wolf, "Hans Kohn's Liberal Nationalism," 655–656.
50. See Hannah Arendt, *The Jew as Pariah: Jewish Identity and Politics in the Modern Age* (New York: Grove Press, 1978). The racial basis of Zionism has since been complicated by the admission of Ethiopian Falashas into Israel on the grounds of their membership in the religious community. See Juan R. I. Cole and Deniz Kandiyoti, "Nationalism and the Colonial Legacy in the Middle East and Central Asia: Introduction," in "Nationalism and the Middle East and Central Asia," special issue of *International Journal of Middle East Studies* 34, no. 2 (2002): 189–203.
51. See Hannah Arendt, "Zionism Reconsidered, *Menorah Journal*, 33 (August 1945): 162–196; Steven Aschheim, "Between New York and Jerusalem," *Jewish Review of Books,* no. 4 (Winter 2011), accessible at http://www.jewishreviewofbooks.com/publications/detail/between-new-york-and-jerusalem.
52. Religious identity and the reality of communalism colored many variants of nationalism extant in pre-independence India. See C. A. Bayly, *Origins of Nationality in South Asia: Patriotism and Ethical Government in the Making of Modern India* (Delhi: Oxford University Press: 1998).
53. See Peter Hardy, *The Muslims of British India* (Cambridge, UK: Cambridge University Press, 1972), 190–197.
54. See Hardy, *The Muslims of British India*, chapter 3. For the two most comprehensive studies of the movement, see M. Naeem Qureishi, *Pan-Islam in British Indian Politics: A Study of the Khilafat Movement, 1918–1924* (Leiden: Brill, 1999); and Gail Minault, *The Khilafat Movement* (New York: Columbia University Press, 1982). As Ayesha Jalal has argued,

membership in the Islamic ummah "was never a barrier to Muslims identifying with patriotic sentiments in their own homelands." See Jalal, "Striking a Just Balance: Maulana Azad as a Theorist of Transnational *Jihad*," *Modern Intellectual History* 4, no. 1 (2007): 95. Jalal argues, "Any new history of political ideas must surely distinguish this discourse on Hindu-Muslim unity from the discourse on secularism. Azad was a key thinker and one of the most sophisticated to represent the former strand in anti-colonial thought that has been neglected by historians imbued with the dogma of statist secularism" (106).

55. The pamphlet was provocatively titled "Now or Never: Are We to Live or Perish for Ever?" See K. K. Aziz, ed., *Complete Works of Rahmat Ali* (Islamabad: National Commission on Historical and Cultural Research, 1978), 1: 4, quoted in Stanley Wolpert, *Jinnah of Pakistan* (New York: Oxford University Press, 1984), 131.

56. See L. Carl Brown, *Religion and State: The Muslim Approach to Politics* (New York: Columbia University Press, 2000), 115–116; Minault, *The Khilafat Movement,* 7–11. On the significance of the abolition of the caliphate and the emergence of the first secular nation-state in the Islamic world as a political anomaly, see Antony Black, *The History of Islamic Political Thought* (New York: Routledge, 2001), 311–319.

57. Jamiluddin Ashraf, ed., *Some Recent Speeches and Writings of Mr. Jinnah,* 2 vols. (Lahore: Ashraf, 1952), 1: 348.

58. Interview with the Associated Press of India on British Policy, Bombay, 2 January 1942, Khurshid Yusufi, ed., *Speeches, Statements and Messages of the Quaid-e-Azam* (Lahore: Bazm-i-Iqbal, 1996), 1508.

59. See, for example, the chapter "The Two Partitions: Of British India and of the Muslim Community," in Hardy, *The Muslims of British India,* 231–239. As Congress Party leader Maulana Abul Kalam Azad recalled during the All-India Congress Committee's consideration of the partition resolution on 14 June 1947, "Partition was a tragedy for India and the only thing that could be said in its favour was that we had done our best to avoid division but we had failed. Now there was no alternative and if we wanted freedom here and now, we must submit to the demand for dividing India." See Azad, *India Wins Freedom* (London: Sangam Books, 1988), 214.

60. According to the notes of the meeting, "[Nehru] then spoke of the fact that there was in this whole matter a very profound ideological issue. Pakistan wished to create a religious state and wished Kashmir to be a part of their nation because the inhabitants were largely Moslems. This he thought struck at the very basis of stability in the Indian sub-continent." Memorandum of Conversation between President Truman, Secretary

Acheson, and Prime Minister Nehru, 13 October 1949, Truman Papers, PSF, Subject File, 1940–1953, Box 157, HSTL.

61. The espousal of particularistic nationalisms grounded in language, religion, or other sources of identity was a significant development in the postcaliphate history of state formation in the Islamic world. As the last Islamic empire receded, the postcolonial territories it vacated sprouted a wide variety of local nationalisms: Anatolian Turkish nationalism, distinct Syrian and Lebanese nationalisms, and others. As scholars like Ayesha Jalal have noted, while this did not preclude nationalists like Azad from appropriating the rhetoric of religious duties like jihad, it represented a fundamental departure from the idea that Islamist governments would have to assume the authority vacated by colonial retreat. That wave of Islamist sentiment did of course arrive in the 1970s, after the failure of both Arab nationalism and pan-Arabism to destroy what they perceived as their Zionist enemy—but not in the immediate aftermath of either world war. See Brown, *Religion and the State,* 119–120; Black, *The History of Islamic Political Thought,* 345; Jalal, "Striking a Just Balance," 96–97.

9. FROM IMAGINED TO REAL BORDERS

1. The extent to which leaders like Jinnah and Ben-Gurion held to precise territorial aims is unclear. Though Jinnah artfully dodged British efforts to define the geographical scope of Pakistan, the widely held view was that he (like other Muslim League supporters) had in mind the six Muslim-majority provinces of British India. Ben-Gurion, Weizmann, and their fellow Zionists based their claim to Palestine on detailed geographic surveys. See Howard Sachar, *A History of Israel* (New York: Knopf, 2007), 116–117.
2. See, for example, "Review of the World Situation as It Relates to the Security of the United States," CIA 1–49, 19 January 1949, President's Secretary's File, Truman Papers, HSTL.
3. Quoted in Peter Hardy, *The Muslims of British India* (Cambridge, UK: Cambridge University Press, 1972), 247.
4. Contrast, for example, the American and British assessments of Pakistan's high strategic importance discussed in Chapter 3, which based that identical conclusion in completely different rationales. See, for example, CIA Report on India-Pakistan, 16 September 1948, President's Secretary's Files, HSTL. Compare with the British assessment in "The Strategic and Political Importance of Pakistan in the event of War with USSR," A. G. S. Davy, 19 May 1948, DO 142/353, UKNA.

5. See Robert Sherwood, *Roosevelt and Hopkins: An Intimate History* (New York: Harper Brothers, 1948), 871–872; Neil Smith, *American Empire: Roosevelt's Geographer and the Prelude to Globalization* (Berkeley: University of California Press, 2003), 299–307.
6. See, for instance, A. P. Thornton, *The Imperial Idea and Its Enemies* (New York: St. Martin's Press, 1959); Miles Kahler, *Decolonization in Britain and France* (Princeton: Princeton University Press, 1984); Robert F. Holland, *European Decolonization 1918–1991: An Introductory Survey* (London: Macmillan, 1985); Lawrence James, *The Rise and Fall of the British Empire* (New York: St. Martin's Press, 1994), 525–534. Piers Brendon argues in *The Decline and Fall of the British Empire: 1781–1997* (New York: Knopf, 2008), xvii–xx that a Gibbonian, macrohistorical view of the imperial life cycle reveals that the very liberal nature of the British constitutional monarchy contained the seeds of its own decline.
7. See Ronald Hyam, *Britain's Declining Empire: The Road to Decolonisation, 1918–1968* (Cambridge, UK: Cambridge University Press, 2006); Peter Clarke, *The Last Thousand Days of the British Empire* (London: Bloomsbury Press, 2008).
8. See Ronald Robinson and John Gallagher, "The Imperialism of Free Trade," *Economic History Review* 6, no. 1 (1953): 1–15; Ronald Robinson and John Gallagher with Alice Denny, *Africa and the Victorians: The Official Mind of Imperialism* (London: Macmillan, 1961). As Roger Louis put it, "Robinson and Gallagher overturned the traditional historiographical assumptions that European expansion originated wholly within Europe; from the time of their work onwards, the history of British imperialism would be the history of the interaction between the British and indigenous peoples." See Roger Louis, *Ends of British Imperialism* (London: I. B. Tauris, 2006), 995–996.
9. On British economic decline as a cause of decolonization, see Peter Clarke and Clive Trebilcock, eds., *Understanding Decline: Perceptions and Realities of British Economic Performance* (Cambridge, UK: Cambridge University Press, 1997); Brian Lapping, *End of Empire* (New York: St. Martin's Press, 1985).

    Weizmann certainly believed that domestic pressures could cause Great Britain to withdraw from Palestine. See Weizmann to Epstein, 21 February 1947, *The Letters and Papers of Chaim Weizmann* (New Brunswick, N.J.: Transaction Books, 1979), vol. 2, 249.
10. On the political changes in the international system as a factor accelerating British imperial retreat, see William Roger Louis, *Imperialism at Bay: The United States and the Decolonization of the British Empire* (New York: Oxford University Press, 1978); Paul Kennedy, *The Rise and Fall of the Great Powers* (New York: Random House, 1988).

11. Elizabeth Monroe's *Britain's Moment in the Middle East* (Baltimore: Johns Hopkins University Press, 1981) and Peter Hardy's *The Muslims of British India* are two works that employ this basic line of argument.
12. Political geographies of the British Empire readily recognized this reality and the importance of the Near East for the Home Islands and India. See C. B. Fawcett, *A Political Geography of the British Empire*, (Westport, Conn.: Greenwood Press, 1970), 272–273.
13. Hyam notes this point in his recent study of decolonization. See the section titled "Geopolitics" in Hyam, *Britain's Declining Empire*, 73–83.
14. One might argue that the profound pragmatism of regionalism and Labour's associated policy of beating an orderly retreat from the Middle East and South Asia were perfectly concomitant with the transition to what Robinson and Gallagher termed "informal empire." It was what John Darwin called "the Price of Survival" in the postwar world that Britain (unlike France and the Netherlands) willingly recognized. See Darwin, *The Empire Project* (Cambridge: Cambridge University Press, 2009).
15. Frank Heinlein's *British Government Policy and Decolonisation: Scrutinising the Official Mind* (London: Frank Cass, 2002). and Darwin's *The Empire Project* are both pertinent examples of recent works in this vein.
16. See Statement by Truman, 25 March 1948, *Department of State Bulletin* 18, no. 457 (1948): 451.
17. See Annex II, Long Term Policy for Palestine, Copy of a letter dated 18 August from the Colonial Office to General Ismay, 18 August 1945, C.O.S. (45), 539 (0), CAB 80/100.
18. Innis Claude, among others, has argued that despite the evolution from the League of Nations to the Security Council, an effective system for organizing collective security still has yet to materialize. See Claude, *Swords into Plowshares: The Problems and Process of International Organization* (New York: Random House, 1984), chapters 1–4.
19. "The Right of Veto," Note by the Foreign Office, Cabinet, Steering Committee on International Organisation, 13 October 1946, I.O.C. (46) 85, PREM 8/377, UKNA.
20. Carter to Grafftey-Smith, 25 March 1948, Box 1, File 1, Grafftey-Smith Papers, Middle East Centre Archive, Oxford University Library.
21. This idea evolved as a brainchild of Truman's new secretary of state Dean Acheson, who conveyed to Loy Henderson that should the UNCIP negotiations over the implementation of the truce agreement fail, the State Department believed that the matter should be referred to international arbitration. See Acheson to Henderson, 18 June 1949, *FRUS*, 1949, vol. 6, *The Near East, South Asia, and Africa*, pp. 1721–1722. Kennan was perhaps the most vocal opponent of employing the Security Council to

resolve international disputes, because of the Soviet Union's participation as a permanent member.

22. See Memorandum of Conversation by Lovett, 4 January 1949, *FRUS, 1949*, 6: 1686.
23. The difficulties of this dilemma are captured in Miles Kahler, "The United States and the Third World: Decolonization and After," in L. Carl Brown, ed., *Centerstage: American Diplomacy since World War II* (New York: Homes and Meier, 1990), 104–120.
24. See Note of the Meeting at the State Department by Cockram, 16 February 1948, FO 371/69711, UKNA. Despite the maharaja's accession, the imperatives of regionalism were clear in Philip Noel-Baker's comments at the meeting: "Mr. Noel-Baker had repeatedly drawn the attention of the [UN Security] Council to the fact that the question before it was not whether Kashmir should go to India or to Pakistan, or the interests of the two dominions in Kashmir, but to remove those conditions in Kashmir which had led to a breach of the peace and a threat of war between India and Pakistan by a free expression of the wishes of the Kashmiris themselves as to their own future."
25. The expression derives from Edward Luttwak's article "Give War a Chance," *Foreign Affairs* 78, no. 4 (1999): 36–44.
26. Robert Jackson holds that the decolonized states of Asia, Africa, and the Middle East, by virtue of the realities of power politics, have emerged as "quasi-states" with insufficient capacity for effective governance, and whose sovereignty is far from absolute by the standards of developed states. See Jackson, *Quasi-States: Sovereignty, International Relations, and the Third World* (Cambridge, UK: Cambridge University Press, 1990).
27. See Marrack Goulding, "The Evolution of United Nations Peacekeeping," *International Affairs* 69, no. 3 (1993): 452. On the development of UN peacekeeping operations, see N. D. White, *Keeping the Peace: The United Nations and the Maintenance of International Peace and Security* (Manchester, UK: Manchester University Press, 1997), 207–223; Norrie MacQueen, *Peacekeeping and the International System* (Abingdon, UK: Routledge, 2006), 43–78. On negative peace, see Jeffrey Kimball, "Alternatives to War in History," *OAH Magazine of History* 8, no. 3 (1994): 5.
28. For a discussion of the operational dimensions of early peacekeeping missions, see John Hillen, *The Blue Helmets: The Strategy of UN Military Operations* (London: Brassey's, 2000), 79–81. The strategy and policy of early observer missions like UNTSO in Palestine and UNMOGIP in Kashmir are covered in Neil Briscoe, *Britain and UN Peacekeeping, 1948–67* (London: Palgrave, 2004), 11–37.

29. See Christine Gray, *International Law and the Use of Force* (New York: Oxford University Press, 2008), 202.
30. See Oliver Richmond, "UN Peace Operations and the Dilemmas of the Peacebuilding Consensus," in Alex Bellamy and Paul Williams, eds., *Peace Operations and Global Order* (London: Routledge, 2005), 85–86.
31. Sadly the disciplinary divide between the historiography of European decolonization and the theoretical literature on peacekeeping has prevented more systematic studies. One exception is Kimberly Zisk Marten, *Enforcing the Peace: Learning from the Imperial Past* (New York: Columbia University Press, 2004). But Marten's brief study fails to draw credible generalizations across contemporary peacekeeping and imperial policing or explore the relevant historical examples with adequate depth.
32. See, for example, Richard Caplan, "A New Trusteeship? *The International Administration of War-torn Territories*," Adelphi Paper no. 341, Oxford University Press (2002), 84; Roland Paris, "Peacebuilding and the Limits of Liberal Internationalism," *International Security* 22, no. 2 (1997): 54–89.
33. Gray, *International Law and the Use of Force*, 201–204.
34. Paul Diehl, "Peacekeeping Operations and the Quest for Peace," *Political Science Quarterly* 103, no. 3 (1988): 486.
35. See, for example, Briscoe, *Britain and UN Peacekeeping*, 16–37; White, *Keeping the Peace*, 210–211; William J. Durch, *The Evolution of UN Peacekeeping: Case Studies and Comparative Analysis* (London: Palgrave 1993), 1. Briscoe does point out that despite "the Cold War's adverse impact on the United Nations' relevance in the security field," some early operations were able to go forward in former British-held territories like Palestine and Kashmir. He attributes these successes to the limits on participation in such missions, which extended only to Western troop-contributing countries, which in turn "helped safeguard British interests" (37).
36. See, for instance, Stephen John Stedman, "Spoiler Problems in Peace Processes," *International Security* 22, no. 2 (1997): 5–53; William Zartman, *Ripe for Resolution: Conflict and Intervention in Africa* (Oxford: Oxford University Press, 1985).
37. Hillen's *Blue Helmets*, Briscoe's *Britain and UN Peacekeeping*, and Evan Luard's *A History of the United Nations*, Vol. 1: *The Years of Western Domination, 1945–1955* (New York: St. Martin's Press, 1982) more or less all employ this line of reasoning.

Thomas Franck has argued that myriad separate developments made it impossible to apply the UN Charter to the letter of the law, namely, the cold war, the rise of proxy civil wars, new weapons systems that helped anticipatory self-defense become a reality, and concern for international justice that accompanied decolonization. Franck's wide-ranging analysis, subsuming technological and ideational motivations, is useful in framing the debate more broadly than through the narrower lenses of exclusively legalistic or political explanations. But he fails to follow through and explore them; the *sources* of these factors remain completely unexplored in *Recourse to Force: State Action against Threats and Armed Attacks* (Cambridge, UK: Cambridge University Press, 2002), which is narrow in its focus as purely an international legal analysis of UN Charter law on the use of force.

A. Mark Weisburd's *Use of Force: The Practice of States since World War II* (University Park: Pennsylvania State University Press, 1997) proposes meaningful analytic categories for various postwar conflicts, including the "postimperial wars" immediately after the Second World War. But like Franck's study, given the focus on the legal rules circumscribing the use of force, the utility of Weisburd's comparative case studies for inferring a fuller set of impediments besetting the Charter's collective security system is limited. Although Weisburd muses about the reasons why the Security Council did not find threats to or breaches of the peace during violent conflicts like the struggle for Indonesian independence, he proffers little in the way of explanation as to why.

38. Bruce Mazlish, one of the early proponents of what has been called "new global history," along with Akira Iriye and others has noted the dearth of scholarship on the development of UN military forces. See Mazlish, "Looking at History in the Light of Globalization," *Yale Global*, 3 January 2003.

39. One of the earliest treatments of the subject was Marshall Singer's *Weak States in a World of Powers: The Dynamics of International Relationships* (New York: Free Press, 1972). A later work examining state-society relations in so-called weak states was Joel Migdal's *Strong Societies and Weak States: State-Society Relations and State Capabilities in the Third World* (Princeton: Princeton University Press, 1988). The proliferation of newly independent states in the post–cold war era facing existential internal security challenges is addressed in Barry Buzan's *People, States and Fear: An Agenda for International Security Studies in the Post–Cold War Era* (Hemel Hempstead, UK: Wheatsheaf, 1991).

40. See, for example, James D. Fearon and David Laitin, "Ethnicity, Insurgency, and Civil War," *American Political Science Review* 97, no. 1 (2003): 75–90. Fearon and Laitin maintain that the Second World War "greatly weakened the main imperial states materially, and the new international legal order (the U.N. system) gave support to anticolonial movements" (87).

41. See, for example, Richard H. Shultz Jr. and William J. Olson, *Ethnic and Religious Conflict: Emerging Threat to US Security* (Washington, DC: National Strategy Information Center, 1994), chapter 2. It is worth noting that scholars like Mahmood Mamdani have argued that, on the contrary, the United States utilized revolutionary insurgency as a cold war tactic to degrade Soviet influence in Africa, Central America, and Southwest Asia. See Mamdani, *Good Muslim, Bad Muslim: America, the Cold War, and the Roots of Terror* (New York: Pantheon, 2004). But the conservative regimes supported by the United States and the communist dictatorships that imposed the Politburo's will vastly outnumbered the states that succumbed to civil wars fueled by cold war superpower patronage.
42. Recent scholarship on what theorists term weak states has attributed their origins to decolonization and the lack of adequate national civilian and military capacity for state administration at the moment of independence, especially in the case of newly decolonized states that emerged since 1945. One sociologist has argued that this lack of capacity doomed many such states to continual civil war. See Ann Hironaka, *Neverending Wars: The International Community, Weak States, and the Perpetuation of Civil War* (Cambridge, Mass.: Harvard University Press, 2008).
43. See J. Samuel Barkin and Bruce Cronin, "The State and the Nation: Changing Norms and the Rules of Sovereignty in International Relations," *International Organization* 48, no 1 (1994): 119–130, especially 122–125. Barkin and Cronin argue that the tension between state sovereignty and national sovereignty has existed throughout history and that the opposing interpretations have alternately risen to prominence as differing manifestations of intersubjective consensus in different epochs.
44. There were, of course, all manner of appeals for the creation of a Jewish state pouring forth from Europe during and after the war. For a sampling of the resolutions passed by Zionist organizations worldwide, see the file titled "Jewish nationalist activities," FO 371/45404, documents 29/6038, 7416, and 7243, UKNA.
45. See, for example, David Newman and Falah Gazi, "Bridging the Gap: Palestinian and Israeli Discourses on Autonomy and Statehood," *Transactions of the Institute of British Geographers* 22, no. 1 (1997): 111–129. Newman and Gazi have described the process of how territorial changes, even when the product of self-determination struggles, have impinged on the self-determination of the inhabitants of the new territories created: "Territorial changes have frequently been justified on the basis of self-determination. Resulting processes of state building often take place at the expense of the national identity and self-determination of groups residing within the territory of the state. This may involve the subordination of

ethnic and other special-interest groups to fit the ideals of the dominant group. At best, autonomy may be granted to national groups residing within the state and constituting a demographic majority within a given territory or region of the state" (112).
46. See Holland, *European Decolonization,* 93.
47. See Joel Migdal, *Strong Societies and Weak States* (Princeton: Princeton University Press, 1988), 279–286.
48. See Mohammed Ayoob, *The Third World Security Predicament: State-Making, Regional Conflict, and the International System* (Boulder, Colo.: Lynne Rienner, 1995).
49. See Jackson, *Quasi-States,* 2. According to Jackson, "The ex-colonial states have been internationally enfranchised and possess the same external rights and responsibilities as all other sovereign states: juridical statehood. At the same time, however, many have not yet been authorized and empowered domestically and consequently lack the institutional features of sovereign states as also defined by classical international law. They disclose limited empirical statehood: their populations do not enjoy many of the advantages traditionally associated with independent statehood. Their governments are often deficient in the political will, institutional authority, and organized power to protect human rights or provide socio-economic welfare. The concrete benefits which have historically justified the undeniable burdens of sovereign statehood are often limited to fairly narrow elites and not yet extended to the citizenry at large whose lives may be scarcely improved by independence or even adversely affected by it. These states are primarily juridical. They are still far from complete, so to speak, and empirical statehood in large measure still remains to be built. I therefore refer to them as 'quasi-states'" (21).

One could argue that Jackson's conception of quasi-states serve to accurately describe postcolonial Pakistan, Indonesia, Syria, Lebanon and Palestine, and Israel.

CONCLUSION

1. On the dynamics of the debate between the defenders of the Monroe Doctrine and hemispheric hegemony and the "universalism" of the United Nations, see Gaddis Smith, *The Last Years of the Monroe Doctrine: 1945–1993* (New York: Hill and Wang, 1994), 46–50.
2. John Gallagher, *The Decline, Revival, and Fall of the British Empire: The Ford Lectures and Other Essays* (Cambridge, UK: Cambridge University Press, 1982), 73.

3. Contrast, for example, Piers Brendon's argument about how the seeds of British imperial demise were rooted in the era of the American Revolution in *The Decline and Fall of the British Empire, 1781–1997* (New York: Vintage, 2007) with the competing claims of the school of imperial history (and adherents like A. P. Thornton) holding that British domestic politics and economic factors hastened the loss of empire under Labour.
4. See Niall Ferguson, *Empire: The Rise and Demise of the British World Order and the Lessons for Global Power* (New York: Basic Books, 2002), 298–301.
5. The roots of American anticolonialism are well documented. Roosevelt himself harbored deep antipathy against European colonialism. Another administration official sharing that sentiment was Undersecretary of State Sumner Welles, a proponent of supporting anticolonial nationalism to pressure America's European allies in the postwar period. See Christopher O'Sullivan, *Sumner Welles, Postwar Planning, and the Quest for a New World Order, 1937–1943* (New York: Columbia University Press, 2003), chapter 6.
6. Consider, for example, Janice Thompson's discussion of the distinct "external" and "internal" meanings of sovereignty. Thompson holds that "interstate relations (or state practices) play as significant a role in constituting the sovereign state as do the relations between individual states and their societies." See Thompson, "State Sovereignty in International Relations: Bridging the Gap between Theory and Empirical Research," *International Studies Quarterly* 39, no. 2 (1995): 213–233, quote on 214. *Self-determination*, of course, was an equally ambiguous term that similarly fell victim to such competing interpretations: the British interpretation of self-determination did not include independence for colonial territories, as compared to the American ideal of universal self-determination, to which President Roosevelt unflinchingly subscribed. See Robert H. Jackson, *Quasi-States: Sovereignty, International Relations, and the Third World* (Cambridge, UK: Cambridge University Press, 1990), 87–88.
7. This may have been because of the difficulties that beset the state-building process in the postcolonial states that emerged out of the Ottoman and Mughal empires. As historian William McNeill explained, "The trappings of modern statehood were a sort of borrowed finery, fitting awkwardly upon the ancient Islamic body politic and in most states commanding a loyalty flawed by profound nostalgia for an irrecoverable past." See McNeill, *The Rise of the West* (Chicago: University of Chicago Press, 1963), 773.
8. Kennedy's widely cited argument that powers expand and eventually subject themselves to imperial or "strategical" overstretch was first put

forth in 1987. See Paul Kennedy, *The Rise and Fall of the Great Powers* (New York: Random House, 1988), 48.

9. Robert Gilpin suggested the idea of differential rates of relative growth determining the rise and fall of competing powers in his classic *War and Change in World Politics* (Cambridge, UK: Cambridge University Press, 1981).

Archives Consulted

ARCHIVAL SOURCES

United Kingdom

Royal Geographical Society, London
    Map Collection
U.K. National Archives, Kew, Richmond
    Cabinet Papers
    Colonial Office Records
    Dominions Office Records
    Foreign Office Records
    Prime Minister's Office: Operational Correspondence and Papers (1937–1946)
    War Office Records

United States of America

Franklin D. Roosevelt Presidential Library, Hyde Park, New York
    Franklin Roosevelt Papers
    Map Room File
    President's Secretary's Files
    Sumner Welles Papers
        Records of the Advisory Committee for Post-war Foreign Policy
Harry S. Truman Presidential Library, Independence, Missouri
    Clark Clifford Papers
    David Niles Papers

Harry Truman Papers
President's Secretary's Files
White House Central Files
Official File
Confidential File
Henry F. Grady Papers
U.S. National Archives II, College Park, Maryland
Department of State Records
Combined Chiefs of Staff Records
Joint Chiefs of Staff Records
National Security Council Records

MANUSCRIPT COLLECTIONS

British Library, London
Department of Manuscripts
Olaf Caroe Papers
Louis Mountbatten Papers
India Office Records
War Staff
Liddell Hart Centre for Military Archives, King's College London
Alan Brooke Papers
Hastings Ismay Papers
Liddell Hart Papers
Oxford University Library, Oxford
The Bodleian Libraries
Clement Attlee Papers
Middle East Centre Archive, St. Antony's College, Oxford
Alan Cunningham Papers
Laurence Grafftey-Smith Papers
Milton Eisenhower Library, Johns Hopkins University, Baltimore
Isaiah Bowman Papers
Library of Congress, Washington, D.C.
Cordell Hull Papers
Gilbert Grosvenor Papers
Leo Pasvolsky Papers
Maps Division

ONLINE COLLECTIONS

Louis Mountbatten Papers Database, University of Southampton Library
Official Document System, United Nations

PUBLISHED DOCUMENT COLLECTIONS

Department of State Bulletin
Foreign Relations of the United States
The Letters and Papers of Chaim Weizmann, vol. 10XI, series A, *January 1943–May 1945.* New Brunswick, N.J.: Transaction Books, 1979.
Palestine Royal Commission Report, CMD 5479. London, 1946.
Post-war Foreign Policy Preparation
Proceedings of the Security Council
Public Papers of Franklin Delano Roosevelt. New York: Random House, 1950.
Public Papers of the Presidents of the United States: Harry S. Truman, 1948. Washington, D.C.: Government Printing Office, 1964.
The Transfer of Power

Acknowledgments

This book proved an ambitious undertaking. I would never have completed it without the support of countless colleagues, friends, and family members who helped make it a reality. Its earliest outlines emerged during my time at Tufts University's Fletcher School of Law and Diplomacy, under the able stewardship of Ian Johnstone. Alan Henrikson and Ayesha Jalal contributed valuable suggestions and insights. My friend and colleague Niall Ferguson not only taught me the nuts and bolts of the craft of history during our Beacon Hill breakfasts but also offered wisdom and steady guidance as the book progressed.

Throughout the research, archivists and librarians at various repositories in the United States and Great Britain helped me track down thousands of documents. John O'Shea and Antonia Moon at the British Library fielded endless questions and requests for India Office Records. Colin Harris at Oxford's Bodleian Libraries helped me secure access to the Attlee Papers. Bob Clark at the Roosevelt Library and David Clark at the Truman Library were indispensable during my research visits and promptly responded to follow-up queries. The staff at the Middle East Centre at St. Antony's College, Oxford not only welcomed me with open arms but also invited me to lunch. Jim Stimpert at Johns Hopkins University's Milton Eisenhower Library located and reproduced a number of useful images.

In the final years of my graduate studies I had the pleasure of teaching motivated undergraduates at George Washington University's Elliott School of International Affairs. But it was the State Department that became my intellectual home. There, Amy Garrett, Adam Howard, David Nickles, Steve Randolph, Steve Galpern, Wes Reisser, and others propelled me with continuous encouragement and allowed me to take considerable amounts of time off to finish the book. All of the views expressed herein are my own, and do not necessarily reflect those of the Department or any other U.S. government agency.

Working with Jason Parker, Marian Barber, and the peerless William Roger Louis to interact with the National History Center's Washington Decolonization Seminar and meet its talented participants over four summers helped me refine key ideas. But I have also benefited from academic insights from farther afield. Having shuttled between Washington and Boston for several years, I must acknowledge the intellectual debt I owe to Harvard University, whose academic and administrative resources I have relied on throughout this project. I am grateful not only for the generosity of the Davis Center for Russian and Eurasian Studies, where I was a graduate student associate for two years, but also for access to the collections at Widener Library and for the patience and generosity of the faculty and staff of the Department of History and the Center for European Studies.

Many specific individuals also contributed suggestions to improve the project, including Evan Luard, Charles Maier, John Darwin, Howard Sachar, Aviel Roshwald, Lucy Chester, Mark Stoler, Elizabeth Thompson, and Matthew Edney. The cafés of Georgetown (and the Four Seasons Hotel) provided relaxing enclaves in which to meditate and write. But it was my friends who sustained me through the research, writing, and editing processes. Theodore Tanoue and Michael Kleinman took time to read draft chapters and share their impressions. Andrew Duggan, Yu-Lan Duggan, Helen Sullivan, George Kuo, Ginger Collier, Alexis Brooks, Mikael Lurie, Alan Alexander, Ryan Jacobs, Jonathan Peccia, Maria Sisk, Reggie Robinson, Brooke Milton-Kurtz, and Hank Tucker—thanks for being there. Fortunately for me, living in D.C. also meant opportunities to bounce ideas about the contemporary relevance of my work off real-world experts and neighbors like Matthew Waxman, Samantha Power, Mat Burrows, and Lee Schwartz.

I was fortunate that this book found its rightful home at Harvard University Press, where Kathleen McDermott and Andrew Kinney managed this project with care and diligence. I thank them, my copy editor, and the manuscript's anonymous readers for their thoughtful suggestions. Over the long process from proposal to publication, my former Harvard colleague and longtime friend Mark Kramer was always generous with his time, fielding my endless questions about the business of academic publishing. My girlfriend, Heather, probably learned more about that business than she ever cared to by going through every step of the long process with me, proving to be an anchor of stability over the past few years.

Most of all I have benefited from the love and support of my parents, Zaheed and Laila Husain, who taught me to embrace and prize scholarship at a young age. This book is really for you. A part of it is also for my other family, at Inter

Milan: President Massimo Moratti, whom I had the pleasure of meeting during the team's 2013 visit to the United States, as well as the players, coaching staff, trainers, and the Fan Club Coordination Centre. It was one of life's greatest joys to wrap up my research in London as we marched toward the historic *triplete* in 2010. We did it—together. Forza Nerazzurri.

Index

Abdul Aziz Al Saud, king of Saudi Arabia, 141
Abdullah, Sheikh Muhammad, 80–82, 87, 96, 232–233
Acheson, Dean, 124–125
Advisory Committee on Postwar Foreign Policy, of U.S., 164–165, 168, 176–178, 188, 194, 265–266, 269; Subcommittee on International Organization, 165–167; Subcommittee on Security, 165
Afghanistan, 12, 96, 99–101, 103, 109–110, 127–128, 184
Africa and the Victorians (Robinson and Gallagher), 247
Airpower, U.S. postwar security and, 188–191, 209–212
Air Transport Command (ATC), of U.S., 209, 215
Alanbrooke, Field Marshall, 292n97
Alexandria Protocol, 135
Ali, Maulanas Mohammad, 238
Ali, Rahmat, 238–239
Ali, Shaukat, 238
All-India Muslim League, 83–96, 134, 232–233, 242
All-India Muslim Students Federation, 239
All Jammu and Kashmir Muslim Conference, 80–82, 87
Ambrose, Stephen, 5
American Empire (Smith), 18

American Jewish Committee, 40
American Jewish Conference, 40
America's Strategy in World Politics (Spykman), 18, 212–215
Amery, Leo, 24, 85
Amritsar, Treaty of (1846), 79
Anderson, Benedict, 233, 336n42
Anglo-American Committee of Inquiry on Palestine, 10, 42–49, 52, 177, 273; *Survey of Palestine* (1945–1946), 30; implications of recommendations of, 49–51, 292n97; impact on India's independence issues, 93–94
Anglo-Egyptian Treaty (1936), 182
Anticolonial nationalism, 6, 18–21, 218–241, 263; nationalist struggles and great power diplomacy, 21–22, 242–246; sovereignty and self-determination issues, 218–223, 228–231; sovereignty's Westphalian origins, 223–227; sovereignty's UN framework, 227–228; sources of and "statist" and "imagined communities," 231–241; drivers of, 246–286; geography and imagined boundaries, 266–270
Arab Higher Committee, 51, 55, 69, 71
Arab-Israeli War (1948), 23, 25, 61–62
Arendt, Hannah, 19–20, 235–236, 246, 271
Argentina, 35
Asabiyya (community), 21

Atlantic Charter, 15, 16, 22, 39, 139–142, 144, 149–151, 159, 229, 231
Attlee, Clement, 216, 230, 264, 267; and Palestine, 11, 40, 44, 45, 48, 50, 53–54, 59, 185; and Kashmir, India, and Pakistan, 93–94, 95, 98–99, 103, 107–109, 111, 117, 120–122, 125, 183, 265, 306n9
Auchinleck, Claude, 97, 100, 106, 184, 304n61
Austin, Warren, 60, 64, 66, 70–73, 110, 115–117, 119, 154, 178, 269
Australia, 153, 155, 179, 181
Aydelotte, Frank, 42
Ayyangar, Gopalaswami, 116
Azad, Maulana Abul Kalam, 87, 90, 91, 237, 238, 246, 300n19, 338n59, 339n61

Balfour Declaration, 24–25, 29, 31, 56, 63
Ball, Joseph, 45
Baruch, Bernard, 49
Baxter, C. W., 37
Bazaz, Prem Nath, 81
Beeley, Harold, 288n48
Belorussia, 175
Ben-Gurion, David: Palestine and Jewish emigration issues, 8, 19–20, 29–31, 43, 48, 55–57, 232–236, 270–271, 286n26; on "absorptive capacity," 26; on Syria, 132; and geopolitics and demographics, 242–246
Berlin, Isaiah, 227
Bernadotte, Folke, 73
Bevin, Ernest, 93, 180, 183, 185, 186, 216, 264, 265, 267; and Palestine, 8, 9, 10, 23, 44–45, 47–48, 50–51, 53–58, 243; and Kashmir, India, and Pakistan, 98–99, 107, 111, 115, 303n57
Bidault, Georges, 143
Biltmore Conference, 31–32, 48, 85
Bloom, Sol, 40
Bodin, Jean, 223–224
Bohlen, Charles "Chip," 196–197
Bowman, Isaiah, 5, 37, 168, 188, 192–194, 199, 211–212, 214, 245
Braudel, Fernand, 322n33
Breuilly, John, 233
Brzezinski, Zbigniew, 281n19

Brown, Wilson, 191
Buber, Martin, 235
Byrnes, James F., 10, 43, 50, 51, 53

Cadogan, Alec, 107–108, 115
Caroe, Olaf, 12, 99, 262
Carr, E. H., 210
Casey, Richard, 87–88
Catroux, George, 133, 135, 138, 264
Chapultepec, Act of, 205–206
Chatterjee, Partha, 19, 336n42
Cheribon Agreement (1946), 148, 150, 152, 155
China: concerns about influence of, 79, 97, 103, 119–120, 152; postwar planning and UN's voting and veto issues, 168–172, 200
Churchill-Samuel White Paper, 25, 26
Churchill, Winston S.: and Palestine, 31, 35–36, 38, 40, 48, 51; postwar planning and, 85, 167, 192, 196, 200, 204, 205; and the Levant, 132, 134, 135, 137, 138; self-determination of peoples and, 228, 229, 230
Clifford, Clark, 40, 45, 50, 60, 63, 76, 177, 265
Coe, Robert, 37
Cohen, Benjamin, 49
Communism. *See* China; Soviet Union
Congress Party, in India, 81–96, 98, 237, 238
Connally, Tom, 64
Cranborne, Lord, 200
Creech Jones, Arthur, 48, 55, 57–58
Cripps, Stafford, 85–86, 91, 92, 98, 299n16
Crossman, Richard, 42
Cunningham, Alan, 49, 52–53, 201, 202
Cunningham, George, 92–93
Curzon, Lord, 80
Cyprus, 2, 180
Cyrenaica, 2

Damascus Protocol, 24
Davis, Norman, 168
Davy, A. E. G., 128
Decolonization. *See* Anticolonial nationalism

DeGaulle, Charles, 14, 132–133, 143
"Distal" and "tacit" knowledge, mental maps and, 162
Dulles, John Foster, 264
Dumbarton Oaks Conference (1944), 6, 16, 172–173, 194, 264, 321n27
Dutch East Indies. *See* Indonesia

East India Company, 78–79, 96
Eddé, Emile, 140, 268
Eden, Anthony, 35–36, 40, 134, 166–168, 190, 192, 202, 205–206
Edwardes, Herbert, 79
Egypt: United Kingdom regional security concerns and, 2, 4, 8–9, 41, 76, 124, 127, 136, 184, 246, 255, 273; United Kingdom policy in Palestine and, 35, 49, 54, 58, 61, 67–68; effect of geopolitics on, 131, 210; the Levant and, 134; Indonesia and, 153
Eisenhower, Dwight D., 215
Elath, Eliahu, 40
Eliot, George Fielding, 183
Embick, Stanley, 197
Evatt, Herbert V., 200, 324n52

Fahmi an Nuqrashi, Muhammad, 68
Fairchild, Muir, 197
Faisal bin Hussein bin Ali al-Hashemi, 130–132
Farouk, king of Egypt, 68, 153, 154
Field, Henry, 245
Forrestal, James V., 61, 63, 73, 188, 198, 205, 213
Fortas, Abe, 197–198
France. *See* Levant
Franck, Thomas, 202–203, 343n37
Frankfurter, Felix, 49
Fraser, Peter, 200, 324n52

Gallagher, John, 247, 266
Gandhi, Mahatma, 84, 89, 90
Geography, perceptions of, 262–274; mental maps and foreign policy, 263–266; anticolonialism and contested boundaries, 266–270; influence of official and popular, 270–272; overstretch and, 272–274

Geopolitics, 17–18, 187–217, 262–263; postwar trusteeship issues and reconciliation of U.S. and United Kingdom interests, 187–201; impact on specific issues, 201–209; supplanting of United Kingdom naval power by U.S. air power, 201–209; mental maps of globalism and, 212–217
George, Alexander, 203
Gerig, Benjamin, 196, 197, 199
Glancy, B. J., 80, 89, 98, 301n28
Glennon, Michael, 203
Glubb, John, 312n5
Goldmann, Nahum, 46, 56
Government of India Acts, 84–85
Gracey, Douglas, 121
Grady, Henry, 51, 113
Graffety-Smith, Laurence, 99, 103–104, 185
Gray, Christine, 255
Greece, 3, 4, 35, 74, 118, 178, 183, 251, 268
Grigg, Edward, 33–34, 288n44
Gromyko, Andrei, 70, 172–173, 175–176

Haganah, 67–68, 71, 74
Halifax, Lord, 35–36, 45, 288n48, 289n54
Hall, George, 201
Hankey, R. M. A., 37, 135
Harriman, Averell, 51, 176
Hatta, Mohammed, 20, 144, 151, 157, 240
Hauser, Henry, 322n33
Haushofer, Karl, 212
Hebrew language, 30, 35, 286n26
Henderson, Loy, 38, 61, 63, 122, 124, 142
Herzl, Theodor, 19–20, 28, 29, 30, 31, 234
Hiss, Alger, 196
Hobbes, Thomas, 224–225, 226
Hobsbawm, Eric, 233
Holland, Robert F., 246, 259
Hopkins, Harry, 176
Hornbeck, Stanley, 188
Hourani, Albert, 20–21
Howe, R. G., 202
Huddle, J. Klahr, 120, 122
Hull, Cordell, 38, 150, 163–170, 174, 188, 189, 211–212
Huntington, Ellsworth, 78
Husseini, Hajj Amin al-, 27

Hussein, Sharif of Mecca, 24, 39
Hutcheson, Joseph, 42

Ibn Saud, king, 3, 38, 41
India: anticolonial nationalism and, 19; United Kingdom concerns about unrest in Palestine, 41; postwar Indonesia and United Kingdom policy, 147–148, 149; effect of geopolitics on, 210; sovereignty and self-determination issues, 218. *See also* Kashmir
Indonesia, 15–16, 129–130; Netherlands' postwar economic condition and, 1; United Kingdom regionalism and Indonesian nationalism, 144–149, 260; U.S. globalism and economic and anti-communism issues, 149–158, 159; UN and, 151–155, 158–159; effect of geopolitics on, 207, 208; sources of anticolonial nationalism and, 232–233, 240; anticolonialism and contested boundaries, 268; official and popular conceptions of geography and, 271; overstretch and, 273–274
Iran, 4, 61, 74, 183
Iraq, 2, 41, 61, 67, 131, 134
Irgun, 31, 48
Ismay, Hastings, 98, 100, 101, 103, 109, 115, 183
Israel: U.S. recognition of, 9, 268, 269; declares independence, 67–68; right of self-defense issues, 69; sovereignty and self-determination issues, 218, 221–222; statehood and national identity, 258–260. *See also* Palestine
Istiqlal Party, 27
Italy, 268

Jabotinsky, Vladimir, 29
Jackson, Robert, 252, 260, 346n49
Jalal, Ayesha, 337n54, 339n61
Japan, postwar Indonesia and, 144–145
Japanese Mandated Islands, postwar trusteeship issues and, 188, 191–192, 194, 202, 209, 213, 327n7
Jebb, Gladwyn, 34
Jewish Agency for Palestine, 31, 51, 53, 55–56, 69, 71, 232, 242

Jinnah, Muhammad Ali: sources of anticolonial nationalism and, 8, 232–233, 236–240; Pakistan self-determination issues and, 20, 82–96, 99, 102–104, 106, 134, 153, 159, 271, 299n8, 300nn23,26; background, 83; death, 121, 123; geopolitics and demographics, 242–246
Joint Four-Nation Declaration (1943), 168–170
Judenstaat, Der (The Jewish State) (Herzl), 28, 234

Karachi Agreement, 126
Karami, Abdul Hamid, 137
Kashmir, 11–13, 78–128; United Kingdom regional security concerns along Northern tier/arc of crisis and, 2, 6–7, 11–12, 59, 77, 79, 83–109, 127–128, 179–180, 183–186, 281n19, 309n9; U.S. global interests and, 6–7, 12–13, 110–127, 178–179; and India's Muslim population, 77, 79, 83–96, 237–240, 339n61; 19th and early 20th century history of unrest in Jammu and, 78–83; UN and, 82–83, 105–126; impact of Palestine issues on, 93–94, 107; United Kingdom's response to violence in, 105–110, 121–123; convergence of United Kingdom and U.S. interests, 118–119, 126–128; effect of geopolitics on, 207, 216–217; sovereignty and self-determination issues, 222; anticolonialism and contested boundaries, 247–253, 268, 269, 342n24; official and popular conceptions of geography and, 270
Kelsen, Hans, 205
Kennan, George, 4, 63–64, 66, 72, 113
Kennedy, Paul, 272
Khan, Zafarullah, 122
Khilafat movement, 84, 87, 237–238, 240
Khoury, Bishara El-, 134
Knox, Frank, 189, 205, 214
Kohler, Foy, 37
Kohn, Hans, 235, 271, 337n48
Korea, 3, 60, 111, 211, 251

Lahore Resolution (1940), 85, 88, 89, 239
Lahore, Treaty of (1846), 79
Langer, William, 214
Latin America, 205–206
Law of Nations, The (Vattel), 226
Lawrence, Henry, 79
Lawrence, T. E., 130, 312n5
Law, Richard, 192–193
Lay, James, 5–6
League of Arab States, 135
League of Nations, 6, 23–25, 41, 69, 113, 130, 164, 174, 192, 195, 197, 200
Leahy, William, 165, 189, 192, 214
Lebanon. *See* Levant
Leggett, Frederick, 42
LEHI (Fighters for the Freedom of Israel), 31
Lenin, Vladimir, 229
Levant, 7, 41, 260; France's postwar economic condition and, 1; France's divided postwar government and, 7, 13–15, 129–130; anticolonial nationalism and, 13–15, 20–21, 129–130, 268; United Kingdom regionalism and national interests, 130–138, 158–159, 180, 183–184; U.S. global concerns and, 138–144; effect of geopolitics on, 208; sovereignty and self-determination issues, 218; sources of anticolonial nationalism and, 232–233, 240; official and popular conceptions of geography and, 271; overstretch and, 273–274
Leviathan (Hobbes), 224–225, 226
Liaquat Ali Khan, 82, 106, 121, 122, 159
Lie, Trygve, 72, 253, 254
Linggadjati Agreement. *See* Cheribon Agreement
Linlithgow, Lord, 84, 88–89
Lloyd George, David, 24
Locke, John, 225–226
London Conference (1946–1947), 52–58
Louis, William Roger, 6, 8, 133, 202, 229, 273
Lovett, Robert A., 125–126, 155, 250
Lucknow Pact, 83, 84
Luttwak, Edward, 252

Mackinder, Halford, 18, 212
Mahan, Alfred Thayer, 18
Manela, Erez, 228–229
Maps: renewed geographic knowledge in World War II, 18, 215–216; representations of British Empire and, 181. *See also* Mental maps
Marshall, George, 71, 72, 73, 115, 121–122, 154, 188
Marshall Plan, 3, 10, 15, 60, 75, 149, 157, 208
McDonald, James, 42
McFarland, A. J., 74
McMahon, Henry, 24
McMahon, Robert, 111, 126, 308nn23, 26
McNaughton, A. G., 121
McNeill, William, 347n7
Menon, V. P., 95, 103
Mental maps, 100, 262; globalism, regionalism and, 7–8, 212–217, 263–265; and shaping of foreign policy, 161–163; "distal" and "tacit" knowledge and, 162
Meyer, Eugene, 49
Military Air Transport Service (MATS), of U.S., 209
Molotov, Vyacheslav, 170
Monroe Doctrine, 170, 205, 210, 213, 263–264
Montagu-Chelmsford Report (1918), 84
Mook, Hubertus von, 148, 264, 274
Morgenthau, Henry, 49
Morris, Benny, 62
Morrison-Grady plan, 56
Morrison, Herbert, 51
Mountbatten, Lord Louis, 185, 262, 265; and Kashmir, India, and Pakistan, 82, 95–99, 101, 103–106, 113, 117, 121, 126, 303nn55, 56, 304n62; and Indonesia, 145–147, 148
M Project, 245, 265–266, 268
Murray, Wallace, 37

Nasakom, 240, 271
National Conference, in Kashmir, 80–82
National Geographic, 5, 18, 215
"Negative peace," 253

362 · Index

Nehru, Jawaharlal, 153; and Kashmir, India, and Pakistan, 81–83, 86–87, 89, 92, 97–100, 102–104, 106–107, 114, 122, 125–126, 236, 239–240, 303n55, 308n36, 326n67, 338n60
Netherlands. *See* Indonesia
New Zealand, 181
Niles, David, 40, 45, 50, 60, 64, 76, 177, 265
Nimitz, Chester, 124, 215
Noel-Baker, Philip, 109–110, 115, 342n24

On Sovereignty (Bodin), 223–224
Ormsby-Gore, William, 24
Ottoman Empire, Damascus Protocol and, 24
Overstretch: of empires, 8, 14–15, 54, 103, 158–160, 219; conceptions of geography and, 263, 272–274

Pakistan: sovereignty and self-determination issues, 20, 82–96, 218, 299n8; self-determination issues and India's Muslim population, 83–96, 239–240, 339n61; vulnerable military position and role in defense of India, 96–106; international policies in Indonesia and, 149, 153, 159; sources of anticolonial nationalism and, 232–233, 236–240; geopolitics and demographics, 242–246; statehood and national identity, 258–260; perceptions of geography and, 262. *See also* Kashmir
Palestine: U.S. globalism and, 6–7, 9–11, 35–40, 63–66, 74–76, 176–178, 268–269, 294n35, 295n39; United Kingdom regionalism and, 6–9, 76–77, 182–186; partition and, 10, 27, 41, 46, 48, 52–53, 59–60, 63, 66–75; United Kingdom mandate and conflicting Jewish and Arab claims to territory, 23–28, 32–39; Nazi persecution of Jews and issues of immigration to, 26–27, 29, 31; Zionism and idea of collective return to Jewish homeland, 28–32, 33, 35, 38–41, 43–46, 55–56, 60–61; Jewish settlement in after World War I, 29; United Kingdom and overstretch in, 47–50, 54; London Conference and British need for UN intervention, 52–58; UN, British regional interests and termination of mandate, 58–59; UN, U.S. global interests and military issues, 60–67; increase in violence in, 61–62, 67–68; impact on Kashmir issues, 93–94, 107; effect on the Levant, 135–136, 141; effect of geopolitics on, 201–202, 207–208, 210, 216–217; anticolonial nationalism and, 232–233, 247–253; geopolitics and demographics, 242–246; mental maps and foreign policy, 265–266; official and popular conceptions of geography and, 270–272. *See also* Anglo-American Committee of Inquiry; Israel
Palestine Liberation Organization, 260
Palestine Royal Commission ("Peel Commission"), 27, 56
Parodi, Alxandre, 70
Pasvolsky, Leo, 168, 188, 195, 197, 264
Patterson, Jefferson, 153
Peterson, Maurice, 37, 193
Pethick-Lawrence, Frederick, 91, 94, 159
Poland, 175–176
Potsdam Conference (1945), 38
Poynton, Hilton, 194–195, 196, 204, 230
Protestant Reformation, self-determination and, 226

Qane, Helen, 335n38
Quigley, John, 69
Quit Kashmir movement, 81
Quwatli, Shukri al-, 142, 151, 232–234, 240, 271

Ratzel, Friedrich, 212
Reisman, Michael, 69
Renville Agreement (1948), 155, 157
Robinson, Kenneth, 194–195, 196, 204, 230
Robinson, Ronald, 247
Romania, 35
Roosevelt, Eleanor, 245
Roosevelt, Franklin D.: postwar planning and origins of globalism, 3, 4, 163,

165–170; Four Policemen and, 5, 170, 171, 176, 190, 202–203; Palestine and, 37, 245; the Levant and, 138, 141; Indonesia and, 149; postwar trusteeship issues and future of U.S. security, 187–194, 209, 211–212, 264; maps and, 215; self-determination of peoples and, 228, 229
Rosenman, Samuel, 45
Ross, John, 60
Ruggie, John, 203

Said, Edward, 287n27
Samuel, Herbert, 9, 25, 32–33, 76, 324n48
San Francisco Conference (1945), 5, 6, 34–35, 39–42, 174–176, 198–199
San Remo Conference (1920), 25
Sargent, Orme, 110, 306n22
Scoones, Geoffrey, 108
Self-determination. *See* Sovereignty
Shertok, Moshe, 56
Sherwood, Robert, 173
Shone, Terence, 98, 109, 110
Silver, Abba Hillel, 45
Singh, Dhyan, 79
Singh, Gulab, maharaja of Kashmir, 78–79, 81
Singh, Hari, maharaja of Kashmir, 79–82
Singh, Ranjit, 79
Singleton, John, 42
Sjahrir, Sutan, 148
Smith, Neil, 5, 18, 204, 206
Solh, Riad al-, 134
South Africa, 181, 199
Southeast Asia Command (SEAC), 15, 20, 145–148, 151
Sovereignty: self-determination issues, 218–223, 228–231, 269, 347n6; Westphalian origins of, 223–227; sovereignty by institution and sovereignty by acquisition, 225; UN framework and, 227–228; postwar reconceptualization of, 258. *See also specific countries*
Soviet Union: concerns about influence in Middle East, 47, 50, 70, 73; concerns about influence in India and Asia, 96, 99, 103–104, 107, 110–118, 122, 128, 178–179, 211, 305n69, 306n22, 308n36; concerns about influence in Indonesia, 151, 156, 158; postwar planning and, 168–176, 199, 205–206
Spears, Edward Louis, 133–136, 137
Spinoza, Baruch de, 225–226
Spykman, Nicholas, 18, 212–215
Stalin, Josef, 138, 169–171, 174–176, 206
Stanley, Lord, 193–195, 199
Stassen, Harold, 199, 264
State failure, 257–261
Stern Gang, 48
Stettinius, Edward, 39, 173–176, 192–198, 221
Stimson, Henry, 188, 195, 198
Suez Canal Zone: United Kingdom policy in Palestine and, 6, 41–42, 58, 77; United Kingdom national interests and, 179–180, 182, 184; UN Emergency Force in, 255, 257
Sukarno, 20, 144–145, 147, 157, 232–233, 240, 259, 271
Sykes, Mark, 24
Symon, Alexander, 103
Syria. *See* Levant

"Tacit" and "distal" knowledge, mental maps and, 162
Taussig, Charles, 192–194, 197, 198, 199
Tehran Conference (1943), 170–171
"The Imperialism of Free Trade" (Robinson and Gallagher), 247
Thompson, Janice, 347n6
Thornton, A. P., 246
Tractatus Politicus (Spinoza), 225–226
Transjordan, 2, 56, 67, 180
Traveaux préparatoires, self-determination and, 230, 231, 335n38
Truman administration: Palestine and, 11, 39, 40, 43, 46–47, 50, 69, 72, 176–177, 208, 245; Kashmir and, 110–117, 179; Indonesia and, 150, 154–157; UN and, 198
Truman, Harry: Palestine and, 10–11, 39, 45, 50, 52–53, 59, 60–67, 76, 265, 290n82; Kashmir and India, 125, 239; UN and, 174

Tsiang Tingfu, 70
Turkey, 3, 4, 74, 118, 178, 183, 268
Two Treatises of Government (Locke), 225–226

Ukraine, 175
United Kingdom: postwar retreat of empire and regionalism in conception of geopolitical interests, 1–8; postwar planning and UN voting and veto issues, 168–176; regionalism, decolonization, and geography of Commonwealth, 179–186, 323n47, 324nn48, 51, 52, 53; postwar trusteeship issues and reconciliation with U.S. interests, 192–197, 199–209; anticolonial self-determination issues, 220–221; regionalism, maps, and foreign policy, 263–266; anticolonialism and contested boundaries, 266–267; overstretch and, 272–274. *See also under* Indonesia; Kashmir; Levant; Palestine
United Nations: San Francisco Conference and, 5, 6, 34–35, 39–42, 174–176, 198–199; United Kingdom regionalism and trusteeship issues, 6, 181–182; U.S. and United Kingdom clashes over structures and procedures of, 6; legal and military considerations for enforcing of Palestine partition plan, 68–75; U.S. global interests and questions of voting and veto powers during formation of, 163–176; sovereignty's framework and, 227–228; self-determination of peoples and, 227–231; peacekeeping and, 253–257. *See also under* Indonesia; Kashmir; Pakistan; Palestine
United States: postwar expansion and globalism in conception of geopolitical interests, 1–8; wartime origins of globalism, 163–176; postwar trusteeship issues and civilian and military aspects of globalism, 187–192, 197–199; postwar trusteeship issues and reconciliation of U.S. and United Kingdom interests, 192–197, 199–209; anticolonial self-determination issues, 220–221; globalism, maps, and foreign policy, 263–266; anticolonialism and contested boundaries, 267–269, 347n5; overstretch and, 272–274. *See also under* Indonesia; Kashmir; Levant; Palestine

Vandenberg, Arthur, 206
Vandenberg Resolution, 114
Vattel, Emmerich de, 226
Villard, Henry, 153–154

War and Peace Studies (WPS) project, of U.S., 163–164
Wavell, Lord, 87, 91, 92, 93, 95, 146, 147, 183
Weak states, postwar origins of, 257–261
Weizmann, Chaim, 28–31, 33, 43–44, 48, 67, 130–131
Welles, Sumner, 163–167, 171, 187, 189, 213, 229, 245, 264, 265
Western Sahara case, 230, 335n35
Westphalia, Peace of, 224–227, 333n15
White Paper on Palestine (1939), of United Kingdom, 27–28, 30, 31, 35, 37–38, 40, 56
Willson, Russell, 197
Wilson, Henry Maitland, 132
Wilson, Woodrow, 24, 25, 228
Wirsing, Robert, 126
Wise, Rabbi Stephen, 40, 53

Yalta Conference (1945), 173, 175, 196

Zionist movement: settlement and sovereignty issues, 19–20; Balfour Declaration and, 24–25; absorptive capacity of Palestine and, 26, 57; United Kingdom's White Paper on Palestine and, 27–28; idea of collective return to homeland and, 28–32, 33, 35, 38–41, 43–46, 55–56, 60–61; growing militancy of, 48; statist aims of, 234–236